Christian and Lyric Tradition in Victorian Women's Poetry

Routledge Studies in Nineteenth-Century Literature

1. Nineteenth-Century Narratives of Contagion
"Our Feverish Contact"
Allan Conrad Christensen

2. Victorian Servants, Class, and the Politics of Literacy
Jean Fernandez

3. Christian and Lyric Tradition in Victorian Women's Poetry
F. Elizabeth Gray

Christian and Lyric Tradition in Victorian Women's Poetry

F. Elizabeth Gray

Routledge
Taylor & Francis Group
New York   London

First published 2010
by Routledge
711 Third Avenue, New York, NY 10017

Simultaneously published in the UK
by Routledge
2 Park Square, Milton Park, Abingdon, Oxfordshire OX14 4RN

First issued in paperback 2014

Routledge is an imprint of the Taylor and Francis Group, an informa business

© 2010 Taylor & Francis

Typeset in Sabon by IBT Global.

All rights reserved. No part of this book may be reprinted or reproduced or utilised in any form or by any electronic, mechanical, or other means, now known or hereafter invented, including photocopying and recording, or in any information storage or retrieval system, without permission in writing from the publishers.

Trademark Notice: Product or corporate names may be trademarks or registered trademarks, and are used only for identification and explanation without intent to infringe.

Library of Congress Cataloging-in-Publication Data
Gray, F. Elizabeth.
  Christian and lyric tradition in Victorian women's poetry / F. Elizabeth Gray.
    p. cm. — (Routledge studies in nineteenth-century literature ; vol. 3)
  Includes bibliographical references and index.
  1. English poetry — Women authors — History and criticism.   2. English poetry — 19th century — History and criticism.   3. Christianity in literature.   4. Lyric poetry — 19th century — History and criticism. I. Title.
  PR585.W6G73 2010
  821'.8093823 — dc22
  2009017871

ISBN 978-0-415-80586-5 (hbk)
ISBN 978-1-138-87836-5 (pbk)
ISBN 978-0-203-86678-8 (ebk)

Contents

Acknowledgments		ix
	Introduction	1
1	"Heirs of more than royal race": The Inheritance of Victorian Women Religious Poets	13
2	"God's interpreters to the sons of misery": Rewriting Master Narratives	38
3	The Woman in the Scriptures: Models of the Christian Female in Victorian Women's Poetry	85
4	"Accept me Lord, for Thee I own": Women's Devotional Poetry and the Development of Relationship	136
5	Virtue and Virtuosity: Style in the Victorian Woman's Religious Lyric	182
	Conclusion	224
Appendix		231
Bibliography		233
Notes		247
Index		259

This book is dedicated to my father, Murray H. Gray

Acknowledgments

This project could not have been completed without generous assistance from many sources. I am deeply grateful to the Royal Society of New Zealand for awarding me a 2005–2006 Marsden Fast Start Grant, without which this book could never have been written. I would also like to thank Massey University's School of English and Media Studies, and Department of Communication, Journalism, and Marketing, and particularly Professor Warwick Slinn and Associate Professor Frank Sligo, for giving me the time, departmental support, and encouragement to work on a research undertaking that absorbed many months. A special word of thanks is due to Professor Paul Callaghan for the long-ago conversation that set me on a tremendously rewarding path.

Some passages in this book have previously appeared in *Victorian Poetry* 42:3, which has kindly given permission to reprint.

I owe a particular debt of gratitude to Drs. Nikki Hessell, Sarah Ross, and Ingrid Horrocks, for many hours of discussion, critical feedback, and collegial inspiration. To paraphrase T. S. Eliot, you have been "the better craftswomen."

Thank you to my mother, Pam Gray, for your painstaking proofreading. Thank you to Katharine Tongs for hours of patient transcription, to Lisa Emerson for many stimulating and wide-ranging discussions about women and faith, and to Christine Morrison and Sharon Benson because NOTHING gets done without you. To Sarah Ross and Andru Isac, Averil Coxhead and Maria Roddick, Robyn and Glenn Mason, Bryan Walpert and Nancy Golubiewski, Virginia Cope, and Deirdre Boleyn: in the course of my academic path you have helped and inspired me in more ways than I can enumerate, and I am humbly grateful. To my students, thank you for the inestimable gift of freshness, for coming to works I've seen many times and provoking me to re-see them as if for the first.

Finally, but most importantly, thank you to my husband, Nigel Edgecombe, for sharing the highs and the lows, helping me bear the pains of this project, and multiplying the joys.

Introduction

In the 1870s, the decade which saw the publication in England of *Middle-march*, *Far From the Madding Crowd*, Arnold's *Collected Poems*, and the first series of Browning's *Dramatic Idyls*, Elizabeth Ayton Godwin published two volumes of pious poetry, *Songs for the Weary: The School of Sorrow and Other Poems* (1873), and *Songs Amidst Daily Life* (1878). Mrs. Godwin's titles, like her poems themselves, are entirely characteristic of the religious verses penned by Victorian women: they seem so 'unoriginal,' so quotidian, so *ordinary*, that they seem barely differentiated from each other, composing a body of work that has subsided into decades of undistinguished, overlooked anonymity. It seems fitting that the now utterly obscure Godwin opens this study. This volume offers a fresh evaluation of the works of many obscure Victorian women religious poets, although its aim is not to issue a call to recuperate masses of their pious verses into undergraduate syllabi (for which thousands of undergraduate students will no doubt be deeply thankful). Rather, my aim in this work is to suggest new ways of reading religious women poets that interrogate the obscurity masking or dismissing their contribution to social, cultural, and Christian narratives, and to contend that the work that these women did, in the form of religious poetry, made a significant contribution to Christian discourse, to lyric tradition, and to contemporary views of womanhood. Mrs. Godwin's poem "Women" plangently voices the combined humility and ambition that infused the religious poetry of a vast, eager, and earnest body of nineteenth-century women.

"We women have so many cares
    Clustering round our way,
And though they may be trifles small,
    They shade the summer day,
And keep the soul from wandering free
In the sweet land of phantasy.

"The daily work to watch and pray
    For wisdom from above,
That every duty may appear
    A mission full of love;
Thus 'midst the cares which fold us round,
A blessing will be surely found.

2   *Christian and Lyric Tradition in Victorian Women's Poetry*

"Man may go forth to mighty deeds,
    To works of power and fame,
Whilst crowds applaud, and wondering own
    The greatness of his name;
But in the shadow of our nest
We find the work that suits us best.

"And if amidst the daily task
    We seek our Saviour's aid,
To help us in each busy hour
    Through sunshine and through shade,
We shall at last, in heavenly rest,
Feel that our labours have been blest.

"'Twas a fair lot, like her of old,
    To sit at Jesus' feet,
And with a calm and quiet heart
    To hold communion sweet;
But busy hand and active heart
May find alike 'the better part.'

"And at the last great judgment-day,
    Names that are now unknown,
Save in the household circle small,
    The Saviour then will own,
And many a timid form will stand
A victor at his own right hand.

"To me it seems a blessed thought
    That when he lived below,
He knew a mother's tenderness,
    Wept for a woman's woe;
And still remembers in his rest
Woman's true heart and faithful breast.

"And he is near in every home—
    The Watcher and the Guide—
To help the weak and troubled ones,
    To comfort and to chide.
Like Bethany, each home may find
Duty and love alike combined."

"At the last judgment-day," prophesies Godwin, women will achieve that measure of power and fame denied them by the society in which she writes: "Names that are now unknown,/ Save in the household circle small,/ The

Introduction 3

Saviour then will own . . . ". Godwin and her Victorian sisters never relinquish their devout Christian faith; far from espousing revolutionary independence, they believe firmly in "the Watcher and the Guide" and in their dependence upon him. And yet their writing enables them to envision and call for recognition from both God and their readers.

The phantom undergraduate student, however, insistently inquires after *the point*. Why *do* we need to examine Victorian women's religious poetry? Is it not deservedly obscure? There's a lot of it; a lot of it is very much the same; a lot of it is quite frankly doggerel; and even when 'good' poets write it, their secular verse holds much more appeal for the modern taste. A starting point may be to examine the assumptions underlying our 'modern taste,' which has led us on occasion to overlook literary works that may have played a significant role in their own culture and time and for their own writers. This oversight may be particularly true of religious literature. John M. Anderson notes how "a canonical bias against religious poetry has necessarily contributed to the historical exclusion of important underprivileged poets, including women poets" (196), and he encourages the modern reader to recognise his or her own over-readiness to expect and to find "complacent or conventional stasis" (208) in religious poetry. Anderson suggests that if we clear our own ideologically loaded expectations, new life may be found in disregarded texts. New perspectives on accepted literary and cultural 'givens' may also open up. Over the last fifty years, scholars of Victorian literature on religious topics have tended overwhelmingly to focus on and privilege the poetry of questioning and of doubt, which I suggest has skewed our understanding of the significance of religious devotion in the century's creative work. This bias needs to be addressed for us to more fully appreciate the breadth and complex ambition of Victorian religious writing, and this is particularly true in the case of Victorian women, for whom ambition in both literary and spiritual arenas was profoundly problematic.

My own goal at the outset of this project was admittedly ambitious: to investigate the consequences of Christian faith for Victorian women's writing, and the consequences of Victorian women's writing for Christian faith. I planned to acknowledge the teeming religious and publishing environments of Victorian England, reading and discussing the poetry of women from a variety of denominational backgrounds, and drawing material from a range of publishing venues. And I planned a literary study that would be appropriately informed by the rich analyses of nineteenth-century theological history that have been undertaken in a number of important scholarly studies. Since Owen Chadwick's wide-ranging and masterly two-volume work on the history of the Victorian Church, our understanding of the Victorian spiritual climate has been developed by works including Elisabeth Jay's studies of Evangelicalism, Edward Norman and D. G. Paz's examinations of Catholicism and anti-Catholic prejudice, and John Shelton Reed's significant study of Anglo-Catholicism (*Glorious Battle*). The work of such scholars has helped me set women's literary works into the social, cultural,

4   *Christian and Lyric Tradition in Victorian Women's Poetry*

and historical context that helped produce them, and that was in turn influenced by them. My own analysis focuses on the cultural influence of Christian religion as it interacted with the creative aspirations of women writers, and on the poetic manifestations of devout women's spiritual and literary ambitions. My work focuses on the 'everyday' face of Christian belief and practice, as experienced and expressed by the majority of its everyday (and largely unsung) Victorian believers, and trains a specific focus on the transfiguration of those practices and expressions into (and by) the genre of lyric poetry. Because Victorian Christianity builds upon and foregrounds specifically gendered cultural expectations, questions of gender also figure significantly in this examination of women's religious literary practice and its impact. And my analysis seeks to complicate the simplistic equation between traditional Christianity and the oppression of women. As Dennis Taylor states, "one of the promising areas of critical religious research is the way in which religious traditions, until recently considered as supporting colonialist and capitalist structures, in fact have supported the aspirations of minority cultures and races and genders" (17). In my reading of Victorian women's verse I investigate how women could find supportive and liberatory models within their Christian faith.

In short, I aim to demonstrate and explicate the multiple functions of Victorian women's Christian poetry. These Victorian women are doing more than 'just writing verse.' They are affirming their belief in and submission to God. They are simultaneously affirming their own membership in a broader community of Christian faith. And they are also affirming their right, as Christians, to write about religious faith and be vitally involved in its practice and transmission. In assessing the multiple operations of Victorian women's religious verse, a textual analysis of a poem as an aesthetic object will provide, clearly, only a very partial assessment of its importance and its 'meaning.' However, even a carefully historicised analysis of the poem within its literary and cultural context may not be sufficient, because part of how such a poem is 'working' is as a blazon of faith. It symbolises self-revelatory self-identification, signifies the poet's witness to anyone and everyone, provides self-reassurance to its author, and self-consciously answers higher authority—this verse is *for God*. This verse is, of course, also *for the writer*, and the particular paybacks for the author of the verse need close scrutiny, but we do these authors an injustice if we fail to recognise the fact that their devout textual acts promote and enact a very sincere faith. Religious sincerity can and does (with rich complexity) coexist with ambition, desire, and an earnest concern for the condition of women.

Given my initial, lofty ambitions for this study, I must state in this introduction my recognition that the scope of such a project—a re-evaluation of the 'cultural work' of Victorian women's religious poetry—is ridiculously huge. The boundaries of the project had to be continually reinterrogated. My first task, defining my parameters, appeared simple: I chose to examine Christian-themed poetry by Victorian women, that is, religious poetry

Introduction 5

that bespeaks a specifically Christian faith, rather than doubt.[1] Yet even this initial, fundamental category suggests a patently misleading manageability: Victorian women adhered to no one Christian faith. Within the Established Church itself were found women of a strongly Evangelical bent who had virtually nothing—theologically, doctrinally, or imaginatively—in sympathy with High Church, Anglo-Catholic women such as Christina Rossetti. Still within the Anglican communion could be found women of a more liberal bent who strove to keep up with scientific and intellectual developments and who would have aligned themselves with neither end of the spectrum, but perhaps could be defined as Broad Church in their inclinations. This isn't even to begin to consider the (very) particular position of Roman Catholic women and the unique ways in which they defined their faith and themselves as distinct from Protestantism and Protestants. Further, there existed the several and various gatherings of Dissenters, amongst whom some reflected Evangelical leanings that might suggest significant (though perhaps strenuously denied) similarities with certain Anglican congregations. And this busy picture of Victorian worship must also take into account outliers like Quakers and soldiers of the newly formed (in 1865) Salvation Army, both of which congregations held views on the position of women that were quite distinct from those of most other Christian denominations. How then, given this bewildering array of beliefs, might Victorian women's religious poetry be discussed in the whole? Can it actually be meaningfully and productively discussed as a distinct, discrete body of work?

In this book I contend that it can, and that it should. Armed with a theologically and historically contextualised appreciation of the differences that appear in many individual women's poems, the reader will find significant similarities in the preoccupations and poetic strategies of women across the spectrum of denominational affiliations. These shared concerns, smothered for so long by the voluminousness and disheartening aesthetic quality of so much Victorian women's verse, have important messages for those of us who desire a better understanding of the role Christian faith played in the lives of nineteenth-century women.

Certainly, appropriate coverage in a book of this nature needs careful plotting. The sheer volume of religious poetry that was written, published, circulated, read, and memorised in the nineteenth century itself provides compelling argument for the recovery of this rich trove of historical and literary artefacts.[2] However, this awe-inspiring volume of works also vastly complicates the critic's task of providing, on the one hand, comprehensive and appropriate coverage and, on the other, succinct and manageable analysis. Women's religious poetry, whether appearing in books or anthologies of devotional verse, or in the numerous periodicals of the period (some of which had readerships in the tens of thousands), was phenomenally popular, to be found in (and, perhaps, created in) almost every middle-class British home. Only a small percentage of this voluminous output was written by Elizabeth Barrett Browning, Christina Rossetti, or names recognisable

6   *Christian and Lyric Tradition in Victorian Women's Poetry*

today; most was produced by ordinary, undistinguished, urban, middle-class women who, like Godwin, are now forgotten. In drawing primary sources for this book I have read as widely as possible, reading over 150 volumes of women's verse and religious and devotional prose, and reviewing uncounted issues of women's periodicals, ranging from *The Christian Lady's Magazine* at the start of the Victorian period to *The Women's Penny Paper* (which became *The Woman's Herald*), which ran from the late 1880s into the 1890s. I have sought to incorporate as many voices as possible in this study, rather than highlighting just a few of the most prominent figures. The reader will thus find analysis of verse by the well-known Rossetti alongside poems by her lesser-known friend, Dora Greenwell; readings of the works of the block-busting Frances Ridley Havergal and Elizabeth Charles beside the works of the entirely obscure Edith Skelton and Emma Frances Bevan. Adhering as closely as I could to my aim of drawing on verse by women from across the spectrum of Christian denominations, my analysis encompasses Augusta Theodosia Drane's Roman Catholicism alongside Mrs. A. Stuart Menteath's stout Presbyterianism. I have also drawn from poetry published either anonymously or under initials only, determining as nearly as I was able the gender of the author (but recognising I may have occasionally erred).

I have of course had to impose limits on my source review. The overwhelming majority of the volumes I consulted contained primarily or solely religious poetry, which means that I have not always read the devout verse that appeared within women's more general volumes. Part of the rationale behind selecting volumes dedicated to religious verse was the related fact that the dividing line between 'religious' and 'general' verse in the Victorian period proves exceptionally flexible and hard to define. Expressions of piety and a distinctly biblical vocabulary inform the majority of women's verse, even those on the seemingly most secular of topics (for example, child labour, as in Dora Greenwell's "The Gang-children," or the Queen's coronation, in Emily S. G. Saunders' "The Accession"). My review of periodicals had to be more stringently delimited again. While Victorian periodicals present researchers with rich sources of cultural knowledge, the utter impossibility of scanning every woman-oriented periodical, or even a representative percentage, for the religious verse they included, dictated the pragmatic delimitation of my reading. I have analysed a convenience sample, choosing several periodicals that were targeted at women and were in several instances edited by women, which provide snapshots of what women were writing and reading at different points in the century. These periodicals and their runs are listed in the Appendix.

Furthermore, and of particular significance to this study, I imposed specific generic parameters. Victorian women's poetry reflects considerable generic variety, ranging from hymn to children's verse to narrative verse to dramatic monody (often all in the same volume), and a number of references to poems in these various forms punctuate the course of my discussion.

However, the most significant genre (quantitatively as well as qualitatively) for Victorian women religious poets is the lyric. Introspective and intensely personal, the lyric poem provides a congenial space for women writers to consider the workings of the spiritual life and affections, and the relationship of the individual to God. The rich history of the religious lyric also provides Victorian women a broad field for creative negotiations. Overall I have aimed to draw as comprehensive a picture as possible of both the variety and the common concerns and strategies to be found in Victorian women's Christian lyric poetry, but I must also state my strong belief that this rich body of work will repay much further study and analysis. For reasons of time and space, I have been able to engage with only a few of the suggestive directions taken by women's religious verse. For example, I have only been able to lightly touch on the broader social permutations of such a widely written and widely read body of work. How did religious poetry enable women's engagement with popular social causes like campaigns against slavery and vivisection? How was religious verse used within the suffrage movement, and in other political causes? I have had to leave examination of these fascinating questions for a later project.

Finally, while discussing the limitations of this study, I should also disclose my own situatedness in regard to the subject of my work. Raised in the Christian tradition by devout parents, and later raised in the feminist tradition by no less devoted university professors, I have spent years studying women's religious poetry because it engages me on a personal level, as well as on an intellectual level. My readings of Victorian women religious poets thus incorporate the personal engagement and the "combination of interest and detachment" that Dennis Taylor, in "The Need for a Religious Literary Criticism," demands from the critic of religious literature (6). Taylor calls for a critical approach to religious writing that is "substantial enough to enter into a productive and competitive relation with the reigning critical discourses" (3). He also requires criticism of religious literature to avoid the twin pitfalls of "softness" (that is, self-marginalising and vague criticism that appeals to unexamined 'accepted' ideals), and of scepticism, the 'approved' but often similarly unexamined deconstructive position. I have worked hard in this study to chart a course between respect and a healthy critical questioning, approaching women's religious writing unapologetically and asserting it as worthy of substantial critical investigation.

This book will describe and discuss the common concerns and features of Victorian women's poetry—subject matter and source material, topoi, imagery, intertextual approach, stylistic and aesthetic characteristics, and mode of engaging with scripture, with God, and with the reader. And it will investigate how women poets deploy those features as a means of exploring their own anxieties and desires.

Repeatedly, Victorian women poets reveal their concern with authorising and charting a relationship with the master narratives that ruled their faith and their experience as persons of faith. The ways in which they sought to

8   *Christian and Lyric Tradition in Victorian Women's Poetry*

reshape their relations to exclusive Christian discourse reveal their understanding of their own suppression, and their attempts to construct a measure of spiritual authority. Women's poetic interactions with biblical texts have important consequences for their self-justification as artists; question in a fundamental way the formation, recognition, and valorisation of concepts of authority and originality; are significantly intertwined with their self-conception as spiritual guides or sages; and are intimately connected with the period's ideas of womanliness.

Repeatedly, Victorian women poets are concerned to find models of womanhood in sacred texts, and they adapt and reshape those models in their own texts. In so doing, I contend, they reinscribe woman into sacred history, making room for women in what they revise into a dynamic and very contemporary 'Christian story.' And at the same time, their operations with these historical/modern figures highlight and question the constructedness and ideological underpinning of all histories.

Repeatedly, Victorian women poets are concerned with finding a way of relating to a masculinised God, and a way of articulating the position that a femininised *I* can be important to God. Women faced serious disadvantages in this project: feminine attributes and ways of knowing seemed to make up no part of the profoundly patriarchal Victorian God. But at the same time, Victorian women could call on particularly helpful resources: the biblical and mystical tradition of the Bride and Bridegroom opened up fruitful imaginative possibilities for the female Christian; and Victorian stereotypes of femininity (such as emotionality, non-intellectualism, and submissiveness) were transformable into aspects of a privileged, gendered relationship with a God who explicitly embraced the 'weak and foolish' of the world. Femininity is, I contend, absolutely central to the quest for relationship that underlies Victorian women's Christian verse, shaping the way relationship is imaginatively constructed. It influences the way Christ is imagined; it informs the deployment of paradigms of romance and submission; and it enables the eroticisation of depicted union.[3]

And further, Victorian women poets repeatedly return to the conundrum of finding a way of 'speaking God,' that is, speaking *of* God and speaking *to* God. The significance of poetic style in women's verse as a means of access to God, as well as a marker or sign of the right to access God, needs thoughtful evaluation. Women's deployment of stylistic and aesthetic elements within a religious poetry had consequences for the development of the lyric tradition that have been little considered, largely due to the marked changes in aesthetic value and taste that have taken place in the last century.

These and other common elements in Victorian women's religious poetry require an investigative approach that does in fact consider this poetry as a distinct body of work, and investigates how it is born out of and helps create a particular literary and spiritual community. Discussing these tremendously various women—the High Church Christina Rossetti, the Unitarian Sarah

Introduction   9

Flower Adams, the Presbyterian Annie Ross Cousin, the Roman Catholic Emily Hickey, the erstwhile Quaker Mary Howitt—as a poetic and religious community is clearly immensely problematic. And yet arguably one of the most significant productions of the now-neglected genre of women's religious verse was a community, and a particular sense of spiritual community. Christian women wrote for other Christian women. And women, in a very real sense, wrote The Christian Woman into being. Responding to and referring to other women's poems, women poets created the rules by which this body of verse was to be read and valued, and they created an identity for a devout, feminine, yet still privileged follower of Christ. In effect, women's religious verse, a voluminous and vigorous body, created its own Christian discourse, not 'dominated' by the powerful edifice of traditional religion but responding creatively to that edifice to contribute to a revised, more inclusive language with which believers could speak of God, speak to God, and construct their own personal relationship with God.

The first chapter of this book provides an introduction to Victorian women poets' inheritance of Christian, cultural, and literary traditions, traditions that both profoundly shaped women's poetic responses and that were in turn shaped by those responses. The chapter discusses how writing in general and writing lyric poetry in particular became an especially congenial way for nineteenth-century women to 'do Church work,' skirting prohibitions on undertaking 'manly' exegesis, and enabling them to take on sometimes unexpected degrees of authority. For Victorian women, Christianity centred every discussion and every endeavour. Our own critical blinders, I suggest, have hidden many of the ways in which Christianity could function for Victorian women as a liberatory as well as an oppressive force, and the chapter suggests Victorian women's poems re-frame, re-vise, and re-write sacred texts in provocative and previously unacknowledged ways.

Chapter 2, entitled "Rewriting Master Narratives," examines how Victorian women poets secured power in relation to the Bible by responding to it as a textual and hermeneutical model. Building on the work of feminist theologians, I suggest that Victorian women poets variously apply, in their poetic responses to the Bible, a hermeneutics of suspicion, which uncovers the biases and assumptions of androcentric scriptural texts, and a hermeneutics of creative actualisation, which uses the Bible as a resource or prototype for creativity. In the undertaking of poetic paraphrases of scripture, Victorian women used an unexceptionably pious activity to create an ongoing critical engagement with narratives of power and orthodoxy. Epigraphy and intertextuality enabled women to wrestle with issues of originality and authorisation by staging the process of transmission and constructedness of holy and inspired messages. I present in this chapter a series of close readings that demonstrate and analyse the particular strategies adopted by women in their poetic negotiations with their sacred originals.

The third chapter, "The Woman in the Scriptures: Models of the Christian Female," applies a narrower focus to women poets' use of particular

10 *Christian and Lyric Tradition in Victorian Women's Poetry*

Christian textual models, examining verse centred on female biblical characters. I build on Cynthia Scheinberg's valuable work on Victorian women's use of Old Testament 'singers,' and reference Ruth Jenkins and Christine Krueger's discussion of women's use of the prophetic model, but I argue that Victorian women found their most useful and suggestive identificatory models in New Testament female characters. I closely examine poetry from a range of authors that portrays the Virgin Mary as "first singer of the church," Mary Magdalene as a transformative and powerful woman, and finally the woman anointer of Jesus, who figures differently in each of the four gospels, as a focal point for the interrogation of narratives of naming and authorisation. The deployment of biblical female characters in verse that did not solely locate itself in a distant past, but argued for contemporary relevance and predicted future expansion of the female role, enabled Victorian women to reformulate their relationship with exclusionary spiritual, secular, and literary histories, and to re-evaluate fame and its gendered construction.

Chapter 4, "'Accept me Lord, for Thee I own': Women's Devotional Poetry and the Development of Relationship," argues the significance of women poets' production of a feminised *I* that could participate in direct relationship with God, and I suggest a redefinition of devotional poetry to illuminate its preoccupation with recognition. The production of a Victorian 'devotional spirit,' and the concomitant focus on the expression of love and intimacy within religious discourse, grow out of and contribute to the period's feminisation of Christianity, which was significantly developed by women's poetry. In devotional verse that explores the bride/bridegroom relationship and eroticises suffering, women poets elaborate upon a provocatively gendered romantic and submissive paradigm to suggest ways in which poetic speakers form particular and privileged relationship with Christ, envisioning a new, mutually fulfilling relationship with God. The chapter concludes by considering how women used devotional verse to improve their own status in relation to their readers, examining the intertwined nature of spiritual and literary ambition.

The fifth and final chapter builds on the contextualisation and thematic analysis provided in the previous sections but focuses on the formal and stylistic choices deployed in this body of verse, examining those choices as deliberate strategies. In "Virtue and Virtuosity: Style and Devotion in the Victorian Woman's Religious Lyric," I examine the challenging stylistic excess characteristic of women's nineteenth-century religious poetry and argue that the verbal and metrical style of women's devotional poetry offers an important way of constructing meaning. Features such as slight vocabulary and cliché phrasing, repetitiveness, metrical monotony, and ornamental excess should be read as a particular and legitimate form of expression, moulded by cultural exigencies, and vividly eloquent about the conditions influencing its own formation. By translating Victorian literalisation of women's expressive lyrics into a religious context, women constructed and participated in a new kind of aestheticism, harnessing lyrical elements as personal religious offerings, and creating a new venue for encounters with God. Profoundly and self-consciously decorative, women's devotional poems present themselves as both tangible artworks and intangible, self-authorising affirmations of contract between the poet and God. Victorian women's deployment of particular tropes and particular prosodic effects, their *way of speaking* about religion as well as just the fact of their speaking about religion, provides them with a way of arrogating power and making meaning.

The book concludes by suggesting the importance of refocusing our critical analysis of Victorian women's poetry. Attempting to develop a critical understanding of major figures like Christina Rossetti and Elizabeth Barrett Browning while shying away from all of their poems that bespeak an 'embarrassing' religious sincerity is a nonsense, and constitutes a serious underestimation of these poets' range and ambition. Similarly, attempting to investigate the writing of a broad range of Victorian women without taking into account the central importance of Christian faith and discourse to their self-conceptions and to their models of self-expression is to diminish our understanding of the breadth of these women's cultural and creative contributions. In 2004 Virginia Blain speculated that a significant new direction for Victorian poetry studies might involve "a new push toward re-opening religious debates from a new knowledge base and a newly sensitized perspective which seeks somehow to put the religion back into the poetry" (73). I fundamentally agree with the need for the reincorporation of the religious back into our considerations of Victorian literature: this volume suggests some ways forward.

1 "Heirs of more than royal race"
The Inheritance of Victorian Women Religious Poets

> Religious literature ... was everywhere in nineteenth-century England.
>
> —Altick, *The English Common Reader*, 103

> Religious poetry is plentiful in our day, and is doing its work even by its very abundance. Perhaps in some cases it has too much of sentiment and too little of praise; too much of man, too little of God. But there can be no doubt that it is telling upon men's minds in all directions; and it is of no small importance that what is genuine and spiritual in it should be carefully sought and perpetuated. It will tell upon the next generation as well as ours. Our children and our children's children will profit by each true song that we are singing now.
>
> —Horatius Bonar, Introduction to Eliza Ann Walker's *Hymns and Thoughts in Verse*, ix–x

> By the principle of adoration, I ... have been hurried into speech.
>
> —Elizabeth Barrett Browning, Preface to 1844 *Poems*

In a verse autobiography published in 1836, Caroline Bowles-Southey, wife of the Poet Laureate, recalled the centrality of Christian texts to her childhood. The Bible, the Book of Common Prayer, *The Pilgrim's Progress*, Foxe's *Book of Martyrs*, and sundry books of sermons dominated her early education, entertainment, and imaginative life. The young Elizabeth Barrett carefully recorded in her diary her own daily chapters of Bible reading, which included the Old Testament in the original Hebrew, as well as staggering amounts of theological literature. Christina Rossetti fell in her teens under the spell of the Tractarian preaching of the Reverend William Dodsworth, pored over Keble's *Christian Year,* and forced herself to give up playing chess because she cared too much about the very unspiritual ambition of winning. In November 1836, the *Christian Lady's Magazine* printed a letter concerning the appropriate writing and reading of poetry by devout women (VI 429–36). A woman should always bear in mind

14   Christian and Lyric Tradition in Victorian Women's Poetry

eternal and unworldly pleasures, states M. A. S., for while sacred poetry "elevate[s] the affections," "worldly poetry [is] a sand-box of Satan" (432). For these and other nineteenth-century women, Christianity and Christian texts offered a guide for all thoughts and actions, and a central focus for social, artistic, and literary projects.

Producing literature was in fact a vital part of Victorian women's practice of Christianity. Women in the Victorian period were acknowledged to be the 'religious sex,' but their relationship to the doctrines, practices, and hierarchies of Christianity was both highly circumscribed, which has been well documented, and complexly creative, which has not. The Victorians themselves delighted in praising women's innate, essential disposition to religious feeling. The Congregationalist minister James Baldwin Brown wrote, "And the women . . . have a deeper insight into spiritual truth, a quicker response to spiritual teaching, and a readier aptitude for spiritual work than falls to the lot of the masculine nature, in any but its highest examples" (175). The Evangelical William Wilberforce agreed when he opined that "that sex seems, by the very constitution of its nature, to be more favorably disposed than ours to the feelings and offices of Religion" (289). And Caroline Bowles-Southey's husband, Poet Laureate Robert Southey, uttered one of the most widely accepted nineteenth-century maxims when he wrote that "if religion were every where else exploded, it would retain its place in the heart of woman" (II 304). That Victorian women demonstrated greater piety than their men folk is borne out by demographics revealing that women made up a disproportionately large number of those attending church, from Dissenting to High Church congregations.[1] In his study of women and Anglo-Catholicism, John Shelton Reed has noted that "a number of demographic and cultural characteristics of Victorian society produced a large pool of unmarried women and of leisured married women, with the time and resources to devote to respectable but largely unpaid 'church work'" ("A Female Movement" 202).

But the nature of the 'church work' undertaken by Victorian women differed materially from the kinds of church work done by Victorian men. The practical work of the church, such as poor visiting, Sunday school teaching, and even arranging flowers for the sanctuary, fell almost solely on female parishioners. Pious belief and activity shaped the social outlets available to women: the Ladies' Committees, the Zenana Societies, the church bazaars, and the social campaiging in which women became increasingly involved from the late 1850s were all inextricably tied to Christian duty. To women also fell the task of extending the church into the home; Barbara Taylor stresses the domestic omnipresence of Victorian Christianity when she states, "God . . . settled into the parlour" (126). Motherhood, domesticity, and piety constituted three sanctioned and intimately related areas of influence for women. In 1848 *The British Mothers' Magazine* counseled women:

"*Heirs of more than royal race*"   15

Let our light so shine before our household. Let the atmosphere of single-hearted piety be breathed in our homes. Let our children detect no inconsistency between our profession and our practice . . . Let them from early childhood be taught to rely on established principles of religion, and to weigh their conduct by the unerring standard of the word of truth—not by the changing policy of the world's maxims. (267)[2]

The Church was preserved and propagated within the family by the patient guardianship of Victorian women. To Victorian men fell spiritual headship, both literally, in the form of the male figure preaching at the pulpit, and symbolically, in the patriarchal authority that handed down spiritual rules and roles. "Let the woman learn in silence with all subjection," proclaimed St. Paul in 1 Timothy 2:11 and 12. "But I suffer not a woman to teach, nor to usurp authority over the man, but to be in silence." While most Victorian divines whole-heartedly agreed, and most Victorian women dutifully complied, the *kind* of silence Victorian Christian women performed deserves closer examination.

Within a few dissenting denominations, including the Quakers and the Methodists, female believers could speak in church, could teach, even preach to the unconverted. Sarah Mallett, for example, received Charles Wesley's approval for preaching in 1787; Mary Bosanquet Fletcher and Sarah Crosby both preached for the Methodists in the late eighteenth century; and on many Victorian street corners Salvation Army women preached the gospel with great vigour. Such women were, of course, denominational exceptions to the general rule. For many more, staying within the spiritual sphere assigned to females meant keeping silence with their tongues but, very often, exercising their pens. Charles Spurgeon may have preached to crowds of over six thousand in the Metropolitan Tabernacle in London, but women could express themselves to an audience many times larger through penning religious verse, devotional manuals, tracts, and moralising columns for periodicals. Such texts were produced in voluminous quantities from innumerable feminine pens, as women wrote out of the single most important aspect of their lives: an inescapably potent cultural and textual touchstone, Christianity centred women's intellectual and imaginative existence. The oft reprinted and excerpted Hannah More counselled her female readers in *Strictures on the Modern System of Female Education*: "There is to woman a Christian use to be made of sober studies"; "serious study . . . helps to qualify her for religious pursuits" (139). Devout writing offered such a religious pursuit, an acceptable outlet for female piety, as the Reverend Morgan Dix states in a chapter entitled "A Mission for Woman" in *The Calling of a Christian Woman and Her Training to Fulfil It* (1884). Dix writes approvingly of women

who have found out ways of helping others, who have learned that love and sacrifice are the greatest words in our language. Some, by their

16 *Christian and Lyric Tradition in Victorian Women's Poetry*

> writings, helpful and wholesome; others, by devotion to philanthropic pursuit ... all these come forward and show us that there is still a mission for any devout and earnest woman who seeks it in faith and patience. (130–31)

It is *how* they wrote their "helpful and wholesome" works, the thematic and generic choices they made, that enabled women to negotiate with their sacred subjects. For, while women's literary engagement with Christian topics was permissible, controls were applied to the shape of that engagement. Dr. John Gregory's *A Legacy to His Daughters*, first published in 1774 and reprinted many times well into the nineteenth century, offered explicit advice to young women as to the ways in which they could explore religious opinion.

> I wish you to go no farther than the Scriptures for your religious opinions. Embrace those you find clearly revealed. Never perplex yourselves about such as you do not understand, but treat them with silent and becoming reverence. –I would advise you to read only *such religious books as are addressed to the heart, such as inspire pious and devout affections, such as are proper to direct you in your conduct,* and not such as tend to entangle you in the endless maze of opinions and systems. (15, my emphasis)

Dr. Gregory advises his daughters to read the kind of religious works that Victorian society allowed women to write: devotional texts. Theological historian Margaret Miles describes devotional writings as "not often argu[ing] theological issues; the advice they give is usually concerned with changing their readers' behavior" (*Image and Practice* 2). An example may be found in one of Christina Rossetti's devotional volumes, *Letter and Spirit* (1883), which gives instruction on how the Ten Commandments should guide the Christian's conduct in every respect, from avoiding idle jesting to thinking only of holy things on the Lord's Day.

Perhaps justly, Christina Rossetti's devotional poetry found more favour than her devotional prose, though in many cases the poetry shows a similarly intense moral scrupulosity. Literary critic G. B. Tennyson has endeavoured to define and categorise devotional poetry as a particularly bounded subset of religious verse. He first defines this broader category as "all poetry of faith, poetry about the practices and beliefs of religion, poetry designed to advance a particular religious position, poetry animated by the legends and figures of religious history, and poetry that grows out of worship" (4). Tennyson's narrower definition of devotional verse emphasises, as do Gregory and Miles, the significant characteristic of focus on conduct: devotional verse is "poetry that grows out of and is tied to acts of religious worship" (6).

Devotional writing, concentrating on worship, directing pious conduct, and regulating the religious affections, was insistently gendered feminine by the Victorians, and as insistently distinguished from 'masculine' theological writing. Nineteenth-century women could properly write devotional forms of literature because, as Miles points out, the devotional mode did not *argue*. Rather, women could take already established theological interpretations as a starting point and discuss their application. Devotional literature functioned to provoke action and stir affective response in its (mostly female) readers; exegetical prose that discussed and debated theological questions exercised, in contrast, contemplation and intellectualism—men's domain. Women's involvement in theological matters was considered not just unseemly but also unnatural—as Ruskin wrote, with famous and barely veiled disgust, in *Of Queens' Gardens*: "Strange in creatures born to be Love visible, that where they know least, they will condemn first, and think to recommend themselves to their Master, by crawling up the steps of His judgment-throne to divide it with Him" (vol. 18, 128). Scholars have begun to interrogate the anxiety (and degree of success) with which Victorians drew and enforced distinctions between masculine exegetical writing and feminine devotional writing; Julie Melnyk, Robert Kachur, and Virginia Bemis, among others, have analysed the variously observed distinction between devotional and exegetical modes within nineteenth-century women's writing, and have suggested that women could and did find ways to extend their devotional writings to 'do theology,' without seeming to exceed the proper bounds. This study will examine in detail the proposition that Victorian women poets could, in their devotional texts, negotiate artfully between prescribed and proscribed genres, to wrest from Christian discourse creative and unexpected modes of speaking.

Any literary undertaking that explicitly drew on the Christian scriptures presented a minefield that nineteenth-century women had to negotiate with enormous care. Victorian Christian women of the middle classes knew their Bibles intimately, carried tracts and baskets of moral earnestness to the poor, and held the solemn charge of raising their children to follow scriptural precepts. Yet Victorian women had a far from simple and straightforward relationship to the Word of God. There were, of course, a small number of women unusually privileged, educated, and ambitious enough to read and seek to contribute to historical and theological debates on the provenance of the scriptures, and even scriptural translations: Elizabeth Barrett, Dora Greenwell, and Frances Power Cobbe all wrote learnedly of such questions. However, women also sometimes felt the need to conceal their learned engagement with the Scriptures: Helsinger, Sheets, and Veeder's wording is telling as they note that Julia Evelina Smith was the first woman to translate the Old and New Testaments into English, in 1853, but "she did not publish her audacious venture until 1876" (vol. 2, 167). Mary Wilson Carpenter, in her study of nineteenth-century Family Bibles, notes the proliferation of biblical commentaries and devotional works by women writers including Mrs. Sarah Trimmer, Charlotte Yonge, and the much-revered Hannah More, but discusses the partial nature and

18 *Christian and Lyric Tradition in Victorian Women's Poetry*

limitations of these publications, limitations imposed by external cultural forces and by the female authors themselves: "Publication of and commentary on the complete Authorized Version appears to have been a space from which women dared not write, or from which they were barred by various economic, legal, and social prohibitions" (9).

In the face of these prohibitions, women used particular strategies in order to write concerning theological and specifically scriptural topics. Melnyk's introduction to an illuminating collection of essays on women writers' negotiations with exegetical and devotional literature suggests a range of strategic generic framings:

> Barred from university and pulpit, [women] were also forbidden to write in the traditional genres of theology, the treatise and the sermon. Their theological ideas appear instead in nontraditional genres, in letters, novels, pamphlets, devotional manuals, and in the increasingly influential periodical press, disguised as uncontroversial religious writings. (*Women's Theology* xii)

The various studies of women's religious writings in Melnyk's volume are significantly helpful for twenty-first century readers and scholars interested in developing a more complete understanding of women's engagements with Christian discourse in the nineteenth century. However, this introductory excerpt, and the volume as a whole, entirely omit consideration of what I contend was a genre of primary importance to women writing on Christian topics: lyric poetry. This omission has been general. Helsinger, Sheets, and Veeder recognise that for women barred from the pulpit, literature may allow a form of 'ministering,' and they comment pithily but briefly on the importance of hymnody:

> When hymn writing, for example, becomes a major enterprise of Victorian women, hymns change in kind and in liturgical function. Unlike earlier religious songs which were largely adaptations of the psalms, the myriad hymns which pour from Victorian pens express individual beliefs and hopes. In turn, the hymn encroaches upon the sermon in Protestant liturgy, as more than one minister realized: Rev. Joel Hawes used to announce caustically after a hymn that 'divine service would now recommence'. (vol. 2, 183)

The authors then immediately proceed, without consideration of poetic forms other than the hymn, to consider the ways women preach through fiction. In the several excellent recent treatments of women's religious writing in the nineteenth century, fiction has been the overwhelmingly favoured focus, and religious poetry has been consistently under-read and under-theorised. Christine Krueger's *The Reader's Repentance* concentrates on Methodist women preachers, and on the novel's adoption of this legacy to

"Heirs of more than royal race" 19

take on a prophet's role for social criticism. Elisabeth Jay's study "Doubt and the Victorian Woman" concentrates, again, on religious ideas in novels. Ruth Jenkins' *Reclaiming Myths of Power* discusses both the ideological ("mythic") underpinning of women's exclusion from spiritual power, and the ways in which nineteenth-century women recreated religious myths, drawing on Gnosticism and on the tradition of the prophetic calling, to "depatriarchalize the language justifying their marginalisation and to reinscribe that language and the companion narratives with female experience" (26). Jenkins' is a fruitful and provocative study, but she, too, concentrates solely on prose, primarily analysing canonical authors including Charlotte Brontë, Elizabeth Gaskell, George Eliot, and Florence Nightingale.[3]

This book argues that in the nineteenth century, poetry provided a particularly significant and congenial genre for speaking on religious topics, and that this congeniality was even more important for *women* speaking on religious topics. The first part of this assertion finds support in the substantial literature on the nineteenth-century fascination with the interrelationship of poetry and religion. Two important examples are Hilary Fraser's *Beauty and Belief* and Stephen Prickett's *Romanticism and Religion*. Fraser systematically explores the "proliferation of religio-aesthetic theories designed to reconcile the claims of Christianity and beauty, morality and art" in the nineteenth century (1). Fraser's comprehensive discussion covers Keble, Newman, Arnold, and Ruskin, as well as Hopkins, concluding with the Aestheticism developed by Pater and Wilde. Prickett's *Romanticism and Religion* begins at a somewhat earlier point, tracing Coleridge's philosophical influence on the poetics and theology of the Oxford Movement and on Newman in particular. Fraser, Prickett, and other critics have proven that in the Victorian period, an age both evincing hyper-religiosity and at the same time absorbing a stunning series of blows to the foundations of Christian belief, poetry became an invaluable prop to faith:

> In this context of the diminishing spiritual authority of the Church, many of the traditional properties and functions of Christianity were transferred to poetry. In its new elevated position, poetry was invested with so many moral and mystical qualities that it became, in the rhetoric of many Victorians, inseparable from religion. (Fraser 5)

Victorian poets themselves often voiced the intimate connection of the two: John Keble called poetry a "handmaiden" to religion, and Elizabeth Barrett Browning maintained that art and faith were inseparable, writing, "Christ's religion is essentially poetry—poetry glorified" (*Brownings' Correspondence*, vol. 5, 220).

Deeply influential for Victorian poets writing on religious subjects were the Tractarian poetics and model provided by Keble. G. B. Tennyson called the attention of Victorianist scholars back to the significance of Tractarian poetics, and of Keble's writings in particular, in his 1981 work *Victorian*

20   *Christian and Lyric Tradition in Victorian Women's Poetry*

Devotional Poetry: The Tractarian Mode. Even for the large majority of Victorians who opposed Tractarianism (also dubbed Puseyism and the Oxford Movement), and who had never heard or read Keble's Lectures on Poetry, the influence of *The Christian Year* was vast. First published in 1828, this best-seller of the Victorian period went through over 158 editions before the copyright expired in 1873; the collection of sweet, simple poems for all the celebrations of the Church calendar could be found in every middle-class English parlour, and was known and valued by High Church and Low Church adherents, by dissenters, and even non-believers.[4] In Keble's formulation, emotionalism and sincerity characterised the truly Christian poem better than striving for originality or effect, and one particularly important aspect of this prescription for his female readers and imitators was furthered by his dictum (and practice): "don't be original." In recent years a number of important studies have focused closely on Keble's literary influence as it shaped the work of women writers. Isobel Armstrong has traced the contribution of Tractarian poetics to an expressive aesthetic that enabled women poets in particular to manoeuvre within the conventions of the affective to critique the cultural construction of the feminine subject (see particularly "The Gush of the Feminine" and "Msrepresentations"). *John Keble in Context,* edited by Kirstie Blair, includes significant essays by Emma Mason, on Keble's influence on a number of women poets, and by Emma Francis, on how Keble's poetic theories relate to a female tradition of expressive poetics. As Scheinberg argues in *Women's Poetry and Religion,* one of the few full-length studies of Victorian women's religious poetry, Tractarian poetics' licensing (and valorisation) of the emotional, the irrational, and the effusive meant that the cultural standards that elided *poetry* with *Christian* and *poet* with *man* came under serious challenge. At the same time, readers must recognise that the intersection of poetry and Victorian femininity presented contradictions as well as congeniality: Scheinberg notes "the deep conflicts that the ideology of Christian womanhood created for women poets" (69), and traces the ways four Victorian women dealt with these conflicts. Scheinberg's book and other studies mentioned previously have contributed to an improved understanding that, in the Victorian period, the feminisation of poetry and the feminisation of religion were not merely simultaneously unfolding processes, they were mutually constitutive processes, and that women were important contributors to these significant cultural shifts.

In "Enfranchisement of Women" (1851), Harriet Taylor Mill sneeringly labeled the restricted field of pious activity open to women as a "sort of sentimental priesthood." Taylor Mill's phrase might be redeployed as a potentially illuminating designation for Victorian women, barred from office and career in the Church, doing God's work through their poetry. Much of their church work and particularly their charitable parish work was grounded in and justified by a nineteenth-century conception of the particular nature of woman as operating from the emotions. But women also

"Heirs of more than royal race" 21

did 'church work' *through* feeling—their writings, and particularly their poetic writings, translated emotional experience onto paper and sought to work on their readers by making their readers *feel*. The sentimental priesthood could have, in fact, a profound emotional and social impact. The Reverend Henry Elliott often said of his sister Charlotte's immensely popular hymn "Just as I am, without one plea," that he believed "she had done more good by that hymn, than he in all his ministry!" (quoted in Bateman 207).[5] Doing good, remaining a womanly woman, loving the Christian faith and scriptures but not overstepping accepted bounds of engagement, the feminine role was made up of a complex mass of dictates, summed up in the broadly used term "Woman's Mission," a phrase itself founded in an ineluctably Christian discourse. Practising femininity became in the Victorian imagination more and more closely identified with practising Christianity. And the production of devotional verse was an integral part of this gendered religious performance.

This study owes a debt to the work of those critics, whose number has slowly grown in the last dozen years, who have both contended and demonstrated that the influence of Christian belief on nineteenth-century literature deserves respectful analysis rather than embarrassed dismissal (among them Janet Larson, Linda Lewis, Julie Melnyk, Jude Nixon, Lynda Palazzo, and Frederick Roden). Christine Krueger rightly observes that feminist readings of women's Christian writings have all too often been one-sided and reflective of our own modern critical perspectives: "we measure the progress of women's literary authority through the eighteenth and nineteenth centuries by their rejection of 'patriarchal' religious beliefs and language" (4). Like Krueger, I dispute the assumption that women writers working with rather than against phallocentric and logocentric texts of Christian scripture and discourse must necessarily preach reconciliation with patriarchy, and find lamentable the exclusion from scholarly study of those women's texts that do not reject or protest. This study seeks to chart new ground in regard to its inclusive approach to women's poetry of Christian devotion. Central to this study is the contention that Christianity offered Victorian women writers more than twentieth and twenty-first century critics have generally allowed. These largely unexamined and often unexpected consolations were not confined solely to the private sphere, but helped define potential avenues for social action—as cultural historians of women's reforming and charitable work have demonstrated—and helped construct a female public identity that could encompass reformer, writer, even sage. It is beyond the scope of this project to fully examine the public face of women's engagement with Christian discourse, but my intention is to argue and analyse as fully as possible the range of 'personal' benefits for women who created literature that engages imaginatively with a Christian discourse. Part of my argument will be that many women saw their writings as 'reforming' in ways that have escaped our notice, and this work will explore the many facets of women's textual re-formations.

22 Christian and Lyric Tradition in Victorian Women's Poetry

Christianity functioned for Victorian women as a liberatory as well as an oppressive force. The conflicts women confronted in the intersection of Christian and poetic discourse could also be productive conflicts, and as Carpenter astutely notes, the Bible "can provide discursive resources for both reactionary and progressive literature—sometimes both in the same work" (148). To look for liberatory aspects within devout Christian texts is not to be blind to the ways Christianity has functioned to oppress the disenfranchised, but neither should criticism of oppression devalue or dismiss the many ways Christian religion aided and enabled Victorian women. Since Mary Daly's *Beyond God the Father*, feminist historians and theologians have built upon and away from her pioneering critique of Christianity's patriarchalism. Daly now calls herself "post-Christian," and a number of writers on women's spirituality agree on the impossibility of recuperating Christian discourse from its inherent and foundational sexism, calling feminists to abandon the Bible and biblical religion.

However, in recent years Michele M. Schumacher and other feminist theologians have called for recognition of the fact that women may make more complex negotiations with traditional religions than either slavish complicity or outright rejection. Bridget Gilfillan Upton, for example, offers a balanced discussion of the arguments concerning feminist readings, interpretations, and even expurgations of the Bible, and calls for nuanced readings of "the ways that feminists can read, challenge, appropriate, hate, or be nourished by the texts that our institutions have sanctioned in some way" (97). The work of Schumacher, Upton, and a number of other feminist theologians including Elisabeth Schüssler Fiorenza, Alicia Suskin Ostriker, and Mieke Bal informs the readings of Victorian women's texts that I undertake in this study. Drawing on Fiorenza's terms, I suggest that Victorian women poets variously apply, in their poetic responses to Christian texts, a hermeneutics of suspicion, which uncovers the biases and assumptions of androcentric scriptural texts, and a hermeneutics of creative actualisation, which uses the Bible as a resource or prototype for creativity, and "allows women to enter the biblical story with the help of historical imagination [and] artistic recreation" (*Bread Not Stone* 20). Ostriker plays with Fiorenza's terms, and, in *Feminist Revision and the Bible*, calls for a 'hermeneutics of indeterminacy,' which acknowledges the multiplicity of possible readings of a text like the Bible, and resists the creation of a replacement meta-narrative. Bal's three books on biblical interpretation insist upon valuing difference over uniformity and urge analysis of the self-interest of every disciplinary and interpretive engagement with scripture. Bal denounces the "centripetal force" of a universalising 'true account,' and presents a mode of reading in which the side story becomes the core story, the marginal character the central character.

The frameworks offered by these scholars offer a way of recognising, valuing, and analysing the creative, multiple operations of Victorian women's devotional verse, for their various transfigurations of Christian texts present un-traditional commentaries that interrogate the political interest-edness of accepted, univocal, 'coherent' narratives. While the majority of the Victorian poets I examine would self-consciously disavow the (anachronistic) label "feminist," their poetry variously and creatively reads, challenges, appropriates, hates, and is nourished by the sacred texts of Christian discourse. As Fred Roden has trenchantly asserted, "religious discourse may function as an alternative avenue to power for those who might otherwise be disenfranchised ... [including] women in Victorian culture by virtue of their gender" ("Kiss of the Soul" 39). In the creation of biblically sourced poetry, women create an avenue to power, finding not a discursive model that silences and suppresses, but rather locating models that permit expanded expression and vision.

Recently, poet and theologian Ostriker and literary critic Sheila Hassell Hughes have called critics to examine women's constructions of theology through the particular lens of literature. Victorian women's religious poetry as a body of literature demands this kind of examination. Kimberly VanEsveld Adams has undertaken one such study: *Our Lady of Victorian Feminism* analyses Victorian women writers' complicated use of what has previously been regarded as an ineluctably oppressive religious model, the figure of the Virgin Mary. Drawing on the arguments of essentialist feminism, asserts Adams, Anna Jameson, George Eliot, and Margaret Fuller use the Madonna to proclaim sexual equality as well as difference. Scheinberg's *Women's Poetry and Religion* makes another important contribution to this field, and concentrates on four Victorian poets, Elizabeth Barrett Browning, Christina Rossetti, Grace Aguilar, and Amy Levy. Scheinberg focuses closely on the four poets' use of Jewish traditions, tropes, and texts, arguing that these women undertook original theological work through their poetry through particular engagement with the Hebrew Scriptures (the Old Testament of the Christian Bible). In her introduction Scheinberg rejects, as do I, an over-simple identification of Christianity with oppressive patriarchalism; she suggests the adoption of Schüssler Fiorenza's kyriarchal model of investigating and understanding power relations, which complicates a dualistic understanding of the determination of authority and identity in Victorian England and foregrounds the contribution of race, class, colonialism, and religion, as well as gender, in the production of a system of domination and subordination.

Janet Larson, in "Lady-Wrestling for Victorian Soul," offers a provocative framework for discussion of nineteenth-century women's texts' conversions of master-narratives. She calls for "a more inclusive, less systematic kind of writing about women's relations to the Divine in the context of Victorian problems and resources" (52). Larson suggests Victorian women produced new words and regenerative visions out of their wrestling with divine texts, but she also acknowledges the limitations and complicities of Victorian women's spiritual writings. Larson emphasises the multivocality of women's texts and cautions, "there can be after all no master-narrative

24　*Christian and Lyric Tradition in Victorian Women's Poetry*

of such phenomena" (61). Larson's framework serves as an important and influential stimulus for my readings of Victorian women's poetry. The women's poems I read in this study, which re-frame and re-vise and re-write sacred texts, may not overtly challenge the male hierarchy that produced, disseminated, translated, and interpreted those texts. Nonetheless, through the act of offering their own textual interpretations (figured by Larson as wrestling), these poets demonstrate a drive for status, power, and creative liberty within that sacrosanct discursive domain.

It will be clear from this preamble that my work does not focus on protest verse, poetry that overtly resists or rejects aspects of Christian belief, Church structure, or textual authority, but rather focuses on *devout* poetry. Thus my goal is in one sense recuperative, but recuperative in a different way from the small but vigorous body of critical work on the religiously radical Victorian women poets to whom Virginia Blain refers as a "new breed of post-Darwinian atheists" (*Victorian Women Poets* 332). These poets include Mathilde Blind, who turned Darwinian theory into verse in the 1889 *Ascent of Man*, Louisa Bevington, who produced in 1879 the Evolution-inflected *Key-Notes*, and Constance Naden, an agnostic who wrote a number of witty, scientific treatments of scriptural texts.[6] Studies of these innovative women have served unintentionally to highlight the dearth of critical attention to the devout religious poetry that was central to the lives and work of numerous women in the nineteenth century. Illustrating this critical lack is the profound under-representation of devout Christian verse in recent anthologies. The anthologised verse of Christina Rossetti and of Adelaide Procter demonstrates the case: while almost all Rossetti's poetry in the second half of her life, after about 1872, is explicitly religious, this half of her oeuvre is very lightly represented in anthologies of the last twenty years; and while Procter's Catholicism is implicitly or explicitly treated in numerous verses, it is usually solely her narrative and feminist poems that have found a place in recent anthologies. Specialised anthologies of women's writing seem to display a uniform neglect of religious verse. Jennifer Breen's slim *Victorian Women Poets 1830–1901* (1994) includes only thirty women—Procter does not appear—and grants Rossetti's religious verse no room whatsoever. Leighton and Reynolds' much more comprehensive *Victorian Women Poets: An Anthology* (1995) reintroduced many forgotten voices, but it prints virtually no religiously themed verse, even that of Barrett Browning and Rossetti. Of the ten Procter poems the editors include, none are religious in theme. Armstrong, Bristow, and Sharrock's 1996 edition of *Nineteenth-Century Women Poets* fares somewhat better; of the ten poems by Procter that are included, five are explicitly religious or implicitly Christian in their morally hortatory content. Margaret Randolph Higonnet's introduction to *British Women Poets of the Nineteenth Century*, which also appeared in 1996, notes promisingly that "the secularization of twentieth-century culture has deflected attention from women's religious poetry; its poignancy and narrative power deserve fresh attention today" (xxviii). Despite this promise, however, this volume is again predominantly secular, including thirty Rossetti poems, just four of religious vein (including "In the Bleak Midwinter" and "Uphill"), and none by Procter.

The Christian ideology and themes reproduced in devout verse challenge anthologists battling questions of exclusion in its many facets. Virginia Blain's *Victorian Women Poets: A New Anthology* (2001) presents a deliberately narrow scope, limiting the poets included to just thirteen, omitting the verse of Procter altogether, and including just two of Rossetti's religious poems. Blain's introduction addresses the influence of Christianity on Victorian women's poetry more directly than most anthologists, but betrays a somewhat contradictory attitude toward it. Blain suggests a possible source of a Christian theme's attractiveness as residing in an inherent spiritual liberation:

> It can be argued that, for the truly devout, the realm of religion was a space marked out separately from the everyday, and that, since souls —unlike bodies—are unsexed, gender hierarchies could be kept at bay in this private space. This might help to account for at least part of the strong attraction towards religion shown by many women poets of the period . . . (7)

However, in an earlier passage of the introduction Blain articulates a more unconsideredly negative view, in her approving description of the way Michael Field "managed . . . to avoid the penitential meshes of conventional Christianity that so troubled many women poets" (6). I am not suggesting that Blain dismisses Christianity as nothing more than a punitive trap for Victorian women—she has elsewhere called for a more thorough investigation of the role Christianity plays in literary production in the nineteenth century.[7] But it has proved easy (and, at a basic level, eminently practical) for many anthologists to avoid fully engaging with the complex tangle of the many facets of Christianity that help shape women's verse—facets which go beyond the penitential and punitive to encompass the stimulating, the nourishing, the mystifying, and the renewing. The selection criteria for anthologies of women's writing have, after all, generally been founded in a feminist ideology unsympathetic to traditional Christian discourse, but additionally, selection necessarily imposes limits: religious verse has arguably been excluded from many anthologies for reasons of space and simplicity as much as ideology.

Even broader-ranging anthologies have displayed only a little more inclusivity. Collins and Rundle's *Broadview Anthology of Victorian Poetry and Poetic Theory* (1999) presents twelve Procter poems, though only one ("The Jubilee of 1850") is explicitly religious in content. Of Rossetti's twenty-six poems in this collection, the only three religious poems are "A Better Resurrection," "For Thine Own Sake, O My God," and "Uphill." On the

26 *Christian and Lyric Tradition in Victorian Women's Poetry*

other hand, Valentine Cunningham's vast, comprehensive *The Victorians: An Anthology of Poetry & Poetics* (2000), which actually includes selections of hymns by Cecil Frances Alexander and Frances Ridley Havergal, offers a slightly more accurate ratio of religious to secular verse: six of the twenty-one Rossetti poems included are religious in theme, and of Procter's four inclusions, one is the pious "Thankfulness." Francis O'Gorman's *Victorian Poetry: An Annotated Anthology* (2004) also includes hymns (four, one of which is by Havergal), and thirteen poems by Rossetti (three explicitly religious) but neither of the two Procter poems included is devout. More recently, Christopher Ricks' commanding *New Oxford Book of Victorian Verse* (2008) prints twenty-four Rossetti poems, of which six are explicitly religious, but from Procter, only the far-from-pious "Envy" appears.

I believe anthologists and scholars of the Victorian period are presently in the interesting position where we need to turn our recuperative efforts to voices not from the margins but from the centre; in the case of Victorian poetry, the centre that has slipped from general view is the verse of religious belief, not doubt; of orthodoxy, not radicalism. Several factors have contributed to this slippage. Jay speaks for many twentieth- and twenty-first-century readers when she points out that both the volume and the conventionality of nineteenth-century religious verse by women is "dispiriting":

> it too frequently display[s] a tendency to narrow the Romantic sensibility into piously sentimental versifying or the expressions of a limited range of acceptable postures and attitudes, where 'Mothers meek' and 'maidens mild' [are] celebrated and heavenly bliss promised to those who learned to 'Wait patiently upon the Lord'. ("Women Writers and Religion" 259)

Jay does not specifically engage, however, with the idea that we find this verse dispiriting *because of the way we read it*, because of our own invisible but powerful 'modern taste.' Feminist and post-colonial theories and Modernist and New Critical approaches have helped shape our attitudes and readerly expectations. Critics looking for obvious or latent subversion have often found little value in texts that staunchly espouse the divinely appointed roles of the sexes, that take a devout rather than antagonistic attitude towards the Christian scriptures, and that reproduce conventional forms. This has meant that a real lack persists in our understanding of Victorian women's devotional writing and its cultural contribution. To ignore or 'read past' the overwhelmingly Christian tenor of most Victorian women's poetry is to marginalise or violate its chief perspective; to abstain from engaging critically with Christian-themed poetry is to surrender the most salient literary position from which women could speak.

As it has been in the anthologies, religious verse has been neglected by most of the critical studies of the last twenty-five years. Its conventionality, its adherence to and promotion of narrow and constraining cultural and literary standards have proved difficult to read critically. Many feminist commentators on women's writing have omitted any analysis of conventional, conformist texts at all. When they have treated the literature of conformity, critics have tended to take one of two approaches. The earlier was a high-minded excoriation of its false consciousness, following the model of Dale Spender:

> Women writers have at times told the male/public what they wanted to hear and have reinforced the dominant group's definition of reality in the process. They have supported the tunnel vision of males and have been accomplices in the reproduction of patriarchal order by portraying females in the distorted forms in which males have cast them, even while they, as women writers, were aware of the falseness of this image. (225)

Spender seems to deny any innate literary or critical value in literature that reproduces cultural 'truths'. The second approach, as adopted in the eighties by Gilbert and Gubar, Annis Pratt, Cheryl Walker, and others, is to assert that much women's writing is characterised by a double-facedness, a simultaneous complicity with and critique of patriarchal cultural and literary standards. Critics attempting to recuperate literatures of conformity from this angle have often resorted to plumbing occasionally uncooperative texts in order to find proof of covert but nonetheless passionate resistance. This approach can prove simplistic, if not reductive, reinforcing a limiting dichotomous relationship between the repressive "society" and the courageously (or timidly) rebellious artist. Looking solely for this kind of polemic in conformist texts limits complete investigation of their full negotiation with social and cultural contexts, making it seem that the nature of the complex interplay between creative artwork and cultural structures is limited to oppositionality.

In the 1990s, two ground-breaking critical treatments of Victorian women's verse were produced by Angela Leighton (*Victorian Women Poets: Writing Against the Heart*, 1992) and Dorothy Mermin (*Godiva's Ride*, 1993). While these works began to right the neglect of nineteenth-century poetry authored by women, both paid scant attention to women's religious verse. Both Leighton and Mermin note the centrality of religion to Victorian women's identity, but present it simply as a restrictive force on women's personal and creative lives. In this way they do not offer much progress from Kathleen Hickok's earlier survey, *Representations of Women: Nineteenth Century British Women's Poetry* (1984). Hickok's work omits study of devotional poetry even though she notes its importance and congeniality as a genre for women of the era. Hickok observes of these minor women poets that "generally . . . the more conventional their poetry, the greater their popularity" (8), but she immediately adds, "and the lesser their enduring value." Hickok, Leighton, and Mermin have tended to concentrate their analysis on women

28 Christian and Lyric Tradition in Victorian Women's Poetry

writers' methods of transcending convention; creatively working within tradition has not merited much attention as a strategy. Isobel Armstrong, while she spends very little time on religious writing in the influential *Victorian Poetry: Poetry, Poetics, and Politics* (1993), does at least suggest its potential illustrative benefits for critics: "often with women writers, the more conventional the didactic lyric, the more accepting of its conventions the writer is, the more it can be used as a way of looking at conformity from within" (336).

Given all its attendant challenges, how can we look at conformity from within? Eric S. Robertson wrote in 1883 in his introduction to *English Poetesses*, "faith is woman-like, doubt is man-like" (xiii). Blinkered and patronising as this statement is, it may suggest a way into the Victorian period, a way to read and consider the literature created by Victorian women that is produced out of their own understanding of (and negotiations with) their fields of interest, engagement, and investment. I aim to read the poetry of "woman-like faith" interrogatively, but to avoid the trap that Mermin (illuminatingly) falls into when she writes of women authors' negotiations with Christian structures: "women could not afford to question the faith that gave them poetic authority" (115). First, this view implicitly valorises questioning and protest in a way that may lead to an exclusionary focus, one that, as deployed in some of the scholarship indicated previously, may skew our understanding of the true range of the literature Victorian women produced. Second, it doesn't open the question of what other possible negotiations with faith were available to and utilised by women, more subtle and creative negotiations with master narratives that might include re-focussed retellings, generic adaptations, or manipulations of expected aesthetic standards. And third, Mermin's statement points to an underlying lack of theorisation of how Victorian women could negotiate their own poetic authority according to an entirely different paradigm, reformulating their relationship to God-words, and creating spiritual and artistic roles in and out of—and supplementary to—existing church hierarchies. This study aims to contribute to such a theorisation. Maintaining a devout Christian faith does not, I contend, equate ineluctably to slavish and uncritical replication of all the structures that have traditionally attended that faith, and women writers "dare" considerably more, even within a structure of sincere belief, than Mermin seems to have considered.

To assess the richness and importance of these artifacts, we need a more nuanced way of reading and evaluating conformity in its various forms, ideological, thematic, and stylistic. The stylistic conventions to which Victorian religious poetry conforms have contributed to the seemingly adamantine barrier to late twentieth- and twenty-first-century assessments of this body of verse: the Modernist and New Critical hermeneutics that dominated literary criticism for much of the twentieth century offered few resources for grappling with a poetry of compliance, devotion, and sentiment. We need, fundamentally, to interrogate the construction of the 'modern taste' that has rendered either "dispiriting" or invisible literature that conforms to earlier, dissimilarly constructed tastes. In Victorian religious verse, these stylistic conventions include didacticism, ornament, repetition, and sentimentality. Religious sentimentality has often been viewed by post-Victorian critics as particularly distasteful. Donald Davie, in his introduction to the 1981 *New Oxford Book of Christian Poetry*, explains his criteria for including or omitting religious poems: "if they are to be worth anything they must not be for instance mawkish or sentimental" (xxi). Not only does Davie neglect to explain precisely why sentimentality renders a poem not "worth anything," he takes it for granted that all readers, both 'now' and 'then,' have applied this incontrovertible standard.[8] More recently, Jane Tompkins and Suzanne Clark have demonstrated persuasively the fallacy of assuming such a standard, arguing for the importance, influence, and transgressive potential of the nineteenth-century sentimental, and this study is indebted to Tompkins' conception of the literary text as "doing cultural work" through its subject matter and style. I contend that in precisely this provocative conjunction of the particular form of sentimental, highly ornate lyric poetry, with subject matter concerning religious belief, observance, and experience, we can find in Victorian women's verse the development of an empowering kind of self-expression. Conventions of style should not be dismissed or excluded as an embarrassment, but rather be taken into account as a vital aspect of a text's cultural work. Style, as Clark points out, has a politics (5).

Recognising the political underpinnings of stylistic features helps us delve deeper into the neglect of Victorian religious poetry that began well before the advent of feminist criticism, as well as helping to explain the usefulness of this body of religious work for its own contributors. In *Distinction*, Pierre Bourdieu insists that artistic practice is socially situated practice, with political functions. Bourdieu outlines the field of literary taste as an arena of struggle, with the establishment of 'taste' an ongoing strategic battle with the aim of recognition, legitimation, and maintenance of cultural and symbolic power. These calculations are, however, masked or concealed: "struggles for the monopoly of artistic legitimacy are less innocent than they seem" (57). It follows that the meaning and value of any artistic work is constantly under challenge and constantly in flux: "the value of the arts, genres, works and authors depends on the social marks attached to them at any given moment" (86). If we recognise, then, that our twentieth- and twenty-first-century aesthetic values, as well as our feminist values, constitute the standard by which Victorian women's religious poetry 'fails' and becomes unreadable (and unread), we must also accept the contention that all aesthetic standards are contingent, arbitrary, and concerned with power. The kind of universal standards that Davie and his cohort espouse in the twentieth century have their roots in New Criticism's efforts to dissociate from Victorian values. In demonstrating the contingency of every set of aesthetic criteria, Bourdieu reveals as untenable theories that 'consecrate' works of art as having transcendental or essential meaning: aesthetic criteria have everything to do with tenuous and vulnerable cultural status

30   *Christian and Lyric Tradition in Victorian Women's Poetry*

and the drive to preserve distance from lower groups. These criteria are in fact the opposite of universal (and disinterested) as they are inescapably tied to the self-interested exercise and maintenance of power.

Bourdieu's explanatory model is particularly apposite to the literary tastes and standards that have waxed and waned in the last hundred or so years. The power processes underpinning the transmission of all taxonomies and typologies become exposed to view, including certain binaries familiar to twentieth- and twenty-first-century commentators on nineteenth-century literature (like distinctive/vulgar, original/derivative, pure/sentimental, and so on). Any arbiter of taste "has to perform a degree of rationalization of what it transmits" (67), because standards of competence and perception are self-justifying and self-perpetuating in a process which Bourdieu felicitously terms "the self-legitimating imagination of the 'happy few'" (31). Literary taste, like many other learned skills, is an acquired cultural competence, in the best interests of the dominant group (in this case, literary critics) to continually replicate and demand. Taste, then, must be recognised as "a distinctive expression of a privileged position" (56). Bourdieu insists we interrogate such aesthetic staples as "the pure gaze," "the taste for formal complexity and objectless representations" (35), and "disinterestedness," (55)—all standards by which Victorian women's religious verse clearly falls short, but all standards representing "an interminable circuit of inter-legitimation" (53).

Most twentieth-century critics have tended to view (or to dismiss from view) women's devotional verse as didactic and/or derivative, but adopting Bourdieu's model to the project of re-examining the literature of conformity from within demands the interrogation of both these terms. Didacticism certainly flourished in this verse, but was by the Victorians valued very differently, and did not necessarily entail the exclusion of other kinds of aesthetic and personal ambition. In this body of poetry, edicts concerning right and moral behavior may be seen to be directed both ways, 'downward' in directives toward the righteously obedient Christian reader and 'upward' in pious reminders directed toward the righteously consistent Lord. Avoiding a reflexive cringe away from didacticism allows recognition that the poet's assumption of a directive role highlights and problematises the role of the didact herself and the nature of her relationship to her God. Secondly, dismissal of this poetry as derivative should also give way to an interrogation of our own (highly contingent) attitudes towards and assumptions concerning 'original' texts and originality. On the one hand, devaluing these poems as derivative of the Bible unwittingly reinscribes a version of the fundamentalist view that valorises Christian belief as an originary force, seminal, monolithic, and univocal—a view which unavoidably derogates poems that draw on the tradition of Christian faith, teachings, and writings as mere secondary imitations of the sole Original. Feminist literary and biblical criticism has taught us to explode this false idea of univocality and recuperate from all sources, including sacred ones, multiple, diverse, and questioning voices. Additionally, as Bourdieu would argue, our contemporary

"Heirs of more than royal race"   31

'derivative' account of Victorian women's religious poetry is acontextual, ignoring or suppressing the period's own prevailing aesthetic standards. Victorian taste was favourably inclined toward respectful replications of model spiritual texts, and was shaped by Keble's influential edicts and example and the entirely different cultural value (from our own) that the Victorian period assigned to poetic "imitations." Nor does a twenty-first-century view take account of the complex ways gender informed aesthetic values, categories, and responses to texts in the nineteenth century.

We need a careful examination of women's devotional verse as a contextualised and coherent body of work, an examination that takes into account the theological and cultural influences that shaped women's beliefs and texts as those texts foreground and thematise the construction of the sacred, and that respectfully analyses the interrelationships of texts that refer to each other and draw from each other. Analysis of the (multiple) forms of power that are constructed, deconstructed, questioned, and reformed in this complex body of work will help re-value the seemingly one-dimensional didacticism of these poems and will open up to view a variety of creative negotiations with sacred sources, the creativity of which is transformative rather than derivative. Women took up the Bible, the Prayer Book, the sermons they heard preached in their places of worship, even the ubiquitous *Christian Year*, and produced re-visions, rewordings, and adaptations that altered genre and characterisation, trained unexpected focuses on or away from strategic plot-points and personae, and manipulated formal and stylistic models. In short, women produced *transfigurations* of source texts.

I mean, of course, to foreground the biblical provenance of this noun. The three synoptic gospels relate Christ's transfiguration on the Mount of Olives, when his human, incarnate face and clothing became unearthly white, bright as the sun.[9] Each of the layers of meaning assigned by the OED to the verb, *to transfigure*, resonates for Victorian women's religious poetry. To transfigure means to change in outer appearance, and this study argues that the lyric form chosen by women poets for their revisions of sacred truth plays a significant role in its re-visioning. To transfigure also means to transform, which connotes a fuller, more mystical and less definable change than simply that of outer shape; this project will assess the subtle and significant ways women poets recast their original subject matter. And to transfigure also means to elevate, glorify, idealise, or spiritualise, all verbs expressing active engagement rather than passive reception, and all connoting an elevation of source material from an earthly, earthy, implicitly inadequate sphere, to a supernatural realm. Transferring the metaphor of transfiguration from Christ's body to women's texts opens up a series of suggestive readings.

Ostriker has suggested a different metaphor for reading women's biblically sourced texts, one drawn from alchemy. She states that in "seizing . . . textual permission, the poet becomes not merely scribe but alchemist. She transforms language . . . in a crucible and flame" to transform the base text and also to transfer the authority of interpretation and revelation to

32   *Christian and Lyric Tradition in Victorian Women's Poetry*

the poet herself (74). While the simplest definition of alchemy is "the pursuit of the transmutation of baser metals into gold," the word's connotations encompass magic and irrationality, a way of thinking that exceeds or escapes the confines of traditionally accepted truth, though retaining entirely traditional materials. I draw on a combination of the transfigurative and alchemical metaphors to discover and articulate the ways women shaped relationship between their conformist, devout verse and the patriarchal theological tradition they inherited. These women poets take up the elements available to them, earthly, 'base,' even contaminated as they are, and create not stark opposition but transformation, elevating, glorifying, and ultimately transfiguring texts into new, unearthly, gleaming forms of truth. Through these poetic operations Victorian women re-figure their works and their roles within Christian structure and Victorian society. I stress here the plurality of works, roles, and forms of truth, because it is through these transfiguring revisions of texts that women poets make their biblical source polyvocal, and as Bal and Ostriker have so persuasively argued, opening up this polysemy is a vital critical and feminist undertaking.

The religious poetry of the widely read and admired Felicia Hemans highlights a number of the primary concerns of Victorian women's religious verse. Dead in 1834, before the teenaged Princess Victoria even ascended the throne, Hemans, her poetry, and her popularity are nonetheless essential to an understanding of the operations of Victorian literature. The posthumous volume of Hemans' *Moral and Religious Poems,* which William Blackwood and Sons published in 1850, reveals not only that Victorian readers maintained an appetite for Mrs. Hemans' verse, but also that this particular genre of religious verse was considered reliably appetising to that market. For the volume does not trade solely on the author's name; few titles could indicate their contents as uncompromisingly as *Moral and Religious Poems.* As Hemans' and many similarly entitled volumes convincingly demonstrate, religious verse maintained its position as an extremely saleable commodity in the Victorian literary marketplace.

Moral and Religious Poems foregrounds the ways in which religious subject matter renders problematic the aesthetic role and ambition of poetry. In a letter written the year of her death, Hemans reflects on the significance of her religious poetry, in a delicate balance of modesty and ambition:

> I hope it is no self-delusion, but I cannot help sometimes feeling as if it were my true task to enlarge the sphere of sacred poetry and extend its influence. When you receive my volume of 'Scenes and Hymns' [of Life, and other Religious Poems] you will see what I mean by enlarging its sphere, though my plans are yet imperfectly developed. (Letter written on May 8 1834; quoted in Jane Williams' *Literary Women of England,* 468)

Articulating a wish to "enlarge the sphere of sacred poetry and extend its influence" indicates the author's high estimation of the potential cultural and social import of this verse; of what this verse—and this versifier—might *be* and *do*. Selection and categorisation in the volume are also revealing of wider Victorian cultural expectations concerning what religious poetry should be and do, because this is not Hemans' own selection but a posthumous editorial arrangement, and thus the volume's structure suggests insights into editorial expectations of the readership. The poems are divided into four sections: Scenes and Hymns of Life; Sonnets (this section further subdivided into five subsections, each with its own title); Hymns for Childhood; and Miscellaneous Poems. The twenty-first-century reader will note the emphasis on both the identification and the somewhat paradoxical interpenetration of specific generic divisions—'lifelike' scenes, hymns, sonnets, children's verse—which clearly did not seem contradictory to the Victorian readership. Conscious aesthetic ambition, in the adoption of the elevatedly poetical form of the sonnet, coexists with the seemingly contrary purpose of the hymn, a form characteristically not merely indifferent to aesthetic aims but even inimical. A hymn's overt purpose is not to attract attention to itself as a work of art, but rather to render itself invisible, directing the reader in effect to cease being 'a reader' and become 'a worshipper,' concentrating solely on God, God's works, God's family, and the required action of the believer as a member of that family. A hymn should deflect attention from its artistic construction; a sonnet invites it. In this volume, artwork and moral work, juxtaposed in sonnet and hymn, render each other problematic.

The "Hymns for Children" section of the volume reveals a particular tension between the aims of entertainment and education. In fact, these hymns seem in their inculcation of a particular moral agenda less poems for children than poems for the guardians of children. While some Victorian women, such as the Taylor sisters, carefully tailored poems to a childish audience by means of simple language and striking image, Hemans' hymns for children render their intended audience problematical—the sentiments are both pious and lofty and the language very little adapted from Hemans' characteristic, floridly ornamental strain.[10] Tone and style beg the questions: who is this poem for? what does it 'do'—and for whom? For example, in the children's section appears "Paraphrase of Psalm CXLVIII." This uninvitingly entitled poem contains a number of elements suggestively characteristic of the broader body of Victorian religious verse. Reading the poem must begin with deciphering the title, which directs attention simultaneously to the original text and to recognition that this secondary text differs: it comprehends its intertext but it goes beyond it, as the psalm's title is comprehended and extended. This poem *says* 'Psalm 148'; the poem *is* Psalm 148 but it says and is also *more*; a self-proclaimed paraphrase, it re-words and words, offering different and additional language to that of the original. Beneath the poem's title appears the epigraph: "Praise ye the Lord. Praise ye the Lord from the heavens: praise him in the heights." This repeats word for word the psalm's first verse, from the Authorised, King James Version. The epigraph offers a further indication of how this text

34 *Christian and Lyric Tradition in Victorian Women's Poetry*

replicates but diverges from the original text: the word-for-word Bible text shows by its inclusion, as an excerpt, that *this* poetic text is not this scripture's usual textual and contextual 'place': the epigraph both familiarises and defamiliarises the text that is to follow. The poem that does then follow provocatively reveres, echoes, supplements, and supplants its original.

> Praise ye the Lord! on every height
> > Songs to His glory raise!
> Ye angel-hosts, ye stars of night,
> > Join in immortal praise!
>
> O heaven of heavens! let praise far-swelling
> > From all thine orbs be sent;
> Join in the strain, ye waters! dwelling
> > Above the firmament.
>
> For His the word which gave you birth,
> > And majesty and might:
> Praise to the Highest from the earth,
> > And let the deeps unite!
>
> O fire and vapour, hail and snow!
> > Ye servants of His will;
> O stormy winds! that only blow
> > His mandates to fulfil;
>
> Mountains and rocks, to heaven that rise!
> > Fair cedars of the wood!
> Creatures of life that wing the skies,
> > Or track the plains for food!
>
> Judges of nations! kings, whose hand
> > Waves the proud sceptre high!
> O youths and virgins of the land!
> > O age and infancy!
>
> Praise ye His name, to whom alone
> > All homage should be given;
> Whose glory from the eternal throne
> > Spreads wide o'er earth and heaven!

What does Hemans' poem borrow from its scriptural original, and what does it transform? How does the poem suggest that borrowing be read as a *way* of transforming? What and/or who is thus transformed? Overall, Hemans' version renders very closely and faithfully the commands issued

"*Heirs of more than royal race*"   35

and the specific beings and elements addressed in the King James version of the psalm, such as fire, vapour, hail, snow, and cedars (though Hemans does not mention the "dragons" that make an appearance in verse seven of the original). The progression of the poem's stanzas matches very closely the content and order of the original biblical verses. Of the fourteen verses of the original psalm, only one disappears from the poetic paraphrase, and that is the last: "He also exalteth the horn of his people, the praise of all his saints; even of the children of Israel, a people near unto him. Praise ye the LORD" (in contrast, the poem's final stanza paraphrases the psalm's verse thirteen, and then closes there). A number of decorative poeticisms characteristic of Hemans and of her many female descendants do intrude, so that the "creeping things, and flying fowl" of the King James Version are beautified into "Creatures of life that wing the skies/ Or track the plains for food"; and "kings of the earth" swell to encompass the weighty accoutrements of power: "kings, whose hand/ Waves the proud sceptre high!"

Hemans' most significant additions are not, however, those of content, but rather those of form, style, and context. Most obviously, the psalm has been transformed formally into metre, and into a stanzaic form—*abab* common metre quatrains—that mandates recognition of its poeticalness. Hemans chooses a markedly more ornamental verbal style than the Authorised Version, deploying noun phrases in the place of a number of simple nouns (as in "mountains and rocks to heaven that rise"), incorporating more adjectives, and choosing words with emotionally loaded connotations (such as "fair" and "proud"). Hemans' stylistic choices help point the reader to the poem's conscious self-contextualisation, its self-incorporation into the affective tradition. The increasing 'pile-up' of pious ejaculations in the second half of the poem, and the cumulative emotive effect of no less than sixteen exclamation marks, help mark the poem as an example of what Armstrong has dubbed "gush"; devout gush, but unmistakably affective gush, as the poem presents a version of the original that is both faithful and unmistakably feminised.

This one brief example helps illustrate the tradition on which Victorian women religious poets drew—a tradition of looking to scripture for subject matter, of negotiating with that subject matter by means of form and style, and of transforming it into an ornamental and sentimental lyric. Importantly, too, Victorian women also created and drew on their own tradition: Hemans was to serve as a kind of sacred authority for subsequent generations of women writing devotional verse, and women poets were to call on other women poets and a womanly audience, as well as on masculine models, to construct an authoritative sacred tradition of their own.

Victorian women's religious poetry is challenging. I use the word deliberately, and mean to apply it in two senses. It is challenging to read, courtesy of our inheritance of an aesthetic and hermeneutics which have taught us to prize intellectualism, complexity, and irony and to cringe at the flowery, the pious, and the sentimental. In this book I endeavour to delineate a new way of reading and evaluating this sentimentalised

36 *Christian and Lyric Tradition in Victorian Women's Poetry*

religious discourse, and as part of this delineation I will explore the second sense in which this poetry can be described as challenging. Conservative and conformist as most of this body of work unquestionably is, it does issue a challenge of its own. While it does not always clearly confront and oppose sexual, social, and religious inequities, women's religious verse consistently investigates and explores the constrictions and the possibilities inherent in women's self-expression in the nineteenth century. As I have already argued, to dismiss this poetry as merely compliant is to ignore its complex relation to its social, historical, and literary context. It manoeuvers within a highly constructed but simultaneously liberating Christian religious discourse; it grows out of and contributes to the aesthetic and theological turmoil of the English Church in the nineteenth century; and it is vitally involved in the development of the lyric genre. Rediscovering and re-reading Victorian women's religious poetry will help broaden our understanding not only of the interests and perspectives of Victorian women, but also of their self-conception and processes of self-construction, and of their varying means of self-assertion as writers and as spiritual sages.

Both universal and particular, religious poetry expresses transcendent desires and simultaneously speaks eloquently of the circumstances of its production. This project examines in depth a poetry that treats God in His Heaven but also women on their earth. In examining the cultural work Victorian women were doing in their production of religious verse, I seek also to illuminate what work *they perceived themselves as doing* in their literary toiling that was simultaneously so humble and so ambitious. While many Victorian women wrote modest and self-deprecating prefaces to their volumes of religious poetry, disclaiming ambition and meekly hoping their verse might be "helpful," these self-deprecating statements need to be reviewed alongside the claims for power articulated in the poems themselves. And many other Victorian women explicitly and forcefully expressed their view of the tremendously important spiritual and even salvific force of their literary undertakings. In "Some Account of the Greek Christian Poets," Elizabeth Barrett writes:

> We want the touch of Christ's hand upon our literature, as it touched other dead things—we want the sense of the saturation of Christ's blood upon the souls of our poets, that it may cry *through* them in answer to the ceaseless wail of the Sphinx of our humanity, expounding agony into renovation. (*The Poetical Works* 600; emphasis in original)

Dora Greenwell was to quote these words of Barrett in her own volume of poems, *Camera Obscura* (1876), thereby suggestively complicating (and extending) the appeal to sacred authority. And Emily S. G. Saunders, also explicitly negotiating with forms of sacred authority in her *The New Christian Year* (1891), includes Morning and Evening Hymns that are subtitled

"*Heirs of more than royal race*"   37

"The Mission of Poets, Individually and Collectively." For Saunders, the poet is the mouthpiece and agent of God for earth's transformation. "Evening Hymn" begins:

> 'Heirs of more than royal race!'
> See ye claim your gift of grace,
> God's interpreters to be,
> To the sons of misery.
> As they sit in darkness dim,
> Let them hear your glorious hymn!
> Praising God for what ye know
> He hath done for man below;
> Singing of the Heavenly Peace,
> Though Earth's wars not yet may cease . . .

And concludes:

> Poets! While endures the wrong,
> As a brotherhood of song
> Praise Him with so clear a voice,
> Earth shall even now rejoice.

These women had no small ambition for their verse, and even those who did not align themselves with Milton as explicitly as Saunders saw themselves as doing God's work in their broader society, in and through their verse.

Horatius Bonar's words, which appeared at the opening of this chapter, also provide the close. Bonar's insistence on the importance of religious verse to the Victorian period issues a challenge and invitation to which this book responds, and the aim of the subsequent chapters is to investigate more closely the significance Bonar saw inherent in "each hymn that has gone out from the most obscure minstrel" (Introduction to Eliza Ann Walker's *Hymns and Thoughts in Verse*, viii).

> They [the writers of these hymns] did a work that is to last. They are not upon the world's roll of poets, but they have struck out notes which have taken hold upon the spiritual history of thousands, and contributed more than volumes of divinity to preserve faith alive, to kindle hope and love, and to infuse vitality into dead creeds, or warmth into frozen forms. (viii–ix)

In declaring that each woman's pious verse "wove itself into the texture of the age," Bonar offers implicit encouragement to twenty-first-century critics and readers seeking to better understand and value the richness and complexity of what Victorian women's religious poetry *did*, both for its authors and for its age.

2 "God's interpreters to the sons of misery"
Rewriting Master Narratives

William Michael Rossetti was a painstaking (if somewhat interfering) post-humous editor of his sister Christina's poetry, and a careful guardian of her reputation: his biographical Memoir takes pains to present her as a morally scrupulous woman and distinguished poet. Nonetheless, he felt the need to sound certain apologetic notes about her work.

> The reader of Christina Rossetti's poems will be apt to say that there is an unceasing use of biblical diction. This is a fact; and to some minds it may appear to detract seriously from her claims to originality, or to personal merit of execution. Without pre-judging the question, I will only remark that the Bible was so much her rule of life and of faith that it had almost become a part of herself, and she uttered herself accordingly. (*Poems of Christina Rossetti* xii)

In the twentieth century, Raymond Chapman has agreed with William Rossetti about what he terms "the linguistic problem" in Christina's work, stating that her close employment of biblical language reflects an inability to articulate religious experience in any original or startling way (unlike Patmore and Hopkins, and the seventeenth-century poets, whom Chapman clearly prefers). "Regrettably," writes Chapman, "the Biblical strain too often dominates what she wants to say. . . . Christina's language too often falls short of her intense feeling" (192).

This chapter seeks to complicate the judgment articulated by William Michael Rossetti and Raymond Chapman, and broadly shared by a number of Victorian and most twentieth-century critics, concerning Victorian women poets' employment of "the Biblical strain," and the subsequent inhibition of merit and originality.[1] Both critics, to give them their due, do suggest biblically based poetry should be read in the context that helped produce and model it. Acknowledgment of the Christianity-centred milieu of the Victorian era is indeed vital for a nuanced reading of the period's literature, as John M. Anderson recognises in a far more sympathetic recent reading of women's religious poetry: Anderson points out the importance for nineteenth-century women of Christian religion "as a social fact and as

"*God's interpreters to the sons of misery*"   39

a source of language and imagery" (196). In recent years, promising signs have appeared of a new critical focus on the rich and complex influence of Victorian Christianity, as, for example, in a special issue of *Victorian Literature and Culture* in 2003, Jude V. Nixon's edited collection *Victorian Religious Discourse* (2004), and innovative studies applying specifically religious lenses to the work of canonical figures including Christina Rossetti (by Lynda Palazzo and Sara Choi), and Elizabeth Barrett Browning (by Linda Lewis and Karen Dieleman): such studies have begun to remedy the late twentieth-century myopia concerning the centrality of Christian belief to Victorian culture, literature, and daily life. These nuanced critical examinations notwithstanding, in studies of women's literature it continues to be of fundamental importance to question and disrupt Chapman's simple, lingering, and inescapably gendered diagram of power relations between Bible and poet, as dominating and dominated elements, respectively. (As Cynthia Scheinberg has trenchantly observed, Milton is never criticised as being 'dominated' by his biblical source.) It is timely to critically investigate the notion that the language of the Bible 'takes over' Rossetti's language, and to consider the ways her poetic language may 'take over' the Bible itself. To borrow Ostriker's metaphor, women presenting retellings of scripture work not as scribes but as alchemists, offering in their retellings neither copies nor necessarily outright revisions, but transformations of source texts. Taking as a starting hypothesis the contention that Rossetti and her many Victorian sisters wrestled with their great Original no less creatively than did their Victorian brothers, a focus on their multivarious poetic strategies will produce insights into the lyrical and cultural importance of their undertaking.

In this chapter I examine an array of Victorian women poets' re-presentations of the sacred text of the Bible, and outline a series of strategies by which Victorian women poets undertook to engage with their awe-inspiring source. These strategies vary in degree of deference and daring. Analysis of these strategies shows how women's religious poetry reveals richly conflicted attitudes: an abiding reverence for Holy Scripture and a keen awareness of exigent cultural dictates jostle with women's strong urge to *make the Bible their own*, to assert possession of it, to wield it as a means of taking on creative and spiritual authority, to teach from it, and to see themselves recognised within it.

The work of feminist theologians helps ground this chapter, underpinning the fundamental assertion that Victorian women, when they produce poetic versions of the Scriptures, offer new interpretations of those sacred texts. Every reading and writing, in short, enacts not passive reception but active engagement and interpretation (see particularly Ostriker, *Feminist Revision and the Bible*). Issues of originality and source of inspiration prove central concerns for Victorian women religious poets, even when—or particularly when—they argue that they are not presenting original interpretations, but rather "reflections," or "responses," and explicitly frame their

40 *Christian and Lyric Tradition in Victorian Women's Poetry*

verses as emotional rather than intellectual engagements with a biblical original. These self-representations as unmediated reflections of scripture deserve scrutiny for what they conceal and reveal about women poets' claims for their texts and for the poems' relationship to the originary texts.

In drawing on feminist theology to offer an explanatory model for what Victorian women poets are doing, I aim to remain clear about what they are *not* doing, and not to attempt to infuse their writings with an anachronistic (and implicitly belittling) twenty-first-century feminism. Rather, my aim is to describe more fully the complexity of the relations between nineteenth-century women poets and their authoritative source. It would be misleading to identify the majority of the women poets I read in this study as either feminists or theologians—most would vigorously reject both labels. Their poetic versions of scripture cannot be uncomplicatedly claimed as examples of feminist biblical hermeneutics, as those versions fail to meet most of the defining features of such a hermeneutics.[2] The overwhelming majority of this poetry does not present self-conscious analysis, nor is it explicitly grounded in the experience of women's oppression. It doesn't, in most cases, set itself specifically to expose androcentric or oppressive intention in those texts. Rosemary Radford Ruether in "Feminist Interpretation: A Method of Correlation" points triumphantly to a new kind of grace made manifest in feminist theology: the "infusion of liberating empowerment from beyond the patriarchal cultural context, which allows [women] to critique and stand out against these androcentric interpretations of who and what they are" (114). While Ruether offers a compelling vision, it remains important to point out the ways in which Victorian women's verse does *not* operate this kind of grace. Emphatically, these women poets do not work or write beyond the patriarchal cultural context; writing on and in tandem with the Christian scriptures, they work explicitly within that context. Nor do Victorian women overtly critique or stand against androcentric definitions of women and women's role. What their poetry *may* do is "highlight the social, religious, and political power of women which has been ignored, overlooked, or hidden by patriarchal hermeneutics" (Upton 100)—but it does so obliquely, often by means of picking and choosing texts and images to represent, highlight, and comment upon, rather than by means of pointed polemic. Victorian women poets do not discard the biblical canon, nor do they set up a new canon; rather, they present and invite new views of the canon, of its formation, and of its interestedness.

In their poetic re-tellings of Scripture, at the same time as articulating humility and reverence for that Scripture, Victorian women poets interfere with the idea of a meta-narrative, disrupting the idea of a single, authorised, correct version by offering "their" version, "another" version, effectively multiplying the possibilities. In the range of individual readings they offer, they present an implicit resistance to systemisation. Building on the definitions of hermeneutical approaches proposed by Fiorenza in the classic 1984 *Bread Not Stone*, Upton dubs such an approach "a hermeneutics of

"God's interpreters to the sons of misery"   41

indeterminacy" and defines this hermeneutics as "insisting on the multilay-ered, contradictory indeterminacy of meaning in texts" which "prefers to offer a range of readings of particular texts rather than the development of some kind of theoretical meta-narrative" (97). Victorian women develop a hermeneutics of indeterminacy by offering multiple readings of particular texts (for example, a number of Jesus' miracles are retold many times in women's religious verse), but also by broadening their poetic focus to take into account overlooked aspects of biblical passages, sidetracks, minor characters, and so on. Women poets take many approaches to the (short) biblical Book of Ruth, for instance: Lucy Bennett writes a series of dramatic monodies voicing Naomi, Ruth, and Orpah, the daughter-in-law who stays behind; Annie Ross Cousin writes poignantly in the first person of Naomi's losses in "Reverses"; Jane Crewdson emphasises Ruth's youthfulness and steadfastness in "The Better Choice"; and Georgiana Taylor, in "Ruth: Or, the Satisfied Soul," chooses to focus on the romance of Ruth and Boaz, turning it into a romantic fairytale of a beautiful maiden rescued. The theologian Mieke Bal in *Death and Dissymetry* models a way of reading and responding to the biblical Book of Judges that helps illuminate Victorian women's broader range of textual engagements: like Bal's, their texts present a mode of reading in which the side story becomes the primary story, or more accurately, one of a range of possible primary stories. In this way Victorian women's texts may be seen to present untraditional commentaries that interrogate the political interestedness of linear narrative.

For most Victorian middle-class women, the Bible was almost always close at hand. Read aloud for household devotions, sought for comfort in the privacy of the closet, and for many families the only acceptable reading material on Sundays: the influence of the Bible as an arbiter of morality and behaviour, a source of imaginative exercise, and a textual model for the Victorians can hardly be exaggerated. As Mary Wilson Carpenter's study of Family Bibles has shown, Victorian women were perceived to be particularly sensitive and impressible consumers of this various and occasionally volatile volume, so much so that expurgated (or, more correctly, delimited) texts were specially produced as suitable reading for the whole family (see *Imperial Bibles, Domestic Bodies*). Drawing on Elizabeth Langland, Carpenter delineates the ways Family Bibles were produced for Victorian women and at the same time helped produce Victorian women themselves. Women were thus positioned as "material angels," simultaneously characterised by the powerlessness of created commodities—that is, the highly constructed pious angel of the home—and also possessing the power of influential consumers.

In this study I am interested in the ways in which Victorian women secured to themselves another kind of power in relation to the Bible, when they responded to this powerful instruction manual and imaginative stimulus as a text and as a textual model. The genre of poetic paraphrases of the Bible is not unique to the nineteenth century. The Christian West has a long history of poetic retellings of biblical narratives penned both before and after Milton:

42 Christian and Lyric Tradition in Victorian Women's Poetry

for example, Francis Quarles wrote extremely popular verse paraphrases of scripture (as in *Hadassa* (1621) and *The Historie of Samson* [in the *Divine Poems*, 1630 and 1633]), Isaac Watts published an imitation of the Psalms (1719), and Charles Wesley published *Wrestling Jacob* in 1742. Women writers also contributed to this tradition: the best-known example of female-authored biblical narrative in the seventeenth century is Lucy Hutchinson's *Order and Disorder,* and in the eighteenth century, Elizabeth Singer Rowe composed *The History of Joseph.*[3] Within the substantial history of women's religious writing, the Victorian period is unique in the proliferation of these writings; literally countless Victorian women sought to make the Bible (and in so doing, their own souls) poetical. In the particular activity of writing poetic paraphrases of scripture, Victorian women took up what could be claimed as an unexceptionably pious activity, and simultaneously created an ongoing critical engagement with narratives of power and orthodoxy.

Attempting the biblical paraphrase elicits from nineteenth-century women a number of statements of anxiety or unworthiness concerning the ambition of the project and/or the poet's inability to live up to the amazing original. An early and ambitious poetical Bible paraphrase was undertaken by the proto-Victorian Hannah More, whose profoundly influential strictures on female education, imagination, reading, and writing continued to shape subsequent generations. Her lengthy *Bible Rhymes* (1821), a work which is modestly (or immodestly) subtitled "On The Names Of All The Books Of The *Old And New Testament:* With Allusions To Some Of The Principal *Incidents And Characters*" (emphasis in original), opens with a contradictory and suggestive prefatory statement. More writes:

> The subject, it is true, admits of little poetical embellishment, even were the Author better qualified to bestow it. Indeed the dignity of the Sacred Volume is so commanding, its superiority to all other compositions so decided, that it never gains any thing by human infusions: paraphrase dilutes it, amplification weakens, imitation debases, parody profanes. (*The Works* 184)

In her balanced periodic style, and to a lesser extent in her word choice, More echoes another quasi-sacred authority, Samuel Johnson, who argued in his *Life of Waller* the impossibility of writing Christian poetry of any value: "Omnipotence cannot be exalted; Infinity cannot be amplified; Perfection cannot be improved ... the ideas of Christian theology are too simple for eloquence, too sacred for fiction, and too majestic for ornament" (292). In composing a grand echo of a great writer writing of (impossibly) great writing, More aligns herself, despite and because of her own protestations, with a tradition of linguistic and stylistic authority. Similarly, within the poem itself More further comments on her inability to deploy language adequate to describe the effectiveness of biblical language. Celebrating this inability then becomes the occasion and justification of her own song, as

"God's interpreters to the sons of misery"   43

when she deploys consciously poetic language to lament her own inability to express, in poetic language, the true "song" of Isaiah:

> 'Twere hopeless to attempt the song,
> So vast, so deep, so sweet, so strong!
> Fain would I tell how Sharon's rose,
> In solitary deserts blows;
> Fain would I speak of Carmel's hill,
> Whose trees the barren waste shall fill;
> Of Lebanon's transplanted shade,
> To sandy vallies how convey'd;
> The noblest metaphors we find
> To loftiest objects there assign'd.
> These splendid scenes before us bring
> Th' invisible, redeeming King.
> In every image, every line,
> Messiah! we behold Thee shine.
>
> But who shall dare these charms to tell,
> One British* bard has sung so well?
> His Christian page shall never die,
> O si sic omnia! all reply.[4]

More's footnoted mention of the one poet (Pope) who, she feels, has managed to 'sing well' of these ineffable glories both undercuts her point about the task's impossibility and renders questionable her posture of modesty concerning her own song. Pope's page is immortal because it is essentially Christian, a character and a condition to which all (explicitly) and the speaking poet (implicitly) may aspire.

More's expressions of inability, along with the other similar protestations that frequently preface Victorian women's poetical paraphrases, are conventional disclaimers that perform a seemingly modest but actually paradoxical function. On the one hand, they deliberately direct attention to the originals, the sacred narratives that, More states, present perfect writing and offer perfect reading. She tells her readers that she, "having long been anxious for their highest interests, cannot consult them better, than by earnestly recommending to their serious and daily perusal, that sacred volume, emphatically called *the book*" (183). The didact More betrays no awareness of the multiple possible referents of her words. Her italicisation of *the book* renders it at one and the same time specific (the Bible/ the Good Book) and suggestively nonspecific. To be pointed to The Book, readers must be reading *this* book; what is more, the reading of these (More's) words replaces the reading of the Bible, in so far as only one can be read at a time. In contradistinction from their own apologia, such poetical paraphrases actually foreground those "human infusions" into the sacred narratives, offer supplements, complements,

44   *Christian and Lyric Tradition in Victorian Women's Poetry*

supplantings; implicit re-evaluations of the relationship between and the mutual positioning of the two texts. More's own wordy title, effectively denoting her work as a supplement to the original, undercuts her suggestion that *the book* renders other writings pointless. In her poem as well as in her preface, More constructs dictates on 'right' writing and 'right' reading and, ineluctably, she asserts control of those standards. More stakes a claim for spiritual authority *by means of* her overtly humble self-positioning in relation to her great scriptural original.

The Authorised Version and the Authorisation of the Poet

Victorian women religious poets construct a complex and multi-faceted relationship with the authorised texts with which they work, and in the process of this construction they negotiate their own authorisation as interpreters of scripture and as poets. Charting the boundary between acceptable and unacceptable female voicing of scripture was an important task and controlling preoccupation for these poets, and they began to position their biblically based poetry relative to the idea of 'originality' even before their readers opened the volume. Scanning the titles of women's devotional verse collections reveals a key initial component of these volumes' self-representation, as numerous titles explicitly relate themselves to the Christian scripture. Examples include *Scripture Spoil in Sacred Song* (Adeline Braithwaite,1886); M.E.B.'s *The Young Child's Gospel, or The Life of Our Lord in Easy Verse* (1880); Mrs. Robert Dering's *Gatherings from the Scripture* (1848), Isa Gillon Fergusson's *Parables in Song* (1889); Harriet R. King's *Thoughts in Verse upon Scripture Texts* (1842, 1846); Fanny Wright's *The Books of the Bible in Verse* (1908); and many, many others. Before the reader glimpses a word of poetry, these titles claim a relationship to sacred texts that is simultaneously primary, a first-hand direct relationship, and also secondary, a relationship of inherent dependence and indebtedness to the Great Original. The Victorians' understanding of the 'originality' of the Bible underwent serious challenges in the course of the period, due to the gradual dissemination (mostly after Eliot's English translations of Strauss and Feuerbach in 1846 and 1854) of the ideas of Higher Criticism. Exponents of the Higher Criticism subjected the biblical account to scholarly historical analysis, in effect questioning the scriptures' veracity; this approach, hand in hand with the popularisation of scientific discoveries concerning the geological history of the earth and the development of species, cast doubt on the status of the Bible as a 'true account.' The publication in 1860 of *Essays and Reviews*, in which a number of churchmen sought to apply the ideas of the Higher Criticism to Christian religion, contained explicit challenges to the idea of the Bible as an original, divinely inspired text. Rather, the Bible was argued to be a product of its time, shaped by its context and the intentions of its various and very human readers. The responses of pious Victorians to these challenges to orthodox faith varied.

"*God's interpreters to the sons of misery*" 45

While some refuted these ideas altogether (branding the authors of *Essays and Reviews* "the seven against Christ"), others, like Philip Henry Gosse, went to some lengths to align new scientific truths with the account laid out in the Bible.[5] The responses of individual Victorians to the Bible *as a text* and as an example of creative inspiration were particularly personal and various, and that variety of response has yet to be adequately studied.

In the context of the widely disseminated but also resisted tenets of the Higher Criticism, the entitlement of women's religious poetry may be read as evidence of a particular kind of assertion: explicitly relating their work to the Original work both conveyed women's affirmation of the inspiration of that primary account and communicated their sense of the inspiration of their own accounts. For devout Victorians who continued to believe in the veracity and divine inspiration of the Word of God, the self-positioning of these women writers in relation to the Bible would have demonstrated sense and a becoming respect. But for a twenty-first-century reader assessing the impact of the cultural context and trained by deconstruction to suspect the unruly powers of the text, these volume titles signal a provocative contradiction. Despite the claims many titles make for a degree of purity and an unmediated re-presentation of scriptural truths, all re-wordings in fact offer mediation of those sacred texts. Explicit entitlement of their verses in relation to scripture renders more rather than less distinct women's active engagement with their holy source, for it draws attention to their co-option of anointing and their implicit assertion of their own entitlement to discuss scripture. Toiling as they do to delineate the relationship of this work to the earlier Work, these book titles have as part of their aim the charting of the boundary between God's words and women's words. Such charting is of course part and parcel of constructing the boundary—and pious Victorian women were keen participants in the process of their own delimitation—but contradictorily, participation in the act of setting boundaries confers its own form of authority, one which contests the clear division between and even the actual divisibility of God's and women's inherently authoritative words.

Not all Victorian women religious poets use the words Scripture or Bible in their volume titles, but most make lesser or greater use of biblical references in their *poem* titles, through this practice simultaneously drawing and problematising that boundary between authorised and unauthorised material. Poem titles are often composed of an indicative few scriptural words such as "Fight the Good Fight of Faith," (*Christian Lady's Magazine* vol. 11, 1839), but even more frequently presenting the unadorned denotation of the chapter and verse, as in Hemans' "Paraphrase of Psalm CXLVIII," discussed in Chapter 1. Such deliberate and bald acknowledgements of exterior originary sources often implicitly conflict with the aesthetic imperative. Consider Christina Rossetti, who drew on scripture for the titles that often vexed her throughout her career, and who adopts explicitly biblical titles almost exclusively in her 1893 *Verses*, whether or not they sound felicitously poetic: compare, for example, the figurative and melodic

46   *Christian and Lyric Tradition in Victorian Women's Poetry*

"They shall be white as snow" with the undeniably unwieldy "That which hath been is named already, and it is known that it is Man."

If a poem's title might conceivably be read without realisation of the biblical context—and George Landow has suggested in *Victorian Types, Victorian Shadows* that for the Victorians such a decontextualisation would be nigh impossible—the inclusion of a scriptural epigraph is an almost mandatory feature of Victorian women's biblical verse. The epigraph itself may take several forms, but most often one of two: it provides either the chapter and verse reference alone, for example, "Mark xiii.2," or the entire verse or passage reprinted in full: "Seest thou these great buildings? there shall not be left one stone upon another, that shall not be thrown down" (both of these examples are drawn from poems printed in *The Christian Lady's Magazine*). Susan Sniader Lanser describes nineteenth-century women writers' epigraphy "as a means for suggesting the scope of their knowledge, giving [their work] a moral and intellectual weight, and lending external authority to their textual stance" (99). Through title and epigraph choice, then, a Victorian writer foregrounds her consciousness of debt to her source, but the paraphrase text also produces dueling claims both to secondariness and to inspiration. Making her verse a scriptural echo-chamber served as a kind of cultural shorthand for a woman poet, indicating piety and modesty in the face of the greatest story ever told. It also enabled a woman poet to do without a classical education, by stressing the adequacy of her biblical education—remembering that while Victorian women were encouraged to study the Bible, that study was to enable them to obey, not question (Flowers 164). Additionally, by so emphatically acknowledging their debt to the Bible, women poets may access the inspiration represented but also *enacted* by the Bible as the Word of God. By acknowledging its secondariness, the poetic paraphrase text can indicate its own parallel nature as a divine communication, divine in origin, inspired and thus unstudied and artless (as Chapter 5 will discuss more fully, this poetry also engages more problematically with aesthetic and religious standards of value).

The presentation of secondariness in this poetry is inescapably vexed and suggestive. On occasion, the scriptural epigraphs multiply, sometimes overwhelming the poem itself: Adeline Braithwaite's "Thou Visitest Him," for example, presents an opening epigraph of text from Job, and then goes on to place between three and five new scriptural references at the start of every quatrain of the poem. Within the body of the poem, many women's verses engineer a sort of reverse epigraphing in the form of diligent and copious footnoting. Verses that take this practice to an extreme can appear quite bewildering to a twenty-first-century reader. Eva Travers Evered Poole references her sources in *Left Alone With Jesus, and Other Poems* (1890) particularly faithfully. Most of her poems have an opening epigraph, and additionally many have scripture verses or references interpolated in the body of the poem, as, for example, in "Ready." This poem has as epigraph "'I am now ready'—2 Tim iv.6," and at the end of each eight-line stanza

"God's interpreters to the sons of misery" 47

appears a separate Bible reference, illustrating each declared readiness—
to fight, speak, work, sit down, give, and wait. Another poem, "Called,
and Chosen, and Faithful" actually supplies note numbers every two lines,
and provides as footnotes scriptural references for even the most glanc-
ingly mentioned ideas. This extremely visible diligence determinedly dem-
onstrates the "faithful[ness] in witness and word" that the speaker of the
poem wants God to find in her. But the supreme example in Poole's volume
of displayed faithfulness to the original must be "Giving and Taking," in
which every single line of the seven trimeter quatrains is footnoted with a
biblical verse reference. This poem now appears positively grotesque.

Take everything from Jesus,[1]
    O needy, laden soul![2]
Give everything to Jesus,[3]
    Oh Him thy burden roll.[4]

His is the free salvation,[5]
    His is the Royal dress,[6]
His is the joy of giving[7]
    To thee His righteousness.[8]

Take everything from Jesus,[9]
    O child of royal birth![10]
Give everything to Jesus;[11]
    Have nothing stored on earth.[12]

His is the golden treasure,[13]
    His is the precious store,[14]
His is the joy of taking[15]
    All that thy love will pour.[16]

First, take the love He offers,[17]
    All undeserved and free;[18]
Then give Him back, with gladness,[19]
    The love He gave to thee.[20]

First take His strength for service,[21]
    Receive His perfect peace,[22]
Then give Him every power,[23]
    And learn thy Lord to please.[24]

Let God have all His glory;[25]
    Contentedly believe[26]
His place to be the Giver—[27]
    Thine, only to receive.[28]

48 *Christian and Lyric Tradition in Victorian Women's Poetry*

1 Rev. xxii.17
2 Rev. iii.17
3 Prov. xxiii.26
4 Ps. lv.22
5 Isa. lv.1
6 Isa. lxi.10
7 Acts xx.35
8 Isa. liv.17
9 John xv.5
10 2 Cor. vi.18
11 2 Sam. xix.30
12 Matt. vi.19, 20
13 Col. ii.3
14 Cant. vii.13
15 Cant. v.1
16 2 Sam. xix.30
17 John iii.16
18 Rom. v.6, 8
19 2 Cor. v.14
20 Rom. v.5
21 Phil. iv.13
22 Isa. xxvi.3
23 Rom. xii.1
24 Gal. i.10
25 Isa. xliv.11
26 Jer. xxxi.11
27 Acts xx.35
28 Ps. lxxxi.10

Disconcerting and awkward to twenty-first-century eyes, but far from rare in nineteenth-century women's poetry, this kind of scriptural source-citing betrays the intensity of women poets' preoccupation with their position in relation to a source so overpowering it must be scrupulously acknowledged (and as scrupulously delimited). Different poems adopt different techniques to yoke their verse to scripture (or yoke scripture to the service of their verse). Frances Ridley Havergal's "I did this for thee! What hast thou done for Me?" and Sarah Geraldine Stock's "The Sweetest of All Music," to name two examples, supply rather than footnotes a full scripture reference *beside* each line of the poem. Slavish citation appears also in the poetry published in women's periodicals. *The Christian Lady's Magazine*, published between 1834 and 1848 and edited for most of that time by the fervently Evangelical Charlotte Elizabeth Tonna, printed religious poetry in every issue, alongside earnest articles on the errors of Popery and on "Female Characters of Scripture." The periodical's verse offers confirming illustrations of many of the defining characteristics of women's religious poetry of

"God's interpreters to the sons of misery" 49

the period, in its range of themes, its emotionality, and in the self-conscious formal and stylistic elements that arise in response to anxiety over acknowledging the poetry's 'appropriate source.'[6] One notable example from *The Christian Lady's Magazine* is "Do You Love Christ?" (vol. 25, 366–67): in this poem of thirty-two lines of rhyming couplets, seventeen footnotes refer the reader to seventeen Bible passages. This footnoting always places the note number at the end of a line regardless of the interruption this presents to the enjambment:

> And if dissevered from the living Vine[1]
> How canst thou dream that thou hast Life Divine![2]
> Sweet is the union true believers feel,[3]
> Into one Spirit they have drunk;—the seal[4]
> Of God is on their hearts,—and thus they see[5]
> In each the features of One family![6]
>
> (1 John xv.1; 2 John xv.6; 3 Rom. xii.5; 4 Eph. iv.4; 5 Eph. i.13; 6 Eph. iii.14)

Other examples of this citation-strained style abound. While the effect of poems like "Do You Love Christ?" is undeniably rather comic, simply dismissing the verse as "bad poetry" means remaining oblivious to an important aspect of how it functions: the reasons for and the result of the conscious and visible strain on poetical structure and linguistic convention need interrogation. This poem is not just "a bad poem," for its function has changed; it is required to work as a poem and to work *as another kind of text* as well.

The primary impact of the kind of scriptural running reference operating in a poem like "Do You Love Christ?" is at a visual level. It constructs a highly constraining relationship with the reader, mandating a reading process that travels out of the poem, returns, leaves the poem, and returns; the reader is confronted with and must put into relation literally multiple texts. But at the same time as emphasising difference and requiring the reader to negotiate that difference, this kind of referencing strikingly breaks down the distinctness between the texts thus artfully arranged. Footnoting of this kind, whether the notes are presented beside the text or below it, suggests an at least visual parallelism between the poem and the source it seems so emphatically to point 'away' to: the source is right there, sharing the same page. Authority diffuses, spreads by proximity, as guidance to one text is offered from a proximate, related, but supplementary other text. What is more, these heavily footnoted (or side-noted) poems strikingly resemble Bible commentaries, popular nineteenth-century versions of which included works by Thomas Scott and John Morison,[7] as well as Bibles that incorporated chain-referencing systems. The cross-referencing to other Bible texts and/or key themes undertaken by such (almost invariably male-authored) guides aided the Christian in studying the scriptures. The proliferation and

50 *Christian and Lyric Tradition in Victorian Women's Poetry*

popularity of such reference guides bespeaks what Landow has noted: the average Victorian reader had such a degree of familiarity with the Bible he or she could reasonably be expected to be able to both recognise and identify virtually any biblical allusion in his or her reading material. Why, then, do many women poets go to such lengths to offer the reader guidance, to specifically identify the texts that their texts allude to? Less, I contend, to help the reader read the Bible, than to help the reader read the poem in a particular way, and thus, and just as importantly, to help the reader read the *poet*. In a copiously footnoted poem, the poet seems invisible: a direct relationship between these words and the earlier words is laid out on the page, effectively suggesting the disappearance of the mediating role of the poet. But the poet is simultaneously completely visible, and completely unignorable: she must be taken into account. The extreme constructedness of this text/these texts, the evident deliberation that has gone into the selection and placement of every word and phrase, continually directs attention to the circumstances and author of its/their construction. The author foregrounds presentation, because these visual markers (numbers, notes) are part of her project: they function for the reader in a familiar way, helping transfer authoritative status to this text and to this text's presenter. Pointing continually to an original Author, the woman poet continually points to her role and to herself, as arranger, artist, and as another author/ity.

Intertextual theory suggests ways of evaluating and analysing the strategies of women poets who incorporate, excerpt, condense, expand, elaborate upon, and otherwise transfigure scriptural texts in their own texts. Theories of intertextuality argue that seemingly 'derivative' texts, those that at a surface level reify a hierarchical origination structure which renders them secondary if not powerless, have in fact a far more complicated relationship to originary text and to reader. Derivation or imitation may in fact be read as an arrogation of power *from* or even *over* the originary text. "Every literary imitation," write Worton and Still, "is a supplement which seeks to complete and supplant the original and which functions at times for later readers as the pre-text of the 'original'" (7). While it may seem deliberate misreading to impute to Victorian women's religious poetry any intention to supplant the authority of the Bible—this would be the opposite of the poets' stated aim—verse that invites a reading of itself as a version of the Bible does implicitly promise but also defer a return to that original, therefore asserting its own (albeit temporary) primacy. It also implicitly promises the 'completion' Worton and Still mention: this text, in these circumstances, in this construction, does a particular thing the Bible does not do, for a particular audience (women poets often deliberately conjure these audiences as children, or servants, or a group in need of a simplified presentation of the Truth, which may be best offered by supplementary texts like these poems). The way in which supplementing may shade into supplanting has implications both for the author (the individual Victorian woman author) and for the continuing but altered original, as "these forms of creative splitting

"God's interpreters to the sons of misery"   51

or catastrophe . . . function both as temporary proofs of the integrity of the writing subject and as transgressive inscriptions of (feminine) fluidity into textuality" (Worton and Still 9). Splitting apart Christian univocality, making versions multiple, provides a way of inscribing the woman into the Bible. Particularly apposite to readings of Victorian women's poetry is the ineluctably gendered aspect of an intertextual reading; beginning with Kristeva's "Word, dialogue and novel," which introduced Bahktin's ideas of dialogism and monologism, theories of intertextuality have regularly incorporated the construction of sexual hierarchies into their accounts.

Thus in their biblically based poetry Victorian women undertake a delicate intertextual balancing act, proffering on the one hand the authority of the original biblical text, and on the other hand presenting their own authority as a shaper and pointer of that text. For, while poetic paraphrases of scripture display considerable variety in the degree of closeness with which they follow the original text, they show a striking uniformity in the presence of an 'application' element, that is, the implicit or explicit lesson which the poet draws from the scripture passage, usually appearing in the second half of the poem. As part of a wrestling for textual and interpretive authority, a woman poet must negotiate the inter-relationship between worshipping, producing worshipful verse, and exerting influence on the readers of the verse. As these roles combine passivity and activity, they foreground the poet's awareness of her own significant, contributive authority.

Frances Ridley Havergal, popular and voluminous hymn-writer and devotional poet, offers an instructive initial example because of her fame, the seriousness with which her verse engaged with the issue of poetry's—and thus the poet's—great religious role and responsibility, and the earnestness with which she attempted to legislate her verse's relationship to God's own words. Born in 1836, the bookish, musical, and linguistically gifted Havergal experienced a passionate conversion at the age of 14, and turned her considerable gifts for singing and for writing poetry to the exclusive use of promoting Evangelical Christianity. She composed many hymns which rapidly found their way into Victorian hymnals and became lasting favourites, including the Consecration hymn "Take My Life and Let it Be" and "Like a River Glorious." Havergal never married and was physically frail for much of her life, but like many Victorian women her earnest piety led her to undertake a phenomenal amount of religious, philanthropic, and literary activity, including the memorisation of the New Testament, the Psalms, and a number of other books of the Bible, as well as the production of many tracts, devotional prose works, and occasional poems. She often said that every line and every tune was given to her directly by God, writing in 1867:

I have a curiously vivid sense, not merely of my verse faculty in general being *given* me, but of every separate poem or hymn, nay every line, being *given*. I never write the simplest thing now without prayer for help. I suppose this sense arises from the fact that I cannot write exactly at

52 *Christian and Lyric Tradition in Victorian Women's Poetry*

will. It is peculiarly pleasant thus to take every thought, every verse as a direct gift; and it is not a matter of effort, it is purely involuntary, and I feel it so. (*Letters* 59; emphasis in original)[8]

Havergal's poem "An Interlude" (in *Poetical Works*, 1884) echoes both the spirit and the expression of the previous statement, describing a relationship of pure, childlike, unmediated receptivity:

> So now, I pray Thee, keep my hand in Thine,
>   And guide it as Thou wilt. I do not ask
> To understand the wherefore of each line;
>   Mine is the sweeter, easier, happier task
> Just to look up to Thee for every word,
> Rest in Thy love, and trust, and know that I am heard. (stanza 3)

In a number of other poems Havergal explores more figuratively the idea of being a receptacle, a mere container and transmitter of what are in very essence God's words. "The Song Chalice" engages explicitly with this question.

> 'You bear the chalice.' Is it so, my friend?
>   Have I indeed a chalice of sweet song,
>   With underflow of harmony made strong
> New calm of strength through throbbing veins to send?
> I did not form or fill,—I do but spend
>   That which the Master poured into my soul,
>   His dewdrops caught in a poor earthen bowl,
> That service so with praise might meekly blend.
> May He who taught the morning stars to sing,
>   Aye keep my chalice cool, and pure, and sweet,
> And grant me so with loving hand to bring
>   Refreshment to His weary ones,—to meet
> Their thirst with water from God's music-spring;
>   And, bearing thus, to pour it at His feet.

The friend voiced in the first line is not exactly correct when she states that the poet "bears" the chalice. The poem makes quite clear that this poet *is* herself the chalice, and her physical body is simultaneously denigrated ("a poor earthen bowl") and exalted, as her purity, her emptiness and lack of contaminating heat and sourness, become the vehicle for a spiritual labour. A new Mary, this handmaiden of the Lord, formed and filled by Him alone, bears the word of God. However, several aspects of the poem complicate its claims of pure, unmediated conveyance of God's words and music. The poet explicitly positions herself *as* a mediator (again like Mary) between God and "His weary ones" who can come to her poetry for holy refreshment. Further, poetic form intrudes into consideration of the nature of this chalice and its contribution to the life it contains: Havergal has deliberately chosen for this 'song' the form of a Petrarchan sonnet, which in poetic terms surely represents the highly wrought opposite of a "poor earthen bowl." Havergal makes virtuosic use of the volta at the end of line eight to move from a humble statement of fact, addressed to a friend, to a prayer, addressed to God, in which she seeks to be consecrated to an elevated purpose; in this formal context, the statement "I did not form or fill" betrays a consciousness that renders highly questionable the poem's purported meekness. Receptivity, as envisioned in and enacted by this poem, takes on suggestive new aspects.

This reading of the "The Song Chalice" suggests avenues to richer assessments of the scriptural paraphrases that make up a significant part of Havergal's vast and exclusively Christian poetic oeuvre. Havergal exemplifies the characteristic standard of Victorian women's religious verse: she generally begins a poem with a Bible verse epigraph or allusion and then delivers a combination of paraphrase and meditation, in exceedingly regular metrical form, with much ornament. In "Luke ix.13" Havergal begins with a focus on scripture that moves to application, a quite particular focus on what the poet herself might do. The gospel story tells of Christ's multiplication of the loaves and fishes to feed five thousand; in Havergal's sonnet version, the octave tells the Bible story and the sestet presents a purely personal application. The speaker prays to God for the transference of a biblical miracle to the contemporary life of the obedient Christian poet.

> The Lord commanded, 'Give ye them to eat,'—
>   Five loaves and two small fishes all their store
>   For hungering crowds. He knew they had no more,
> And He had called them to that wild retreat.
> They gave it as He gave them, piece by piece,
>   Where on the green grass grouped the great and small
>   Till all were filled. So not theirs at all
> But His, the glory of that grand increase.
> Master, I have not strength to serve Thee much,
>   The 'half-day's work' is all that I can do,
> But let Thy mighty, multiplying touch
>   Even to me the miracle renew.
> Let five words feed five thousand, and Thy power
> Expand to life-results one feeble hour.

Marrying the scriptural-historical with the contemporary and personal, the poet uses her Bible source as a way of reflecting upon herself, her vocation, and her ambition, in this poem using the Bible story as an analogy for her self and for her own transformation. In an appeal very similar to that of "The Song Chalice," she prays that her words, few as they are and feeble

54 *Christian and Lyric Tradition in Victorian Women's Poetry*

vessel as she is, will result in 'grand increase.' In asking for an extension of the biblical miracle to and into herself, the speaker uses phrasing that echoes Havergal's own previously quoted words concerning how she composed poetry, every line and every word asked for, received, and written down. "They gave it as He gave them, piece by piece," writes the speaker of Christ's disciples. She implies that, as a participant in a like miracle, she is included in the description: "not theirs at all/ But His, the glory." Yet the poem's several implicit comparisons (poet with the dispensing disciples; poet with the nourishing Christ himself) make such an expression of humility, at the very least, double-edged.

Havergal also produced a large number of brief, often impromptu "Verses on Texts," which were so labeled and collected together in a subsection of her posthumous collected works, edited by her sister Maria Havergal. (These may have been what Maria had in mind when she defended the reproduction of even her sister's "lowliest lays," "even the spray of her pen" ["Introduction" viii].) Very often these verses are a single stanza in length, and often have no title. On occasion the scriptural epigraph appended is lengthier than the actual poem; elsewhere the poem outweighs the scripture; the poet's verses and the Bible verses maintain a swinging balance of original and reflection, or original and condensation, or original and extension. The grouping formed by the editor thus creates a new kind of cumulative identity for these slight poems by drawing attention to the relationship that is being continuously formed, reformed, and adjusted between the originary source and the series of poetic 'responses.' Page 735 offers an illustrative example of the verse in this section of the volume.

'Casting down imaginations, and every high thing that exalteth itself against the knowledge of God, and bringing into captivity every thought to the obedience of Christ.'—2 COR.x.5

> Let every thought
> Be captive brought,
> Lord Jesus Christ, to Thine own sweet obedience!
> That I may know,
> In ebbless flow,
> The perfect peace of full and pure allegiance.

'Even so, Father: for so it seemed good in Thy sight.'—MATT.xi.26

> And if it seemeth good to Thee, my Father,
>   Shall it seem aught but good to me?
> Thy will be done! Thou knowest I would rather
>   Leave all with Thee.

"God's interpreters to the sons of misery" 55

'Moreover also I gave them my Sabbaths to be a sign between me and them, that they might know that I am the Lord that sanctify them.'—
EZEK.xx.12

> The token of His truth and care, the gift that He hath blessed,
> The pledge of our inheritance, the earnest of His rest;
> The diamond hours of holy light, the God-entrusted leisure:
> Oh for a heart to prize aright this rich and heavenly treasure!

Their placement in a sequence gives these brief poems the appearance of a call and response series, with the poems serving as companion or complement pieces to the scriptures they follow. Visually and formally, the poet constructs a kind of participatory relationship between Bible and speaker/poet, including the reader as a bearer of witness and a respondent. In fact, the poems' layout on the page somewhat recalls the antiphony of the Litany's series of responses, as recorded in the Book of Common Prayer.

As opposed to these "lowliest lays," a number of Havergal's most substantial poems engage very fully with extended biblical passages. In such examples, the artistry with which the biblical text is co-opted and transfigured into poetic form again directs attention to the poet's conception of the significant religious role of poetry, and of her own significant religious role. "The Thoughts of God" is a lengthy poem of fifteen pages that begins with substantive interpolated passages taken word for word from Psalm 139. Havergal's title itself is suggestive of a diffused authority, and throughout the poem the poet elides herself with the Psalmist and with a prophet figure. The first four stanzas are reproduced here, with the word for word replication of the King James Version indicated in bold type.

> Thy thoughts, O God! O theme Divine!
> Except Thy Spirit in my darkness shine,
>   And make it light,
>   And overshadow me
>   With stilling might,
> And touch my lips that I may speak of Thee,—
>   How shall I soar
> To thoughts of Thy thoughts? and how dare to write
>   Of Thine?
>
>   Thou understandest mine
>   Far off and long before.
> Thou searchest, knowest, compassest! Thy hand is laid
>   Upon me. Whither shall I flee
> From Omnipresence and Omniscience? **If I fly**
>   **To heaven, Thou art there: and if I lie**
>   **In the unseen land,**

Behold, Thou art there also! If I take
The wings of morning, and my dwelling make
In the uttermost parts of the great sea,
Even there Thy hand shall lead me, Thy right hand
Shall hold me. If I say
Surely the night
Shall cover me, it shall be light
About me. Yea, the shade
Of darkness hideth not from Thee,
Night shineth as the day;
The darkness and the light are both alike to Thee.

Thee I will praise: for I am fearfully
And wonderfully made.
My substance was not hid from Thee
When I was made in secret, curiously wrought
And yet imperfect. Then
Thine eyes did see me. In Thy book
Were all my members written, when
Not one of them was into being brought.
Such knowledge is too wonderful for me,
Too excellent, too high. Yet 'tis but one
Keen ray of Thy great sun
Touching an atom in a dusty nook!

One ray! while others traverse depths profound
Of possible chaos; and illume
The boundless bound
Of space; and vivify worlds all unguessed,
To whom
Our farthest eastern spark,
Caught by the mightiest telescope that ever pierced the dark,
Is farthest west.
One ray! while others overflow
The countless hosts of angels with celestial blaze;
With still diviner glow,
Flooding each heart with adoration sweet,
And yet too glorious for the gaze
Of seraphim, who cover face and feet
With burning wings,
While through the universe their 'Holy, holy,' rings.

The first stanza, dense with biblical echoes and allusions, shows Havergal's crafting of a web of references and intertexts. In announcing the conditions by which she can speak/write of God, the speaker incorporates into

"God's interpreters to the sons of misery" 57

her own passage Jeremiah's humble avowals of his inability to speak of God—and God's touching of his mouth in anointing.[9] The intertext of the opening chapter of Jeremiah itself contains an interpolated passage from Psalm 139. Furthermore, the poem's speaker's opening discussion of her unworthiness to put into words the glories of God echoes several additional biblical passages: Isaiah 55:8 and 9, where the Lord states that his thoughts are higher than man's thoughts; David's words of humility in other psalms including Psalm 145:3 ("Great is the LORD, and greatly to be praised; and his greatness is unsearchable"); as well as verse 6 of Psalm 139 specifically, which reads, "Such knowledge is too wonderful for me, too lofty for me to attain." (It is worthy of note that the speaker even echoes another influential sacred father, Milton, in her opening line.) The Bible frequently references itself in an ongoing and circular assertion of its own authority; "The Thoughts of God" contributes to and participates in this self-reinforcing ascription of authority and inspiration.

Stanzas two and three, of irregular length, metre, and rhyme, are primarily exact verbal copies of Psalm 139, but poeticised and 'form-alised' in a way that recalls Yeats' famous poeticisation of Pater's essay on the "Mona Lisa." Havergal chooses strategic line-breaks and creates lines of different lengths to emphasise otherwise hidden internal rhymes, or to pause on particular images or phrases of pathos (as in "In the unseen land" or "Shall hold me. If I say ... "). Despite Havergal's protestations elsewhere of being a mere receptacle, this poem clearly demonstrates the mediating role of language in the construction of meaning, as re-formation of the content mandates reconsideration of that content. "Poem-lines" enforce consideration not only of the content but also of the *way* these words are written, and demand the reader recognise the intrusion of the poet. Towards the end of the third stanza Havergal 'exits' the biblical psalm text and moves to her 'own' psalm. Even if the resumption of regular rhyme weren't sign enough, the intrusion of metaphors of noticeably Victorian inflection make clear the new context in which these words now operate (the atom, the mightiest telescope), and these images again indicate the presence of the poet in this text.

"The Thoughts of God" intently foregrounds and dramatises its own textuality. Consistently concerned with the role of transmitting words in the exercise not just of faith but also of salvation, Havergal here *stages* the process of transmission and the constructedness of holy and inspired messages. All of the statements in the first stanza concern *how*, not *what*, the poet may write. In the opening self-conscious invocation, Havergal, like Milton, invokes an explicitly heavenly muse. Dramatising her unwilling willingness, the speaker asks to be literally enlightened but at the same time overshadowed, touched, and stilled with might. Her posture of weakness and humility enables her to seek empowerment through heavenly inspiration that is out of herself as well as within herself, and to herald her theme "Divine." Despite this dramatisation of the transmittal process, however, Havergal is not writing Higher Criticism in verse. While Victorians in the

58 Christian and Lyric Tradition in Victorian Women's Poetry

1860s frothed with agitated responses to the view of the Bible expounded by Jowett in *Essays and Reviews*, Havergal's previously quoted 1867 letter makes clear her belief that God himself is the ultimate source of all inspiration and truth. At no point in this poem or any of her others does Havergal's reverence for the scriptures or her belief in their holiness and reliability waver. The implicit thematisation of the hermeneutical process in "The Thoughts of God" does not call into doubt the verity of sacred texts or of the belief system they help construct, but rather it 'makes room' in that belief system as it makes room for new words, Victorian words, Victorian *women's* words, beside and within the original sacred text. The rewriting of scripture into verse enables the woman poet to participate in the sacred and sacralising work of producing inspired and authorised texts. Authorisation, as Havergal demonstrates in her work, is extendable.

Poetic Parables

Jesus' parables are among the most commonly 'retold' Bible stories within Victorian women's poetry, and present another way of following an unexceptionable spiritual textual model, Jesus' own. The parables provide a particularly apposite and potent model for women writers, as Jesus' texts made a virtue of simplicity, elevating it over learnedness as a vehicle for truth. His tales, shaped for a simple and working (rather than pharisaical) audience were characteristically picturesque, operating by analogy or even more simply, by presenting a direct exemplar. He shaped lessons around common, comprehensible activities like planting and harvesting, and around everyday objects like salt and candles; he depicted men working in vineyards and women sweeping the house. While Jesus' parables are never fantastic in a fabular sense, they often use exaggeration or surprise, and employ a certain disarming quality, a simplicity that penetrates resistance. The parables present profoundly important illustrative examples of a scriptural text of great use to Victorian women trying to write on religious topics: "He has made the foolish things of the world to confound the wise" (I Corinthians 1:27).

In *Ballads and Other Poems* (1847) Mary Howitt makes interesting creative use of a number of parables. She draws on both her own childhood love of the ballad tradition and her deeply felt imperative to communicate moral virtues to a working-class audience, to produce poems that, like Jesus' model, combine stirring narratives and appealing, homely form. Raised a Quaker and marrying the prominent Friend and writer William Howitt, she and her husband eventually became disillusioned with the Society of Friends, and experimented with both Unitarianism and spiritualism. Toward the end of a long life of considerable literary variety and religious questing, Mary Howitt converted to Roman Catholicism. She incorporated parables into her popular ballads with brio as well as with serene moral authority, a notable example being "Dives and Lazarus." "Dives and

"God's interpreters to the sons of misery" 59

Lazarus" proves an invigorating read, with its well-paced dramatic trajectory and ballad meter compressed into rhyming couplets. In this poem Howitt takes the parable of the rich man and the beggar Lazarus (see Luke 16:19–31) and treats it like any other folktale source material, reciting the rich man's riches with relish and detailing his eventual tragic fate with equal relish. True to ballad tradition, it draws on the reader's emotions, striking a dramatic contrast at the outset between Dives' material comforts, particularly his food and wine, and the beggar outside: "'Twas in the dreary winter, and on a stone he sate." A similar contrast is painted at the end, but by then the characters' fortunes have been signally reversed.

> Dives put on his purple robes, and linen white and fine,
> With costly jewels on his hands, and sate him down to dine.
> In a crimson chair of state he sate, and cushions many a one
> Were ranged around, and on the floor, to set his feet upon.
> There were dishes of the wild fowl, and dishes of the tame,
> And flesh of kine, and curious meats, that on the table came;
> From plates of ruddy gold he ate, with forks of silver fine;
> And drank from out a crystal cup the bright and foaming wine.
> Behind him stood his serving-men, as silent as might be,
> To wait upon him while he dined amid his luxury.
>
> Now Lazarus was a beggar, a cripple weak and grey;
> A childless man, too old to work, who begged beside the way;
> And as he went along the road great pain on him was laid,
> So on a stone he sate him down, and unto God he prayed.
> 'Twas in the dreary winter, and on a stone he sate,
> A weary, miserable man, at Dives' palace gate.
> There many servants out and in were passing to and fro,
> And Lazarus prayed, for love of God, some mercy they would show;
> And that the small crumbs might be his that fell upon the floor,
> Or he must die for lack of food beside that palace door.
>
> Now Dives on a silken bed in sumptuous ease was laid,
> And soft-toned lutes and dulcimers a drowsy music made;
> But he heard the voice of Lazarus low-wailing where he lay,
> And he said unto his serving-men, "Yon beggar drive away!"
> "He is old," said one; another spake, "He's lame, and cannot go."
> Said a third, "He craveth for the crumbs that lie the board below."
> "It matters not!" said Dives; "go, take my blood-hounds grim,
> Go, take them from their kennels, and set them upon him;
> And hunt him from the gate away, for while he thus doth moan
> I cannot get a wink of sleep." And so the thing was done.
> But when they saw the poor old man who not a word did say,
> The very dogs had pity on him, and licked him where he lay;

60 *Christian and Lyric Tradition in Victorian Women's Poetry*

And in the middle of the night, sore smit with want and pain,
On the frosty earth he laid him down ne'er to rise up again.
And Dives likewise laid him down on a bed of soft delight,
Rich silver lamps were burning dim in his chamber through the night;
But a ghostly form stole softly in, and the curtains drew aside,
And laid his hand on Dives' heart; and Dives likewise died.
Then burning guilt, like heavy lead, upon his soul was laid,
And down and down, yet lower and lower, to the lowest depth of shade
Went the soul of wicked Dives, like a rock into the sea,
To the depths of woe, where troubled souls bewail their misery.
His eyes he wildly opened in a gulf of flaming levin,
And afar he saw, so green and cool, the pleasant land of heaven;
A broad, clear river went winding there, and trees grew on its brim;
There stood the beggar Lazarus, and Abraham talked with him.
"Oh! father," then said Dives, "let Lazarus come along,
And bring one drop of water to cool my burning tongue,
For there is torment in this flame, which burneth evermore."
Said Abraham, "Dives, think upon the days that now are o'er:
Thou hadst thy comfortable things, water, and food, and wine;
Didst deck thyself in costly robes, purple and linen fine;
Yet was thy heart an evil heart amid thy pomp and gold,
And Lazarus sate before thy gate, despised, and poor, and old;
A beggar whom thy dogs did hunt, and whom thou didst revile,
Wretched and weak, yet praising God with thankful heart the while.
Now in the blooming land of heaven great comfort doth he know,
And thou must lie 'mid torment, in the burning seas below.
Beside all this, there is a gulf that lieth us between,
A boundless gulf o'er which the wing of angel ne'er hath been."
So Dives saw them pass away from the clear river's shore,
And angels many, on snowy wings, the beggar Lazarus bore.

This poetic retelling makes Dives' lack of charity more simply selfish and more petty than it seems in Luke's original account—he can't sleep for the beggar's moaning, he complains. The concreteness of this detail adds an element of 'fairy-tale logic' to Howitt's parable narrative. Other fairy-tale elements appear in various traditional trappings of courtly life, such as the golden plates and silver forks, and the dogs of the gospel story become Dives' unmistakably British bloodhounds. Exaggerated pathetic elements also appear in Howitt's rewriting: the reader's heartstrings are plucked by the fact even the dogs pitied poor Lazarus; a supernatural frisson is felt as personified Death draws aside Dives' bed-curtains and reaches a hand to his heart. The narrative yokes the parable text with ghosts of other fantastic texts very successfully; certain elements of course characterise both genres, particularly the use of extremes and extreme reverses, as here in the exchanging of places, low for high, torment for rest on angels' snowy wings.

"God's interpreters to the sons of misery" 61

The poet's variations upon the biblical version deserve careful consideration. While the facts of the story remain unaltered at the most fundamental level, Howitt has extended the tale, making it longer and much more elaborate, and has taken conscious measures to increase the entertainment value for her Victorian readers. The ballad-revision takes straight-forward aim at the reader's emotions, and invokes perhaps a greater range of emotions: envy and *schadenfreude* are provoked, as well as compassion. And the details Howitt incorporates make the setting simultaneously more distant and more up-to-date. The baronial Dives has medieval trappings of wealth about him, but the complicated emotional work of the verse conjures a specifically Victorian reader, through the poem's simultaneous fascination with and disgust at ostentatious consumer wealth, as well as in the naked pathos. The alteration of generic context also plays a role in Howitt's engagement of her reader. While both parable and ballad are primarily oral forms, the parable sets itself forth as a teaching tool; the appropriate receptive attitude is one of reflection and consideration of how one's life might be better lived. The ballad, on the other hand, presents at least at a surface level an entertainment; the moral does not have to be attended to with the same seriousness; the reader (or hearer) can revel in the more or less illicit pleasures conjured by the text. Howitt's extension of her biblical original, then, goes beyond simply changing the setting. Her play with genre enables a certain titillation as well as teaching of the reader.

This kind of extension, incorporating a range of additional elements into the scriptural paraphrase, diversifying its emotional range and the possibilities for feeling and judgment that it offers to both writer and reader, may be found in the poems of a number of other Victorian women. Eliza Maskell, in *Gospel Themes: A Series of Sacred Poems* (1860), produces poetic versions of several parables, including the Rich Man/Lazarus story that Howitt utilises. One of Maskell's most considerable extensions is undertaken in her treatment of the parable of "The Foolish and the Wise Builders," which provides her poem's title, and the scripture reference "Luke 6:47, 48, 49" is appended as an epigraph. Maskell's lengthy elaboration of the parable permits her to develop a thorough-going and pointed rebuke to Christians falling into what Maskell considers error. Granting to the speaker the authority to rebuke and to instruct, the poem undertakes a very particular construction of the speaker as authoritative and learned. It does so, fascinatingly, by reverse-engineering the parable's structural and syntactic simplicity. The first twelve lines of the blank verse poem, which focus on Jesus' words as recorded in Luke, actually bear scant similarity to Jesus' parable presentation. Archaic in its use of apostrophe to mark unsounded vowels, the poem *looks* learned; elaborately multisyllabic in word choice, it *sounds* learned, too, so that while Jesus talked of a man who built his house on sand and of a storm that blew it down, Maskell speaks of a man who rashly rears his edifice upon the changing sand, where it is assailed by tempest violent, etc.

62 *Christian and Lyric Tradition in Victorian Women's Poetry*

> The blest Redeemer, while He sojourn'd here,
> Compar'd the persons who not only heard
> His heav'nly words, but did what they enjoin'd,
> To one who built his house upon a rock,
> Which firmly stood when winds and waves arose;
> For its foundation was secure and strong.
> While they who listened to His precepts pure,
> And strove not His commandments to obey,
> He likened to a man, who rashly reared,
> Upon the changing sand, his edifice;
> Which when assailed by tempest violent
> Shook on its base, and fell immediately.

Having established a linguistically elevated persona, the speaker spends the rest of the poem—another hundred lines—methodically rebuking particular groups of Christians, each of which, she claims, is building on the sand of a different kind of doctrinal error. While the poem concludes with a passage praising those who do take Christ as their foundation and who keep their eyes fixed above, the most vigorous language appears in these pointed denunciations (on one occasion the pronoun slips and instead of an impersonal "they," the author's jab goes straight to the reader: "Deluded souls, your ruin is as sure"). The poem identifies the first group of deluded souls as those who think mistakenly that God is "too merciful,/ To any creature He has made, t'award/ The fearful doom of everlasting woe." The speaker denounces this belief and identifies God as a God of justice, wielding extremely strong language of sin and redemption, using words such as "heinous," "penalty enforc'd," "vile rebellion," and "God out of Christ is a consuming fire." While the term "Pharisee" never appears in the poem, the speaker clearly intends that identification, as to describe these people the poem incorporates recognisable allusions from other parts of the gospels. These "souls presumptuous" display great good works and are applauded for their deeds, but "their proud hearts, with vanity puffed up" reveal their mistake: they think they can save themselves by their own efforts. Again, the language with which the speaker warns them of the destruction to come is full of sound and fury:

> His violated law will justice claim,
> And like a mighty torrent sweep away
> The edifice your hopes so vainly rais'd,
> And only desolation leave behind.

Finally, the speaker denounces those who contend that only believers of their particular denomination will find salvation. While the message here seems anti-sectarian, the rebuke is more truly directed at those who engage with their faith intellectually: "They've much head knowledge and possess

"God's interpreters to the sons of misery" 63

the pow'r/ Deeply to argue on religious points," but intellectual pride is the downfall of these "vain presumers." They too will find, "To their souls' cost, fallacious were their hopes,/ And be themselves in utter ruin lost." The speaker only grants acceptance to those whose prayers are simply "th' effusions of a heart,/ That feels God's mercies are unmerited," those who, in the final section, acknowledge that they cannot do any salvation work for themselves, instead "seeking His Spirit's aid with humble heart."

Certainly there exists Gospel precedent for this kind of rebuke of intellectualism: Christ told the Pharisees on a number of occasions that they were blind guides, wise in their own eyes, and full of sin (see, for example, Matthew 23:13–33). But Maskell's poem shifts the focus from Christ's positive instructions to build on the rock, to a negative catalogue of errors and punishments, uttered with considerable detail, relish, and the calm assumption of the right to judge. Maskell's whole volume is unified by a concentration on what to do and what not to do; profoundly practical and deeply concerned with the human rather than the heavenly condition, the poems in *Gospel Themes* transform the gospels into a poetical instruction manual. In one final parable poem, Maskell's focus on the application of Christ's words completely displaces Christ's words themselves. Maskell entitles this poem "The Unprofitable Servant" and gives it the epigraph "Matthew xxv.30," but not a single line directly refers to Christ's narrative, which tells the story of a man who gave three servants money to invest. Instead the poem leaps straight into the speaker's own 'lesson'—which also contains a self-application:

> Whatever talents we enjoy,
>   Their gracious Giver has design'd,
> We carefully should them employ
>   To aid and benefit mankind.
>
> [. . .]
>
> Have we ability to write?
>   The talent should to God be giv'n:
> 'Tis sacred—we should not indite
>   One page to lead a soul from heav'n.
>
> Science and art are we skill'd in?
>   Whate'er the knowledge we possess,
> Should not be used t'encourage sin,
>   But to promote men's happiness

Without mentioning the parable directly, the poet turns its subject matter and its specific terminology to her own account and uses it in her own defense. The unprofitable servant of Christ's story had buried the money (in

64 *Christian and Lyric Tradition in Victorian Women's Poetry*

the denomination of one talent) loaned him by his master, instead of investing it, or otherwise turning it to account. The poem here foregrounds a different meaning of talent, in order to make a monitory comment on how humans should use their skills, including the skill of writing. Writing should not draw souls away from heaven, toward sin, but rather focus them constantly on the path above and on the action required to get there. For this poet, then, true writing is literally 'righting' of the erring human. Every poem in Maskell's volume reveals the seriousness with which she addresses the use of her talent and her role, as paraphrases of Bible stories give way to her own unique efforts to lead her readers to heaven. These readers remain in an important sense Christ's readers and followers, but additionally become in a particular sense the speaker's own readers and followers.

As illustrated in Howitt and Maskell's verse, the particularly pedagogical textual model of Christ's parables offered ready means for women poets to emotionally engage their readers and also to transfer to themselves a form of moral authority. As these poems work to produce their own authority, and their own authorisation, they render questionable the identity of the person(s) for whose benefit they are created. In effect, women poets reconstructing biblical texts make cultural capital out of confining stereotypes, constructing from their traditional posture as devout poets a heightened status as better and holier conduits for God's truth, and suggesting they can render that truth itself to readers in a 'better' form.

Scripture Made Easy

Even when not explicitly drawing on parable texts, Victorian women's verse on biblical topics regularly aligns itself with a key parable principle, that of simplicity. Even the most casual scan of volumes of Victorian women's religious verse reveals how often women draw on one of the most common and time-honoured techniques for justifying writing on sacred texts: the presentation of poetic versions of scripture with the aim of making it 'easy to understand.' To quote from a poem by Emily S. G. Saunders, herself quoting and adjusting a line of Milton, Victorian women poets see themselves acting as "God's interpreters . . . / To the sons of misery" (84). Women's 'helpful' interpretations were very often directed at audiences that might be expected to be deficient in understanding of sacred truths and to be in need of patient instruction, particularly children, but also the working class. The titles of many volumes clearly signal this ambition, and very often the intended audience. The pre-eminent example is C. F. Alexander's prodigiously popular *Hymns for Little Children*, first published in 1848, which was continuously reprinted throughout the Victorian period. Alexander's volume itself proves an influential model and intertext for numerous other works, such as the Honorable Mary Emma Lawrence's *Hymns and Poems for Very Little Children* (1871); M. E. B.'s *The Young Child's Gospel; Or, The Life of Our Lord in Easy Verse* (1880); and Rosa Raine's *Verses for Church Schools* (1861),

"God's interpreters to the sons of misery"   65

to name only a few of a vast number of specifically child-oriented volumes. Some women held different groups of learners in mind, including servants, sailors, and soldiers. Mary Sewell's *Stories in Verse for the Street and the Lane* (1861) was the second series of the popular *Homely Ballads for the Working Man's Fireside*, and despite the lack of indication in the title, these were unavoidably moral and usually explicitly Christian tales.

Irrespective of their overall title, many volumes of women's poetry contained particular sections labeled as children's verse. Sometimes, as in the case of the Hemans volume discussed in Chapter 1, such labelling seems purely arbitrary, with little distinguishing these 'children's' verses from the surrounding poems, but other poets demonstrate a clearly held objective and a sincere attempt to render the religious content of the verse attractive to an infant mind. The Preface to Harriet R. King's *Thoughts in Verse upon Scripture Texts, to which are added Miscellaneous Poems and Nursery Hymns* (two volumes, 1842 and 1846) illustrates the general aim:

> The *Nursery Hymns* are submitted, in much deference, to Mothers and Teachers, in the hope that they may be found conducive to that early and practical understanding of the Creed, the Lord's Prayer, and the Ten Commandments, which the Baptismal Service of the Church enjoins. (vol. 1, v–vi)

King reveals a very systematic intent in her Nursery Hymns. She separates the words of the Creed and the Lord's Prayer into distinct passages and then illustrates each passage with a poem in simple quatrains, usually in hymn metre. She follows a similar model with the individual instructions of the Commandments, and with paraphrases of other biblical passages. Language, rhyme, and metre render the poems easily memorisable. For example, the poem "2 Corinthians I. 3, 4" gives as epigraph those verses from the Bible in full, and then presents the ideas in six-line stanzas of three pairs of rhyming lines. The last couplet in each stanza rings the changes on a disyllabic rhyme, with considerable relish.

> "Blessed be God, even the Father of our Lord Jesus Christ, the Father of mercies, and the God of all comfort; who comforteth us in all our tribulation, that we may be able to comfort them which are in any trouble, by the comfort wherewith we ourselves are comforted of God."

> God of mercy! God of grace!
> From Thine high and holy place,
> As a Father hear our prayers,
> When we bring to Thee our cares;
>   By Thy Son, vouchsafe salvation,
>   By Thy Spirit, consolation.

66   *Christian and Lyric Tradition in Victorian Women's Poetry*

Pilgrims through a gloomy way,
Lighten Thou our clouded day;
When we tremble, hush our fear;
When we falter, whisper cheer;
  When we pass through tribulation,
  Sanctify the dispensation.

Father, thus sustain'd by Thee,
Unto others let us be
Instruments of joy and peace,
Which may never, never cease,
  To proclaim, with adoration,
  Gifts beyond our computation.

Thou! at whose right hand above
Jesus sits, supreme in love;
Send the Spirit of Thy grace
Thence to bless our ransom'd race,
  By adoption, by salvation,
  Guidance, counsel, consolation.

Generally, all King's biblically based poems take as titles only the scriptural reference that serves as their starting point—the verse is given in full, and quite often there are two or more verses providing the topic for the poem. King provides copious and diligent footnoting even of readily recognisable biblical ideas, thus demonstrating the "deference" she avows in her Preface. Similar earnestness characterises her hymns on the Lord's Prayer and on each of the Ten Commandments, and throughout King takes care to keep the language and concepts accessible to and suitable for children: for example, in one of the poems on the Commandments, adultery is rendered no more explicitly than as "sin coming from the heart."

Insisting on their nature as humble, simple, and easy to understand, such poetic versions of biblical texts operate in a dialectic of pride and humility. This dialectical operation may be observed in Jean Sophia Pigott's "Divine Childhood" (in *A Royal Service and Other Poems*, 1877), which at a surface level reduces all Christians, including herself, to the level of infants.

Oh, sweet school! Where God's belovèd
  Come to be as babes in heart;
There to learn of Him, my spirit
  Seeketh as its better part.

Lowlier there to sit, and lower,
  Ever lower, at His feet,—
This is my Divine ambition,
  This my lesson, strangely sweet . .

"God's interpreters to the sons of misery" 67

Poems such as King's and Pigott's express a radical kind of ambition: an ambition to deference and an ambition to (artless) sincerity. The aspirational humility expressed in and symbolised by these texts extends the claim of problematic humbleness to their authors: Pigott asks God to "perfect and develop in me/ This sweet infancy of soul," and Saunders sees women acting as conduits, specifically, as "God's interpreters." These humble petitions and statements hint at the authors' lofty, potentially discomforting desire for perfection. Another indicator of this aspirational humility may be found in the diminutives that characterise the titles of so many women's volumes, from Ann Butler's *Fragments in Verse* (1826) and Sophia Streatfield's *A Little Garland of the Saints* (1877) to Rachel Jane Fearnley's rather charmingly entitled *Crumbs From the Master's Table* (1899), and Elizabeth Cheyne's *A Little Book of Saints* (1906). Even the redoubtable feminist Frances Power Cobbe published in 1887 a slender volume of pious verse entitled *Rest in the Lord, and Other Small Pieces*. Cobbe's *are* small pieces; the whole volume is only fifty pages long, and for a good number of other women's volumes, too, a diminutive in the title quite literally describes the work's physical size. But reduced physical dimensions are not the only feature women seek to denote with these titles: such modest entitlement provides another method of codedly but consciously disavowing any spiritual pride or over-reaching. Avowedly humble in purpose and limited in scope, these poetic efforts present themselves as merely 'fragments' of a very large truth; partial, they offer at best complements to the sacred original, and, state their authors, they in no way present a replacement text. As Fearnley's volume title suggests, her words offer mere crumbs while Christ offers the entire feast. However, this title's intertext also directs us to an underlying and more assertive meaning. The title echoes the words of an unnamed woman in the Bible, variously identified in the gospels of Matthew and Mark as a Canaanite or a Syrophoenician woman, who combined humility with considerable assertion (and is praised for it). She appealed to Christ to free her daughter from demon-possession, and when he responded that he was called to help only the children of Israel, she replied: "'Truth, Lord: yet the dogs eat of the crumbs which fall from their masters' table.' Then Jesus answered and said unto her, 'O woman, great is thy faith: be it unto thee even as thou wilt.' And her daughter was made whole from that very hour." (Matthew 15:27–28). Crumbs from the Master's table, then, might be all that falls to a woman's portion, but they may serve as a marker for great faith and the no less great achievement of Christ's recognition and praise.

Exegesis in Verse

The implicit link between littleness, feebleness, and femaleness underlies a wide range of self-descriptions and self-conceptions of women writers on biblical topics. However, a more complicated situation arises when the feeble and female little verses, with the avowed aim of 'making it easier to understand,' present explications that come close to exegetical engagements

68 Christian and Lyric Tradition in Victorian Women's Poetry

with the Bible. The degree of interpretive authority that these poems claim, and the means by which that authority is claimed, require careful analysis. While women's religious poetry reveals a preoccupation with the boundary between the right and wrong ways for women to engage with Holy Scripture, women's efforts to chart this boundary paradoxically help produce and reinforce it at the same time as they open it up to challenge. A particularly significant element of the boundary concerns the deployment of biblical material in order to interpret and teach, and women's poetry wrestles with self-conceptions of its teaching role.

As Chapter 1 has shown, referencing the work of Melnyk, Miles, and other scholars, Victorian Christian culture strictly limited the kinds of teaching in which women were permitted to engage, and forbade women from engaging exegetically with the scriptures. It is important to note that a number of individuals and groups argued against these limitations, including the denomination that provided the Victorians with the noisiest support for (and examples of) female public ministry: the Salvation Army. Catherine Mumford Booth, wife of Salvation Army founder William Booth, published in 1859 a slim but forceful one-penny tract entitled "Female Ministry; or, Woman's Right to Preach the Gospel." With great vigour, but also with a carefully systematic grounding in the scriptures and in the writings of eminent biblical scholars, Mrs. Booth debunks the arguments against women's preaching and prophesying in the Church. Her own epigraph is "And your sons and daughters shall prophesy," a text from Joel 2:28, which Booth reads as not merely providing women an excuse for speaking, but also issuing a positive command to speak. She trounces two leading arguments against women's public preaching, those of unnaturalness and unseemly publicity, and spends the bulk of the tract analysing the passages of scripture traditionally used to bar women from preaching. Quoting liberally from authorities on church history and the Greek language, she boldly argues that key passages from the New Testament, in the course of the transmission of the Scriptures, were deliberately partially translated and even mis-translated; these key passages would support the view that women and men are called equally to prophesy, which, using St. Paul's definition, means "speaking unto others to edification, exhortation, and comfort" (19). Booth argues an interpretation of scripture for her cause, then uses it against those (mis-)using scriptural evidence for their exclusionary position, and her ultimate assertion is emphatic: "not only is the public ministry of women unforbidden, but absolutely enjoined by both precept and example in the word of God" (5).

Mrs. Booth, for all her vigour, represents an outlier viewpoint. Most Victorian women, many of whom yearned to speak (or write) "unto others to edification, exhortation, and comfort," took more carefully circuitous routes than climbing to the pulpit, or to the street corner. Women's strategies to interpret and teach from the Bible in their poems are many and varied. Some

"God's interpreters to the sons of misery" 69

women poets present the interpretation of scripture as akin to a meditation, a rhythmical repetition of or dwelling on certain words or phrases, which produces a deeper understanding of the whole, without 'questioning.' This anti-controversial model is often used by Havergal, as, for example, in "He is thy Lord" and "God the Provider." In each of these poems, the speaker takes up the biblical verse that's either indicated in the title or supplied as an epigraph, and considers each word, for a stanza at a time. Thus in "Isaiah xxxiii.17":

> *Thine* eyes shall see! Yes, thine, who, blind erewhile,
> Now trembling towards the new-found light dost flee,
> Leave doubting, and look up with trustful smile—
> *Thine* eyes shall see!
>
> Thine *eyes* shall see! Not in some dream Elysian,
> Not in thy fancy, glowing though it be,
> Not e'en in faith, but in unveilèd vision,
> Thine *eyes* shall see!
>
> Thine eyes *shall* see! Not on thyself depend
> God's promises, the faithful, firm, and free;
> Ere they shall fail, earth, heaven itself, must end:
> Thine eyes *shall* see! (emphasis in original)

And so on. Clearly, the mode here is consciously devotional: Havergal focuses on meditative consideration of the scripture and its meaning to the individual life. As she closely ponders each word and each element of meaning within the verse, the poem proffers an unexceptionable, humble, receptive, feminine treatment of scripture.

Other poets, however, spend more time engaging with consciously learned complexities than with careful devotional formulae, and their ambition, more immediately visible, collides more overtly problematically with concepts of humility and receptivity. Adeline Braithwaite's *Scripture Spoil in Sacred Song* (1886), for example, demonstrates considerable depth of biblical knowledge and quite ingeniously constructed scripture teachings. The poem "Joseph" opens the volume and its subtitle, "(A Type) or, Seven Steps to the Throne," indicates its typological message. Braithwaite develops the comparison of Joseph with Christ with some skill and in great detail, exploring her case over the course of fifteen pages of dense blank verse. "My Witnesses" is another long and complexly structured poem in four sections, meditating on a number of scriptures about blindness, deafness, and dumbness: it links Old and New Testament passages to application to a modern Victorian audience, deploys the analogy of Eve's fateful decision to describe the contemporary plight of Victorian Christians, asserts that Christ took on human sensory deprivation in his sufferings, and explains

70 *Christian and Lyric Tradition in Victorian Women's Poetry*

how salvation frees the Christian to vision, hearing, and speech. The complexity of the argument and the variety of biblical sources are skillfully linked and controlled through the central metaphor of the senses; the poem resembles a particularly well-crafted and imaginative sermon. While the poet displays in-depth biblical knowledge throughout the volume, "My Witnesses," particularly, seems to proffer an entirely original interpretation of scripture. In the face of this unsanctioned exegetical originality it is no accident that Braithwaite's volume takes enormous care to indicate the scriptural grounding of every poem. Every poem presents a biblical epigraph in full beneath the title; most have more than one epigraph; a few present scriptural epigraphs that are longer than the subsequent poems. And some have in addition to the biblical epigraph an explanatory note referring the reader back to the Bible: for example, beneath "As He is, so are we," which is glossed "(1 John iv.17)", appears this note:

> TO THE READER—If these are "the true sayings of GOD" (see Rom. v. to viii., 2 Cor. iv., Gal. ii. 20, Eph. ii., Col. i. to iii., 2 Tim. ii.), shall they not also be the language of *our* heart, the expression of *our* faith, and the description of *our* experience? So shall we "set to our seal that GOD is true". (emphasis in original)

Such attempts to deflect attention to the 'true' original paradoxically also highlight the female-sourced 'new' original, and the author's awareness that some might deem it unacceptable.

Marian Saunders Wright undertakes exegesis through poetry via a different approach, in her *Paraphrases on Sermons Preached By Professor Elmslie [in verse]*, published in 1891.[10] On numerous levels Wright guards her work against the charge that the woman author does any preaching of her own. In the Introduction she writes of her poems:

> Most of them were printed for private circulation in 1887, having previously been brought under Dr. Elmslie's notice; and they elicited the following comments from him:

> "It was a surprise and a pleasure to me to see the Sermon Paraphrases in print. It is singularly curious and instructive to me, to read them, and to note how your mind has worked on the ideas, and, in many cases, enriched them. Many of the turns of phrase are so happy and expressive, that I suspect they will emerge in future preaching, on the themes you have so gracefully versified."—*Extract from a letter from Professor Elmslie, June 2nd, 1887*

> "I prefer your Paraphrases to verbatim reports. *They* try to get all the words, and somehow miss the spirit—and *you* get that."—*Professor Elmslie, June 30th, 1889*. (emphasis in original)

"God's interpreters to the sons of misery" 71

The Author hopes that to very many who loved him, these echoes of the beloved Teacher's words may be welcome and helpful.

The quoted extracts from Dr. Elmslie, and Wright's Introduction as a whole, are deeply provocative. From the outset, this volume makes it clear that it presents holy verse at two removes: the verses do not merely paraphrase Scripture, but paraphrase another's (a man's) own interpretation of Scripture in his sermons. The Introduction begins to blur the layers of authority, as it is not completely clear whether the phrase "the beloved Teacher's words," in Wright's final sentence, refers to Professor Elmslie or to Christ. Both fathers, both authorities, their individual distinctness in fact takes a secondary position to the Introduction's key focus: the woman poet's own relationship to these sources of authoritative speaking.

In charting this relationship, the question of how and why the Professor's approving words are transferred to the reader looms large. Professor Elmslie vouches for the fact that the female author has worked on pre-existing ideas, that is, she has not produced her own exegesis. Everything he says reinforces contemporaneous gender divisions within the church: magnanimously, the doctor suggests that the woman poet's words might inspire another (man) to preach. Also worthy of note is the inherently gendered assessment of what "you have so gracefully versified," as well as the less visible gendering in the Professor's second statement, in which words and spirit are counterposed, and the woman can, even when missing lexical exactness, convey spirit. Professor Elmslie does acknowledge, ever so briefly, the creative and additive power of the poet who, "in many cases, enriched them [the sermon's ideas]." Graceful arrangement of another's exegesis is an acceptable and secondary feminine undertaking, but this phrase suggests, however glancingly, that something has been added to the original.

Wright's own words work hard to undercut this suggestion. Every formal element at her disposal emphatically points to the original, not just the volume's title and introduction but also each poem: the body of each is followed by a date and usually by a place also, which refers not to the date of poetic composition but to that of the sermon's first preaching (Wright makes this clear by the oft-repeated phrase: "Preached at . . . "). Without transcripts of the original sermons it is impossible to analyse exactly how or where the poet has diverged from the original and "enriched" the ideas therein, but Wright's ventriloquising efforts certainly stretch the distinction between sermon and verse. The slim volume of nineteen poems (all but four of which treat Jesus' ministry, miracles, and words) provides nineteen pointedly expounded lessons. "Elijah" tells the Old Testament tale of Elijah outcast, fed by ravens, complaining to God.

> The great temptation of exalted minds
> And lonely, is to think themselves alone.
> The cause of God so self-identified,

72   *Christian and Lyric Tradition in Victorian Women's Poetry*

That without them it hardly can succeed.

The poems definitely sound like sermons, and most contain very prosey sections which, despite Professor Elmslie's compliment, really haven't yielded their original form to "graceful versification." For example, into the poem "Jesus Washing the Disciples' Feet" intrudes a comment both fundamentally prosaic and also evaluative of the original gospel sources:

John's spirit was a shrine for his dear Lord,
Wherein reflected, Him whom he adored,
More clearly through his story we can see
Than in the evangels of the other three . . .

The author's repeated efforts to portray herself as solely versifier and not preacher are, then, of limited success, and through the gaps between articulated goal and actual achievement may be seen the pressures of cultural and creative proscriptions warring with devout women's urge to master their biblical narratives.

The Intrusion of Self into Scripture

As Victorian women poets unsettle the solidity of notions of authority and of authorship, the reader of their verse is redirected to seek authentic truth from a broadening array of sources. Ties to originary scripture are on occasion stretched enough (although never entirely released) to allow insertion of the poet's own history, experience, feelings, and responses as additional and arguably equal sources of authority. In a poem of this kind, the characteristic turn from paraphrase to application is so rapid or so subtle that it suggests the poem's primary focus may lie not in the biblical story or text but rather in the description of or production of a personally found revelation or personally grounded truth. This technique foregrounds subjective experience, transfiguring personal truth into the likeness of scriptural truth.

Certain biblical passages lend themselves particularly readily to women poets' efforts to transform and elevate individual experience to the level of Scripture. Among these are the plangent, passionate cries of the individual, lyrical Psalms, which model the emotional utterance as scripture and allow a number of women poets room to expand and personalise the sacred 'cry of the heart.' Jane Euphemia Browne rewrites David's famous Psalm 51 in "Renew a Right Spirit Within Me" (in *The Dove on the Cross, and Other Thoughts in Verse*, 1849), recasting it in perfectly regulated common metre. In her echo of David's personal cry, Browne simultaneously makes it her own cry and 'cleans it up'—she presents herself, through the poem, as a rival speaker of Scripture, and a more demonstrably dutiful one. Unlike David, who speaks out of an anguished awareness of his sin (adultery with Bathsheba), this speaker is both more

"God's interpreters to the sons of misery"   73

moderate and more plaintive, asking God, as though he is a cross Victorian papa: "Why art Thou wroth with me?" Avoiding the starkness and self-flagellation of the original psalm ("Against thee, thee only have I sinned, and done what is evil in thy sight" v.4), the speaker departs into a prim, ultra-principled cataloguing of possible sins. Rewriting her holy model, the speaker performs holiness through the stringency with which she lists (and disavows) her own possible wrongdoings.

> My Father, Thou hast hid Thy face;
>   Why art Thou wroth with me?
> Take not from me Thy love and grace,
>   Though I have grievèd Thee.
>
> Lord, I have communed with my heart,
>   And I have tried to pray,
> Kneeling in solitude apart,
>   Yet found not what to say.
>
> If I have sinned through heedlessness,
>   And injured or offended
> Some little one whom Thou dost bless,
>   Whom angels have attended . . .

In its display of correctness, metrical as well as moral, the poem presents a more convincing case for the speaker's rectitude than for her venality. She presents an über-biblical, list-checking moral vigilance, as well as incorporating the typically Victorian sentiment in stanza three that conjures the "little one" the speaker fears she may have offended. Browne's new psalm undertakes both a kind of contemporisation and a kind of self-justification. The poem concludes with the eighth stanza:

> And in this faith I come to Thee
>   To seek forgiving grace:
> From secret sin, oh cleanse Thou me,
>   And let me see Thy face.

Both the anguish and the immediacy of the sin have been tidily erased from Browne's version, and what remains is an entirely self-focused, almost self-congratulatory exercise in reflection and dutiful repentance.

Similarly, Browne's "Blessed Are the Pure in Heart" turns a scripture verse to a devotional meditation in which the speaker's subject almost instantly turns inward. While the poem makes clear its biblical provenance in its title, which is drawn from the Beatitudes as reported in both Matthew 5:1–12 and Luke 6:20–23, the poem eschews paraphrase in favour of an extended application of that particular verse ("blessed are the pure in

74 *Christian and Lyric Tradition in Victorian Women's Poetry*

heart") to herself. Made personal, the promise at the close is boldly claimed by the speaker.

> O God of purity, my soul
>   Most earnestly desires to be
> Subdued to perfect self-control,
>   Chastened to perfect purity.
>
> Let truth be written on my heart,
>   And so transparent let it be,
> That light pervading every part
>   Would only shew sincerity.
>
> Oh, let each wish and each desire
>   Be fully satisfied in Thee;
> And let Thy love, as holy fire,
>   Refine my spirit inwardly.
>
> Let every thought and every aim
>   Be simple as a child's might be—
> And let each motive be the same,
>   Perfect in its simplicity.
>
> Oh, sweetest promise! made most sure
>   By Him who gave Himself for me,
> That they whose inmost hearts are pure,
>   Shall see the God of purity.

Scripture can thus be turned by women's poetry to purely personal account. Victorian women poets simultaneously personalise and universalise biblical texts, as they make scripture 'real' by emphasising its relevance to common, contemporary, and individual concerns. A scriptural original turned into an intensely personal meditation, while this personalisation is simultaneously justified by its universal applicability, may be found in Dinah Mulock Craik's "David's Child" (in *Poems,* 1866), which takes for an epigraph the exchange: "Is the child dead?"—And they said, "He is dead." While Craik doesn't include the scriptural reference for this epigraph, this verse is taken from 2 Samuel 12:19. King David had committed adultery with Uriah's wife Bathsheba, and then sent Uriah to be killed on the battlefield; this is the sinfulness David bewails in Psalm 51. God's punishment on David was to strike down the infant son Bathsheba had borne him. While it struggled for life, David fasted and prayed, but on the seventh day, his courtiers told him the child was dead. David stopped praying, got up, washed, and ate, telling his dismayed courtiers that as the worst had come, there was no point in further protest.

"God's interpreters to the sons of misery"   75

In face of a great sorrow like to death
How do we wrestle night and day with tears;
How do we fast and pray; how small appears
The outside world, while, hanging on some breath
Of fragile hope, the chamber where we lie
Includes all space. —But if sudden at last
The blow falls; or by incredulity
Fond led, we—never having one thought cast
Towards years where "the child" was not—see it die,
And with it all our future, all our past,—
We just look round us with a dull surprise:
For lesser pangs we had filled earth with cries
Of wild and angry grief that would be heard: —
But when the heart is broken—not a word.

Craik's version omits all biblical back-story, and, other than the title, makes no mention of the character of David. David exits the poem entirely, as the actor or sufferer becomes a universalised "we"; even "the child" is de-particularised arguably to the point that the quotation marks render it a pure symbol, representing any thing of value that any human loves and clings to, and loses. A particular Bible story becomes an everyman's or everywoman's story, although as Craik's poem powerfully demonstrates, extracting the particulars does not necessarily entail any diminishment of emotional intensity. Craik's sonnet, rigidly controlled, recalls both in theme and form Elizabeth Barrett Browning's "Grief," Craik's last line recalling most strongly Barrett Browning's first: "I tell you, hopeless grief is passionless." Thus in addition to the biblical intertext, another authority is recognised and incorporated into the poem, as Craik's sonnet shifts on its biblical foundations and positions itself in the recognisable emotional landscape of Victorian England. The poem's porous relationship to its historical source (to borrow Isobel Armstrong's phrase) reveals the poet's wrestling with her originary text, her effort to make the Bible story function in a different way, at a different time, to a different reader. The projected reader, too, expands. Craik's universalised account encompasses the woman reader, making room for the grieving mother who in the biblical account of King David's loss is never considered. This poem, then, recollects the vanished biblical woman by placing her in relationship with the contemporary woman reader of biblical texts. A shared but deeply personal experience becomes the true originary text as a new kind of emotionally based authority is asserted, one that is presented alongside scriptural authority.

Craik's poem can be seen to 'swerve' to the personal immediately after the biblical epigraph. This kind of swerve from focus on scripture to focus on subjective experience is an important characteristic of Victorian women's religious verse, and one further example will help illuminate how the subjective swerve could enable the significant intrusion of a female Self into a biblical tradition that had traditionally failed to recognise that female

76 Christian and Lyric Tradition in Victorian Women's Poetry

Self. Ann Butler's "Difficulties Removed" (in *Fragments in Verse,* 1826) begins with two stanzas that deal explicitly with the biblical story indicated in the epigraph, but the poem then swerves to a purely personal application that turns the key feature of the original text—the enormous stone in front of Jesus' grave—into a flexible metaphor of insistently personal application to the (implicitly female) speaker.

> "And they said among themselves, Who shall roll us away the stone from the door of the sepulchre? And when they looked, they saw that the stone was rolled away: for it was very great." Mark xvi.3,4*

'O 'tis a Stone immensely large,
  How shall we get it rolled away?'
Thus as they sought their mournful charge
  The sorrowing Marys doubtful say.

They *looked*: behold no stone was nigh:–
  '*Twas* rolled before the Almighty's hand;
Nor wonder this, –for the mountains fly,
  Or melt to air at his command.

–Thus in this world of grief and sin,
  (As anxious, mournfully I stray,)
How oft my aching eyes have seen
  Some vast obstruction bar my way.

'O *this* I never can break through—
  This is the greatest, worst I've known:
It hides my last faint hope from view;
  O, who shall roll this mighty stone?'

Thus have my unbelieving fears
  Against all better thoughts prevailed;
Thus have I wet my couch with tears,
  And faith, and hope, and peace have failed.

I quite forgot who 'twas that died,
  The dreadful weight of sin to move:
I quite forgot whose love supplied
  The care-free tenants of the grove,

But though so doubting, wicked, vain,
  My Saviour had not me forgot;
He kindly bade me 'look again;'—
  I did—behold, my griefs were not.

"God's interpreters to the sons of misery" 77

Touched by his hand, they shrunk to nought,
    Or turned to blessings 'fore my eyes;
Gone was the fear that 'whelm'd my thought,
    Before me new and full supplies.

'Tis thus the weary Traveller sees
    Huge hills in prospect check his way;
And, worn with toil, and courting ease,
    He dreads ascent,—yet fears delay.

But what in prospect seems so vast,
    Recedes, as farther on he goes;
He mounts the hill, and troubles past
    Are lost in charms its views disclose. (emphasis in original)

*Composed after hearing a sermon from the above text by the Rev. J. N. Goulty.

This poem doesn't so much tell the story as reflect on the uses of storytelling. Butler treats the biblical story not just as Truth, but also explicitly as a literary device; Butler's speaker holds the scripture at a sufficient distance to *trope* it, thematising the (essentially literary) use the poem's speaker makes of the biblical passage. The speaker here draws a parallel between herself and the Marys who quailed before Jesus' tomb, as she considers her own "unbelieving fears." She also draws a less obvious but still potent parallel between herself and the somewhat similarly prostrate, generalised Psalmist, who regularly bewails in the Bible that *his* couch is wet with tears, and that *his* faith has failed.[11] Butler makes the familiar gesture to the male authority (here the Rev. J. N. Goulty) to guarantee her text's correctness, even as she adjusts the scriptural original to make her parallels serve her own purposes. In her retelling, Jesus, rather than the angel, encourages the women to take a second look at the obstacle: the revelation is thus made personal and immediate to the first-person speaker, rather than being filtered through either the angel's or the apostles' agency, as in the different gospel versions of the Bible story. And while the poem concludes with a broadening of the message to the third person, it is the insistent first-person pronoun, the speaker who actually quotes herself as she consciously turns her own response to the story into art, who takes on the central role of this verse.

Butler starts with a third-person Bible story, and then swerves to a first-person meditation; she invites comparison of her case to that of biblical characters, while taking care to maintain the separateness inherent in the figure of the simile: *this, as this*. Many other women's biblically based poems similarly construct themselves about simile as a way of incorporating self into scripture. For example, Winifred Iverson's "God's Touch" (in *God's Touch, and Other Poems*, 1890) systematically draws

78 *Christian and Lyric Tradition in Victorian Women's Poetry*

parallels between the speaker's own case and those of the lepers Jesus healed, the despairing Elijah, the suffering Job, and several other Bible characters. M. O. W.'s volume *Rhymes from the Book and From Life* (1900) includes a section of long blank verse poems about biblical characters, most of whom are women and several of whom speak in the first person, including "Rachel on the Birth of Joseph," "Leah," "Ruth," and "Michal." Charlotte Elliott writes many such first-person 'identificatory' Bible-based poems, in which she inserts a self into scripture as a means of creatively reworking that scriptural original. Elliott, who lived from 1789 to 1871, was a genuine star of Victorian religious literature, displaying astonishing literary productivity despite lifelong invalidism. She edited the annual *Christian Remembrancer Pocket-Book* for 25 years, wrote some 150 hymns, including the enduring popular "Just as I am, without one plea," and published several volumes of verse that went into numerous editions and sold tens of thousands of copies. Hugely popular and unimpeachably correct, Elliott nonetheless articulates a strong sense of her own authority within her biblically based verses, drawing parallels between her speakers and Bible characters, and then problematising those parallels in ways that suggest sometimes novel, sometimes daring interpretations. In one notable poem Elliott presents a rather shocking character parallel, one far from characteristic of Victorian women's scriptural verse: the speaker identifies with the woman caught in adultery and dragged to Jesus for judgment (John 8:3–11). How the speaker manages to identify with this character and yet maintain a distance of conscious fiction, turning sordid source material into a highly correct devotional appeal, is a fascinating enterprise.

"Go and Sin no More" (in *Selections,* 1873)
  John viii.11

Speak, my Saviour, speak to me,
  With divine effectual power—
Weeping, I look up to Thee—
  Bid *me* "go and sin no more."

Thou art full of pardoning love,
  Thou canst grant what I implore;
Now Thy pitying mercy prove,
  Bid me "go and sin no more."

Thou upbraidest not Thy child;
  Deeply I the past deplore,
Now with gracious accents mild,
  Bid me "go and sin no more."

Nothing can I see but sin,
  It has tainted my heart's core;
There it spreads, without, within,
  Can "*I* go and sin no more?"

'Tis for man too hard a task,
  But Thou *canst* my soul restore;
Saviour! this alone I ask—
  Bid me "go and sin no more."

Self-condemned—without a plea,
  Guilty—lost—like her of yore,
Mine may her acquittal be!
  Bid me "go and sin no more."

Oh, how blest will be that day
  When, while I Thy love adore,
I shall never need to say,
  Bid me "go and sin no more!" (emphasis in original)

While the declared extremity of guilt, the sense of sin and lostness voiced in this poem may be found commonly enough in Victorian women's religious verse, identifying with such an overtly immoral biblical character is not common at all. A poem such as this, which requires such an identification to produce meaning, but simultaneously requires a clear identificatory break between the speaker and the biblical persona to which she compares herself, raises significant questions about its dramatisation of a sense of sinfulness. The problematic parallel Elliott constructs between character and speaker works in two ways. On the one hand it functions as a dramatic technique—the speaker pleads with Christ, speak to *me like her*; forgive *me like her*—but on the other hand, paradoxically, it provides a method of foregrounding the speaker's earnestness and righteousness. That is, the parallel actually points to the *difference* between speaker and the character she only very partially inhabits. The identification offered in the first stanza—"Weeping, I look up to Thee"—is immediately undercut by the italicised pronoun *me*, which emphasises the fact that this speaker, pleading to receive Christ's merciful words, is distinct from the other (original, expected) recipient. As with that original woman, who was caught in adultery by the Pharisees and dragged to Jesus, Jesus speaks no word of blame: "Thou upbraidest not Thy child." Yet this parallel, too, is no sooner raised than it is deflated: the poem's speaker declares herself distinct from that biblical woman with every word, most significantly through the fact she literally speaks for herself. The nameless and voiceless original was the passive subject of others' spite and bid for power: she was caught in sin, dragged

80 *Christian and Lyric Tradition in Victorian Women's Poetry*

to Jesus without her own volition, and cast speechless on the ground in an attempt to trap Jesus. The poem's speaker, on the other hand, herself implores pity and forgiveness. An active participant in her own regeneration, she repents: "deeply I the past deplore," and in stanza four she utters her loathing of her sense of sin.

All of these elements work unexpectedly but effectively to undercut the explicit comparison drawn in the sixth stanza, where the speaker declares she is "like her of yore." Elliott's subtle adaptation of the gospel story shows, rather, that the speaker is quite different from "her of yore." Her sin generalised and thus sanitised, her sincerity signalled, her repentance clearly voiced, her appeal for mercy loud, clear, and repeated; the poet speaker insists on her own righteousness. Her repeated request for mercy, emphasising the speaker's sincerity, itself swerves from Jesus' singular utterance, and is unusual given Jesus' actual instruction: "go and sin no more." The speaker appeals to be continually given grace, which in an economy of redemption based on forgiveness means continually being bidden not to sin again (which therefore suggests she must be repeatedly sinning to be thus repeatedly engaging with Christ). The speaker's absolution is structured around repeated acts of speaking to and being spoken to by Jesus. In this poem, then, Elliott presents a different kind of redemptive operation to that found in John's gospel: here redemption is based on ongoing relationship and therefore its production depends upon the participation and active engagement of the (woman) speaker.

In the hands of poets like Elliott, such intertwinings of biblical material and subjective experience present daring extensions of the scriptural source. In *Bread Not Stone*, Elisabeth Schüssler Fiorenza proposes a many-faceted model of feminist critical biblical interpretation: the hermeneutics of creative actualisation, she argues, "allows women to enter the biblical story with the help of historical imagination, artistic recreation, and liturgical ritualization" (20). Fiorenza's articulation of the importance for women of creative engagement with the biblical tradition, echoed by feminist theologians such as Hughes and Ostriker, makes her critical model particularly congenial for assessing the importance of Victorian women's poetic negotiations with scriptural authorities, and the significance of their artistic recreations of biblical scenes, stories, and characters. Going beyond identificatory comparisons of the kind analysed here, a number of Victorian women extend their imaginative explorations of the biblically based subjective lyric towards the territory of the dramatic monody. Recreating biblical narratives from a first-person viewpoint that erases the insistence on separate characters and separate categories of texts, some poets directly adopt the persona of a character in the Bible story itself. This signaling of total imaginative identification has particular consequences for a woman poet setting her voice inside and against an authorised text.

Georgiana M. Taylor in *Lays of Lowly Service: And Other Verses* (1889) heavily favours the first-person retelling of scripture, and adopts a diverse array of personae. "Ruth: Or, the Satisfied Soul" presents a short first-person narrative that focuses on Ruth's romantic relationship with "the Master,"

"God's interpreters to the sons of misery" 81

who at a primary level is Boaz, but in a typological reading (indicated by the capitalised nouns and pronouns), is Christ. Many other women poets retell biblical events from the first-person viewpoint of female biblical characters: Elizabeth Charles composes poems spoken by women including Leah and Rachel, both of whom married Jacob; Rossetti writes "Mary Magdalene and the Other Mary" in the first-person plural; Emily Hickey composes a dialogue spoken by Eve and the Mother of God in "Eve waiteth for Mary"; and at the close of the Victorian period, Michael Field writes a number of urgently passionate biblically sourced poems from the first-person point of view, including "Bibe, Domine," spoken by Rachel, and "A Mother of Bethlehem of Juda." The Bible characters that women poets choose as speakers are, on occasion, male as well as female, the dramatic strategy allowing the woman poet to explore broadened vistas of identification and experienced grace. Such a dramatisation of a male speaker may remain unproblematically orthodox, as, for example, in Georgiana Taylor's "The Path of Faith." This poem takes as epigraph Peter's cry to Jesus: "Lord, if it be Thou, bid me to come unto Thee on the water" (Matthew xiv.28), and tells a first-person narrative that signals the speaker to be a Peter/Christian wishing to "venture forward unto Thee." The persona identifies fully with Peter in her analogous state:

> Even if I should fail,
>   Through looking at my weakness, or around,
> One faltering cry to Thee,
>   And in Thine arms I know I shall be found.

Drawing a parallel between the individual Christian and the tribulations (and often rewards) of a character from Bible times is a perfectly acceptable traditional, devotional move, practised by generations of Christian poets. But in the hands of Christina Rossetti, the character of Peter allows the poet to explore the daring limits of identification and identity. In "I followed Thee," the speaker looks at the cross, and sees Christ looking back—but also sees himself/herself. Rossetti's retelling of this Bible story proposes a revolutionary Christian identity model, one that paradoxically breaks down all individuation and difference—between the sinner and his Lord, between the artist and her subject, and between exercise of imagination and exercise of worship.

In this poem, Rossetti's speaker is the apostle Peter, wracked with guilt as he looks up at Jesus, who looks back at him, knowing everything he's said and done. The first-person dramatisation emphasises the emotional intimacy and the horrifying physical immediacy of the scene.

> I followed Thee, my God, I followed Thee
>   To see the end:
> I turned back flying from Gethsemane,
> Turned back on flying steps to see
>   Thy Face, my God, my Friend.

82 *Christian and Lyric Tradition in Victorian Women's Poetry*

Even fleeing from Thee my heart clave to Thee:
    I turned perforce
Constrained, yea chained by love which maketh free;
I turned perforce, and silently
    Followed along Thy course.

Lord, didst Thou know that I was following Thee?
    I weak and small
Yet Thy true lover, mean tho' I must be,
Sinning and sorrowing—didst Thou see?
    O Lord, Thou sawest all.

[...]

Ah Lord, if even at the last in Thee
    I had put faith,
I might even at the last have counselled me,
And not have heaped up cruelty
    To sting Thee in Thy death.

Alas for me, who bore to think on Thee
    And yet to lie:
While Thou, O Lord, didst bear to look on me
Goaded by fear to blasphemy,
    And break my heart and die.

[...]

Lord, I am standing far far off from Thee;
    Yet is my heart
Hanging with Thee upon the accursed tree;
The nails, the thorns, pierce Thee and me:
    My God, I claim my part

Scarce in Thy throne and kingdom; yet with Thee
    In shame, in loss,
In Thy forsaking, in Thine agony:
Love crucified, behold even me,
    Me also bear Thy cross.

The poem conveys the Peter-speaker's psychological conflict and distress through a series of metaphoric and linguistic paradoxes, foremost among which is the paradox of the cross, which simultaneously symbolises the distance that humankind placed between itself and Christ, and also represents how close the two parties can approach. The poem examines and re-examines these two poles of distance/difference and closeness/identification. Peter's emotional

"God's interpreters to the sons of misery" 83

tergiversations match his physical peregrinations: he followed Christ, after initially running away; he "turned back on flying steps to see/ Thy Face, my God, my Friend." Rossetti simply juxtaposes these simple nouns, God and Friend, to present in that collision the paradox central to the poem—Peter, and whoever speaks the "I" of this poem, can look in the face of a being who is both almighty God, unapproachable, and also "my friend," intimately known and loved. Rossetti figures the human relationship to God with her typical submerged violence, as she meditates on the fact that through love the believer is both set free by and ineluctably bound to the Saviour: "I turned perforce/ Constrained, yea chained by love which maketh free;/ I turned perforce . . ." Poor Peter, even after all his betrayals, has to follow his God. He is compelled, he is owned, by the friend he betrayed—who is still his Lord.

In the third stanza Peter utters the despairing question: does Jesus know he (Peter) has been following him up the hill to Golgotha? Did He see him? In answering his own question, Peter adopts God's own omniscience; he knows, of course, that the answer is yes: "O Lord, Thou sawest all." Knowing that Jesus did in fact see everything agonises Peter, because he recognises (again, seeing and understanding all) that his betrayals wounded Jesus as profoundly as the scourging and the nailing to the cross: Peter has "heaped up cruelty/ To sting Thee in thy death." Peter is horrified by what he's done, and the source of the horror—as well as, ultimately, the source of his redemption—comes through the same imaginative act, that of comparing himself to Jesus. He, Peter, contrived to think about Christ but still lie and deny him, "goaded by fear to blasphemy," but Christ his great parallel, in his own great suffering, nonetheless "bore to look on me."

In Rossetti's faith economy, restructured to be based on identification, redemption is subsequent to and intimately related to recognition. Thus the poet's/Christian's primary goal is to construct a relation through which that all-important recognition may occur. The result of this speaker's conflicted but persistent following is that Christ looks and sees and knows the penitent sinner. In the last two stanzas of the poem, with the words, "Lord, I am standing far far off from Thee," the speaker loosens the identification with Peter and could be anybody, even—particularly—the Victorian reader, at a great historical distance. And yet, Rossetti asserts, no real distance exists at all, because Jesus' sacrifice effectively broke down the barriers separating humans from God. For Rossetti, that means an awesome and awful responsibility, as recognition merges into mutuality: the speaker of the poem steps forward, after all those denials, and claims his or her share of Christ's sufferings. In effect, she responds to Christ's call to pick up her cross and follow him, and says *yes I will*. Thus those last two stanzas express a desire to participate in a horrifying fate—the speaker imagines herself hanging on the cross, with Christ, pierced by the same nails and thorns, sharing the shame and loss and agony. "Love crucified" she says to Jesus, "behold even me, me also bear Thy cross." Holding Christ as her great example, she declares her willingness to live up to him, to become like him—a difficult, terrible, and miraculous transformation. When Rossetti's speaker looks at the cross, she sees Jesus recognise her. In this poem, being face to face with God is agonising for the poor sinning human. But, as Dolores Rosenblum has shown, the act of mutual looking and mutual recognition, for Rossetti, empowers the individual believer ("Watching, Looking, Keeping Vigil"). Beholding and being beheld represents ultimate victory: face to face, the difference between God and human disappears. Thus the intrusion of a first-person self in this poem reveals thematic as well as dramatic intent and achievement. It demonstrates the operation of redemption, the cancelling of difference, the transformation of the human from a sinful, particular, and gendered being to a purified being freed from earthly trappings and resembling nothing other than God.

In my readings of the poems here, the speakers' fluidity, constructed through adoption and adaption of differing biblical voices, indicates in its complexity (and, occasionally, its seeming incoherence) a broader significance to women poets' first-person indwellings of biblical texts. Women poets do not restrict themselves solely to a focus on female characters in scripture, although the particular importance of their deployment of those female characters will be analysed in Chapter 3. Rather, as the array of analyses in this chapter have demonstrated, Victorian women poets create a number of innovative strategies for refocusing biblical personae and texts, as well as refocusing ways of responding (imaginatively and stylistically) to those biblical originals, in so doing diffusing and multiplying sources of authoritative speaking. Their poetry may be read as a constructive, active expression of women's engagement in and creation of what they assert to be a discipleship of equals. And this creative transfiguration is as valid and as worthy of study as male-authored engagements with the biblical prototype that have produced the creative responses, embellishments, and celebrations which the Christian community has traditionally heralded as 'correct' and 'original.' Women's similar creative responses, their formulations of new stories, poems, versions, rituals, and wordings, also claim originality, by foregrounding the contingency of originality. Victorian women do not question the inspiration of the scriptures. Rather, they claim a diffusion of inspiration, an expansive renewal. Believing fervently in God and in God's word, they interrogate the Bible in ways quite different from the Higher Criticism, perceiving it and using it as a model of Christian faith and life that, as a living and dynamic model, continues to function in their times, to their communities, in various, inclusive, and nourishing ways.

3 The Woman in the Scriptures
Models of the Christian Female in Victorian Women's Poetry

> . . . Come with the voice, the lyre,
> Daughters of Judah! With the timbrel rise!
> Ye of the dark prophetic Eastern eyes,
>   Imperial in their visionary fire;
> Oh! steep my soul in that old glorious time,
> When God's own whisper shook the cedars of your clime.
>
> —Felicia Hemans

In these lines, from the opening of the series "Female Characters of Scripture," Felicia Hemans invokes the "Daughters of Judah," the women of the Bible who owned and uttered "visionary fire," and who are held up by Hemans as models for women of later times. Hemans and the female poets who followed her found that by recreating "that old glorious time" when biblical Daughters of Judah sang and spoke out, they found present reason and justification to themselves speak and sing, and to encourage other women to do likewise, extending their influence and agency and suggesting bold new paths. As the latter part of the previous chapter suggested, the Bible's galleries of characters for potential identification offered Victorian women opportunities to insert a female subjectivity into male-dominated narratives. This chapter focuses more closely on how certain female biblical figures were deployed by Victorian women poets to politicise, feminise, and make contemporary the biblical narrative. In those poems on biblical women, Victorian womanhood remains a significant presence; poets expand biblical texts to incorporate the Victorian woman into a living text of ongoing significance.

Victorian women knew, with an often painful clarity, that they lacked a tradition. "I look everywhere for grandmothers, and see none," Elizabeth Barrett Browning famously lamented.[1] Florence Nightingale, appalled by the narrow horizons hemming in her gender, voiced a not-dissimilar plaint, denouncing the lack of "types" for strong women (Boyd 235). Barrett Browning longed for a model of creative endeavour and success, Nightingale for a model of active endeavour and success; the problems were related ones, and some Victorian women found the means to respond to both in one source: the Bible. The forerunners sought by Nightingale, Barrett Browning, and other literary women could be and were found in and formulated from biblical sources, and furthermore these types significantly combined the active

86 Christian and Lyric Tradition in Victorian Women's Poetry

strength, the spiritual status, and the creative song that enabled women poets to envision an expanded artistic and spiritual role for themselves.

Whether or not the Christian tradition offers a source of encouraging or liberating role models for women has, however, been vigorously debated by modern scholars, many of whom have taken the negative view. Marina Warner's groundbreaking *Alone of All Her Sex* (1985) surveys Marian symbology throughout history, arguing that the figure of Mary has served as an overwhelmingly constricting and oppressive archetype. More recently but in a similar vein, Julie Melnyk has observed a lack of empowering archetypes within the Christian tradition: "Christianity in nineteenth-century England offered women no forceful female religious symbols, no images of women's spiritual power" ("Mighty Victims" 134). In a provocative account of Victorian women novelists' use of biblical symbols, Ruth Jenkins suggests these women could in fact engage creatively with biblical characters and symbols in response to the period's spiritual crisis (*Reclaiming Myths of Power*). However, even as Jenkins constructs an argument about Gaskell's creation of a Christ-like female protagonist, a redeemed fallen woman, Jenkins frames this creation as essentially a negative or reactive act, part of Gaskell's critique of the nineteenth-century Church's refusal of power to women: "Nightingale, Brontë, Gaskell, and Evans all point to the patriarchally complicitous relationship between their culture's sacred and secular institutions, a dynamic that divests women of power and authority" (155). While these three scholars offer markedly different readings of nineteenth-century women's responses to the circumscribed role offered by the Church, they are united in observing, in the traditional narratives and casts of characters presented by nineteenth-century Christianity, the withholding of power and authority from women.

A small but significant number of scholars have, however, suggested that certain aspects of Christianity, particularly prophetic models, served as an enabling structure for nineteenth-century women's articulation. In *Prophetic Sons and Daughters* (1985), Deborah Valenze examines the significance of the rise of female preaching and 'cottage-based evangelicalism' in the industrial upheaval of the nineteenth century, arguing that evangelical ideology permitted women to expand both their private and public voices. Christine Krueger's *The Reader's Repentance* (1992) draws attention to Victorian women novelists' use of the scriptural prophet figure in their fiction, looking at models of female preachers in writers including Gaskell and Eliot. More recently, Charles LaPorte has offered an illuminating account of the elision, this time in Eliot's poetry, of the roles of the (Victorian) poetess and the (biblical) prophetess. Cynthia Scheinberg is one of few scholars to have offered a sustained discussion of the biblical prophetess model in women's poetry, surveying how biblical heroines of the Old Testament (the Hebrew Torah), including Miriam, Esther, and Deborah, appear in the poetry of Hemans, Rossetti, and the Jewish poet Grace Aguilar as prophetically inspired female figures exercising a public voice ("Measure to

The Woman in the Scriptures 87

Yourself"). Generally, those scholars who argue biblical models functioned positively in Victorian women's writing have focussed on a small gallery of leading nineteenth-century authors, reformers, and proto-feminists. George Eliot, as noted previously, is a favourite. Josephine Butler is another. Lucretia Flammang writes on Butler's cooption of the rhetoric of biblical prophecy and the examples of bold biblical women who followed God's "calling" regardless of social disapprobation or cost. Helen Mathers has also written on Butler's use of Christian and specifically Evangelical discourse in her campaign against the Contagious Diseases Acts. While these are persuasive accounts of Victorian women's creative uses of Christian discourse, the suggestion remains that these few, leading figures are exceptions, unusual in their ability to wrest from an otherwise constricting tradition paradigms transformable to their own creative self-envisioning.

In fact, nineteenth-century women found a whole gallery of forceful female characters in their Bibles, characters that could be drawn on to help justify multiple social and creative ambitions. The biblical restrictiveness posited by a number of critics does not recognise the variety of literary treatments Victorian women applied to female scriptural characters, who made appearances in fiery political pamphlets as well as in conservative sentimental verse. Examples of scriptural women were frequently produced to support women's broader engagement in society, in philanthropic endeavours, and even in expanded roles of authority within the Church of England itself. F. K. Prochaska, in his study of women's charitable activity in the nineteenth century, offers a handy gallery of biblical examples found useful by Victorian women:

> Mary Magdalen at Calvary was the model of fidelity; Phoebe of Cenchreae, 'a servant of the church,' compassion incarnate; Dorcas of Joppa, who made clothes for the poor, synonymous with good works; Rebekah was the personification of industry and piety; Lydia an example of benevolence and self-sacrifice; Priscilla an active Christian; Mary a contemplative one; Esther a patriot; and Ruth a friend. (16; see also n.53 and 54)

Women prose writers often drew didactic lessons from female characters in the Bible, lessons that ranged from the conventionally patriarchal and prescriptive to the radical. Mrs. Donaldson's *Home Duties for Wives and Mothers, Illustrated by Women of Scripture* (1882) offers pious, kindly lessons drawn from Bible stories of heroism and villainy.

> In these pages I have endeavoured, by Divine help, to set before them the examples of women of old, who have had difficulties and trials, joys and sorrow, such as theirs; some of whom shone forth as bright lights, not only to be admired, but to be hopefully and patiently followed. Others, on the contrary, serve only as sad and awful

88 *Christian and Lyric Tradition in Victorian Women's Poetry*

examples of duty neglected, opportunities wasted, and of responsibilities abused. (viii)[2]

On the other hand, Mrs. Susannah Meredith's *Wanted: Deaconnesses for the Service of the Church* (1872) takes a more politically radical tack. Meredith uses the example of Phoebe, described in differing translations of the Bible as a "servant" or "deacon" of the Church (Romans 16:1), to argue vigorously that Victorian women should, following this precedent, be allowed positions of greater responsibility in the Church. Donaldson and Meredith both, in their very different works, capitalise upon the emotional and symbolic force attached to these sacred female figures. Other writers, harnessing the potential of that symbolic power, turned to political account even those biblical characters that have seemed to critics like Warner ideologically irrecuperable. Anna Jameson's popular *Legends of the Madonna* (1852) introduced thousands of English Protestant readers not just to the reverence accorded to the Madonna in European art but also to the idea that contemporary women's status should be elevated and her social role developed. Writer and campaigner Frances Power Cobbe wrote in 1864 that adoration of Mary means adoration of motherly and feminine tenderness and virtue, and that Protestants can "ill dispense" with honouring such characteristics and, by extension, womanhood itself.[3]

In Victorian women's poetry can be found a still largely unexplored wealth of biblical female characters and 'honouring' treatments of those characters. Thoughtfully examining the creation and deployment of these figures requires re-reading and re-analysing the relationship between religious traditionalism and feminist aspirations. In her comprehensive account of nineteenth-century feminisms, Barbara Caine notes the internal contradictions as well as the vitality and development of feminist thought in the Victorian period, observing that "for much of the nineteenth century, feminists reworked and rethought conventional ideas and images as a way both of articulating and gaining widespread acknowledgement of their views" (82). Victorian women's relationship to a particular set of conventional ideas and images, the biblical historical sources they mined for poetic subject matter and devotional encouragement, is ineluctably constrained and situated, but because of its very constraints and situatedness it is also revelatory. The influence of our own situatedness on our investigative frame of reference has often prevented thoughtful analysis of these historical factors, as Fiorenza cautions: "Historical interpretation is defined by contemporary questions and horizons of reality and conditioned by contemporary political interests and structures of domination" (*In Memory of Her* xvii). What, then, do Victorian women religious poets, working as amateur, proto-feminist biblical historians to offer readings of the female figures of the early Church, reveal about their own preoccupations, aspirations, and cultural and historical context? In what ways do their negotiations with the biblical past shape their negotiations with their present, Victorian circumstances?

The Woman in the Scriptures 89

How can we read their work aright? Kimberly VanEsveld Adams, in her study of the centrality of Mary the Mother of God to the essentialist/difference feminisms developed by Jameson, Fuller, and Eliot, offers an example of balanced, historically informed criticism (*Our Lady of Victorian Feminism*). A similar close analysis of poets' uses of female scriptural figures will be illuminating in the important and overdue task of assessing Victorian women's various, creative attempts to claim status and power within Christian discourse.

In her work on Victorian women poets' use of Bible characters, Scheinberg focuses her argument almost entirely on Old Testament women, specifically Jewish biblical heroines, claiming that these figures help "resolve[] the contradictions of Christian women's literary identity" ("Measure to Yourself" 277). Scheinberg argues her case strongly, but the role of New Testament biblical female figures, the specifically *Christian* woman model, demands similar attention and analysis. I am not convinced by Scheinberg's contention that "Christian women found it somehow easier to construct an authoritative female poetic identity out of the Old (potentially Jewish) rather than New (clearly Christian) Testament" (*Women's Poetry and Religion* 69). The New Testament in fact provided a rich resource for Victorian women poets, presenting female Christian models that did not require such convoluted (albeit richly suggestive) manoeuvrings with Other-ness;[4] in fact, as Clara Balfour wrote in 1847, Victorian women found in New Testament women particularly useful models precisely because they were generally less "remarkable." In her popular prose work *The Women of Scripture*, Balfour wrote:

> The characters of the illustrious women of the New Testament have less of external incident, and more of internal principle, than those of the Old. Woman's outward life is exhibited in the charming and gorgeous narratives of the ancient dispensation. In the more spiritual pages of the Gospel record, the inward life of vital piety is exquisitely displayed: not startling situations, not unusual authority, not worldly rank, not human influence; but the deep emotions of the heart, the sacred principles of moral conduct, the lofty spiritual aspirations of the soul, are the characteristics exhibited for our instruction. *It is obvious, therefore, that the New Testament female characters are more valuable as models for imitation, from the fact of their illustrating moral principles, rather than remarkable situations; the principles being important to all, wonderful situations peculiar to a few.* (221–2; my emphasis)

Victorian women's poetry reveals these New Testament female figures to be, as Adams argues of Mary, contested figures; they are not fixed categories but flexible ciphers capable of manipulation, expansion, and other unexpected treatments. Acknowledging their inherent flexibility helps demolish the narrow view that the Bible only offered Victorian women

90 *Christian and Lyric Tradition in Victorian Women's Poetry*

constricting or limiting models. Female Christian models were deployed in women's poetry to express multiple meanings and emphases, a multiplicity explored both through the employment of many individual characters and additionally through the presentation of many facets of individual characters. At a primary level, these proliferating poems on biblical women reinscribe women back into sacred narratives that had often been used to exclude them; in this way these poets may be seen as pioneering one of the foremost drives of twentieth-century feminist theologians.[5] These reinscriptions also wrote woman in multiple forms: pure, maternal, sexual, powerless and powerful, nameless and named. This was significant, and fraught, work: Scheinberg rightly draws attention to "the high stakes involved for women when they challenge hegemonic representations of scriptural figures" (*Women's Poetry and Religion* 77). For Victorian women poets, no less was at stake than the right to see themselves within Christianity's most sacred narratives.

A number of poems depicting these characters support a reading of the work as feminist in a close-to-modern sense. But just as important as proto-feminist verses are the poems that contributed to powerful constructions of sexual difference. Voicing 'difference feminism' allowed the exaltation of womanhood in general and of certain women in particular. Biblical characters were occasionally presented as markedly idealised figures of leadership (Deborahs and Jaels), or more generally as figures to aspire to (in *Image as Insight*, 149, Miles makes the important point that such figures can present compensations for current realities as well as alternative possibilities). But, importantly, they were also figured not as distant ideals but as real and realistic women, 'real' both as historically situated actual persons and as relevant artefacts with an ongoing existence in the Victorian here and now. This practice has clear correlations to contemporaneous secular emulation literature. Feminist periodicals of the middle and late Victorian period regularly featured portraits of famous and honoured women through history, exposing their audiences to the achievements of women from Madame de Staël to Elizabeth Fry to Lydia Twining, and holding them up as aspirational models.[6] Numerous hortatory biographical volumes published in the period sought to reproduce in their Victorian reader the qualities of their subjects, and religious poetry can be seen to operate very similarly. Poetic depictions that stress the integrity, veracity, and historical distinctness of these female models also link the condition of ancient biblical women, seemingly paradoxically, to the condition of the contemporary Victorian woman. My analysis will encompass treatments of famous, infamous, and anonymous female figures from the Bible, as not all Victorian women concentrated on Deborah-like leaders of nations, but often also on those who, as in Balfour's description, were less "remarkable" (but, perhaps, thus more 'Victorian'). Suggestively numerous in Victorian women's poetry are treatments of New Testament women who are not primary actors but who are acted upon: women who ask for or otherwise elicit miracles; women who cause Christ to act like Christ; women who bear witness to the gospel. These seemingly passive (and often nameless) women characters are portrayed as the occasion for the Christian message, the parchment on which miracle and salvation are ultimately written, the bearers of the record—without whom nothing could be read or confirmed as true. Such women offer a different kind of heroism and history, a distinctly feminised form particularly congenial for nineteenth-century women.

"First Singer of the Church": Mary the Mother of Jesus

The figure of Mary the Mother of Jesus in Victorian England was, as Carol Marie Engelhardt writes, "symbolically charged and highly visible" (159). Sally Cuneen, in her review of Marian legend and symbolism throughout the millennium, closely examines the explosion of attention Mary received in the nineteenth century, in the form of devotions, apparitions, the new papal doctrine of the Immaculate Conception in 1854, and, somewhat unexpectedly, Protestant women's appropriation of Mary in their efforts to elevate women's social and spiritual status. Engelhardt discusses the ways Mary's role elided with but also contested the idealised cultural figure of the Angel in the House in the critical areas of motherhood and virginity, setting Anglican discomfort with Mary's idealisation in the historical context of nineteenth-century anti-Catholicism. While Engelhardt states firmly, "no Anglican upheld her as the feminine ideal," a questionable position, Engelhardt does concede that "the Virgin Mary was understood by Catholics and Protestants alike as a powerful figure" (160). Adams' *Our Lady of Victorian Feminism* agrees with Cuneen concerning the vibrancy and contestation of the Mary figure in the nineteenth century, as opposed to the flat depiction of Mary's subordinate and passive goodness that has been assumed by the majority of scholars in both literary and historical religious studies. Adams argues that the Victorian period's 'multiple Marys' reveal her appropriation and redefinition by a number of nineteenth-century writers, including proto-feminists, for a number of different ends.

This recognition of Mary's power finds varied and vivid shape in Victorian women's poetry, as verse from across the denominational spectrum expresses admiration, sometimes overtly celebratory, sometimes somewhat anxious, for the Mother of Jesus. It is nonetheless important to note that Roman Catholic poets present a concentration on and veneration of Mary distinct in degree and in quality from Protestant figurations. Protestant portrayals of Mary avoid petitions for aid and (for the most part) personally directed expressions of worship, and generally take care to emphasise Mary's honoured but still human status. It is rare to find in Protestant verse extended consideration of Mary's personal beauties and qualities, while Roman Catholic women poets, deeply concerned with Mary's iconicity, frequently concentrate on Mary's appearance as well as her virtues. Both parties are deeply concerned with Mary's status, but they figure her power differently.

92   *Christian and Lyric Tradition in Victorian Women's Poetry*

In the poetry of Catholic women in the Victorian period, we find overt, worshipful venerations of Mary's womanly supremacy. Roman Catholics like Emily Shapcote and Emily Hickey produce entire volumes dedicated to the adoration of Mary, and their works echo Mary's own titles (for example, *Mary: The Perfect Woman; Ancilla Domini;* and *Our Lady of May*). In numerous other volumes and poems Roman Catholic women meditate on different aspects of Mary's sanctity: her purity, her compassion, her sorrow, her faithfulness, her queenliness. Some poets are more successful than others in introducing fresh perspectives on narrowly delimited subject matter, and creating a living dialogue with a tradition of centuries' standing. Augusta Theodosia Drane was a redoubtable Victorian convert who as a young woman joined the Dominican convent at Clifton, took the name of Sister Francis Raphael, and eventually became prioress and then in 1881 Mother Provincial of her Order. Intellectual and indefatigable, Drane wrote substantive historical and biographical works as well as poetry, and a number of her poems on Mary draw vividly on literary tradition. "Our Lady of the Sacred Heart" uses an unusual stanzaic form and lushly physical descriptive language to offer Mary various adorations, describing her as a lily with silver wings, a "ruby Gem," and the "choicest of vines." "A Prayer to Our Lady," indicates the sub-titular note, is a paraphrase of an original found in *Typographical Antiquities*, and while Drane retains just the one obvious archaism of "Ladye" the poem, in its simple rhymes, unornamented trochaics, and directness of address has an immediate, primitive charm:

> Ladye! I will trust in thee
> That my prayer shall granted be;
> I shall, Ladye, then be blithe,
> Thee to greet with Aves five!

The period's best-known Roman Catholic poet was Adelaide Procter, reportedly Queen Victoria's favourite poet,[7] who enjoyed great popularity in the mid-century. Much of her most explicitly religious poetry appears in *A Chaplet of Verses*, which she published in 1861 to benefit a Catholic-run night refuge for homeless women and children. "The Names of Our Lady" is representative of the majority of the volume's verse in general, and of Procter's treatments of Mary in particular. After a brief preamble at the start of the poem, each neatly rhymed common metre stanza begins with an italicised 'title' for Mary, ranging from *Star of the Sea* to *Our Lady of the Rosary* to *Fair Queen of Virgins*, and meditates on what that title communicates about her nature. The sentiments are devout and conventional, even formulaic; the changes rung on a repeated formulary suggest the chapters of a rosary. The poem concludes by suggesting that of all her many names, "Mary" is the holiest and the dearest, because it is the closest to our humanity. Thus stylistically as well

The Woman in the Scriptures 93

as thematically, the poem seeks to render the relationship between Mary and the worshipful human speaker concrete and tangible. (Procter's use of ritual and repetitive language will be discussed in greater detail in Chapter 5.)

Even as they draw on certain recognisable formularies, Roman Catholic women adopt a wide variety of approaches to Mary. May Probyn offers in *Pansies* different poems of Marian veneration; one of the more complex, "Ballade," sets Mary and Eve in dialogue, presenting Mary as the New Eve who will redeem mankind (and specifically womankind) from the legacy of Eve's first dreadful sin. Harriet E. H. King's "Mater Dolorosa" concentrates on Mary's specifically motherly sufferings, and hymns her transformation into Mother of all Sons of Man. Many Victorian poems of Marian devotion retell apocryphal tales or attributed miracles; the Irishwoman Katharine Tynan, for example, retells a Welsh story in "The Dream of Mary," in which Mary tells to Jesus her dream of the fate that awaits him, and every detail of her vision proves true. The poem ends:

> Over the hill, and a cold, cold hill,
>> I saw Mary dreaming and weeping,
> Making a space betwixt souls and ill,
>> Snatching men from hell and its keeping. (*Ballads and Lyrics*, 1891)

The portrayal of the extent of Mary's agency in humanity's salvation— whether or not she actively 'snatches men from hell'—most clearly demarcates between Roman Catholic and Protestant believers. Shapcote's Mary, like Tynan's, has visions of Gethsemane and Calvary, and Mary 'wills it' as much as Christ does (her willing of Christ's death, argues Shapcote, is necessary for its accomplishment). The part divisions of Shapcote's volume *Mary: The Perfect Woman, One Hundred and Fifty Rhythms in Honour of the Mystical Life of Our Lady* (1903), reflect a typically Roman Catholic, exalted view of Mary's role: Part II is entitled, "Redeemer and Co-Redemptrix," and ends with her assumption to heaven; Part III is entitled, "The Kingdom of God and Queenship of Mary." Emily Hickey renders Mary in "Our Lady's Crowns" an equal participant in Christ's own sufferings:

> And next He crowned thee with his sorrow—thee
>> He called upon His crucifixion morn,
>> And girt thy brows with His own piercing thorn,
> And clothed thee with His purple of mockery.

And in the second part of "Any Child to the New-Found Mother," Hickey portrays Mary as acting in every way like Christ: wielding judgment and punishment; showing identical love and intent towards human beings; embodying his tenderness.

94 Christian and Lyric Tradition in Victorian Women's Poetry

> Ever one with Him in will, His heart, His bride,
> Thou defied art He defied;
> Thou beloved art he beloved; and in thy face
> Is the fullness of His grace.

Mary's status is also often emphasised by Protestant poets, but they figure her power differently, deploying a variety of poetic strategies to depict but also to contain this female figure's powerful attributes. The Anglo-Catholic Christina Rossetti, who was deeply influenced by Tractarianism as well as by the Roman Catholic heritage of her Italian father, writes several poems on Mary that reflect a richly complicated attitude to the Foremost of Women, seeking solutions to the conundrum of honouring Mary but also avoiding honouring her over much.[8] In "Feast of the Annunciation," Rossetti's subject veers from Mary herself to language about her and language spoken to her, tracing the difficulty of finding metaphoric language that doesn't trespass on metaphors belonging solely to a supremely honoured Christ.

> Whereto shall we liken this Blessed Mary Virgin,
> Fruitful shoot from Jesse's root graciously emerging?
> Lily we might call her, but Christ alone is white;
> Rose delicious, but that Jesus is the one Delight;
> Flower of women, but her Firstborn is mankind's one flower:
> He the Sun lights up all moons thro' their radiant hour.
> "Blessed among women, highly favoured," thus
> Glorious Gabriel hailed her, teaching words to us:
> Whom devoutly copying we too cry "All hail!"
> Echoing on the music of glorious Gabriel.

Rossetti here ponders and then discards a number of poetic strategies, arguing that the use of traditional Marian symbols (lily, rose, "flower of women") is fundamentally flawed. Ultimately Rossetti's opening question, "whereto shall we liken this Blessed Mary Virgin" is left unanswered, unanswerable, as she shows that Christ is the ultimate metaphor and symbol, and that all language ultimately points to him. He is the supreme one, alone, a central star with a number of reflective satellites. Rossetti aligns poets, then, with Mary herself; they like she can only reflect back and echo Christ's perfection; all that is left for the believer is what might be termed devout copying.

Other Protestant poets find differing ways to suggest the containment of Mary's problematic power. Using a similar strategy to Rossetti, though with less subtle execution, K. E. V. in "The Conception" takes up the familiar figure for Mary, the lily, in order to show its limitations. The poet contrasts the symbol of the lily with that of Christ, the Tree, in order to draw clear conclusions about true power, lasting influence, and fruitfulness. A more direct critique is presented by Emily Saunders, who puts into Mary's own mouth a rebuke of Mariolatry, insisting on her humanity rather than divinity ("Annunciation of the Virgin Mary").

Making thee blessed above all
    Others of womankind,
Why did God's choice upon thee fall?
    Can we the secret find?

[...]

Holding thyself in small esteem,
    God so exalted thee.
How little thou didst ever dream
    That one day thou wouldst be

By human folly placed on high,
    Till unto thee, at length
Was lifted many a sinner's eye,
    If not for life, for strength!

If grief were ever felt above,
    The unexpected sight
To horror would thy spirit move,
    And shadow Heaven's delight.

And thou wouldst say, "Ah! was it I
    Who for Earth's rescue died?
Ye madmen! with me magnify
    My Lord, the Crucified."

Another Protestant treatment of Mary, displaying a more measured and generous approach, may be found in Elizabeth Rundle Charles' "The Crown." The young Elizabeth Rundle was drawn to the Oxford Movement, and while she never converted to Roman Catholicism as she was reportedly tempted to do, her Anglicanism remained broad and tolerant, informing her diverse friendships and her many charitable activities.[9] *The Women of the Gospels, The Three Wakings, And Other Verses* (1868) is divided into several sections; the first, "The Women of the Gospels," groups poems in headed divisions, including divisions for Mary the Mother of Our Lord, Mary Magdalene, and Salome. The fifth poem in the Mary section, "The Crown," offers her numerous coronations, including the crown of motherhood and "the victor's crown of fadeless life." While every stanza begins with the same statement of acclamation, "Thou shalt be crowned!", the final stanza shows that Mary is not alone

96   *Christian and Lyric Tradition in Victorian Women's Poetry*

in her future glory—and that she is still clearly subject to (not the equal of) God:

> Thou shalt be crowned! But not alone,
>   No lonely pomp shall weigh thee down;
> Crowned with the myriads round His throne,
>   And casting at His feet thy crown.

Clearly, the various manifestations of Mary's power in this poem necessitate this ultimate delimitation. Of particular interest is the form that power takes in the second stanza, in which Mary is granted a specifically literary crown, and is heralded as the ultimate religious poet:

> Thou shalt be crowned! More fragrant bays
>   Than ever poet's brows entwine,
> For thine immortal hymn of praise,
>   First Singer of the Church, are thine.

The reference to Mary's "immortal hymn" is significant, as the contestation of Mary's power, in Victorian women's poetry, may be brought into sharper focus through the lens of the key issue of Mary's *speech*. While Mary is so often depicted as watcher and sufferer, what Mary does and does not, can and cannot *say*, is a profoundly significant conundrum for women seeking to envision an historical tradition in which women are significantly active, knowledgeable, and authoritative. Here the verse of both Catholic and Protestant women converges on a significant shared focus: Victorian women poets from a range of affiliations repeatedly analyse and reconstruct Mary's voice. Scheinberg has described the Virgin Mary as "perhaps the most important, and most traditionally silent of Christian female figures" (*Women's Poetry and Religion* 76), and argues that literary depictions of Mary as a Jewish woman grant her prophetic voice, but constructions of her as Christian woman render her silenced. My findings, however, support quite a different reading: Victorian women poets certainly present Mary the mother of God as the foremost Christian woman, but they also regularly present her as the foremost Christian singer, finding in Mary's voice a primary model of holy, anointed, and authoritative speech.

Scheinberg's assertion that the majority of poetic depictions of Mary represent her as silent object is then complicated by her own discussion of Elizabeth Barrett's long, rich dramatic monologue, "The Virgin Mary to the Child Jesus," first published in *The Seraphim and Other Poems*, 1838. Scheinberg constructs a daring reading of the poem, arguing that its central concern is the problem of a woman speaking to God. Scheinberg links Mary's linguistic power to her spiritual power, claiming Mary's utterance enables her to "position[] herself at the center of religious history, as leader and spiritual prophet" (*Women's Poetry and Religion* 79). Section X of the poem reads:

The Woman in the Scriptures

And then the drear sharp tongue of prophecy,
With the dread sense of things which shall be done,
Doth smite me inly, like a sword: a sword?
That "smites the Shepherd." Then, I think aloud
The words "despised,"—"rejected,"—every word
Recoiling into darkness as I view
    The *Darling* on my knee.
Bright angels,—move not—lest ye stir the cloud
Betwixt my soul and His futurity!
I must not die, with mother's work to do,
    And could not live—and see. (emphasis in original)

While earlier in the poem Mary compares herself to Moses, in this stanza she quite explicitly and radically identifies herself as a prophet, taking into her own mouth Isaiah's words about the Messiah, who was to be "despised and rejected," and applying them both presciently and maternally to the "darling" on her knee. Throughout the poem Mary identifies the importance of her role through her actions, stating, "I bear," "I look," and "I know"; Barrett has her Mary articulating her understanding of the centrality of her own spoken witness to a right viewing and understanding of the Christ.

Scheinberg sees Elizabeth Barrett as the exception to the general rule, but Barrett is not in fact alone in her focus on Mary's speech acts and their significance in authorising female prophetic/poetic speech. Elizabeth Charles, in her prose work *Sketches of the Women of Christendom*, dwells at length in her chapter on Mary upon "The Song of Mary."

> Her nation had a rich treasury of sacred song, and many women of her people had been poetesses and prophetesses.
>
> Two songs especially by Jewish women were well known in their Sacred Books—one a grand war-song of thanksgiving for victory over an oppressor, the other a mother's song of joy and praise for the birth of her firstborn son.
>
> But this song of the Blessed Virgin's was the very first song of the Christian Church, and it is sung every afternoon in many parts of Christendom by men, women, and children. The first singer of the Church was the mother of our Lord.
>
> [...]
>
> You see, when Mary speaks of herself it is not to exalt herself, but her God and Saviour; it is simply of herself as of "low estate," as among the hungry, the humble, and meek.
>
> [...]

98 *Christian and Lyric Tradition in Victorian Women's Poetry*

"All generations shall call me blessed," she sings. And so indeed she has been blessed, throughout Christendom, daily, for nearly two thousand years.

For her blessedness is not that she had a special gift to lift her apart from all. It is that the unspeakable gift given through her is a blessing for all, —for all the hungry, all the humble, of all time. (21–22)

Like other commentators, Charles notes the earliest Hebrew singers of the Bible were Miriam and Hannah. But Charles emphasises Mary's membership in the *Christian* faith, and thus presents her as a role model for all Christians, right down to the present day, who echo her words "every afternoon in many parts of Christendom." Thus Mary's song, a "gift given through her," really belongs to all Christians, "of all time"; of the people yet above the people, Mary is simultaneously the embodiment of humility and—through her song—the focus of thousands of years of blessing.

Emily Hickey was a late Victorian of considerable independence of thought and action, a gifted teacher and a varied and productive writer whose poetry, even before her 1901 conversion to the Catholic faith, shows her fascination with the subtleties of Mary's humility and exaltation. *Ancilla Domini*, a slim volume privately printed in 1899, presents fourteen poems following Mary through her life, from "Her Conception" to "Her Repose." *Our Lady of May and Other Poems* (1902) reprints a number of the *Ancilla Domini* poems and adds several more, similarly emotionally tender. In both volumes appears "She stands without, seeking to speak to Him," which retells the story found in Mark 3:31–35, Matthew 12:46–50, and Luke 8:19–21. Jesus, embarked on his public ministry, is teaching a large crowd, and his mother and brothers cannot get into the building to talk with him. Hickey's poem meditates, as the title indicates, on Mary's speaking, both on her humility in waiting to speak and also on the occasions of her active speaking. The poem collects and rewords various words of Mary recorded in the Bible, here replayed to suggest the centrality of her words to the birth, development, and miraculous ministry of Christ.

Without the blessed Mother stands:
She of the loving reverent hands
That wrapt our Lord in swaddling bands:

She of the holy brow, the eyes
That saw the light o' the world arise
In her Babe's Face, 'neath Bethlehem's skies:

She who had watched the gates of sense
Expanding fair and, issuing thence,
High wisdom, pure intelligence;

Since on her bosom He was laid;
Hers, whom the Word that all things made,
God's Self, implicitly obeyed.
But now, the ministry begun,
That time for evermore is done,
And she who bare the Eternal Son,

Like any soul that strives to climb
To His obedience' height sublime,
Must stand without and wait His time.

At Cana was the word breathed through
That soul of hers in meekness due,
Whate'er He saith unto you, do;

But first that word of duteous breath
She spake in holy Nazareth,
God's handmaid she, for life, for death,

Her will with God's in blest accord—
Unto the handmaid of the Lord
Be it according to thy word.

That self-surrender absolute,
(Faith's holiest flower, Love's fairest fruit,)
That sealed her God's from head to foot,

Is not annulled: she waiteth meek,
Until the time be come to speak
With her Desire, whom all men seek. (emphasis in the original)

A delicate balance is achieved here between the characters of Mary and Jesus, who in many ways mirror each other. At the opening of the poem the mother Mary guards and raises the dependent child Christ, their paradoxical relationship of power and subjection portrayed in terms of language: the all-powerful creative Word obediently subject to the instructional words of his parent: "Hers, whom the Word that all things made,/ God's Self, implicitly obeyed." As he reaches maturity their roles reverse and Mary submits to him, "Like any soul that strives to climb/ To His obedience' height sublime." The poem emphasises their similarities syntactically, in the repetition of forms of 'obey,' but most significantly in the multiple iterations of "word," teasing out multiple layers of signification. Both are animated by the Word, and Hickey suggests constituted by it—though Christ *is* the (capitalised) Word, and Mary serves as a vessel for it, bearing the child, and "breathed through." The poem

100   *Christian and Lyric Tradition in Victorian Women's Poetry*

records Mary's words in italics, both those she spoke at the Annunciation—words of meekness and acceptance—and those she spoke at the wedding at Cana. At that wedding her speaking catalysed Christ's first recorded miracle, the turning of water into wine. Before he'd given any sign that he would miraculously intervene in the situation, Mary's words directed attention to his words: "*Whate'er He saith unto you, do,*" thus recording her implicit faith that he would speak/perform a miracle. Here the miraculous performance inheres in the speech act, as does recognition of miraculous potential. Finally, at poem's end, it is Mary's turn to wait, meek and obedient, for his will; she mirrors her son at the poem's opening, but also reflects back his own exact purpose: "Her will with God's in blest accord."[10]

The most famous of Mary's speakings is the Magnificat. As already mentioned, Elizabeth Charles heralds Mary as "first singer of the church," and Charles dedicates an entire section of *Sketches of the Women of Christendom* to explicating the importance and novelty of the Magnificat. "[Mary's] nation had a rich treasury of sacred song, and many women of her people had been poetesses and prophetesses ... But this song of the Blessed Virgin's was the very first song of the Christian Church" (21). Victorian women poets ring many changes on this song to produce commentary on their own songs and their own roles as 'singers of the Church.' Proto-Victorian Felicia Hemans focuses on Mary's song to consider the "divinest chords" of religious poetry and her frequent topic, female literary fame. Scheinberg has suggested that Hemans' poem on Miriam's song becomes a meditation on the operation of the woman's public poetic voice (*Women's Poetry and Religion* 91). I contend that for Hemans, Mary's song, too, provides the occasion for a meditation on poetic renown. "The Song of the Virgin" focuses on Mary's words, once spoken, enduring eternally: Mary's is lasting fame.

> Yet as a sunburst flushing mountain snow,
>   Fell the celestial touch of fire erelong
> On the pale stillness of thy thoughtful brow,
>   And thy calm spirit lighten'd into song.
>   Unconsciously, perchance, yet free and strong
> Flow'd the majestic joy of tuneful words,
>   Which living harps the quires of Heaven among
> Might well have link'd with their divinest chords.
> Full many a strain, borne far on glory's blast,
> Shall leave, where once its haughty music pass'd,
>   No more to memory than a reed's faint sigh;
> While thine, O childlike virgin! through all time
> Shall send its fervent breath o'er every clime,
> Being of God, and therefore not to die.

The Woman in the Scriptures 101

As constructed here by Hemans, Mary embodies the perfect solution to the conflict between maintaining perfect femininity and procuring lasting renown. Literally inspired by the Lord, she accords perfectly with the early nineteenth-century model of the effusive female singer: Thoughtful, still, and pale, Mary is a passive and sexless channel; the words flow through her "unconsciously, perchance" as artless and unmediated pure emotion; the words, it is clear, are voiced by her but are not actually her own, rather belonging in heaven, "being of God." For these reasons she is the perfect Hemans poet. Her perfectly pure and feminine strain, fervent but modest, contrasts with an essentially masculine model characterised by showy engagement in the public sphere—accompanied by "glory's blast" and "haughty" in its pride. Distinct from those ephemeral, noisy utterances, Mary's song will live eternally, continually uttered throughout the world.

At the end of the period, Margaretta Ayres Karr's long, mystical volume, *The Heavenly Voice, a Life of Christ in Blank Verse: His Work and Word in Sonnet* (1905) explicitly links the continuing utterance of Mary's song with the utterance of Karr's own song. The volume has an ambitious and complicated poetic structure. The section entitled "The Mystery," which describes Nazareth, the Virgin Mary, the annunciation, and Mary's visit to Elisabeth, concludes with the Magnificat, versified. Karr's reproduction of Mary's words reflects back to the volume's preface and its earnest defence of Karr's own inspiration to bear the exalted word. The preface begins: "In the sere and yellow leaf of 1899, when clouds as a thick darkness spread over the sky of the author, it pleased the Lord to bestow upon His lowly handmaiden a gift of light, to irradiate the inner and outer life with increasing glow" (v). The phrase "lowly handmaiden" unmistakably identifies the author with Mary, and Karr goes on to describe two particular visions vouchsafed to her, both of which reinforce the parallel between her experience and Mary's. In descriptions reminiscent of Dante Gabriel Rossetti's depiction in the painting *Ancilla Domini* of a girl on her bed, crouched against the wall in her room, Karr relates that her visions both took place in her bedroom. One was of a window of light against the wall, one of a window of light in the ceiling, through which mystical apertures light streamed upon her in a "radiant manifestation of His approval" (vi).

Karr also emphasises the parallels between Mary and herself as songmakers. Mary's Spirit-filled utterance stands out from the rest of the blank verse poem as 'song' as Karr crafts it into regular quatrains, each with three rhyming lines and a closing refrain.

> "My soul doth magnify the Lord
> With whom my spirit doth accord:
> My life shall e'er obey the word
>   Of God my Saviour.

102 *Christian and Lyric Tradition in Victorian Women's Poetry*

> "My spirit hath rejoiced in Him,
> Since He o'erlooked estate so slim:
> Lo! I'll be blest to ages dim
> Through God my Saviour.

> "Holy, most holy is His name:
> A mighty God! I now proclaim
> The great things done in this poor frame
> By God my Saviour.

> [. . .]

> "He empty sent the rich away:
> For mercy, Israel helped alway,
> To keep the word none may gainsay
> Of God my Saviour."

Karr emphasises that she, like Mary, may "proclaim the great things done in this poor frame," concluding her long Introduction with the words: "The writing and completion of this work has been attended by such manifestations of heavenly light, as to convince the author of the unfolding of a divine purpose in its publication" (xii). Both Mary the Mother of God and Karr the inspired poet are impregnated with divine purpose: both must bring to birth the Word.

Emily Shapcote's unusual, rhapsodic *Mary: the Perfect Woman: One Hundred and Fifty Rhythms in Honour of the Mystical Life of Our Lady* bears certain similarities to Karr's work. In these 150 "rhythms" Shapcote systematically considers every possible facet of Mary's character. In this volume Mary quite literally is made into Everywoman: every other female character in scripture is a type of her; she embodies perfect maiden, mother, intercessor, comforter, queen, and so on. Shapcote's very long introduction disavows any conscious artistic intention on her part; she claims the work was originated outside of her and she was merely the humble vessel that translated it from the heavenly to the mortal realm. This construction, and Shapcote's use of the language of conception and birth, invites a comparison of Mary and herself.

> It was on the 3rd of January, 1894, that I began *this labour of love*—for such it was—and I wrote continuously until April 21st. Each morning as it came unfolded the picture as I went on. I was simply painting the beauty of a glorious creation, as I conceived it by my spiritual eye, far more plainly than I could see any visible object with my physical eye. Every Rhythm stands in the original place it first occupied; and every thought exists as it was then developed. *I did not appear to be the originator, but only the agent of the work. I had no cause to reason on*

the subject; nor did I choose the colours of the palette. All was there ready to my hand; and as it was produced then, so does it appear now. (xxii; my emphasis)

The first poem in the volume, "The Incarnation," is subtitled "Invocation"; the two very similar words blend together and elevate the status of both Mary and her poet. Shapcote invokes Mary's aid for her own kind of Incarnation, giving birth (into verse) to Mary herself, with Mary taking a role as originator, inspirer, model, and teacher. The penultimate stanza reads:

> Then teach my failing voice to sing of thee;
> Let my last music ring in praise of thee;
> Let these last humble rhymes be full of thee
> That, swan-like, this my latest song may be
> A sweet and mystic melody to thee.

The Magnificat is Mary's defining speech-act, uttered in response to her cousin Elisabeth's heralding of her unborn child, but in Victorian women's poetic depictions it regularly escapes the confines of one place or time or even specific occasion. Hemans' phrase "through all time" finds many echoes as the Magnificat is presented as a mobile, fluid representation of Mary's ongoing divine inspiration. In Hickey's *Our Lady of May*, "Her Assumption" has Mary still singing the Magnificat in Heaven. The poem concludes:

> In the everlasting city, paved with love, with gladness tiled,
> He thy Son and thou His Mother, He thy Father, thou His Child,
>
> Satisfied with His likeness, and exceeding glad thereat,
> Still the song upon thy lips is thy divine *Magnificat*.
>
> In the rapture of the will that meets His will in sweet accord,
> Thou rejoicest in thy Saviour, thou dost magnify the Lord.

This identity of Mary as a singer, like her song, is unsilenceable and perpetual, and the ongoing life of her words, representative of the woman's continuing "rapture," is assured.

Mary's words may be repositioned in other mouths as well as in other sacred contexts: by echoing her words, all Christians can participate more fully in the recognition and figurative conception of Christ. Mildred Beresford Hope's "Festivals of the Blessed Virgin Mary," in *Eucharistic Hymns* (1892), places Mary in a central position at the Eucharist, punctuating every aspect of the observance with phrases from the Magnificat and encouraging the celebrant to follow Mary's example of singing, confessing, and proclaiming.

104 *Christian and Lyric Tradition in Victorian Women's Poetry*

> The Blessed Virgin said, when told
>   She Mother of the Lord should be,
> "Be it according to Thy word,"
>   She questioned not the mystery.
> Grant us like faith, God's Presence here
>   To see, then sing, on bended knee,
> Before this Sacrament adored,
> "My soul doth magnify the Lord."

As the stanzas consider different aspects of Christ's redemptive mission (his incarnation, his crucifixion and winning of pardon for sinners), each stanza concludes with a phrase from the Magnificat, which show how Mary's words anticipate and appropriately respond to every aspect of Christ's holy career. The poem closes with a return to the communion scene in which the Magnificat becomes the one true song of every Christian:

> And here we take that sacred food,
>   Christ's Body giv'n to man below,
> And drink His precious Blood outpoured,
>   And thus refreshed, rejoicing shew
>
> Our joy, in glad Magnificat,
>   Like Mary we God's love do know,
> "And He," the Church with Mary sings,
> "Hath filled the hungry with good things!"

Not all Victorians, however, found in the Magnificat a model for liberation into speech. Countering the paean of authority and fame that these poets read into/create out of Mary's song, American Episcopalian clergyman Morgan Dix offers a reactionary reading in which the Magnificat becomes a call to submission. Dix's *The Calling of a Christian Woman and Her Training to Fulfil It* was published in London in 1884, and in it Dix urges women to reject the modern, "degraded" agitations and campaigns claiming for women equal status with men and a public role. He advises women "tired of the incessant drumming for attention, and the unseemly actions of some of your sex, and feel[ing] as if you needed something to clear the thoughts and purify the intention" (48), to meditate on the words of the Magnificat. Those words, which Dix quotes in full and helpfully capitalises, remind women of the accepted, orthodox "story of their exaltation and the way of maintaining their influence and their honour among us" (49), and direct women to their true mission: dedication of themselves to piety, service, and sacrifice. Upon "loyalty to God, and loyalty to the home-idea . . depends the salvation of society" (24) declares Dix. Dix takes at face value Mary's calling herself a "lowly handmaiden," but as we have seen, women poets tend to plumb the declaration for its paradoxes and alternate truths. The political agendas of the two parties, while founded on identical words, could not be further apart.

The Woman in the Scriptures   105

To illustrate this, and to close the discussion of Mary's song, we can see a late Victorian transferring to herself Mary's power by a transferral of her singing and her most famous song. Crossing the end of the nineteenth century, Edith Nesbit's lush "Magnificat" in *Ballads and Verses of the Spiritual Life* (1911) offers her own hymn of praise, a rival to Mary's.

> This is Christ's birthday: long ago
>   He lay upon His mother's knee,
> Who kissed and blessed Him soft and low—
>   God's gift to her, as you to me.
>
> My baby dear, my little one,
>   The love that rocks this cradling breast
> Is such as Mary gave her Son:
>   She was more honoured, not more blest.
>
> He smiled as you smile: not more sweet
>   Than your eyes were those eyes of His,
> And just such little hands and feet
>   As yours Our Lady used to kiss.
>
> The world's desire that Mother bore:
>   She held a King upon her knee:
> O King of all my world, and more
>   Than all the world's desire to me!
>
> I thank God on the Christmas morn,
>   For He has given me all things good:
> This body which a child has born,
>   This breast made holy for his food.
>
> High in high heaven Our Lady's throne
>   Besides her Son's stands up apart:
> I sit on heaven's steps alone
>   And hold my king against my heart.
>
> Across dark depths she hears your cry;
>   She sees your smile, through worlds of blue,
> Who was a mother, even as I,
>   And loved her Child, as I love you.
>
> And to her heart my babe is dear,
>   Because she bore the Babe Divine,
> And all my soul to hers draws near,
>   And loves Him for the sake of mine!

106 *Christian and Lyric Tradition in Victorian Women's Poetry*

Nesbit chooses to voice and identify with Mary's power and rapture, as her version of Mary's Magnificat triumphantly hymns her own child and her own body.

Through this array of readings, I argue that Victorian women's religious poetry does not support a reading of Mary the Mother of God as a purely passive, repressed, and silent figure. Rather, women poets use her as a figure by which to imagine not mere passivity, and not submissive silence, but rather active engagement in the key tasks of loving, recognising, and praising Christ. Mary's activity is primarily embodied in her singing, and it is significantly through her singing that her authority is produced. This authority is ongoing, and may be transferred to other Christians; women poets of all denominations make creative use of the model of Marian power, by focussing on Mary's voice, and by linking their own songs to Mary's famous Magnificat, the first song of the Christian church.

The Transforming Woman: Mary Magdalene

> Of all the personages who figure in history, in poetry, in art, Mary Magdalene is at once the most unreal and the most real—the most unreal, if we attempt to fix her identity, which has been the subject of dispute for ages; and the most real, if we consider her as having been for ages, recognised and accepted in every Christian heart as the impersonation of the penitent sinner absolved through faith and love. (Anna Jameson, *Sacred and Legendary Art*, vol. 1, 343)

The other Mary: whore, demoniac, penitent, lover of Christ. Shackled by centuries of tradition to a sinful character nowhere to be found in the Bible, multiply identified and misidentified, the figure of Mary the Magdalene came in the nineteenth century to embody a tantalising blend of fiction and fact, a morally mercurial figure in feminine form. As such she provides an illuminating focal point for analysis of the ways in which Victorian women poets discuss the challenge of transforming female power within Christian discourse.

For Victorians, the word "Magdalen" was widely used to signify a sexually fallen woman, and by extension the rapidly proliferating institutions that sought to 'reform' such women.[11] The euphemistic term, loaded with biblical connotations of Christ's tender redemption, shielded the middle classes from the harsh realities of prostitution and the desperate situation of the thousands of unfortunate women who had 'lost their characters,' for whom even the most earnest attempts at reformation offered but scant possibility of social reclamation. Eric Trudgill has traced the changing fortunes of the symbolic figure of the Magdalen in Victorian England, demonstrating that the figure was far from static. The ways in which writers, reformers, politicians, and increasingly the general public viewed and discussed the fallen woman changed significantly in the period, as she transformed from a figure of harrowing squalor to a figure of sentimentalised pathos to an almost glamourised portrait of a delightedly wicked courtesan. Foregrounding this changeability, Patricia Kruppa has analysed depictions of the Magdalene in Victorian literary and visual arts, using portrayals of the figure to highlight contradictory attitudes toward gender, sexuality, and social class. The symbolic figure of the Magdalene, vilely sinful yet utterly pure, repulsive yet compelling, represents a fundamental challenge to the inherent contradictions of Victorian moral culture and to the religious discourse that underpinned it.

This section focuses on depictions of the Magdalene as they operate in the devoutly Christian discourse of women's religious verse. In this particular context, the Magdalene figure is never glamourised, but she may nonetheless achieve certain kinds of glorification. The figure of the biblical Magdalene presented devout women writers with a provocative array of possibilities: religious women poets could and did explore unexpectedly positive aspects of the character's mutability and unignorable female sexuality. The biblical Magdalene opens up a space for reconsideration and reevaluation of these characteristics, and of the radical possibility of retaining and combining those characteristics with a close, privileged relationship to Christ. Even the ways in which the character of the Magdalene has been utilised for oppressive ends—her alternate histories suppressed and her sexual sin magnified in the service of the systematic suppression of an active, powerful female role in the Christian tradition—may be used as ways of highlighting and interrogating those very oppressive operations. In multiple forms, the Magdalene is used by Victorian women poets as a vehicle to challenge univocal history, to discuss female multiplicity and transformation, and to suggest an alternate tradition of women's power within the Christian tradition.

Arguably more than any other biblical character, the figure of Mary Magdalene provided Victorian women poets with a huge scope for creative and critical license. Not only did they exercise considerable imaginative diversity in their engagements with historical 'facts' in their depictions of this woman, women poets seized the opportunity to thematise the creative and fictional aspect of all historical facts, including those of the biblical record. For several reasons, the Magdalene is uniquely suitable for opening up this kind of critical discussion. Susan Haskins' extremely readable *Mary Magdalen: Myth and Metaphor* provides a detailed account of how the developing Christian Church in the early centuries of the millennium created a history for the character of the Magdalene that was not founded on the gospel accounts, at all. The gospels' mentions of Mary of Magdala reveal very little: she was an important member of the group of women who followed Christ (Luke 8:1–3); she was present at Christ's crucifixion (Matthew 27:56; Mark 15:40; John 19:25); and three of the gospels name her as the first to whom the resurrected Christ appeared (Matthew 28; Mark

108 *Christian and Lyric Tradition in Victorian Women's Poetry*

16:9; John 20). It is also mentioned that Christ cast out of her 'seven devils' (Luke 8:2); early Bible commentators read the seven devils as a moral and specifically sexual sinfulness, and linked her to the sinful woman who anointed Christ's feet in Luke's gospel. It was this identification, rather than that of her ministry and leadership roles, that was retained, expanded, and handed down in Church commentary, so that "Mary Magdalen, chief female disciple, first apostle and beloved friend of Christ, would become transformed into a penitent whore" (Haskins 15).

In establishing this 'authorised version' of the Magdalene's character, the Church Fathers suppressed other, competing accounts of her importance to Christ and the First Church, accounts that emphasised the important support ministry she provided to Christ during his life, and her witness to the resurrection. Mary Magdalene's importance was richly elaborated in the Gnostic tradition, particularly in the *Gospel of Mary* and the *Pistis Sophia*, which show her as Christ's beloved, leader of the apostles, and embodiment of the spirit of wisdom. While Gnosticism was largely eradicated in the early centuries AD, traditions and myths of Mary grew and persisted across Europe. A number of Victorian women would have been familiar with these stories; some may have visited famous sites such as St. Maximin, in Provence, purportedly the Magdalene's burial place. As Mrs. Jameson's words show, the Victorians were becoming more aware of the conflicting histories of the Magdalene and of the innate constructedness of the figure. In an 1842 pocket edition of the annotated Authorised Version of the Bible, for example, the ubiquitous biblical commentator Rev. T. Scott appended the following Note to Luke's version of the story of Christ's anointing, in chapter 8, verses 37–39:

> Whilst our Lord was at the Pharisee's table, a woman, an inhabitant of the city, who was of known bad character, having formerly been a harlot, as it is generally supposed, came into the room. Tradition reports that this was Mary Magdalene, but there is no other proof of it; and, indeed, what is said of Mary Magdalene, or Mary of Magdala, in other places, renders it improbable; she is spoken of rather as one who had been remarkably afflicted, than peculiarly wicked. (719)

Haskins suggests that Clara Balfour's popular *Women of Scripture* (1847) was particularly influential in clarifying the absence of any link between the characters of the Magdalene and the penitent harlot, thus foregrounding for the Victorians the inherent variability of this 'historical' character. In a chapter entitled "Fidelity. Mary Magdalene and the heroines of the Cross," Balfour writes:

> A popular error has confounded the name of Mary Magdalene with that of the penitent mentioned in the preceding chapter. Hence, public institutions for penitent women have been very erroneously called by

the name of one, whose life, so far as the gospel narrative unfolds it, was pure and spotless. (320)

The figure of the Magdalene, attended by many myths, traditions, and attempts to legislate apocryphal from canonical accounts, opened up to the Victorians the possibility of acknowledging and exploring a number of alternate Church histories. A number of Victorian women poets took the opportunity of contributing their own versions of 'the history of the Magdalene.' Sarah Dana Greenough, for example, in *Mary Magdalene, and Other Poems* (1887), creates in the title poem a sixty-six-page blank verse narrative epic, with the Magdalene as heroine. The poem styles itself as both epic and authoritative: it is structured in three parts, with each part divided up into numbered sections, and while Greenough interpolates no biblical epigraphs, she includes a number of passages which are so close to the original that the language is instantly recognisable as 'scriptural.' And yet Greenough departs quite radically from scriptural and traditional depictions of Mary Magdalene. Part First introduces the Magdalene as no street prostitute, but as a kind of celebrity, with an impressive marble palace, full of luxuries, revelry, and "sumptuous banquet room":

> It was the home of Mary Magdalene,
> The beautiful and the unholy one,
> The Magdalene, that sinful city's boast,
> The Magdalene, that sacred city's shame.

She is described as a queen among courtiers, as surpassingly beautiful (and essentially Northern European, with golden hair and violet eyes), and as seemingly unconscious of her sin and shame. The history that Greenough creates for her explains this lack of shame, and, while not contradicting the tradition of the Magdalene as guilty of fornication, recasts her sin as fundamentally a sin of ignorance: Mary of Magdala is Greek; as a child she was taken to be a priestess for Aphrodite (the rites, which she dutifully and even reverently undertakes, have an unspecified sexual component). After her father was killed, she travelled to Judea, mourning, and once established there in her palatial dwelling continued to fulfil Aphrodite's rites. Greenough insists that throughout this period of her life Mary retains a kind of innocence: "so sinful and so sinless!" Then the Magdalene hears tale of Christ's teaching:

> "Oh ye, my weary ones, behold your rest!
> Lay down your burden, lay it on my neck,
> And I will bear it for you. Cast aside
> Your sins: learn love and holiness and peace!"

110   *Christian and Lyric Tradition in Victorian Women's Poetry*

She is struck by the words "holiness and peace."

> "... I dimly feel
> There is a something better than this life
> Which I have led till now."

She seeks out Christ, learns from him, and then is awakened to a sense of her sin and her desperate need for redemption. Repentant and transformed, she becomes a leader amongst his followers. At the crucifixion, states the poem, the Magdalene's sufferings exceed even those of the Madonna, because Mary's foreknowledge of her son's death helps protect her from the worst agonies. Then, as the Magdalene weeps by the tomb, Christ appears to her and sends her to the disciples with the news of his resurrection. The poem ends with a simple acclamation of her central importance to the Christian tradition:

> ... We know but this,
> When Jesus Christ was risen from the dead
> He first appeared to Mary Magdalene.

Greenough's poem transforms the Magdalene into a fully contextualised, deeply sympathetic heroine. Her sexual sin, while acknowledged, is rendered less offensive by the mitigating circumstances of her youth and lack of understanding. And Greenough also suggests a re-evaluation of the Magdalene's sexuality by incorporating statements of the woman's beauty (there are many descriptions of her hair, her eyes, and her womanly figure) into the trajectory of a romantic narrative that sexualises both Mary and Christ. When the two first see each other, their mutual recognition is cast in intensely physical language:

> The Jewish Prophet looked a Heaven-born King!
> Calm on his smooth, broad brow, command sate throned,
> His clear, full opened eye with powerful glance
> Seemed through the secrets of each heart to pierce
> With vision supernaturally keen,
> Yet filled with a compassion all divine . .
>   ... And he saw!
> Jesus of Nazareth saw the Magdalene!
> The eye that loved the beauty of the flowers
> Rested upon that flower-like face. His look,
> Piercing and puissant, clove that pearly breast
> And saw the struggling human soul within
> That blindly yearned for purity and love.
> He saw her past, he knew her as she was,
> And a divine compassion stirred his heart.
> A look of mournful pity gave response
> To her imploring eyes.

The Woman in the Scriptures   111

All the traditionally gendered romantic elements are present here: the woman imploring, submissive, white-breasted; the man powerful, knowledgeable, penetrative, and keen to rescue. Paradoxically, this highly conventional romantic construction, when applied in this particular gospel context, helps produce a radical reconstruction of the woman's significance, both to the central Christian story of Christ's death and resurrection, and also to Christ the man, on a personal and essentially sexual level. In creating her own version, Greenough complicates the dominant iconographic representation of the Magdalene. While the Victorians generally identified the Magdalene as the penitent whore, regarding her as a passive sexual commodity, this poem casts both her sexuality and her agency in a revised, expanded, and positive light.

Christina Rossetti, on the other hand, spends no time highlighting aspects of the Magdalene's sexuality or individuality, yet she too produces a provocative meditation upon the figure's innate power, which suggests the expansion of the active role of all (including female) Christians. Unlike Greenough, she does not construct an extended context or alternate history for the character; in fact, Rossetti radicalises the figure of the Magdalene not by insisting upon but by discarding her unique and individual reality. In "Mary Magdalene and the Other Mary. A Song for All Maries," Rossetti takes for her subject the recorded presence of Mary Magdalene with Mary the mother of God at and after the crucifixion. But, as so often is the case in Rossetti's verse, she takes her scriptural original as a creative starting point to be developed in unexpected ways. Rossetti extends the operation of the character, placing her in an ongoing history of keeping vigil: a history in which all Christians are Maries, a history that eludes traditional constraints of time and that encompasses and values every believer.

> Our Master lies asleep and is at rest:
>   His Heart has ceased to bleed, His Eye to weep:
> The sun ashamed has dropt down in the west:
>   Our Master lies asleep.
>   Now we are they who weep, and trembling keep
> Vigil, with wrung heart in a sighing breast,
>   While slow time creeps, and slow the shadows creep.
>
> Renew Thy youth, as eagle from the nest;
>   O Master, who has sown, arise to reap:—
> No cock-crow yet, no flush on eastern crest:
>   Our Master lies asleep.

The poem, spoken jointly by the two Maries, meditates on existence and action—and their worth—inside and outside of conventional measures of time. The first stanza focuses on "Our Master"; with each line weightily end-stopped, it emphasises the cessation of certain recognisable units: the day has ended; Christ's physical existence has ended. Effectively, this is a

112 *Christian and Lyric Tradition in Victorian Women's Poetry*

dead record. The centre section, in contrast, centres on "we"; it throbs with present tense verbs and verb-based adjectives and adverbs, the enjambed lines conveying ongoing, even excessive awareness, sensation, and action. Countering the stasis of historical fact, what has been recorded and what has ended, Rossetti posits a new reality: *"Now we are they."* These "we" are new Maries, extended from Mary Magdalene and Mary the Mother of God to include all Christians, not past historical characters but present, living believers who persistently keep vigil, persistently trembling and sighing, paradoxically constant in the face of the entropic depredations of 'creeping' time. While the final stanza looks forward to a future state when chronological and historical time will be defeated and undone—as the speaker petitions the dead/sleeping Christ to literally turn back the clock, to "renew Thy youth, as eagle from the nest"—at the end of the poem he still lies 'asleep.' The Maries, however, continue, seeming to exist out of time, maintaining the vigil that recognises Christ and that effectively, by defining him as sleeping rather than dead, keeps him alive. This Mary Magdalene, along with other Maries that include contemporary Christian women, is essential to the continuation of Christianity.

Male Victorian poets on occasion also took up the figure of the Magdalene. My reading indicates they seem to have done so less frequently than women poets, and they omit the focus on the Magdalene's power that so often characterises the verse of women poets. For the most part, male poets follow a strong literary tradition that focuses on the Magdalene's emotional nature, her sensitivity, and particularly her tears.[12] For example, Henry Francis Lyte's "The Complaint of Mary Magdalene" is effectively a long lament, the tone of which is set in the first two lines: "She sat far off,—she sat and wept,/ Heart-broken Magdalene!" Lyte's piteous Magdalene bravely observes Christ's sufferings on the cross, until finally he dies and is borne away, at which point she gives way to her true feminine nature.

> The shades of evening round her head,
> > Now gathered thick and fast;
> And forth her burthened spirit fled,
> > In louder woe at last.
> Upon the ear of silent night,
> > Her plaintive murmurs broke,
> And sorrow seemed to grow more light,
> > As thus she wept and spoke . . .

Twelve stanzas of complaint follow, and the poem ends not on a note of triumph, with the Magdalene bearing witness to Christ's resurrection, but simply with her sitting by the tomb, sighing, and passively waiting for daybreak. Lyte abstracts all agency and all self-determination from the figure of the Magdalene; he emphasises the passivity of her fidelity rather than her active engagement with Christ.

The Woman in the Scriptures   113

Female poets' representations of the Magdalene, on the other hand, consistently acclaim the character's agency, power, and capacity for change. Rossetti multiplies the Maries in her title for her particular poetic ends, but the same kind of multiplication of Maries may be found in the gospels themselves, as several characters share the same name (not only Mary the Mother of God, but also Mary the sister of Martha and Lazarus, Mary the wife of Cleophas, Mary the mother of John, and Mary the mother of James the Less). Additionally, because the writers of the gospels often told the same story in different ways, or identified different characters as primary players in similar narratives, Mary Magdalene and Mary of Bethany (sister of Martha and Lazarus), have become elided with each other and with the figure of the woman who anointed Jesus' feet. On Luke's description of this anointing woman as "sinful" (though he does not name her; only John's gospel names her Mary) rests much of the subsequent identification of Mary Magdalene as a sexual sinner. The provocativeness embodied by the woman who anoints Jesus will be discussed at length in the third section of this chapter, but here I want primarily to highlight the fact that the gospels themselves present in Mary Magdalene a model of a various, multiply identified, transforming character who eludes capture in a single definition.[13] The transforming woman, as she appears in Victorian women's religious poetry, has a number of scriptural mothers, including Eve, Miriam, and Esther in the Old Testament, as well as the Magdalene in the New. The fundamental suggestiveness for Victorian women poets of this mobile character ultimately lies in no one particular identification of the many available, but in the *mobility itself*: Mary Magdalene represents essential changeableness, as she is simultaneously one of the most vile and one of the most holy women in scripture, the sinner transformed into Christ's faithful follower. A number of poets specifically highlight this changeability. Hemans, for example, centres her sonnet "Mary Magdalene at the Sepulchre" upon the contradictory directions of the Magdalene's character.

Weeper! to thee how bright a morn was given
After thy long, long vigil of despair,
When that high voice which burial-rocks had riven
    Thrilled with immortal tones the silent air!
    Never did clarion's royal blast declare
Such tale of victory to a breathless crowd,
        As the deep sweetness of one word could bear
Into thy heart of hearts, O woman! bowed
By strong affection's anguish! one low word —
"Mary!" and all the triumph wrung from death
Was thus revealed; and thou, that so hadst erred,
So wept, and been forgiven, in trembling faith
Didst cast thee down before the all-conquering Son,
Awed by the mighty gift thy tears and love had won!

114 *Christian and Lyric Tradition in Victorian Women's Poetry*

Hemans composes a scene of striking contrasts: the bright morning is set against the woeful night; the thrilling voice cuts through the silence; and Hemans also incorporates multiple linguistic oppositions: "triumph [is] rung from death"; a trumpet blast is figuratively contrasted with the low, sweet, single word Christ speaks to the woman. These syntactic and figurative variations upon the essential paradox of the Christian faith, the concept of victory emerging from death, find in the Magdalene a centre point. She that had so erred has been so forgiven; she still trembles but she has the strength of faith; she casts herself down in submission to Christ but she receives the ultimate reward. The poem opens by apostrophising the Magdalene as the traditional weeper, as in Lyte's depiction. At the end, however, she is changed, has become a winner, her life exemplifying the Christian's transformation from despair to bright hope.

Another example of a poem using the Magdalene as a means of focusing on transformation may be found in K. E. V.'s *The Circle of Saints. Hymns and Verses for the Holy Days of the English Calendar* (1886), which presents, as the title suggests, a poem for every saint "in the hagiology of the English Church." "This little book will serve as an invaluable companion to the Calendar of our Book of Common Prayer," states Reverend T. B. Dover in the preface; " . . . each poem will illustrate some special feature in the life on which we are bidden to dwell" (n.p.). The special feature of the life of "S. Mary Magdalene," whose day of observance is July 22, seems to be her changeability. The poem begins with these four stanzas:

> O Magdalene, the lost and found,
>   We love to think of thee,
> Whom Jesus lifted from the ground
>   And from sin's power set free;
> A jewel, thou didst lie debased
> Till Jesus thee in safety placed.
>
> He saw in thee the power of love,
>   The power of penitence,
> With His great love thy heart did move,
>   Grieved o'er lost innocence;
> From thee had gone the lily white,
> Love's rose was precious in His sight.
>
> O Magdalene, with flowing hair
>   And steadfast tear-dimmed eyes,
> The gladness we can scarcely bear
>   That in thy story lies;
> Thee as a weed the Gardener found,
> Placed thee a flower in His own ground.

The pure estate we cannot reach
    Of Mary, queen of flowers,
But oh, thy story us doth teach
    Repentance may be ours;
For all who will themselves abase
Christ in His garden finds a place . .

From the first line focussing on the contrasts embodied in the "lost and found" Magdalene, the poem uses the figure as a representative/idealised Christian who may move between abasement and elevation, sorrow and gladness, despoilment and purity (ideally, this movement is one-time and one-way, but part of the provocative nature of the Magdalene figure is the never-eliminated possibility *she may change back*). Her changeability connects to the "power" Christ recognises within her, of love and of penitence; key to her redemption is her key possession, that of a heart capable of 'moving.' And in the fourth stanza, the speaker suggests that while Saint Mary Magdalene is not as "good" as Mary the Mother of God, the "queen of flowers," for reader Christians the Magdalene may in fact be better, because she presents a more realistic and potentially emulated model for our own frail human natures: "oh, thy story us doth teach/ Repentance may be ours."

In fact, the Magdalene represents a potent alternate female model to that provided by the Madonna. Trudgill entitles his study of the development of Victorian sexual attitudes *Madonnas and Magdalens*, noting that "by 1853 [the Magdalene] was establishing herself as a feminine archetype almost equal to the Madonna," an essential element of Victorian sexual idealism (289). Countless nineteenth-century writers, including Rossetti, construct pairings of the two; in theological writings across the centuries both have been dubbed "the Second Eve." Adams, pointing to the long tradition of viewing the two Maries as counterparts, representing the spiritual and the fallen nature of woman, suggests the Victorians' fascination with the "interchangeability" of the two (5). The Victorians in fact often deployed the two as representational competitors, fronting duelling claims as to what may represent 'true' Christian womanhood. Courtesy of the tradition of her fallenness, the Magdalene, unlike the Madonna, displays an undeniable, unignorable sexuality (which Greenough, as we have seen, claims as a positive attribute).[14] Mary Magdalene may then be proposed as the true Bride of Christ, as for example in the undeniably romantic relationship sketched by Greenough in her epic poem. Many of the earliest Magdalene traditions, including a number of the Gnostic gospels and Rosicrucian accounts, depict a physical and even sexual relationship between Christ and the Magdalene; in our own century a blockbuster best-seller is founded on the suppressed history of that sexual relationship and the child that eventuated.[15] The Magdalene in such traditions is a partner to Christ in a way his mother cannot be; the Magdalene's sanctified femininity can encompass, rather than suppress, female sexuality.

116   *Christian and Lyric Tradition in Victorian Women's Poetry*

While I have found no Victorian women religious poets who depict an explicitly sexual relationship between Christ and the Magdalene, many highlight the unique and privileged relation the two enjoyed, and several underscore this through implicit comparisons between the Magdalene and the Madonna. Elizabeth Charles, who includes several poems on the Magdalene in *The Women of the Gospels*, presents her not only as a significant companion of Christ, but also as a significant witness to Christ's dealings. The witness borne by the Magdalene rivals the biblical description of Mary the Mother of God as the original keeper of record, observing what Christ does and says and "keeping all these things in her heart" (see Luke 2:19 and 51). The third of Charles' Magdalene poems begins with the somewhat ungrammatical epigraph, "And certain women, which had been healed of evil spirits and infirmities, Mary, called Magdalene, . . . which ministered unto Him of their substance" [sic]. The poem's first stanza relates the close companionship with Christ that Mary Magdalene enjoyed as she travelled "from day to day" "by His side," and systematically shows how she "ministered unto Him." The poem progresses by describing Christ's various miracles, but most stanzas begin by indicating the lens through which the reader witnesses the miracles, which is that of the Magdalene's witness. Thus "She saw," "She heard," and "She knew" open most quatrains, and are repeated within many, with a key pronouncement appearing in the ninth stanza:

> She saw His brow its light regain,
>   And strength reknit each wearied limb,
> All to be spent for man again;—
>   A woman's service succoured Him!

Bounded by attention-grabbing punctuation, a dash on one side and an exclamation mark on the other, the last line confronts the reader with the significance of the Magdalene's assistance. Charles may be drawing on a now antiquated definition of succour, "to relieve or remedy a state of want, weakness, etc.," to suggest that the succour the Magdalene provides to Jesus actually enables him to be renewed, to continue his miraculous and redemptive dealings. As she appears in this poem, Mary Magdalene is not only an important witness to Christ's work, she may even be indispensable to the conduct of that work.

The final three stanzas, however, present a change in focus, as the reader is asked to consider what may come next, after the close of Mary Magdalene's witness record.

> And are those days for ever o'er?
>   Must earth be of that joy bereft?—
> The sights and sounds are here no more,
>   And yet the very best is left.

The Woman in the Scriptures   117

Still may we follow in His way,
    And tread this earth as by His side;
May see Him work from day to day,
    As in His presence we abide:

See Him shed light on darkened eyes,
    The bowed and fettered heart set free;
May succour, serve, and sacrifice,
    And hear from heaven His "unto Me."

As stated in the first stanza, the Magdalene experienced the "joy" of walking with Christ and hearing his voice; Charles' rhetorical questions in the third to last stanza suggest that that joy may in fact continue to be the Christian's. By repeating phrases from the opening stanzas' descriptions of the Magdalene, the poem suggests devout followers may go on as she did, treading the earth "by His side" "from day to day." Like her, Christians may "see him" on an ongoing basis; Christ's significance, clearly, continues, but so does the Magdalene's: the poem transforms Mary Magdalene's role into an ongoing, living tradition. Explicitly like her, the believer "may succour, serve, and sacrifice"; implicitly like her, the believer (and, unignorably, the poet) may take on her role as bearer of record. The Christian can reproduce former days by reproducing the role of Mary Magdalene; arguing a case similar to Rossetti's "Mary Magdalene and the Other Mary," the poem suggests that Christians can in fact recycle and reconstitute biblical history, as the poet herself here demonstrates.

Of the two Maries, the Magdalene arguably offers a more realistic and inspiring example than does the Mother of God, as K. E. V. suggests. More than one poet suggests that the Magdalene may even rival Mary the Mother of God's claim to be foremost singer of the Christian tradition, as demonstrated by a proto-Victorian poet persistently fascinated by the female poetic tradition and its genesis. Letitia Landon's long poem "The Magdalen" casts the character as an instantly recognisable Landon heroine: she muses, grieving, on the hopes and dreams and betrayal of her youth, and the unspeakable weariness that followed from the pleasures of former days. However, this Landon heroine meets a different kind of fate from the usual: she meets Christ, and her life is transformed. The whole poem is uttered in the first person, but the lengthy appended "Hymn of the Magdalen," which ends the poem, has as a clear forerunner and rival the only hymn actually uttered by a woman in the New Testament: Mary the Mother of God's Magnificat. Other biblical intertexts include Miriam's song of triumph in Numbers, and the poem's other obvious progenitor is Ecclesiastes, as the Magdalene's conversion transforms her into a source not just of praise but also of sage wisdom.

118 *Christian and Lyric Tradition in Victorian Women's Poetry*

. . . For I have learnt, my God, to trace
Thy love in all things here;
How wonderful the power and grace
In all thy works appear.

The vineyard dim with purple light,
The silvery olive tree,
The corn wherewith the plains are bright,
Speak to my soul of thee.

This loveliness is born to die;
Not so the race, for whom
The sun goes shining thro' the sky,
The world puts forth its bloom.

We know that to this lovely earth,
Will sure destruction come;
But though it be our place of birth,
Yet it is not our home.

For we are God's own chosen race,
Whom the Lord died to save;
This earth is but a trial-place,
Whose triumph is the grave. (ll.135–54)

Landon's Magdalene possesses the singing prowess of the Madonna, the wisdom of the Preacher of Ecclesiastes, and the salvation-preaching authority of the apostles. Though Landon's depiction is neither particularly complex nor politically incisive, her "Hymn of the Magdalene" crystallises the provocative nature of the Magdalene, as developed in Victorian women's poetry. Set in an historical context which reveals the way traditional histories have tried to suppress aspects of her character, and simultaneously set in a contemporary context in which not just her sexuality but also her agency, witness, and fame jar against Church-sanctioned feminine roles, the figure of the Magdalene in Victorian culture embodies a series of challenges through her identities as close companion of Christ, apostle, and leader. Most threateningly of all, because it underpins all of these challenging roles, *the Magdalene is a speaker*. Three of the gospels present Mary Magdalene as the first to spread the news of Christ's resurrection (Matthew 28:7; Mark 16:9–10; John 20:18); in Matthew's gospel she is specifically bidden to report the news. The Magdalene's special ability to speak Christ, and her roles as first witness to the resurrection and bidden messenger, were generally suppressed in traditional iconography in favour of that one-dimensional characterisation as weeping, penitent whore.[16] However, Victorian women choose to highlight the elements of her voice and her witness in their poetic rewritings of conventional tradition. Caroline Noel, for example, centres her poem "Woman's

The Woman in the Scriptures 119

Commission" (in *The Name of Jesus*, 1878) on Mary Magdalene's witness at the tomb, and calls the Christian women who follow the Magdalene's example as much pillars of the Church as the Apostles themselves.

> O Woman, take thy stand
>   Upon this high position,
> And faithfully hand on,
> Till Death itself is gone,
>   This great Commission.

> The Apostolic Line
>   No higher message bear;
> They who the world must roam,
> And thou, within thy home,
>   One glory share.

Annie Johnson Brown's very different poem "S. Mary Magdalene" (in *Rejected of Men, and Other Poems*, 1890), takes the form of a lengthy dramatic monologue, and opens with the words, "Nay, but first hear me!" Her interlocutor seems unwilling to hear, but Brown's Magdalene insists on telling her version of her own life. Noel's and Brown's poetic redirections, foregrounding voice, and witness, may be read both as re-discoveries of the 'true' Magdalene of the scriptures and as new 'versions' of the Magdalene myth, which call into question the truth of any version, and which draw attention to the politically interested underpinnings of the creation of any version.[17]

Two final poems will close this discussion, both focussing on what the Magdalene has to say, and both foregrounding the significance of *the act of saying* within the Christian tradition. Hemans' "Mary Magdalene Bearing Tidings of the Resurrection" makes a stunning claim for the Magdalene.

> Then was a task of glory all thine own,
>   Nobler than e'er the still, small voice assigned
> To lips in awful music making known
>   The stormy splendours of some prophet's mind.
> "Christ is arisen!" — by thee, to wake mankind,
> First from the sepulchre those words were brought!
>   Thou wert to send the mighty rushing wind
> First on its way, with those high tidings fraught —
> "Christ is arisen!" Thou, thou, the sin-enthralled!
> Earth's outcast, heaven's own ransomed one, wert called
>   In human hearts to give that rapture birth:
> Oh raised from shame to brightness! there doth lie
> The tenderest meaning of His ministry,
>   Whose undespairing love still owned the spirit's worth.

120 *Christian and Lyric Tradition in Victorian Women's Poetry*

Repeatedly apostrophised and conjured by "thine," "thee," and "thou," Mary Magdalene is granted multiple kinds of recognition and veneration in this poem. Hemans pronounces her as surpassing all previous prophets and even suggests her as agent of a new Incarnation. Other prophets are almost scornfully dismissed, even those of the stature of Elijah, to whom the still, small voice of God spoke (I Kings 19)—his prophecies are described as only "the stormy splendours of some prophet's mind," far inferior to the amazing message the Magdalene has to speak. Multiple scriptural allusions work to magnify the scale of the Magdalene's achievements: she is called "to wake mankind," "to send the mighty rushing wind" of the Holy Spirit, even, rivalling the supreme task of the Madonna, "to give that rapture birth." Expressed with frantic expostulations and breathless enjambment, the message of the Magdalene is one of deeply emotional triumph. Hemans' message here is double, as the poem recognises twin triumphs: the resurrection is the good news, but so is the fact that it is the Magdalene who may bear the good news.

While still focussing on the Magdalene's unique message, Dora Greenwell's far more ambivalent poem "Quid Dixit, Maria?" (in *Carmina Crucis*, 1869) injects Mary Magdalene's message with a unique, complex note of resistance. Beginning with the title, which means, "What did he say, Mary?", the poem questions the veracity of the record, the troubling gaps between a spoken and a written record, and the indeterminacy of truth and authority behind multiple refractions of an original speech act. The poem's title, "Quid Dixit, Maria?" is placed in quotation marks, indicating its nature as a dramatic utterance, and begging the question of who asks this. The title forces the reader of the poem to ask a further question, whether the dramatic utterance of the speaker Mary actually conveys what He did say. Does what she says equate to what He said? Does she represent or misrepresent Him? How can the reader or her interlocutor know this? She is the only witness—which means she is the only possible source of 'truth,' despite what seem to be the interlocutor's assumptions that an original truth may be ascertained. Further, Greenwell poses her opening question in Latin, the language of centuries of Church 'authority,' in so doing deliberately connoting an original and unmediated utterance. But the poem undercuts that position of (implicitly gendered, implicitly masculine) originating authority in two ways. First, as Greenwell well knew, the New Testament was composed in Greek, not Latin, so she draws attention to the fact that even this 'original' speech is a translation and a version. Second, this seemingly authoritative voice has in reality *no* authority, because it petitions the woman to share what she alone knows, what it itself clearly does *not* know.

Greenwell's Mary Magdalene, questioned at the tomb, maintains what she has to say and do with what appears to be recalcitrance, but which is gradually revealed to be unshakeable, unsettling faithfulness to her call, and an iron-willed insistence upon the primacy of her own version of what

The Woman in the Scriptures 121

Christ said. The poem's form, like its main speaker, bears a surface resemblance to convention but moves unexpectedly within those conventions: the stanzas vary in length and the rhyme scheme moves flexibly between couplets and alternating lines. Initially, the stanzas alternate between the two speakers, the unidentified questioner and Mary Magdalene herself, but even that alternation soon breaks down and we must read carefully to identify who, exactly, says what.

> What said He, Mary, unto thee?
> For it was thine His voice to hear,
> When thou wert waiting in the gloom
> Of twilight dawn, and by the tomb,
> He talk'd with thee when none were near;
> Oh, happy thus thy Lord to see!
> What said He, Mary, unto thee?

Mary Magdalene responds, with an explicit echo of St. Luke's description of Mary the Mother of God:

> "Few words He said to me, I hide
> Each word He said within my heart . .
>
> [. . .]
>
> And by His tomb He bade me stay
> Until the breaking of the day!"

What the Magdalene here reports, of what Christ said to her, veers away from the gospel accounts in which Christ bid her to go and tell his disciples of his resurrection. She claims she was told to stay where she is, "until the breaking of the day"—which seems to indicate, on its face, biding one night, till dawn. Upon this answer, her questioner begins to try to dissuade her and to make her go out and act. He points to the sunrise and the light on the hills, and urges her attention to "What flowers unclose! what herbs of price!/ What costly gums for sacrifice/ Are dropping now!" He seems to tempt her to fulfil a 'better' form of service than her passive waiting, but she rejects the implied valorisation of action and costly sacrifice: " . . . by His cross He bid me dwell/ Until the evening shadows fell." With this second report of what Christ said to her, she prolongs the period of her waiting; now it seems she must wait the additional length of a day.

"Yet rise, thy Lord hath risen!" her interlocutor urges. He seems to reproach her for living a half-life: "Why linger 'mid the shadows dim?/ Why watch the place where Jesus lay?" To this the Magdalene responds sharply, referring to the authority of Christ's words to her, and also to the authority of her own experience.

122 *Christian and Lyric Tradition in Victorian Women's Poetry*

"Beside His tomb, beside His cross
He bade me rest! Ye speak in vain
Who have not known my gain nor loss;
The Master's words are kind and plain,
He calls the wounded not to pain . . . " (emphasis in original)

In the course of this dialogue, the reader's opinion of the relative voices of the interlocutor and Mary Magdalene undergoes a subtle change. At first the interlocutor's voice seems both just and pious, as he encourages Mary to go forth and engage with the world in the service of righteousness. But as she resists him, maintaining what Christ said to her, and advancing her own experience as undeniable authority, she comes to seem the more honourable character. The pointed contrast she draws between Christ's merciful call and this speaker's non-comprehending exhortations, "*He* calls the wounded not to pain,/ The weary unto conflict sore," reveals not just the underlying brutality of these dictates, but asserts, like Milton, "they also serve who only stand and wait." From this point, the interlocutor is silent and Mary speaks unopposed. The poem concludes:

To me He said not, 'Thou shalt rise
With Me, thy risen Lord this day,
And be with Me in Paradise,'
Beside the cross He bade me stay;
He met me in the garden's gloom,
But to that garden, sweet and dim,
Or through its angel-guarded gate,
He sent me not! I wait for Him
Beside His cross, beside His tomb;
I wait for Him, my soul doth wait,
And by the cross I will abide,
And keep the word my Lord hath given.
Except the cross and Him who died
Upon it, now in earth or Heaven
What own I, claim I? now below
I seek no further, here is woe
Assuaged for ever; now above
I look no longer; here is love!

The Magdalene quotes Christ's words to the repentant thief, by so doing asserting that His words *to her* are unique *to her*, and insisting she will not adhere to anyone else's idea of what is reasonable or right. Her resistance, her inaction, thus reveal her faithfulness. The poem concludes with Mary achieving an ecstatic experience independent of the action-reward model proposed by her interlocutor: in the Magdalene's paradigm, there is no owning, claiming, seeking, or in fact earning, only keeping watch,

The Woman in the Scriptures 123

maintaining, and enduring. "Here is love!" she concludes triumphantly, achieving this triumphant state by means of her determined hold on her own understanding of Christ's words.

Greenwell's resistant Magdalene defies the expectations and definitions of her questioner: in her faithfulness to Christ she insists on her own individual interpretation of Christ's call and her own inalienable 'truth.' In Greenwell's version, the Magdalene figure dramatises the *creation of versions*, highlighting the gap between what (or who) is told and the telling of it (and who tells it), and insistently diffusing and relocating authority. The Magdalene's passivity becomes the site of resistance, thus fundamentally recasting that stereotyped and constraining feminine characteristic. In various and related ways, many Victorian women poets offer recastings of stereotypical versions of the Magdalene. While they regularly depict the Magdalene as essentially female, drawing attention to her beauty, her sexuality, and her loving service, their poetry also demonstrates how the figure maintains within that femininity an assertive, transformative power. Dubbed by Elizabeth Charles "Prophet through love's tenacity" (in the fifth of her Mary Magdalene poems in *The Women of the Gospels*), the Magdalene is a both/and figure: faithful follower of Christ, she also takes on the role of a prophetic speaker and leader.

An historical figure used to embody messages of particular relevance to the contemporary nineteenth-century reader, the Magdalene is deployed in Victorian women's poetry to challenge traditional narratives, to suggest the interestedness of the constructions of those narratives, and to produce new, more inclusive versions. For a biblical figure so startlingly out of step with Victorian mores, the Magdalene proves in fact very much the woman for the times. As demonstrated in this section, Victorian women poets find a number of creative ways to interrupt the traditional iconography of this figure, emphasising beside the traditional (although non-gospel) penitent whore the many possible counter-realities of the figure from the biblical and Gnostic gospels. The transforming woman is at one and the same time faithful follower, minister to Christ, sexual woman, Bride of Christ, leader, and speaker of Truth.

The Nameless Woman: She Who Will Be Remembered

The two Maries, and their many reincarnations in Victorian women's poetry, help illustrate how devout Victorian women used the source material of the Bible in an ongoing battle to secure themselves an acknowledgement in spiritual, secular, and also literary histories. Paradoxically, some of the most significant battles in this literary offensive were undertaken by means of the (seemingly) least significant of biblical characters, those women who remain unnamed and largely unheralded in the scriptures, apparently blank canvases which nonetheless record extraordinary narratives. In my reading of Victorian women's devotional verse I discovered a surprising number of poetic refigurings of nameless biblical women, with certain characters

124   *Christian and Lyric Tradition in Victorian Women's Poetry*

recurring frequently, particularly "the widow of Nain," "Jairus' daughter," "the Syrophonecian woman," and "the Canaanite woman." Each of these New Testament figures, identified not by name but by her place of birth or her relation to a man, interacted with Jesus and became the reason for or the site of a miraculous event. Recorded in the Bible not for what they themselves did, or for their own 'name,' but rather for what they instigated and served to record, these female figures may be deployed to problematise the nature and production of fame and of the historical record, the gendered expectations undergirding these processes, and the hiddenness of women's contribution. Their deployment may also suggest ways to uncover women's ongoing contribution to Christian tradition.

Poems concerning these unnamed women characters were penned by well-known poets including Annie Ross Cousin, Elizabeth Charles, Cecil Frances Alexander, and Katharine Tynan, as well as by more obscure poets such as Emily Brewster, Emily Saunders, and M. E. B. Their poems depict the widow of Nain eliciting Jesus' tears and compassion; the daughter of Jairus revealing Christ to be the bringer of joy; and the Canaanite woman 'talking back' to Jesus and winning his unequivocal approval. A number of poets explicitly identify with particular praiseworthy characteristics of these unnamed women; Jean Sophia Pigott in "One Touch," for example, aligns herself with the woman with the issue of blood, who touched Jesus' robe and was instantly healed because of her faith.[18]

Foremost among these unnamed female characters, a woman whose suggestive potential provides feminist theologian Elisabeth Schüssler Fiorenza with the title and the thematic centre of her 1983 work *In Memory of Her,* appears in the gospels of Matthew and Mark, and in different forms in Luke and John. Mark's version, found in chapter 14, verses 3 to 9, is here quoted in full.

> And being in Bethany in the house of Simon the leper, as he sat at meat, there came a woman having an alabaster box of ointment of spikenard very precious; and she brake the box, and poured it on his head. And there were some that had indignation within themselves, and said, Why was this waste of the ointment made? For it might have been sold for more than three hundred pence, and have been given to the poor. And they murmured against her. And Jesus said, Let her alone; why trouble ye her? she hath wrought a good work on me. For ye have the poor with you always, and whensoever ye will ye may do them good: but me ye have not always. She hath done what she could: she is come aforehand to anoint my body to the burying. Verily I say unto you, Wheresoever this gospel shall be preached throughout the whole world, this also that she hath done shall be spoken of for a memorial of her.

St. Matthew's version is very similar. Most biblical commentators agree that St. Luke's account really relates a separate event: Luke tells of a (still unnamed) "sinful woman" who anoints Jesus' feet, rather than head, and Jesus tells her that her sins are forgiven. St. John's gospel alone identifies the woman (whom he does *not* call sinful) as Mary of Bethany. She anoints Jesus' feet and is rebuked by Judas, but defended by Christ. All four gospels record Christ's defence of the woman's actions, but only Matthew and Mark record the key statement when Jesus predicts that what the woman has done will be told as a memorial of her.

As Fiorenza and more recently Upton have argued, this story and particularly the memorialising words in Matthew and Mark present many suggestive possibilities for feminist commentators seeking to re-establish and revalue a female tradition within the androcentric Christian text. The woman's anointing of Christ holds significance not only as a pre-emptive act, in that she anoints him for his subsequent burial, but also as an act of prophetic recognition: she anoints him as king. This particular sacred function was reserved solely for priests, exclusively male in the Judaic tradition; but Christ himself defends not only her right to function in this role but also her initiative and insight to take it upon herself; and Christ himself instructs that she be made part of the historical account, part of the living text of Christianity. Fiorenza argues that this woman represents the ideal of faithful discipleship, and suggests that in early Christianity there existed a far more egalitarian community of belief than that which later developed and was formalised into patriarchal structures. Upton, while more cautious, does still see the promise this biblical story holds for subsequent generations of women:

> Women in an androcentric world, where men still own most of the resources of land, power, politics, and the church, can engage with a Jesus and with a woman like this, and respond by acting positively in their own right, empowered by this nameless exemplar of long ago. (107)

Victorian women poets were fascinated by the account of this nameless exemplar, and they retell it over and over. They variously highlight the rebukes the woman suffers for her service, Jesus' defence of the importance of those seemingly humble ministrations, the woman's recognition of Jesus' special calling to which the others at the table are blind, and the lasting fame she is granted. And they highlight ways in which her humility, her namelessness, and her fame resonate for the Victorian woman. For example, Harriet R. King entitles a poem "Mark XIV. 8, 9." (in *Thoughts in Verse*, 1842 and 1846) and presents the scriptural text in full as the epigraph, to make explicit her focus and her 'lesson':

> "She hath done what she could; she is come aforehand to anoint my body to the burying. Verily I say unto you, Wheresoever this gospel shall be preached throughout the whole world, this also that she hath done shall be spoken of for a memorial of her."

O! Joyful hearing for the humble soul!
No high achievement, painful martyrdom,
Nor superhuman excellence of life,
Distinguish'd her for whom her Lord decreed
This record, lasting as His own free grace;
The simple record is but briefly this,
That what she could, she faithfully perform'd.
    How little, yet how much, to win from Him,
The Lord of Glory, such enduring praise!
Take, O my soul, the lesson home to thee;
Make it the rule and measure of thy life;
Do what thou canst; and leave the rest to Him,
Who bore thy heavy burthen on the cross;
Suffer'd the bitter pangs of death for thee;
Enter'd, for thee, the precincts of the grave;
Ascended thence triumphantly on high;
And now, from His own place at God's right hand,
Show'rs down the Spirit's gifts upon mankind,
Thus sanctifying those He died to save;
Thus leading them unto His Father's throne,
And claiming for them thus, adoption there.
Do what thou canst, and leave the rest to Him;
But then, be sure that thou do all thou canst;
Be not lukewarm in the important work;[19]
Be diligent in prayer, in watchfulness,
In earnest study of God's holy word,
In prompt obedience to the Spirit's voice.
Do what thou canst; but, whatsoe'er thou do,
Let all be done in the Redeemer's name;[20]
No merit pleaded, and no strength assum'd,
But that Himself hath won, His Spirit giv'n.
    How little, yet how much, have I to learn!
Teach me, O Holy Spirit, for I feel
That human wisdom is confounded here;
That which I can, oh! prompt me still to do;
That which I cannot, let Thy grace supply.

In this poem King performs the expected, conventional turn from the scriptural story to the self-application of a "lesson." However, when the speaker encourages herself to "Take, O my soul, the lesson home to thee" and to "Make it the rule and measure of thy life," the lesson she's considering has a less-expected, even self-aggrandising facet: the creation of a "record, lasting as His own free grace": "enduring praise." It might be possible to miss the self-arrogation of fame within the earnest humilities of the poem, but even the almost over-determinedly correct formulae of "Be not lukewarm" and "Be diligent in prayer, in watchfulness" cannot obscure the suggestion that eternity for this speaker-poet, though it is glossed later in the poem as a more conventionally featured adoption into God's kingdom, may in fact be read as literary renown. "Do what thou canst," an instruction oft reiterated by the speaker-poet, is also a function enacted by the speaker-poet in the production of this consciously humble, somewhat edged literary exhortation. "This record," decreed by the Lord, may also be read as *this poem*. Bearing eternal memory of the humble woman, this poem and its poet constitute part of the everlasting record, and participate in carrying out Christ's own decree. This kind of veiled self-referential function proves a common feature in Victorian women's retellings of this story: women poets self-consciously write themselves into the biblical record, their poems the legible marks of their faithfulness and obedience to Christ's instruction, and their literary selves constructed as followers of this rewarded, recorded exemplar, producing the memorial which simultaneously memorialises their own contribution.

Citing the scripture reference as an epigraph, Lucy Bennett takes up Mark's version of the story in "Let Her Alone" (in *Poetical Works*, 1930), not only foregrounding the woman's relationship with Christ, but also insisting on recognition of its particular and special nature. The poem strenuously defends a woman's right to relate to Christ, directly and emotively. Bennett personifies the unnamed woman as Love, and sets her in opposition to "cold" Suspicion and "calculating" Reason, who chide her. Love is "burning" with the sacred fire; she is "lavish," "glowing," fired with "vehement hot haste"; bluntly put, she is essentially passionate, and essentially feminine. Suggestively, Bennett's descriptive figures break down the differentiation between this fiery female embodiment of Love and the Christ whom she honours: "Love winneth from the lips of Love/ The highest meed of praise;/ A sweet 'memorial'." Like King, who noted "that human wisdom is confounded here," Bennett emphasises that Reason cannot grasp what "her heart hath understood"; the woman exemplifies a different and far superior way of knowing and relating to God. Subsequently, hers is a privileged relationship to Christ.

> Where'er the Holy Name is named
>> Let this remembered be,
> That to the hands of Love was given
>> The sacred ministry.

Also significant is Bennett's description of the woman's ministry, which renders "The house [. . .] filled/ With perfume sweet and rare." This description has a literal significance, as the story specifies the woman anoints Jesus with perfume, but Bennett also makes the perfume function symbolically, as a metaphor for the faithful woman: "For fragrant are the deeds of Love,/ Pervading everywhere." Loving, passionate, fragrantly perfumed:

128 *Christian and Lyric Tradition in Victorian Women's Poetry*

both the exemplary Christian act *and the exemplary Christian* depicted here are emphatically feminised. The memorial, too, is subtly feminised, described as tender and "sweet," and when the poem states that the Saviour loves "the labour which the world esteems/ A labour of excess," the poem suggests a reflexive comment upon its own sweet, ornamental, possibly scorned nature. Feminised ministry, memorial, and ornamental verse are thus conflated.

Upton points out, and her observation rings particularly true of a Victorian audience, that "many who hear this story hear, behind a particular rendition, echoes of all the other available versions" (105). A number of Victorian women blend the various versions of this story in their poetic retellings (the section on Mary Magdalene has already mentioned the linking of this nameless character to that of the Magdalene). Elizabeth Charles, in one example, entitles her poem "The Sisters of Bethany II," which links the story to John's account in identifying the women as Mary of Bethany, but Charles gives as epigraph the last two verses from Mark's version, those that decree the woman's eternal memorial. And, while the poem begins by apostrophising Mary of Bethany by name and praising her humility, the most forceful message of this three-stanza poem closely resembles Bennett's in its salute to the woman's achievement, which is grounded in her particular way of knowing and communicating Christ. The key stanza is the second:

> Whilst evermore the heart obeys
> > The sermon of thy listening looks,
> Learning religion from thy gaze
> > Better than from a thousand books.

"The heart" of the generalised Christian hears and comprehends this Mary's particular sermon, which she preaches wordlessly. She teaches religion just by looking with love, which, Charles asserts, is far superior to a masculine written tradition of theological exegesis. Two modes of communication are here opposed, and Charles' own particular 'memorial of her' aligns itself with the living, oral tradition, against that of rigid, dead, written histories that spring from the intellect rather than from the heart. Mary is remembered forever because she is spoken forever: "from His lips thy name distils,/ And, dropping like thy precious balm,/ Ever His house with fragrance fills." While this take on fame seems to suggest a link between retellings of this story and Catholic venerations of the Madonna, a confusing gambit as Mary of Bethany is a biblical character quite distinct from Mary the Mother of God, Charles (again like Bennett) makes her poem stand in the same place as the woman's perfect offering: each reiteration of the woman's name and story is "like thy precious balm." Aligning her own eternal poetic memorial with the woman's original fragrant gift, Charles thereby aligns herself with that woman who will be forever honoured.

The Woman in the Scriptures 129

M. E. B.—who, interestingly enough in a discussion of the production and perpetuation of fame, obscures her own identity behind initials—also offers a poetic conflation of gospel accounts in "Mary Anointeth the Lord." M. E. B. identifies Mary of Bethany by name (and names her siblings, Martha and Lazarus), but concludes with a resounding retelling of Christ's memorialising words, conveying to herself the task of furthering this woman's fame. In this most specific of accounts, M. E. B. also names the villain of the peace, "wicked Judas," who "murmuring said,/ 'Why was this waste of ointment made?'"

> . . . But Jesus kindly looked on her,
>   He knew her heart's intent:
> "The poor ye always have with you,
> And when ye will may kindness show.
>
> But I am leaving you—this deed
>   Of love hath now been wrought,
> Preparing for my burial day:
>   Where'er the gospel's taught,
> Throughout the world, there shall this be
> Made known that she hath done to Me."

The metre of this poem is unexceptionably smooth, the language unremarkable, the characters named and their roles clearly demarcated; the poem is well shaped for the youthful audience targeted by the volume's title: *The Young Child's Gospel; or the Life of Our Lord in Easy Verse (Also Children's Morning and Evening Prayers and Hymns for a Week)* (1880). M. E. B.'s intended audience helps explain the particular formal aspects of the poem but renders even more suggestive her blending of gospel accounts and the deliberate (and technically erroneous) inclusion of Christ's specific words regarding the woman's future fame. The author, choosing to reproduce these words, enacts Christ's bidding, consciously enacting as part of her didactic aim regarding her young readers the dictum that "where'er the gospel's taught . . . there this shall be/ Made known that she hath done to Me." The poet spreads the word, and thereby builds fame.

Felicia Hemans, devoted female singer of the heartbreak and lasting renown of the female singer, returns to the anointment story more than once, in "The Memorial of Mary" and in "The Penitent Anointing Christ's Feet." The first of these not only records Jesus' memorialising words, but makes them, and the woman's subsequent mythologisation, the particular subject of her poem. The second defines the anointing woman as a singer and as an object of song, the nature of which signally changes after her action of loving recognition towards Christ.

130　*Christian and Lyric Tradition in Victorian Women's Poetry*

"The Memorial of Mary"
"Verily I say unto you, Wheresoever the gospel shall be preached in the whole world, there shall also this that this woman hath done be told for a memorial of her."—Matthew, xxvi.13. See also John, xii.3

Thou hast thy record in the monarch's hall,
　　And on the waters of the far mid sea;
And where the mighty mountain-shadows fall,
　　The Alpine hamlet keeps a thought of thee:
　　Where'er, beneath some Oriental tree,
The Christian traveler rests—where'er the child
　　Looks upward from the English mother's knee,
With earnest eyes in wondering reverence mild,
There art thou known—where'er the Book of light
Bears hope and healing, there, beyond all blight,
　　Is borne thy memory, and all praise above.
Oh! say what deed so lifted thy sweet name,
Mary! to that pure, silent place of fame?
　　One lowly offering of exceeding love.

Here Hemans draws a very particular geographical and historical context, deliberately placing in relation the woman of Jewish history, the contemporary woman ("the English mother") reading her story and passing on her memory to her child, and the woman poet retelling the story which helps to constitute this ongoing relationship, history, and reality. The poet's retelling helps constitute this ongoing relationship, traditional narrative, and historical 'reality'; the repeated word "where'er" effectively implies that the woman's story, and her fame, is in fact everywhere. Hemans' deployment of these varied contexts shows that this storied woman in fact exceeds all the constraints of geography and history. By means of her many memorials, she is a world traveller; she is a constant presence and in a constant present, "beyond all blight," everywhere praised.

"The Penitent Anointing Christ's Feet"

There was a mournfulness in angel eyes,
　　That saw thee, woman! bright in this world's train,
Moving to pleasure's airy melodies,
　　Thyself the idol of the enchanted strain.
　　But from thy beauty's garland, brief and vain,
When one by one the rose-leaves had been torn,
　　When thy heart's core had quiver'd to the pain
Through every life-nerve sent by arrowy scorn;
When thou didst kneel to pour sweet odours forth
　　On the Redeemer's feet, with many a sigh,

And showering tear-drop, of yet richer worth
    Than all those costly balms of Araby;
Then was there joy, a song of joy in heaven,
For thee, the child won back, the penitent forgiven!

This second penitent seems at first barely distinguishable from Hemans' extensive gallery of passionately loving, ultimately wronged and scorned female singers. Clearly, this woman is an 'entertainer' of dubious character, of bright, beautiful appearance, hymned in song ("the idol of the enchanted strain") and herself actively musical, "moving to pleasure's airy melodies." It is clear, however, that she has been spurned, with her beauty and acclaim lost; Hemans' description of her as quivering in pain, pierced by scorn, elides her with a literary figure of much utility to a number of nineteenth-century women novelists and poets, Madame de Staël's Corinne.[21] In contrast to the tragic Corinne, however, this woman's action leads to triumph. She reasserts Christian values over those of paganism ("those costly balms of Araby" are shown inadequate), and reclaims her self as pure girl, as she was prior to her life of pleasure, winning back the state of childhood. Perhaps most importantly, she reclaims music for holy purposes, as the false enchanted strain gives way to true song, "a song of joy in heaven." Earthly music is misleading and temporary, but as figured by this penitent woman—and by the woman poet who hymns her—heavenly song is eternally renewed and renewing.

Historically, a number of commentators have elided the character of the "sinful" woman who anoints Christ's feet with Mary Magdalene, although none of the scripture versions make this specific identification (only one, Luke, even calls the woman "sinful").[22] By incorporating the Magdalene into the story, women poets engage in a different way with questions of fame and notoriety. K. E. V.'s poem "S. Mary Magdalene," already discussed, makes mention in the penultimate stanza of the Magdalene's pouring of ointment at Christ's feet, in order to draw a parallel between the penitent's great and acceptable offering and the offering of this poet and her fellow believers: "But Thou poor worthless gifts wilt take/ And from them sweetest odours make." Christ, in other words, transforms not just the character of the penitent woman, but also transforms her gift/her works/her words. Sarah Greenough's long poem "Mary Magdalene," also mentioned in an earlier section of this chapter, presents the scene in which the Magdalene enters the Pharisee's house, anoints Christ, and is recognised by him, as the centrepiece of the poem, in certain ways more climactic than the crucifixion scene, and certainly more sensually and sexually charged. Unlike the Hemans' poem, in which the woman's actions allow her to purify herself and revert to a sexless, childlike state, Greenough's concentration on the physical beauty of the Magdalene, her insistent identification of her femininity and sexuality, become the means of heralding and praising the character. In her warmth and passion she serves as the counterpart of Jesus: She kisses his feet repeatedly, "the while/ She bathed them with her warm,

132 *Christian and Lyric Tradition in Victorian Women's Poetry*

fast-flowing tears"; he is hot-blooded too, his feet "fevered with loving toil," and she and Jesus together are set in opposition to the contemptuous, loveless coldness of the Pharasaical guests. The two are a romantically figured couple; she has a "lovely face" and is crowned with "the gold of her long hair"; Jesus responds to her with "deep, vibrating voice" and "tender, yearning pity." When he speaks to her directly, "Woman, thou art forgiven; go in peace!", part of the primary force of his words is in his recognition of her as "woman"; it is arguably her womanliness which is recognised and redeemed in this poem. Her beauty, her passionate nature, and her sexuality are redeemed from notoriety (which Greenough figures as "the look/ Of scornful wonder running round the board") and translated into features of a reverential memorial: she is remembered and recommended to future generations as "woman."

A significant number of other women poets who take up the story of the woman who anointed Christ, but omit his specific words of recognition and memorialisation, nonetheless retain memorialisation as their implicit focus. They reshape their poetic versions of the story to include themselves in the cast of characters, thematising the memorialisation of their own song. Eliza Ann Walker, in "The Penitent's Place" (in *Hymns and Thoughts in Verse*, 1864 and 1887), gives Luke vii.38 as the epigraph and inserts herself into that familiar narrative.

> Mine be the penitent's place,—
>   Low, Jesus, low at Thy feet!
> Waiting Thy pardoning grace,
>   Waiting Thine accents sweet.
> Mine be the penitent's place,
>   Mine be the penitent's tears . . .

The poem curiously conflates supplication with assertion in a way that mines penitence for the full range of possibilities it opens up (the OED includes supplication as part of the defining action of a penitent: "a person seeking forgiveness of sins and reconciliation to the Church"). This active seeking or supplication is foregrounded by numbers of Victorian women poets, in repetitions of verbal acts which seek to engage Christ in a particular kind of contract. That is, the poems require from him specific action in response to repentant statements: remember *me*. Ultimately, of course, the penitent's place, that of humility and abjection, will translate to the place at Christ's right hand in heaven—a translation that Walker's speaker specifically points out in the last stanza:

> Soon shall the penitent's place
>   Be at Thy right hand above,
> With all Thy redeemed to trace
>   The heights and depths of Thy love.

The Woman in the Scriptures 133

Mary Ethel Granger's "Peace: A Thanksgiving after Holy Communion," in the volume of the same name (1886), also constructs a kind of penitence contract that demands the speaker be remembered. Stanza four reads:

> Like Mary, I have brought in tears my perfumed tribute small;
> Accept me, Lord! for Thee I own, and Thee my Master call;
> And meekly kneeling at Thy Feet, I cast before Thy Throne
> The idols that I treasure most, and hail Thee God alone.

Granger treats her source material in this poem with considerable creative flexibility; she conflates the identification of Mary in John's gospel with Luke's statement of Christ's forgiveness, and like numerous other women poets she correlates the "perfumed tribute" brought to Christ by the woman who will be remembered, with the perfumed tribute that is her own poetic offering. These poetic words represent her faith and love; they also represent, quite literally, the way in which she herself will be remembered. This idea complicates the speaker's statement that she is casting away treasured idols; within the poem's assertion of humility (itself paradoxical) lurks another more prideful assertion, that of the ongoing renown of this tribute.

Both humble and assertive, Emily Hickey's "An Offering," in her 1896 *Poems*, writes the speaker both into and out of the anointing narrative, explicitly declaring her own poetry as the equivalent of the original woman's wordless gift. The value of "just a song" is transformed into a gift of no less worth than that famous biblical offering, partly through the agency of Christ as recipient, but also through that of the poet, who glories in the humility of her identification with the anointing woman, recognising and translating the value of her own work.

> Suffer me, O my Lord, my God, to bring
> And lay before Thy feet some offering!
>
> This poor hard heart forbids my tears to flow:
> I cannot wash Thy feet, my Master, so:
>
> And precious nard I cannot pour upon
> Those lovely feet, whose toil my ransom won:
>
> What shall I give Thee, then? For shame and wrong
> Freely forgiven, I offer—just a song:
>
> I offer just a song to Thee, whose gift
> Of love has known nor measuring nor thrift.
>
> To Thee, O Giver of all precious worth,
> A song that rises dulled through mists of earth!

134   *Christian and Lyric Tradition in Victorian Women's Poetry*

> Yet in Thy love be it accepted free,
> And heard as Thou would'st have it sung for Thee.

Hickey and her fellow rememberers of the nameless anointing woman suggest that this nameless woman is made a text, initially written by Christ himself, and then on an ongoing basis written by those who continue to write and sing her. They suggest their own identification with this character and with her enduring offering, and assertively connect themselves to the original memorialising 'author,' Christ. In so doing, they find a new significance for the tale as an extended and inclusive model of participatory faith.

As a final illustration of the creation of this expanded and liberating model, Elizabeth Rundle Charles includes in *The Women of the Gospels* a poetic sequence called "The Unnamed Women," structured around Luke's version of the penitent woman's story. The first of six poems suggests a reason for this woman (and a number of others) remaining unnamed in the gospel accounts that record them: Christ deliberately withheld their names, as an act of kindness to protect them from future calumny.[23] The second poem begins with the epigraph, "And stood at His feet behind Him weeping, and began to wash His feet with tears," and suggests that the woman's love and grief mirror, in a small way, the love and grief Christ is about to show in giving up his life (the woman is thus constructed, very unusually, as a kind of type of Christ). Charles' third and fourth sections highlight different parts of the same story, where Christ turns to the anointing woman, defends her actions, and shows he *prizes* her and her love. The fifth and sixth explicitly rewrite the past and future of the woman (the epigraph for Five reads "Thy sins are forgiven thee"; that for Six repeats Christ's parting words to her in Luke's version: "Go in peace"), and the series concludes with a rapturous depiction of the woman dressed in white, in a state of bliss, the Bride of Christ.

Crystallised in Charles' sequence on "The Unnamed Women" may be found some of the key issues with which Victorian women poets struggled in their negotiations with female biblical characters. Of central concern is the exclusion of women from orthodox Christian histories, and this concern is intimately related to the conundrum of how being published or put on record has often meant, even for devout Christian women, disrepute. Charles and the other poets reviewed in this section search for poetic solutions as to how women poets might redefine the fame/infamy puzzle to 'make a name for themselves' in Christian discourse, and, as Charles demonstrates, even namelessness and lack of recognition may be redeployed to re-envision an empowered, glorified woman. Even while the sequence title "The Unnamed Women" draws attention to these characters' lack of knowable identity, and to the way in which a traditional narrative 'overlooks' them, it also heralds them, recognises, recuperates, and values them. The sequence itself writes their history, expanding the discursive tradition to grant to women a past, present and future of their own devising.

Clara Balfour concludes her *Women of Scripture* with a full peroration, with ringing summary of the roles women have played in the Christian history and the roles they can continue to play. Balfour's aim, she states, has been

> To show that women have now, as in former times, a mighty work to perform; that trivial pursuits, petty aims, neglected talents, are unworthy of them; that the exigencies of the present age have claims on them of no unimportant kind; and that, *as the spiritual descendants of these sacred heroines*, it is their duty to be "thoroughly furnished to every good word and work." (368; my emphasis)

This chapter has focussed on three significant New Testament women and their multiple incarnations in Victorian women's religious verse, demonstrating the ways in which women poets drew on and helped construct a vigorous model of Christian female singers and witness bearers. In so doing these poets wrote themselves into an ongoing tradition, consistently (and increasingly assertively) drawing relationships between contemporary and biblical women. The poets I have reviewed drew creative connections between the devout Victorian female and her faithful, recording, singing, biblical "type," and thereby revealed themselves to be "the spiritual descendants of these sacred heroines." Deploying New Testament female characters in verse that did not solely locate itself in a distant past, but that suggested the contemporary relevance and potential expansion of the female role, enabled Victorian women to reformulate their relationship with exclusionary spiritual, secular, and literary histories, and to question fame and its construction within a masculinist, partial tradition. These undertakings indicate far more complicated attitudes on the part of Victorian women religious poets to their female biblical models than most scholars have considered. While these poets certainly cannot be claimed as proponents of a critical theology of liberation, their works offer devout and creative commentaries on biblical narratives that reveal Christian history to be women's history too, showing women as well as men to be initiators and inheritors of a living and dynamic Christian tradition.

4 "Accept me Lord, for Thee I own"
Women's Devotional Poetry and the Development of Relationship

"The intercourse between God and the human soul cannot be poetical"
— Samuel Johnson, *Life of Waller*

Long did I toil, and know no earthly rest;
  Far did I rove, and found no certain home;
At last I sought them in His sheltering breast,
  Who opes His arms and bids the weary come.
With Him I found a home, a rest divine;
  And I since then am His, and He is mine.

— Henry Francis Lyte

In 1879, shortly after its author's death, Frances Ridley Havergal's *Kept for the Master's Use* was published, a companion volume of devotional prose to her famous, beloved Consecration Hymn, "Take My Life and Let it Be." In the first chapter, Havergal meditates both on the Christian's need for complete submission to the Lord Jesus Christ, and on the rewards that come from such utter self-abnegation.

> Consecration is not a religiously selfish thing. . . . Not for 'me' at all, but 'for Jesus'; not for my safety, but for His glory; not for my comfort, but for His joy; not that I may find rest, but that He may see the travail of His soul, and be satisfied! Yes, for *Him* I want to be kept. Kept for His sake; kept for His use; kept to be His witness; kept for His joy! Kept for Him, that in me He may show forth some tiny sparkle of His light and beauty; kept to do His will and His work in His own way; kept, it may be, to suffer for His sake; kept for Him, that He may do just what seemeth Him good with me; **kept, so that no other lord shall have any more dominion over me**, but that Jesus shall have all there is to have. . . . (20–21: original emphasis in italics; my emphasis in bold)

"That He may do just what seemeth Him good with me," muses Havergal, striking unmistakably erotic notes as she explores what it means to be kept and to be owned in a Christian economy. In its passionate rebuttal of relational one-sidedness, the passage suggests that keeping and owning goes

"*Accept me Lord, for Thee I own*"   137

both ways between the two relationship participants: the devout Christian brings Christ glory, joy, and satisfaction, and, for the submissive and feminised Christian, 'owning' Christ as Master opens up a number of suggestive possibilities for emotional and creative fulfillment.

Chapter 3 discussed important female biblical models for Victorian women poets; a number of poets feminised Christ himself, turning him into a role model for the most feminine of activities: weeping, bleeding, caring for the sick, even mothering.[1] However, while several studies have investigated the ways in which Christ presented an important figure of identification for Victorian women,[2] I contend that he represented even more importantly a figure with whom women poets might construct relationship, and thereby construct themselves *through* relationship. The composition of personal relationship, forging the 'I-God connection,' is a central concern of women's religious poetry of the period. Victorian women's verse focuses most consistently not on woman taking Christ's place, but rather on woman taking a place at Christ's side, and this chapter will analyse the mechanisms, processes, and repercussions of this relation.

There is, of course, a long tradition in English poetry of the personal appeal to a personally known God. Fore-runners include the many sixteenth- and seventeenth-century imitators of the Psalms,[3] Philip Sidney and Mary Sidney Herbert, John Donne, George Herbert, and their many followers. In the eighteenth century, Wesleyan Methodists put the trope of relationship with God to specifically doctrinal uses, as they developed a hymnody that emphasised a close personal and sometimes even physical relationship between the Christian and Jesus, and that foregrounded the Christian's need to examine her standing before her Lord. In her foundational work on the seventeenth-century religious lyric, Barbara Lewalski describes devotional poetry as centring about this sense of spiritual self-examination: devotional verse treats "the painstaking analysis of the personal religious life," in which the poet "explore[s] such questions as his relationship to God, the state of his soul, and his hopes of salvation" (13). I contend, however, that within a specifically Victorian and specifically gendered context, devotional poetry requires a more multi-faceted definition and investigation. Analysis of this distinct sub-genre will illuminate the religious self-positioning, self-identification, and entwined spiritual and literary aspirations of women in this unique historical period.

Formulating a fully contextualised definition of 'devotional poetry' will reveal how Victorian women's lyric poetry constructed and standardised particular kinds of relationship with Christ. To this point, this book has (for simplicity's sake) generally used the umbrella term of 'religious poetry,' meaning all poetry expressive of devout Christian belief. Devotional poetry, the subject of this chapter, stands as a distinct subset of that broader category, and has particular functions. One of the few critics to have treated this sub-genre as a distinct body of work, G. B. Tennyson links devotional poetry in rather a wholesale way to his particular focus, the fruits of the Oxford movement.

138   *Christian and Lyric Tradition in Victorian Women's Poetry*

> Such poetry exhibits an orientation toward worship and a linkage with established liturgical forms, especially forms associated with High-Church Anglican or Roman Catholic religious practices. By devotional poetry I mean, therefore, poetry that grows out of and is tied to acts of religious worship. (6)

I suggest a refinement of Tennyson's definition that will be both more inclusive and more descriptively accurate of the broad body of Victorian women's devotional poetry. This body of work is indeed sometimes linked to established, identifiable liturgical forms, but not always. It is sometimes poetry of the Cathedral, but may also be poetry of the Chapel; and it is highly likely to be poetry of the closet, that is, homely, personal verse of homely and personal worship, quite distinct from formal and sectarian regulation. Fundamentally, in their poetic focus on worship, Victorian women maintained a consistent *relational* emphasis on personal intimacy between Christian and God, rather than on a distant relation of numinous awe. The devotional poetry I read in this chapter consistently valorises an emotive and non-intellectual understanding of and expression of faith in God. And, while I will suggest that this poetry always *acts*—to construct different kinds of status and relative position for its speakers—it is not always about 'acts.' Worship, in women's religious poetry, is only sometimes constructed as an external activity; very often it is a practice of mind, constructing an emotional rather than behavioural contract with God and also, in suggestive ways, with the reader who accepts the sincere testimony of the speaker. This body of verse might usefully be termed "the poetry of relationship." Thus, devotional poetry as I will be using the term in this chapter connotes expressiveness and affectivity, the construction of relational intimacy with God, and the performance of an emotional and spiritual sincerity which invites 'true understanding' of the poem's speaker.

Because the nature of devotional verse as *lyric* poetry is foundational to its function, devotionality's generic construction deserves due consideration. Devotionality's creation of intimate colloquy may be seen in fact to be generic as well as thematic. Part of the devotional poet's project to establish intimacy is undertaken through textual and technical means traditional of lyric, through a speaker implicitly requesting dialogue, 'in her own voice.' As Lewalski points out, the Psalms provide the great example of lyric verse (39), and the first-person singular pronoun has always predominated in the devotional lyric. Subjective, personal and particular, the lyric poem also allows the speaker to thematise her relationship with and emotions toward her God. However, as Frye writes, even the most subjective Psalms also display "the sense of an external and social discipline" (*Anatomy of Criticism* 294), and the lyric genre, even while constructing an intimate address, suggests that personal intimacy and communality (or universality) are not necessarily exclusive. The devotional lyric foregrounds communality somewhat more insistently: the individual speaker's relationship with God, the

"Accept me Lord, for Thee I own" 139

primary focus, is triangulated by the speaker's relationship with his or her readers and co-believers—an unignorable secondary focus. As Douglas Gray observes, the devotional lyric poem shares with the biblical Psalm the use of "the poet's 'collective I', where the Psalmist 'speaks in the name of the many'" (10). The lyric genre, then, helps promote but also problematise devotionality's particular concerns.

Given the simultaneously intimate and communal functions of devotionality, the close relation of the devotional poem and the hymn deserves brief consideration. In truth, no separate classification can be entirely maintained: the language, imagery, and prevailing themes of hymns, as well as the uses to which they were put, rendered them to their Victorian readers almost indistinguishable from devotional poems. Two of the most popular and widely sung hymns of the century, the Evangelical Frances Ridley Havergal's "Take my life and let it be" and the Unitarian Sarah Flower Adams' "Nearer, my God, to Thee," might easily stand as representative examples of Victorian devotional verse, as both focus on intimate and individual relation between the Christian and her Lord. The robustly assumed communality of the hymn genre may seem to exceed the parameters of the intimate relational focus described here; in fact, Tennyson differentiates the two sub-genres along those very lines, defining hymnody as public and communal, and devotional poetry as private (5).[4] However, Duncan Campbell's 1898 work on *Hymns and Hymn Makers* expresses more nearly the Victorian view, stating that the nineteenth-century hymn retains a profoundly individual focus, with poets writing a hymn in order "to embody moods of spiritual analysis, the desire to express the individual's consciousness, to show the soul to God as well as God to the soul" (xvi). In fact, the Victorian hymn had to be both individually and communally 'true.' Mary De Jong's analysis of the construction of what she terms "the (im)personal I of nineteenth-century hymnody" argues that on the one hand clergy and hymnal editors praised hymns that could express a universal Christian experience and exemplary formulations of selfhood. The hymn's singer (or reader) was expected to be able to identify with the *I* of the text. However, De Jong also notes the Victorian fervour for identifying hymns as very particular lyrics; specifically, as their authors' spiritual autobiographies: "laypeople as well as clergymen did understand the sung text as a testimony and the 'I' of hymnody as a self-representation" (202). The elision between writer and speaker was thus very broadly accepted in this genre. The *I* of the lyric is therefore simultaneously fictive and factual; the hymn/devotional lyric is simultaneously universal and entirely individual; the thoughts and feelings conveyed are simultaneously 'sincere' of the elided writer/speaker and 'true' of the reader or singer.

Campbell also stresses personal feelings as essential to a hymn, describing the genre as emotive and non-intellectual: "A good hymn is not necessarily informing. It is not the function of a hymn to instruct or awaken thought, *that* should be the function of a sermon. A hymn has to do with

140   *Christian and Lyric Tradition in Victorian Women's Poetry*

the emotions rather than with the intellect..." (xvi, emphasis in the original).[5] James Edmeston, Victorian poet and hymnodist of some renown, also stresses the highly personal and affective nature of the hymn. In the preface to his own volume of *Closet Hymns and Poems* (1846), he explicitly counters the mandating of communality or publicity:

> I have been induced to compile this manual of Closet Hymns from the impression, that there was nothing of the kind in existence, and yet that there are many thoughts, feelings, encouragements, and cautions which, thrown into hymns, would be highly useful and applicable to closet reading—particularly at the seasons of devotional retirement— which are not proper for singing in public, nor even, in all cases, for family reading. In the form of a hymn, there is something more particularly commending itself to the affections than even in the best written prose.[6]

The Victorians, then, had a ravenous appetite for and a markedly flexible attitude to both the composition and consumption of hymns, which were read for their universality and as unique expressions of autobiographically expressive writers, and which were considered useful for both congregational singing and individual meditation. Both the Havergal and Adams examples use the first-person singular rather than plural pronoun ("take my life"; "nearer, my God"), and while the hymn sung in congregation clearly does render its use of the singular pronoun highly elastic, the exclusion from a discussion of Victorian devotional poetry of any poem that either entitles itself a hymn or was set to music and sung communally as a hymn would mean creating distinctions that Victorian poets themselves neither perceived nor practised.[7]

This chapter focuses primarily on women's devotional verse (including some self-identified hymns) that centres upon the first-person singular pronoun, and that does not present distant, overtly didactic exhortation, but rather styles itself as personal and 'private.' This posture of privacy is richly, suggestively problematic. On a surface level, these lyrics are written as just between woman and Lord, as, for example, in "Take my life and let it be/ Consecrated, Lord, to Thee." Here, as in most other women's devotional poetry, protagonist and antagonist are readily recognisable: the addressed Lord is generally identified as Christ the Saviour, and the speaker is regularly elided with the author herself, the woman poet. Devotional poetry, in short, extends the identificatory possibilities of the lyric genre to its ultimate degree: in the particular context of expressions of religious sincerity, the devotional poem (like the hymn) seems to dissolve the difference between speaker's and poet's voice. This sincerity poetics holds particular significance for the way in which the devotional poem, however 'private' its posture, seeks to act upon the reader, as will be discussed in the final section.

"Accept me Lord, for Thee I own" 141

Devotion, then, and devotional writing more particularly, function on multiple levels. The Oxford English Dictionary offers a precise but static definition of *devotion* as "The fact or quality of being devoted to religious observances and duties; religious devotedness or earnestness; reverence, devoutness"; and more specifically it identifies devotion with worshipful activity: "Religious worship or observance; prayer and praise; divine worship." Mary Heimann's study of Catholic devotion in the Victorian period offers a more fully developed definition, while at the same time acknowledging the difficulty of delimiting the term.

> Devotion in its broadest and most fundamental sense implies an earnest and deep love for God, and can hardly be measured. Although devotion is a private matter impossible for the contemporary, let alone the historian, to judge, manifestations which were generally thought by contemporaries to suggest a pious bent, or a serious religious commitment, are more open to scrutiny. (38)

Following Heimann's prompt, I argue that the literary manifestations of Victorian devotionality are both open to and richly deserving of scrutiny, and that they depart in illuminating ways from the bland definitions of the OED. Broadly speaking, Victorian devotionality can be understood as the practice of traditional piety that was at the same time private *and* popular. For the Victorians, devotionality encompassed the undertaking of everyday, "mundane" observations private to oneself: prayers, readings, meditations on the Bible, the Prayer Book, other holy texts (or indeed hymns), the consideration of one's own conduct and salvation. But additionally, literary practice—and specifically publishing—was an important aspect of Victorian devotionality. Devotional volumes proliferated in the period and very often reflected a kind of compendium approach, into which readers could regularly dip, and to which aspiring writers could frequently contribute. For example, *The Golden Year* (1887), compiled by Emily Orr, combines short extracts from various divines, commentary from *The Imitation of Christ* and other religious prose works, occasional prayers, and a number of poems and hymns from an array of authors. Compiling a devotional volume allowed women to insert their own writing alongside extracts from some of the most popular authors of the day: Emily Elliott's *Wayside Pillars: Religious Meditations in Prose and Verse* (1866), for example, combines contributions from poets and hymnodists including the Reverends Henry Lyte and Horatius Bonar, as well as Cowper and Bishop Heber, with self-authored and very extensive passages of devotional prose. Thus literary devotional practice offered suggestive possibilities for extending the public voice (and public regard) of the devout scribbler.

Such multivarious devotional publications also help demonstrate a different kind of diffusion of power. Victorian devotionality was not located solely in a weekly attendance at the seat of religious power (whether that

142 *Christian and Lyric Tradition in Victorian Women's Poetry*

was Church or Chapel), and did not have to be undertaken under the constraining instruction of a sermonising priest or minister. Rather, Victorians could engage in Christian devotion under their own roof, under their own auspices. Devotional practice provided a way for the Victorian woman to reassure herself of her relationship with God, rather than receiving that reassurance from another's mouth (or pen). For all these reasons, devotion may loosen ties to authoritative rubrics and present provocative possibilities for self-determination.[8] Further, the growth of devotionality in the Victorian period (given its emphasis on conduct and relationship) entailed increasing acceptance of Christian faith and practice being conceptualised in feminised terms. As such, devotionality made an important contribution to the broader culture's feminisation of religious practice, described by Sue Morgan in numerical and conceptual terms (1). Victorian women's devotional poetic texts help demonstrate how devotionality is consistently and provocatively gendered feminine, as devotional practice was constructed as essentially non-authoritative, anti-dogmatic, both individualistic and intuitive, and widely perceived as sentimental.[9]

It is important to emphasise that Victorian devotionality was not monolithic but variable, and incorporated a number of different denominational, doctrinal, social and literary influences. Lewalski has argued that the growth of a specifically biblical poetics in the early modern period is ineluctably linked to the Protestant Reformation, and that "the poetics of much seventeenth-century religious lyric derives primarily from Protestant assumptions about the poetry of the Bible and the nature of the spiritual life" (5). In women's verse in the nineteenth century, however, the devotional lyric was far less tightly linked to what Lewalski identifies as a specifically Protestant aesthetic, and it transcends denominational delimitation. Certainly, important characteristics of Victorian devotionality show clear links to Evangelical emphases. Evangelicalism valorised individual, intimate, and emotive knowledge of Scripture and of Redeemer, and the doctrine of sanctification promoted the kind of daily dutiful practice of piety espoused by such influential Evangelicals as Hannah More, whose essay "Thoughts on Private Devotion" was frequently reprinted in the Victorian period:

> For private prayer sweetly inclines and disposes a person to a cheerful performance of every other religious duty and service; and the power of godliness in the soul flourishes, or decays, as the private duties of the closet are attended to, or neglected. This, in conjunction with the precept, promise, and example of the Saviour, furnishes the true Christian with powerful motivates for continuing instant [sic] in private prayer even unto the end. . . . (quoted in *The Book of Private Devotion*, 1845, 30)

However, despite its links to aspects of Evangelical belief, the prevalence and popularity of Victorian women's devotional poetry militates against its being easily mapped onto any one particular denominational or doctrinal emphasis. Victorian women poets' general acceptance of and reproduction of a model of intimacy between Christian woman and her Lord found echoes across the denominational spectrum.

For example, at the opposite pole to Evangelicalism within the Church of England, Anglo-Catholicism contributed significantly to the rise in Victorian devotionality and the value ascribed to worshipful observances. G. B. Tennyson has drawn critical attention to the prominence of liturgical observance in Tractarian writings and the influence of this preoccupation in religious poetry more broadly; as already mentioned, Tennyson suggests that 'devotional poetry' is ineluctably linked to the Tractarian mode.[10] The Roman Catholic Church, too, saw the popularity of fervent devotional demonstrations explode, as Mary Heimann, Ann Taves, and Edward Norman note in their examinations of the changes in observances and rituals, as well as in doctrine, that took place in the second half of the nineteenth century. Heimann hypothesises, suggestively, that an important contributing factor to the nineteenth-century growth of Roman Catholic devotionality may have been devotional literature (31).[11]

Without downplaying the doctrinal differences to which all middle-class Victorians would have been keenly attuned, I suggest that women's devotional poetry of the period requires a reading that does not foreground denominational difference. Rather, this poetry supports the argument that the broad growth in Victorian devotional focus and expression raises to prominence a set of new concerns. The production of a Victorian 'devotional spirit,' and concomitant focus on the expression of love and intimacy within religious discourse, significantly contribute to the period's ongoing feminisation of Christianity, and the literary and specifically poetic roots of this production deserve interrogation. As subsequent close readings will show, the intimacy paradigm appears very similarly in the poetry of women as diverse as the Methodist Lucy Bennett, the Roman Catholic Augusta Drane, the Presbyterian Annie Ross Cousin, and the High Church Anglican Christina Rossetti. All construct a poetry which, in the intensity of its focus on the intimate relationship between woman and Christ, renders their separate affiliations often impossible to detect, and instead highlights a concerted and suggestive interaction with the gendered hierarchies of broader Victorian religious discourse and its paradigms of the Christian's 'standing' before God.

In short, devotionality, emotionality, and gender became inextricably linked in the period, contributing to the richly complex religious climate of the Victorian period. The earnest religiosity which twentieth- and twenty-first-century scholars (perhaps too casually) hold to characterise that large segment of the Victorian public that continued faithful Christian believers[12] was itself a nuanced, mobile, and developing phenomenon. As the century progressed into the 1860s, and notwithstanding the enduring grimness of some sects,[13] Victorian Christianity in general may be seen as becoming 'kinder and gentler' in many ways relating to observances. In her discussion

144 *Christian and Lyric Tradition in Victorian Women's Poetry*

of English Roman Catholicism in the second half of the nineteenth century, Heimann discusses the "new piety," examining the popular growth of such "flowery" devotions as the Quarant'ore, the Stations of the Cross, and the recitation of the rosary (7; 35–36). Heimann also quotes Gibson's postulation that Catholicism was shifting away from a religion of fear to becoming a religion of love (33).[14] Gibson's view of this amelioration is interestingly similar to Elisabeth Jay's description of the 'softening' of the harsher aspects of English Evangelical belief as the century progressed (*Religion of the Heart* 87–88).[15] These observable mellowings of religious discourse in the nineteenth century, and the growing emphasis on the softer emotions over the intellectualised legalism of regulation and judgment, intersect in suggestive ways with the rise of women's ventures into religious writing, and with women's growing confidence in inserting into religious discourse specifically feminised treatments of religious topics.[16]

The role of gender in manifestations of devotionality is unavoidably contentious because it seems to flirt with essentialism. Heimann, for example, explicitly refuses to engage with the question of identifying a 'female' piety, and with the question of its differentiation from a general picture of pietistic practice (30). Yet to the Victorians, 'feminine piety' was a natural, uninterrogated category: the feminine character was almost universally perceived to be naturally devout, with feminine devotion closely linked to feminine emotionality. William Wilberforce, quoted in Chapter 1, wrote, "that [female] sex seems, by the very constitution of nature, to be more favourably disposed than ours to the feelings and offices of Religion . . . the wife[] habitually preserving a warmer and more unimpaired spirit of devotion" (289). And when in 1888 Yeats advised his friend, the poet Katharine Tynan, "your best work . . . is always where you express your own affectionate nature or your religious feelings" (Kelly and Domville vol.I:119), his linking of women's poetry, devotion, and affectivity is characteristic of the general Victorian reception of women's pious verse.[17] While the relation of sentimentality, femininity, and devotional observance provides the grounds for much debate for twentieth- and twenty-first-century critics, both male and female Victorians firmly associated the two.[18]

Felicia Hemans' preface to *Scenes and Hymns of Life* (1834) deliberately discusses the affectionalisation and feminisation of religion to which she acknowledges she contributes.

> I trust I shall not be accused of presumption for the endeavour which I have here made to enlarge, in some degree, the sphere of religious poetry, by associating with this theme more of the emotions, the affections, and even the purer imaginative enjoyments of daily life, than may have been hitherto admitted within the hallowed circle.
>
> It has been my wish to portray the religious spirit, not alone in its meditative joys and solitary aspirations (the poetic embodying of which seems to require from the reader a state of mind already separated and

"Accept me Lord, for Thee I own" 145

exalted), but likewise in those active influences upon human life, so often called into victorious energy by trial and conflict. (vii)

Hemans explicitly incorporates into religious verse emotional and relational activity, and the language of her apology is not particularly apologetic. She states her aim is both to "enlarge . . . the sphere of religious poetry" and also to enlarge the potential readership of such verse, targeting not just privileged, Romanticised, masculinised readers who exist in a lofty state, with time for solitude and meditation, but also feminised readers for whom the "trial and conflict" of everyday life and everyday concerns inevitably inform the experience of Christian faith. Such an undertaking seems profoundly democratic, and not, perhaps, particularly humble. The massive quantity of devotional poetry by the women writers who followed Hemans made a significant contribution to the century's production of a new, more inclusive, more emotive, distinctly feminine Christian. Devotional poetry provides a space in which women may ponder and debate not just religious texts and practices, but also what it means to be a reader and writer of religious texts, and what it means to be a practiser, a religious devotee, a *Christian*.

For example, Jane Euphemia Browne's "Blessed are the Pure in Heart" turns a scripture verse into a poetic devotional meditation that actually dictates the terms for the relationship between Christian and Christ. The poem offers less of a paraphrase of the well-known verse from the Beatitudes than a self-application; made personal to the speaker, Christ's promise is boldly claimed at the close. Thus the speaker moves from the humble self-abnegation of the first stanza:

> O God of purity, my soul
> > Most earnestly desires to be
> Subdued to perfect self-control,
> > Chastened to perfect purity.

To the triumphant (self-)assurance of the last:

> Oh, sweetest promise! made most sure
> > By Him who gave Himself for me,
> That they whose inmost hearts are pure,
> > Shall see the God of purity.

In a second example from a far more widely read poet, Havergal's "By Thy Cross and Passion" offers an insistently personal meditation on the famous redemption contract passage from Isaiah 53, verses 4–6:

> Surely he hath borne our griefs, and carried our sorrows: yet we did esteem him stricken, smitten of God, and afflicted. But he was wounded for our transgressions, he was bruised for our iniquities: the

146 *Christian and Lyric Tradition in Victorian Women's Poetry*

chastisement of our peace was upon him; and with his stripes we are healed. All we like sheep have gone astray; we have turned every one to his own way; and the Lord hath laid on him the iniquity of us all.

Havergal's devotional poem version turns all the plural first-person pronouns into singular ones, presenting quite literally a poetic translation of 'what this passage means *for me*.' Stanzas three and four, for example, read:

> Wounded for my transgression, stricken sore,
> That I might 'sin no more;'
> Weak, that I might be always strong in Thee;
> Bound, that I might be free;
> Acquaint with grief, that I might only know
> Fulness of joy in everlasting flow.
>
> Thine was the chastisement, with no release,
> That mine might be the peace;
> The bruising and the cruel stripes were Thine,
> That healing might be mine;
> Thine was the sentence and the condemnation,
> Mine the acquittal and the full salvation.

In this poem, Havergal strips back the Christian faith experience to just two participants: Christ, and this individual speaker-poet. Incorporating the tradition of biblical parallelism into her verse, Havergal's use of antithesis ("Weak, that I might be always strong in Thee;/ Bound, that I might be free") communicates the inescapable bond between the two characters even as it stresses their difference. Lines pivot about the echoing possessive pronouns of Thine and mine, and employ disyllabic rhyme and precise metricality to construct linguistic mirror images: "Thine was the sentence and the condemnation,/ Mine the acquittal and the full salvation." This speaker uses multiple formal techniques to demonstrate how she can take Christ's sacrifice to herself, for herself alone: the devotional poem, centred about relationship construction, becomes an exercise in possessiveness.

Viewed through this particular lens of possessiveness, devotional poetry may be seen to enable a female poet to focus on "me" and to extend her claims as to what is "mine" in a Christian economy. The invitation in a sincerity poetics to identify the speaking *I* with the poet herself, inserts an implicitly female self into orthodox Christian discourse. This insertion permits the writer to explore her power in and over a discourse that has traditionally excluded her. The emphasis upon individual expression that is elevated by Victorian devotional poetry accords to the woman writer/ speaker a right both to action and to reward, in and through a relationship with God that no one else can mediate or control. Virginia Blain notes that poets constructing forms of relationship with God may in so doing challenge other kinds of oppressive relationship, highlighting self-assertion rather than self-abnegation. We need to recognise, Blain argues,

> the limitations of the common belief that most female poets of the Victorian age devoted themselves singlemindedly to God. Even when they do write religious or devotional lyrics . . . the space afforded to a woman by this mode of discourse, fashioning itself out of a communion between an individual soul and its Maker, could in itself offer an escape from the power of the domestic patriarch. (*Victorian Women Poets* 15–16)

I read the devotional poems in this chapter not only for ways in which they offer 'escape' but also for the more complex ways in which they offer Victorian women opportunities to redraw relationships, to reposition themselves in regard both to God and to man, to express assertive possessiveness, and to gain access to spiritual and erotic power.

The first and longer section of this chapter examines the poetic means by which Victorian women sought to revise their own status through constructing a relation to God that was regularly characterised by romance and/or eroticised suffering. Foundational to Victorian women's poetry of relationship is the lengthy tradition that figures Christ as Bridegroom and the Church as feminised Bride. In their devotional poetry, Victorian women poets elaborate upon this provocatively gendered romantic and submissive paradigm to suggest ways in which poetic speakers may choose to place themselves in particular and privileged relationship with Christ. The second section considers another, seemingly paradoxical but intimately related form of relationship-construction undertaken through the genre of devotional poetry: I analyse how women published the privileged, 'private' relationship in their devotional verse to improve their own status in relation to their readers. Fundamentally, Victorian women's devotional poetry centres about a preoccupation with recognition. This body of verse articulates intertwined spiritual and literary ambitions; the devotional poetry of relationship, then, helps the Victorian woman poet reconstruct her 'standing' before God and her 'standing' before men.

"My Beloved Is Mine, And I Am His"

The metaphors and figures that repeatedly appear in Victorian women's devotional verse help illustrate the increasing prominence, within nineteenth-century Christianity, of humanity over legalism, and these figurations also help produce that change in emphasis. At the same time, these literary figures develop the construction of a privileged, profoundly feminine relationship with Jesus. Women poets draw their relational models most frequently from the Bible, and, as previous chapters have already suggested, women's selections and emphases help them shape very particular meanings from their biblical sources. While the New Testament several

148   *Christian and Lyric Tradition in Victorian Women's Poetry*

times figures the Church as the Bride of Christ,[19] it is in the passionate figurative language of the Old Testament Song of Solomon (or Canticles) that Victorian women devotional poets source most of their depictions of the individual Christian standing in a bridal relation to Christ. Even as contemporaneous Protestant preachers sought to universalise (and de-feminise) that Bride,[20] these women poets frequently highlight the gendering of "my dove, my sister, my spouse" in the original text, exploiting the potential usefulness of *overt* femininity in their devotional poetry.[21] Certainly, the gendering of the Christian as female, solidly grounded in biblical and patristic tradition, was broadly culturally accepted in the nineteenth century. In a study of same sex desire in Victorian religious culture, Frederick Roden discusses the gender roles entrenched in biblical and mystical Christian writings:

> As in [Christina] Rossetti, the devout embracing the Heavenly Spouse in Christian mysticism is usually depicted as female, feminine, or feminized in soul, accepting a male Deity. If the Holy Spirit or Shekhinah might be conceived as 'feminine,' its method of entry—penetration—is profoundly masculine. The Divine Lover in this tradition is therefore represented as male. Hence the devout is female. . . . (*Same Sex Desire* 107)

Roden is primarily interested in how a male devout Christian potentially disrupts what Roden terms a "heterosexist paradigm"; my focus is on how Victorian women writers could and did turn this gendered relationship paradigm to particular account. Many Victorian women poets who make use of Song of Solomon imagery enforce the gendering of the partners with almost overdetermined characterisation and emotive gush, as, for example, in Georgiana M. Taylor's "Wilderness Rest." This poem quotes "Song of Solomon viii.5" as its epigraph: "Who is this that cometh up from the wilderness, leaning upon her Beloved," and within the poem the woman speaker does not so much lean on her Beloved as recline supine, eschewing all activity and indeed agency to be passively clasped and carried by Him.

> Only just to rest upon His bosom,
>   Only just to lean upon His arm!
> Calm from all the fretting and impatience,
>   Safe and confident from fear of harm.
>
> 'Tis no effort I can make will bring me
>   To this place of sweet and blessèd rest;
> But He holds me, keeps me there for ever,
>   Folded closely down upon His breast;
>
> Carries me o'er mountain, hill, and valley . . .

"Accept me Lord, for Thee I own"   149

This particular construction of the Song of Solomon woman as a dependent, feeble, essentially feminine leaner is also deployed by A. M. Hull in "The Bride," the eponymous heroine of which is "so fondly nourished day by day,/ So soothed and cherished all the way" that she comes to resemble a kind of feminine parasite: "For though with weakness much beset,/ Thou hast in Jesus succour met." This kind of meek, needy, and feminised dependence also characterises the Christian speakers of a number of male devotional poets, as can readily be seen in the poem by Henry Francis Lyte, quoted as epigraph to this chapter (which closes, "With Him I found a home, a rest divine;/ And I since then am His, and He is mine"). The seemingly sexist hyper-feminisation that characterises poems like these, while perhaps disconcerting to twenty-first century readers, serves an important purpose for women poets. The model works to justify women poets' deployment of the speaking subject position within an explicitly biblical discourse, for, although Hull's poem adopts an authoritative third-person speaker, the majority of Victorian women working with this trope adopt (as Taylor does) the Bride as first-person speaker.

This authorised, feminised subject position offered in the Song of Solomon provides a logical and congenial model for these female artists. Several such first-person accounts may be found in the poetry of the Roman Catholic Augusta Drane, who begins to suggest for the female speaker an expanded degree of agency and self-determination. In "The Search for the Beloved," for example, the intellectual, widely read Drane draws upon the language of both the Song of Solomon and also St. John of the Cross's "Spiritual Canticle," dramatising a passage from Song of Solomon's third chapter, in which the woman and man are apart and the mournful woman seeks urgently for him. In "The Fairest Fair," Drane provocatively highlights the female speaker's gender. Taking a far more active role than the passive females discussed previously, Drane's speaker also takes authority over a pastoral literary tradition in which, now, it is she who issues the coaxing invitation to her male lover:

> Come forth into the woods; in yonder valley,
>> Where rippling waters murmur through the glade,
> There, 'neath the rustling boughs of some green alley,
>> We'll watch the golden light and quivering shade:
> Or couched on mossy banks we'll lie and listen
>> To song-birds pouring forth their vernal glee;—
> Wave on, ye woods! ye fairy fountains, glisten!
>> But more, far more, is my Beloved to me.

Giving her female speaker the power to praise and woo her own beloved, Drane turns both Song of Solomon and secular pastoral lyric traditions to new account, through their combination. The speaking position offered by the figure of the Bride of Christ thus offers opportunities to articulate

150   *Christian and Lyric Tradition in Victorian Women's Poetry*

an unexpectedly enlarged range of ambition and desire, including (here quite explicitly) the conscious appropriation of a particularly androcentric lyric tradition. Drane makes use of the previously noted capacity of devotionality to loosen the constraints of authoritative rubrics, choosing to explore a self-determined and self-scripted faith experience. As we can see in this poetic example, a woman's "speaking for myself" is both positively enjoined by devotionality and also made possible *through* devotionality. As an anonymous writer in the 1845 *Book of Private Devotion* observes, "It is impossible that a serious Christian can present to God in secret prayer all his wants, all his sorrows, all his dearest and most important concerns, in a few general sentences pre-composed by another" (78). In her manipulation of her Song of Solomon model, Drane rejects 'pre-compositions' and presents a self-determined voice and agency.

In addition to a useful model of an authorised, feminised subject position, the Song of Solomon also makes available to Victorian women poets a suggestive flexibility of speaking position within the romance/desire narrative. Annie Ross Cousin explores this mobility in a poem sequence with the general title, "Songs of the Beloved," in the 1876 volume *Immanuel's Land, and Other Pieces*. Making full use of the Canticles' eight chapters, in which the Bride, her friends, and her Lover all variously take up the speaking position, the four separately titled poems in Cousin's sequence speak in a range of voices, switching in and out even within the same poem, and exploring a mobile and mutual desire. "Sighs for the Beloved," the first poem in the sequence, begins with an omniscient narrator: "The bride is sitting lonely,/ In the absence of her Lord." The longing bride herself speaks in the eighth and ninth stanzas of the poem, in which she urges her beloved to make haste and come to her:

> 'Beloved, my heart is waking!
>   Help me to watch and pray,
> Till, morning lustre breaking,
>   I rise and come away,
>   By Thee embraced.'

And in the final two stanzas of the poem, her Lord replies, telling the bride the marriage feast is nigh, and "then shall mine arm embrace thee." This first poem, in its narrative progress as well as in its presentation of a dialogue, resembles most closely the original model of the Song of Solomon. However, as Cousin's poem sequence continues, the two speakers seem to multiply, their varying characterisations disrupting straightforward readings and dramatising conflict as well as harmony. The second poem, "The Beloved's Voice," is spoken throughout by an exultant, puissant male Lord.

> I've bounded o'er the hills, my love,
>   O'er Bether's barrier hills,

"Accept me Lord, for Thee I own"   151

Like roe that seeks the rills, my love,
    The rushing, rippling rills.
For lo, the winter is past, my love,
    Its drearness all is past;
I've brought thee Spring at last, my love,
    Bright, balmy Spring at last!

The third, "The Night Song", also employs a male speaker, but in very different mood. Appealing to his beloved: "Open to me, my sister,/ My dove, my undefiled!", his tone here is pleading, plaintive, as though often rebuffed:

My head is wet with dew-damp,
    My locks with drops of night.
Thou knowest not thy Bridegroom's voice,
    His knocking at thy door;
Strange on thine ear His pleadings fall,
    They melt thy heart no more.

And this third poem makes explicit the typological connection popular in nineteenth-century commentaries on this book of the Bible, seeing this pleading Lord of the Song of Solomon as a type of Christ: "The thorny crown my visage marred,/ The sharp spear pierced my side."

The fourth and final poem in the series, "The Night Search," spoken by the woman, seems to respond directly to the man's pleadings in poem three, but in such a way that disrupts the identification with Christ explicitly drawn in that third poem. For this woman is seeking a lover who has gone away, who after knocking and appealing to her, is no longer to be found—profoundly *unlike* the omnipresent and ever-faithful Jesus, who assured his followers he would never forsake them. In her fear and overtly sexualised longing, the speaker bears little resemblance to the waiting but already (bloodlessly) triumphant New Testament Bride of Christ, and is far more tightly identified with the Song of Solomon woman, and with that character's provocative capriciousness and desire.

'I am sad, I am sick with hope deferred;
    I pine, I languish with love's delay;
I yearn, I thirst for the voice I heard,
    That died from my door away!'

As Cousin's poem sequence illustrates, the diverse speakers of the Song of Solomon permit poets to deploy a variety of speaking subjects, and this mobility of speaking subject position enables a flexible articulation of authority and desire, a model in which a female speaker may be protagonist as well as antagonist, actor as well as rescuee, and subject as well

152 *Christian and Lyric Tradition in Victorian Women's Poetry*

as object of a desiring gaze. In the hands of Victorian women devotional poets, adoption of the Song of Solomon's Bride/Bridegroom trope permits an exploration of romantic partnership and of voice and voicing that builds upon and complicates the nineteenth-century view of woman's role within Christian religion. In such a context, a romantic relationship offers a female participant exactly that, a participatory, rather than simply abjectly passive, model of faith experience.

The use of dialogue in devotional poetry offers women a further avenue to explore the conundrum of authoritative and autonomous voicing and its role in constructing a model of participatory relationship with God. Cousin's Song of Solomon sequence alternates speakers' voices to complicate their identities and roles. Other women poets go further, using poetic dialogues to thematise the potentially fluid access to power revealed in speaking subjects' relative positions.[22] For example, Mary Kendrew's comforting, conventional, pastel-toned little volume *Lyra Sacra* (1894) includes "Jesu, Thou art to me," a poem in which the romantic possibilities of the woman/Lord pairing are explored in a dialogue that foregrounds and unsettles authentication and authority. Each of the three elaborately constructed stanzas begins with four lines of conventional protestation in the voice of the Christian; each of these complaints is then answered, in the same stanza, by seven lines spoken by the loving and companionate Christ. Kendrew draws attention to the poem's use of voice in several specific formal ways. She encloses Christ's words in quotation marks, whereas the Christian speaker's words appear unquoted, suggesting they are the seemingly 'unvoiced' or unmediated words of the poet. This use (and non-use) of visible indications of speech immediately highlights the question of 'authentic' speech, as who says what and who reports what are presented within the poem as explicitly identifiable—and thus implicitly examinable and questionable—categories. The poem also clearly differentiates the two speakers by the use, on the part of each, of different metrical and rhyme schemes, all the more distinct for being yoked together in the same stanza. And finally, the two speakers employ notably distinct poetic registers: the Christian speaks/thinks simply, whereas the loving Christ speaks in high-flown metaphor heavily salted with biblical allusion and contorted syntactic structures. Interestingly, the poem seems to demonstrate that Christ is more 'poetic' than the speaking Christian, whose simplicity may be read as a marker of her sincerity. He is certainly a more consciously constructed speaker.

> Jesu, Thou art to me
>> The sweetest and the rarest,
>> The altogether fairest—
> Art everything to me!
> 'As the apple of My eye I will keep,
> With My counsel I will ever guide My sheep,
>> Till that day
> When the mountains melt away,

> And the rocks their silence break;
> Then My loved ones I will take
> To Myself for evermore!'

Such a dialogue, while it clearly serves the traditional devotional goal of relationship reassurance, raises more questions than it answers about the power dynamic depicted. While it presents Christ in personal and intimate conversation with the devout believer, the Christ who responds in high-flown poetic cliché to the bidding of the first four lines appears in some ways a conjured Christ, with the exaggerated formal aspects of his speech serving to highlight his almost puppet-like deployment. Precisely because Christ is quoted, those quotation marks work paradoxically on the reader: on the one hand the marks serve as assurances of veracity, and on the other hand they raise the spectre of the reporting poet, the possibly editorialising poet, the poet who is creating a Christ who serves her particular purposes.

The first speaker appears in the course of the poem to be trying to compel her Christ into moving from general consideration of all Christians—"My sheep," "My loved ones"—to consideration of this *one* Christian; to perceive her and respond to her as an individual. In the second stanza his response to her call, "Ah, make me love Thee more,/ Thou glorious King!" includes a specific recognition of her: "In the hollow of My hand/ Thou shalt stand." And by the third stanza Christ is responding to his follower with a statement of comprehensive one-to-one relationship that sounds echoes of the marriage contract: 'Thy stay in grief, thy help in strife,/ Thy peace in death, thy joy in life,/ All the way!' The first speaker's insistence upon and creation of relationship with that second speaker through the course of this dialogue poem point to common devotional concerns in the period: the production and maintenance of privileged intimacy with Christ, and the rewards for the devout woman that may be procured through that production.

Christina Rossetti's devotional poetry, which is of considerably greater stature than that of Kendrew, reflects these same concerns, and demonstrates some of the same strategies, as Rossetti's speakers wrestle with the compulsive need to create, recreate, assert and reassert intimacy with their Lord. Throughout her oeuvre, Rossetti displays a deep concern with the possibility of balancing the fulfillments of the communal voice of heavenly unison, depicted in some of her more triumphant poems, and the insistent, intimate concerns of the suffering, imploring individual. Her devotional verse reaches towards the satisfaction of *we* but cannot ever fully relinquish the pressing needs and wants of the solitary *I*. Rossetti's speaking *I* directly and intimately addresses Christ throughout the entirely religiously focused 1893 *Verses*. As a means of negotiating the claims and the insistent individualism of the speaking *I*, Rossetti composes a number of dialogues between woman speaker and Saviour, including "Thou, God, seest me" (II.190), and "Lord I am here" (II.194). Both feature a speaker expressing

154 *Christian and Lyric Tradition in Victorian Women's Poetry*

her inadequacy and fear, and finding encouragement in the responsive voice of Christ. "Thou, God, seest me" is particularly provocative on both thematic and formal levels. Each stanza presents a dialogue in miniature, in which the speaker's initial plaint is answered by Christ showing that the terms in which she expresses her fear actually contain the form of the answer to that fear. The fourth and final stanza closes:

> . . . Without a pool wherein
> To wash my piteous self and make me clean.—
>> "My Blood hath washed away
>> Thy guilt, and still I wash thee day by day:
>> Only take heed to trust and pray."—
> Lord, help me to begin.

The last line of each stanza expresses the speaker's acceptance; hers are the last words as well as the first. The speaker's unquoted, seemingly unmediated speech encloses and contains Christ's quoted response. This dialogue, then, presents Christ's as a (formally) interiorised voice but also as the speaker's *own interior voice*, as the speaker speaks herself toward the ability to undertake her Christian walk and Christian identity.

Rossetti's suggestion of the (self-scripted) love and reassurance which may be articulated in and through a participatory relationship, however, is somewhat unusual in its overtness. At least at a surface level, the characteristic posture of a great deal of Victorian women's devotional poetry is that of self-prostrating dependency. The argument that Victorian women's devotional poetry systematically presents an *I* seeking and constructing intimate relationship with God must take into account the expressions of passivity and dependence that characterise so many poems. My discussion of these less easily recuperable poems analyses how passivity and dependence may be interrogated by the poems, and be redeployed for paradoxically empowering purposes. My claim is not that these verses 'are not really about passivity and dependence,' but rather that the poems reevaluate these states in an explicitly Christian economy. In surveying the forms that passivity can take in Victorian women's devotional poetry, explanatory models provided by feminist theology and feminist religious history may illuminate the 'payback' of a submissive posture.

Victorian women's expressions of dependency on occasion verge on almost groveling utterances of self-effacement. Sarah Geraldina Stock's "Whose I Am, and Whom I Serve," for example, literally makes poetry out of self-subjugation, with the first six couplets of the poem limited to repeating variations on a theme of humble renunciation: "I would not have," "I would not call," "I would not speak," "I would not use," "I would not seek," and so on. Frances Ridley Havergal's "Enough" (709–10) explicitly voices the humility of a woman seeking and finding fulfillment solely in relationship with Christ. She states that without Him she is empty and incapable:

> "*Accept me Lord, for Thee I own*" 155

> I am so weak, dear Lord, I cannot stand
> > One moment without Thee!
> But oh! the tenderness of Thine enfolding,
> And oh! the faithfulness of Thine upholding,
> And oh! the strength of Thy right hand!
> > That strength is enough for me!
>
> I am so needy, Lord, and yet I know
> > All fullness dwells in Thee;
> And hour by hour that never-failing treasure
> Supplies and fills, in overflowing measure,
> My least, my greatest need; and so
> > Thy grace is enough for me! (stanzas 1 and 2)

Going even further than such quivering acquiescence, to avow a passivity so profound that the speaker seems to seek nullification, is Jane Euphemia Browne's "Submission" (13). Here the suffering speaker doesn't counsel her unruly will to accept God's chastening; rather, she voices the abandonment of personal volition altogether.

> Do with me what Thou wilt,
> > Submissively and still,
> I will lie passive in Thy hands;
> > Do Thou Thy holy will.
> 'Tis Thine to choose—my portion let it be
> To acquiesce with deep humility.

In the second stanza the speaker imagines being "absorbed" entirely into the Lord; the poem concludes with the utterly abject lines, "let me see/ Thee only, and forget my misery."[23]

In her article "Feminist Experience and Faith Experience," Michele Schumacher complicates the perceived passivity of religious faith. Schumacher considers the meaning of religious faith "both as object and act, as gift and response" (170), arguing its essentially participatory nature, and explicating how much faith demands of and claims for the devout believing subject.

> Receptivity is hardly an honourable concept in a modern intellectual environment that has equated it with passivity, even to the extent that it is perceived as infringing upon human freedom. . . . In contrast, however, to the derogatory notion of receptivity understood as *passive passivity*—where something is simply undergone or suffered—a new feminism challenges us to reappraise the value of receptivity as *spiritual (or active) passivity*, so named because the powers of the human spirit are active: this experience is characterized by 'an element of expectation and appeal, of acceptance and consent'. (Mouroux p.12) (178–9; emphasis in original)

156 *Christian and Lyric Tradition in Victorian Women's Poetry*

Schumacher's argument helps us understand what Victorian women's devotional poetry is working to achieve through those repeated tropes of relating and being known, which compose a seemingly passive and inactive experience of faith. In 'being known,' being recognised and partnered, the subjectivity of both relationship partners is preserved. Schumacher takes care not to dispense with the distinction between objective and subjective redemption—God gives faith, Christians receive by faith—and Victorian women poets never challenge the foundation of redemption in Christ, even as they suggest their own expanded contribution to the redemptive project. Schumacher argues, however, the inextricably linked contributions of human and divine action within any act of faith (185): "One *cannot clearly distinguish faith as God's gift from faith as our response*, God's coming to us from our coming to God" (185, emphasis in original). A significant aspect of coming to God is acknowledging him—what he has done, presently does, and will do. The Christian's repeated acknowledgments express faith, a faith that is neither a refusal to question nor a purely intellectual assent, but rather "a giving of the self . . . 'wedding' the believing subject with the object of [her] faith: the divine subject who gives himself, in an act of love, as an 'object' to be known and loved" (171). Schumacher develops the metaphor of the mutual knowledge of spouses who give themselves to each other in love, the same romantic paradigm so regularly called upon by Victorian women devotional poets. These poets' articulations of faith, then, express an "active passivity" that suggests mutual benefit for both faith partners.

In the light of this argument about mutually constitutive acts of recognition, we should read expressions of humility in Victorian women's devotional poetry particularly carefully, whether that humility connects to relational or literary ambition (as we will see, the two are closely intertwined). Schumacher's concept of spiritual or active passivity helps explain the movement in Georgiana M. Taylor's "Oh to be Nothing" (which appeared in the pointedly titled volume, *Lays of Lowly Service*, 1889) from humble self-nullification to mutually loving fellowship. The preface to the volume explicitly decries both literary ambition and any belief in an equal partnership between Christian and Lord, as the poet describes how her verses have been "gathered together and sent forth in the hope that He who has in the past deigned to comfort and help some of His 'little ones' through their instrumentality, may further use them for His glory, as He often does 'the weak things of the world'" (n.p.). The poem "Oh to be Nothing!", one of Taylor's most popular, articulates a similar rejection of any desire for *spiritual* glorification. This poem was praised by Frances Ridley Havergal in a letter that is reprinted in full at the end of Taylor's volume: the textual feature of this reprinted praise, whether the author's or the publisher's decision, clearly renders problematic all the volume's expressions of humility. The poem itself utilises and problematises the romantically inflected relationship paradigm that was so available and useful to Victorian women, as it explicitly verbalises the speaker's passive abnegation of will and indeed, all identity.

"Accept me Lord, for Thee I own"   157

Oh to be nothing—nothing!
    Only to lie at His feet,
A broken and emptied vessel,
    For the Master's use made meet!
Emptied that He may fill me,
    As forth to His service I go;
Broken, that so, unhindered,
    Through me His life may flow.

The theme of being a simple conduit for God's love, grace, or words is a common one in Victorian women's poetry (see, for example, the discussion of Havergal's "The Song Chalice" in Chapter 2), but in Taylor's hands the 'mere container' idea is revised so the passive container suffers violence, being broken down, seemingly to the point where all independent identity or potential usefulness is obliterated. Stanzas two and three follow in an identical vein to stanza one, the opening line of each repeating the cry, "Oh to be nothing—nothing!" However, in the fourth stanza this line suddenly disappears. The final three stanzas modify the apparent extinguishing of the speaker's individuality, as the speaker explores the paradox central to the concept of receptive Christian humility: that the meek, lowly, and valueless will be exalted.

Yet e'en as my pleading rises,
    A voice seems with mine to blend,
And whispers, in loving accents,
    "I call thee not 'servant,' but 'friend;'
Fellow-worker with Me I call thee,
    Sharing My sorrow and joy—
Fellow-heir to the glory I have above,
    The treasure without alloy."

This poem dramatises and complicates the speaker's choice to adopt (or assert) a posture of passive self-abnegation for, through this choice, she earns a response of love ("in loving accents") and an elevation from nothingness to friendship and fellowship, becoming "fellow-worker" and "fellow-heir." The abnegation of self voiced so vividly in the first three stanzas is thus not abandoned but rather reframed, brought into paradoxical, constitutive relationship with aspirations of future reward and shared glory, as "a voice seems with mine to blend." Taylor's poem links in interesting ways to Schumacher's model of active passivity, postulating as it does the rewards for the devout Christian woman of surrendering will and self-determination to her Lord. Through acknowledging God's greatness and acting upon faith in that greatness, the Christian is promised in return not servitude but full partnership, a share in duty, emotion, and inheritance.

Should we query, then, even such expressions of humility as appear in Stock's and Havergal's poems, which seem on the surface almost self-annihilating in

158 *Christian and Lyric Tradition in Victorian Women's Poetry*

their insistence on the all-sufficiency of one partner and the non-existent contribution and complete self-abnegation of the other? Here and elsewhere in Victorian women's devotional poetry, the prevailing romantic paradigm becomes infiltrated with figures of self-abasement that draw heavily on the language and imagery of suffering, often emotional, but very often additionally figured as intensely physical. The figure of the piteous, suffering Christian is extremely popular throughout nineteenth-century women's poetry. Elizabeth Barrett deploys this figure of the submissively chastened Christian in a number of her earlier poems, including "Bereavement" (in her 1838 *Poems*), which closes with a loving depiction of "my great Father, thinking fit to bruise." The durability of this particular suffering model, even co-existing with a proto-feminist stance, may be seen in its appearance in the poetry printed in the late-century, staunchly suffragist *Women's Penny Paper* (later *The Woman's Herald*). Running between 1888–1893, the periodical incorporated alongside its overtly political orientation a number of orthodox religious and devotional poems, including "A Prayer," which begins familiarly: "Chasten me not too sore I pray,/ Nor smite me with thy sword . . . " (May 5, 1891). While articulations of a female desiring subject, such as may be found in a number of devotional poems drawing on the Song of Solomon model, prove fairly readily recuperable to twenty-first century feminists, there is less obvious material to admire in devotional works figuring a relation that explicitly embraces repression, oppression, and pain. A representative work may be found in Margaret E. Darton's *Words in Season for the Weary*, (1850), the dedication of which sets the tone for the entire collection: "To those who have known much sorrow, and who have been chastened because they were loved, this little book is affectionately inscribed." Every poem in the volume, most of which are written in the first person, concerns suffering and patience, and the speaker interprets that suffering as a sign of God's love. Most are extremely confessional, containing laments and brave self-reminders to be strong; many are framed as prayers, praying for patience to bear God's discipline, as in the allusively titled "Thy Will Be Done."[24]

Posing similar hurdles to a feminist reading, as it interprets infliction of suffering as extremity of favour, is a large portion of Charlotte Elliott's oeuvre (two of her volumes, for example, are entitled *Hours of Sorrow* [1836] and *Hours of Sorrow Cheered and Comforted* [1869]; both went into multiple editions). In one of Elliott's most dramatic paeans to suffering, "Paternal Chastening" (in *Selections*), the speaker utters the encouraging cry, "Cheer thee, cheer thee, suffering saint!", and counsels her reader: "While in the furnace to lie still,/ This is indeed to do His will." Extending this figure of suffering as a flame which "consumes thy suffering, wasted frame," the speaker develops the metaphor of purification, all the while continuing to use intensely physicalised and immediate images of burning, agonising torture. As the poem closes, the speaker explicitly conjures "the martyr's white-robed throng" and urges her reader to accept the glory and delight of that martyrdom. The overall effect is genuinely brutal. Another brutal example, even more startling in its first-person directness, may be found in Lucy Bennett's "Though He Slay Me, Yet Will I Trust in Him." The title, taken verbatim from Job 8 v.15, gives fair indication of the passionate tenor of the poem, which reiterates the speaker's willingness to be (even delight in being) quite graphically slaughtered by her Lord.

> "Though He slay me," I would lie
>   Quiet, calm, and still;
> That the Blessed One may strike
>   Where and how He will.
>
> "Though He slay me," I would cling
>   To Himself, my Life;
> Loving still the pierced Hand,
>   Though it holds a knife.
>
> "Though He slay me," I would be—
>   By His matchless grace—
> For the very slaying, hid
>   In His close embrace.
>
> [. . .]
>
> "Though He slay me," yet on Him
>   Would my heart be stayed;
> Grateful that no stranger-hand
>   Hold the unsheathed blade . . .

Lying quiet and still, clinging to her beloved, longing for his embrace and unfailingly faithful, this quintessentially passive feminine speaker quivers at the thought of the knife, the "unsheathed blade" with which her hyper-masculine Lord will strike her, doing exactly what he wills with her.

Rossetti, too, occasionally posits as a final goal a quiveringly sensitive but nonetheless complete submission to the will and rulings of God, which may only truly be achieved through enduring suffering. The first stanza of "What is that to me? follow thou me" conveys a sense of wounded bewilderment, addressing in turn the speaker's self, then other people, and finally God himself: "Thy hurt a help not understood." This confusion as to interlocutor accords with the confused syntax and agency throughout the first two stanzas, but the third and final stanza of the poem, in which the speaker's will is properly relinquished in complete submission, is suddenly completely clear:

160 *Christian and Lyric Tradition in Victorian Women's Poetry*

> Lord, I had chosen another lot,
> But then I had not chosen well;
> Thy choice and only Thine is good:
> No different lot, search heaven or hell,
> Had blessed me fully understood;
> None other, which Thou orderest not.

These verbs, "had chosen," "had not chosen," "had blessed me," all appear in the conditional perfect tense; the suffering speaker speculates that she would have chosen otherwise, if left to herself. Yet the heavily end-stopped phrases and paratactic structures of these lines convey a learned-by-heart sense of indoctrination, a closure and finality which shuts the door on any other speculative possibilities, ultimately enfolding the speaker into an identity that is "only Thine," and concluding with "not," a final negation.

Schumacher's formulation of active passivity enables a more nuanced reading of women poets' expressions of faithful submission and acknowledgements of God's greatness. Such a reading uncovers voices of assertion and aspiration within reiterations of the submissive devotee's 'return' for her submission. A strategic reading must also take into account a more overt and overtly eroticised demand for a 'return.' In women's devotional poetry of relationship, explicit figurings of the speaker's sufferings appear akin to contract negotiations, in which suffering is displayed both as a sign of the woman's extreme love for her Lord and also as a guarantee or marker of his reciprocal love (as is so clearly argued, for example, in Bennett's "Though He Slay Me"). As this element plays out in the poetry of those Victorian women who daringly incorporate a desiring voice into their devotional verse, the eroticisation of the relationship with God is regularly explored through a particular model of dominance and submission.[25] Illustrating this model, Harriet Eleanor Hamilton King provides a fascinatingly explicit and complicated depiction of a woman battling her own unwillingness to suffer the marks of the Lord's loving, punishing rod, in "The Bride Reluctant" (in *The Hours of the Passion*, 1902). At first this Bride resists the invitation to meet her Bridegroom within her chamber, complaining of the "fixed, and fast, and wearisome" relationship. The voice of her guardian, who clearly takes the side of her Lover, continues to urge her, as she continues to search for an escape.

> 'Come to thy chamber, for He stands
>   Tearful, and seeking only thee;
> With ravished eyes, and outstretched hands,
>   And he commands resistlessly.
> Come to thy chamber, though it be
>   Narrow, and dark, and full of pain;
> He paid a heavy price for thee,
>   And can He let thee go again?'

"Accept me Lord, for Thee I own" 161

'My Bridegroom's bed is cold and hard,
   My Bridegroom's kiss is ice and fire,
My Bridegroom's clasp is iron-barred,
   I am consumed in His desire:
My Bridegroom's touch is as a sword
   That pierces every nerve and limb;
"Depart from me," I moan, "O Lord!"
   All the night long I spend with Him.' (stanzas 3 and 4)

The sexual charge of this anticipated consummation is unmistakable, but so is a sense of shrinking horror. In response to her guardian's promotion of the Bridegroom's passionate ardour, the woman refutes the idea that there can be any love in such a possessive, dominated relation:

'Rather am I His bondmaiden,
   Compelled by law and not by love.
Oh, would I were enfranchised; then,
   With wings of silver, like a dove—
Then would I flee, past heaven's far bound,
   The unendurable embrace;
Then would I hide in earth's profound
   From the strange terror of His Face!' (stanza 6)

Yet, despite these passionate refusals, it eventually appears that the Bridegroom's commands are indeed "resistless." At the very end of the poem, when it seems the resistant Bride really is about to declare her freedom from her Bridegroom, she looks upon his face and suddenly sees "nought in heaven or earth but Thee!" Calling him "my Lord, my Life, my Love," she asks him to comfort her upon his breast, a tender closing image that sits extremely uneasily with the twin impulses of desire and fear of pain that throb throughout the poem.

King's exploration of her female speaker's shrinking away from and simultaneous compulsion towards submissive suffering, and the intensely problematic 'happy ending' the poem offers, help shape a pressing question that faces twenty-first-century readers of this explicitly self-subjugating devotional poetry. How can we rightly read poems that seem to propound such an oppressive, masochistic, anti-feminist message? How might these poems—seeming devotional masochism manifestos—be read to reveal what they actually *do* for Victorian women poets?

The model of a human-divine relationship cast in terms of dominance and submission, with God as master/punisher, and the speaker of the poem as submissive, suffering victim, follows a long tradition in which Christian mystics, including most famously Theresa of Avila and John of the Cross, cast their relationships with God in frankly erotic and masochistic terms. Rightly reading this model within Victorian women's devotional

162   *Christian and Lyric Tradition in Victorian Women's Poetry*

verse demands its examination within the specific cultural and Christian context in which these women conceived of submission and conceptualised gender roles. Caroline Bynum's work on women's spirituality in the Middle Ages has important implications for studies of women's interactions with religion well beyond the medieval period. Bynum reinterprets the functions of asceticism and voluntary suffering, and of the significance of gender in relation to those practices, within women's experience of religion. Applying Bynum's explanatory model to nineteenth-century Christian women's thinking about their spirituality suggests ways towards a better understanding of the implications of eroticised suffering and submission in Victorian women's piety and poetry.

The standard interpretation of ascetic and self-abnegating practice in women's religious lives (which has been common to all historical periods, and as commonly decried by twentieth- and twenty-first-century scholars) has stated that ascetic or submissive practice is masochistic, reflecting an internalised misogyny and self-hatred, and is basically dualistic and pathological. However, Victorian women's eroticised submission to suffering expresses ways of finding value and giving meaning that were clearly important enough to be repeatedly iterated: rather than responding with an acontextual moral sneer, Bynum reminds us that we should investigate these models in their cultural context to learn more about how women used them to find value and give meaning. Interrogating the roles and symbolism dramatised by Victorian women's devotional poems of relationship produces readings that suggest a speaker's submission indicates not the denial of her desire, but rather, the transformation of that desire. A submissive speaker in this economy *wants*, and, arguably, *gets*.

Bynum's central argument is that women's accounts of female suffering, in a Christian economy, don't shut down but rather open up possibilities for female desire. She suggests that in these models of suffering the female body is neither despised nor effaced, but rather that "efforts to discipline . . . the body should be interpreted more as elaborate changes rung upon the possibilities provided by fleshliness than as flights from physicality" (6). In such models, women do not reject the cultural identification of woman as fleshly and human; rather, they embrace it. Countering scholarly arguments that self-hating religious women aped maleness as a way of approaching God, Bynum suggests that women embraced "the great reversal at the heart of the gospel: the fact that it is the contemptible who are redeemed" (284) and the humble who are magnified. What goes on in Victorian women's poetry of religious submission, then, may be not merely a simple reversal of symbols (which might suggest that women sought to reverse the normative distribution of authority), but a more complex thing. Bynum's analysis of medieval women's practice also resonates for Victorian women poets' practice: "Women's symbols did not reverse social fact, they *enhanced* it" (279; my emphasis). As a number of examples in this chapter have shown, Victorian women took up the socially accepted image of the weak, meek,

"Accept me Lord, for Thee I own" 163

submissive woman not to explode it, but to mine it for its full significance in the Christian symbolic universe. If to be a woman meant being identified with flesh, fallibility, weakness, and suffering, then woman is the essential human in need of salvation, the representative Christian. Human because they are women; redeemable *because* they are women; Victorian women in their poetry do not so much reimagine gender roles as they radically reassign value to them. The paradigm of suffering female submission is a peculiarly enabling model for this, not a denial of weak, contemptible female nature, but an extension of it to its symbolic, powerful limit.

Thus the postures of submissive suffering that women adopted (often physical in medieval times; usually poetic and metaphoric in the Victorian period) are "not, at the deepest level, masochism or dualism, but, rather, efforts to gain power and to give meaning" (Bynum 208). A key component of Bynum's argument concerning medieval women's religious life centres upon the control (over family, spouse, and also clergy) that was offered by manipulating body, food practice, and symbol. Control and aspiration are similarly key aspects of my reading of Victorian women's manipulation of a submissive/suffering paradigm: Victorian poets manipulate a poetic, imaginary body in an explicitly submissive relationship with an incarnate Christ. By these means their speakers assert a measure of control in the relationship, gaining from their submission (which Schumacher might term "active passivity") powerful and privileged connection with God. As already seen, the female speakers of poems like "Though He Slay Me," "What is that to me?" and "Submission" variously explore the dominant/submissive relation, positioning God as a disembodied but nonetheless physically and spiritually demanding partner for an essentially female (frail, fleshy) Christian. In such poems, the submission articulated by women's devotional poetry may be seen as aspirational, in so far as these poems assert their abnegation as a means to explore mutual recognition, in an ongoing search for intimate relationship between a dominant God and a weak, fallible human Christian, whose femaleness plays an essential role in structuring this relationship.

Many of Rossetti's devotional poems take on new facets of meaning when examined through this explanatory model. In her numerous poems in which speakers embrace suffering and force themselves to submit, the partner is always identified as a masculine, dominant Heavenly Bridegroom. The woman addresses her Lord directly, often beseechingly; when he answers, she accepts anew her suffering role, because the mutual bond between them has been reaffirmed. The provocative love sonnet "Why?" presents a direct exchange between the submissive woman and her stern master. In the octave, she questions why her suffering is necessary, claiming that her love for her master is already complete. "Why need I any more these toilsome days," she asks; "If all my heart loves Thee, what need the amaze, /Struggle and dimness of an agony?—" (ll.2, 7–8). At the turn of the sonnet her master answers, but predictably enough, he doesn't alter his demands:

164   *Christian and Lyric Tradition in Victorian Women's Poetry*

Bride whom I love, if thou too lovest Me,
Thou needs must choose My Likeness for thy dower:
 So wilt thou toil in patience, and abide
Hungering and thirsting for that blessed hour. (ll.9–12)

The female speaker must endure a night of pain, figured as deprivation or separation, before achieving eventual satisfaction in "that blessed hour,/ When I My Likeness shall behold in thee,/ And thou therein shalt waken satisfied" (ll.12–14). The speaker submits in expectation of a reward; the prize for her endurance is eventual consummation, figured in her transformation, recognition by her Master, and satisfaction of her desires. A triumphant and transformative vision will have superseded the partial vision spied "through a glass darkly."

"Why?" provides a convincing picture of a dominating relationship, and its concluding vision shows that willingly adopting a position of suffering submission leads to a mutual recognition that reveals the separateness *and also the likeness* of the two. The relationship formed between the submissive Christian and her Master in a poem like "Why?" works towards co-feeling, not the dissolution of one identity into the other but, daringly, a partnership that will grant equal power to two who recognise their difference *and* their sameness. In Rossetti's exploration of the erotic relationship between submissive and God, she presents provocative suggestions of the rapprochement between human (female) nature and God-nature.

Dolores Rosenblum has drawn attention to the importance in Rossetti's devotional work of what Rosenblum terms "the visual metaphor[,] whereby 'seeing' stands for knowing, loving, and having" ("Christina Rossetti's Religious Poetry" 36). I suggest that Rossetti's frequent poetic explorations of mutual, literal regard and recognition represent a stylistic 'footprint' revealing a psychological imperative toward spiritual and erotic fulfilment, which Rossetti contemplates and figures with a virtuosic complexity. The beautiful, desperate sonnet "Cried out with Tears" begs a magisterial Lord not to despise or shun the abject speaker but to recognise her grief and sense of guilt and ultimately, to recognise *her*. The self-abasement gathering in the poem, coming to a head in the "dust" in which the speaker grovels in the twelfth line, paradoxically becomes the means of a powerful assertion of intimate, reciprocal regard:

Lord, I believe, help Thou mine unbelief:
 Lord, I repent, help mine impenitence:
 Hide not Thy Face from me, nor spurn me hence,
Nor utterly despise me in my grief;
Nor say me nay, who worship with the thief
 Bemoaning my so long lost innocence:—
 Ah me! my penitence a fresh offence,
Too tardy and too tepid and too brief.

"Accept me Lord, for Thee I own"   165

Lord, must I perish, I who look to Thee?
   Look Thou upon me, bid me live, not die;
       Say "Come," say not "Depart," tho' Thou art just:
       Yea, Lord, be mindful how out of the dust
I look to Thee while Thou dost look on me,
   Thou Face to face with me and Eye to eye.

At the poem's close Christ reflects back the speaker's sufferings, but the analogy works both ways, as the speaker in turn mirrors him as the two steadily regard each other. The closing couplet brings to bear a battery of formal poetic resources to construct and illustrate the concept of intersubjective partnership. Rhyme reflects the two lines back upon each other, as internal rhymes strike with the repetition of "Thee," "me," and "me," while the closing sight-rhyme of "me/Eye" formally enshrines difference within sameness. The couplet's monosyllabic words strip back the possibilities of even pronunciation variations, and Rossetti further limits syntactic variation by repeating pairs of verbs and nouns: look, face, eye. Only the disruption of iambic regularity provides an exception to the lines' essential sameness, and Rossetti places her stresses to emphasise her actors and their identical actions: I, Thee, Thou, look, me,/ Thou, Face, face, me, Eye, eye. Balanced and parallel in multiple formal ways, the closing couplet embodies coupling, the mutual recognition of separate but equal subjects. This fulfilling vision closing an anguished poem presents a characteristic portrait of a Rossetti speaker who struggles to re-place herself in an actively passive position, who strives to know and be known.

Like Rossetti, Jean Ingelow depicts the process of achieving mutual recognition or "union" with God as an anguished process, suggesting that suffering offers the only means of translation to God's side and Godlikeness. Ingelow's "O Christ of God, in my good days" (in *One Hundred Holy Songs, Carols, and Sacred Ballads,* 1878) uses as epigraph the verse fragment, "*To know . . . the fellowship of His sufferings*" (Philippians 3:10). Sweet fellowship with Christ, according to the poem, may ultimately be gained if the Christian pursues Him faithfully along His own path of suffering.

O Christ of God, in my good days
I found Thee, both in work and praise;
But now the cup of pain I drink
And fail to find Thee there,—and sink.

Sore is the weight doth on me lie,
Jesu, I shall not live but die;
Thee have I loved, yet fear is now,
And though Thou diedst, I find not how.

166   *Christian and Lyric Tradition in Victorian Women's Poetry*

In toil for Thee in holy strife
Thy death was hid from me by life;
Now sinks my heart, now fails my breath,
Thy life is hid from me by death.

I faint, and at Thy Cross lie low;
There is no resting, Lord, but so!
The abhorrèd nails my lips do meet,
My arms embrace Thy bleeding feet.

O depth of pain: forget, my soul,
Thy little part; behold the whole.
O Christ, Thy thorns have woundèd me,
Of Thee redeem'd, I bleed with Thee.

What dost Thou tell me, dying Lord,
Am not I near to heed Thy word?
I mourn for God, I make my cry
In union with Thy death to die.

My soul drawn nearer sweetness finds;
The fellowship of suffering binds;
In this dark hour Thou teachest me
My soul is in the dark—with Thee.

I will lay hold, O death divine,
Till all my will is lost in Thine;
Till grief a balm in union prove,
And suffering be assuaged with love.

Like many of Rossetti's plaintive speakers, Ingelow's speaker can see at the outset of the poem no point to her suffering at all; in fact, it seems to her initially to prevent her from seeing God himself: "Thy Life is hid from me by [my own] death." But through the course of the poem she learns to rightly read suffering and to rightly see the Christ to whom she comes very, very close. The fourth stanza sounds an echo of Donne, as the speaker discovers there is no rest except in the opposite of rest, and she embraces Christ's cross and wounds, and kisses the nails that pierce him (although the syntax here makes ambiguous the direction of the approach: "the abhorrèd nails my lips do meet"). By experiencing a physical contact with Christ's sufferings, the speaker gains perspective: hers is but a little suffering; his comprehends all. As the speaker imaginatively participates in Christ's sufferings, his pangs become her own and the two are unified in pain: "O Christ, Thy thorns have woundèd me,/ Of Thee redeem'd, I bleed with Thee." Mutual experience

"Accept me Lord, for Thee I own" 167

leads the speaker to reevaluate a (mutual) death: like the women in the gospels, near enough to hear Christ's dying words, the speaker is now able to utter her own (eroticised) appeal to his ears: "my cry,/ In union with Thy death to die." Having reached this crisis or climax of union, the speaker can now perceive, despite the darkness about her, "sweetness," for "the fellowship of suffering binds" her to Christ more closely and intimately than any other path. Anguish enables Ingelow's speaker to know a hitherto unknown mutuality: "grief a balm in union prove[s]."

Lucy Ann Bennett's poem "Subjection" works toward a similarly ecstatic final vision, offering beneath a seemingly uncomplicated textual surface a thoughtful questioning of the benefits of voluntarily assuming a submissive position. Bennett returns to several key themes across her very large oeuvre, one of the most significant the idea of the Christian being God's particular property.26 This particular poem opens with two epigraphs: "Yield yourselves unto God," (Romans iv. 13), and "I am the Lord's" (Isaiah xliv.5). Seven of the nine stanzas begin identically, echoing the second epigraph in the emphatic exclamation: "I *am the* LORD'S!" (emphasis in the original). Stanzas also repeat this phrase internally: stanza two, three times; stanzas three and five, twice apiece. The poem appears an absolutely consistent, committed declaration of willingness to be a holy possession, wholly possessed.

> *I am the* LORD'S! Yet teach me all it meaneth,
>   All it involves of love and loyalty,
> Of holy service, absolute surrender,
>   And reserved obedience unto Thee—
> They nearest draw to joy's sublime perfection
> Who seek it in the depth of full subjection. (stanza six)

The seventh stanza calls on God to prove and develop this relationship through verbs of physical mastery: take, mould, come, renew, subdue. The eighth stanza strikes an even more dramatic note, issuing a cry for violent discipline and domination:

> By any means and every means conform us
>   To the blest image of the Son of God;
> And if the rebel heart refuse Thy leading,
>   Then, spare not for our crying, take Thy rod—
> Compel each wayward heart to swift contrition,
> Constrain each broken will to full submission.

But the complete breaking down of will and being, to the point of extinction, is not the ultimate end of this speaker, or of this poem, for Bennett's final two stanzas quite explicitly claim the reward or "afterward" of submission, which is triumphant indeed.

168 *Christian and Lyric Tradition in Victorian Women's Poetry*

> Not joyous for the present, Lord, but grievous,
>   We know, indeed, Thy chastening would prove;
> But, ah! we crave the precious fruit it yieldeth,
>   The "afterward" of blessing, through Thy love.
> And so we would not shrink from Thy correction—
> The sure, sweet pledge of Fatherly affection.
>
> *I am the* LORD'S! Yes; body, soul, and spirit,—
>   Oh, seal them irrevocably Thine;
> As Thou, Beloved, in Thy grace and fullness
>   For ever and for evermore art mine;
> The everlastingness of love transcending
> In everlastingness of glory ending!

"As Thou, Beloved . . . for ever and for evermore art mine," states Bennett's speaker, balancing this claim against the earlier repeated assertions of "I am Thine." Echoing the famous Song of Solomon declaration, "My Beloved is mine, and I am His," an intertext for so many Victorian women's devotional poems, this poem concludes with an ecstatic revelation of transcendent loving recognition and ultimate partnership.

Partnership and possession, concerns fundamental to Victorian women's poetic project, are worked towards by means of intertext, trope, and syntax. In women's devotional poetry of relationship, the verb "To own" becomes particularly significant, its homonymity permitting direct play with concerns of mastery and authority. Women poets explicitly state, and demonstrate, that they 'own' God as Lord, admitting or recognising him as such in their verse, lauding and honouring him. At the same time, their poems may suggest they 'own' God in the sense of possessing him, internalising him, or comprehending him. In Mary Ethel Granger's poem "Peace: A Thanksgiving After Holy Communion," from the volume of the same name (1886), Granger shows one of the most significant facets of the Eucharist to be the reconstruction of the relationship between the communicant and her God (and she uses the highly significant anointment story, analysed in Chapter 3, in her construction).

> Like Mary, I have brought in tears my perfumed tribute small;
> *Accept me, Lord! for Thee I own, and Thee my Master call;*
> And meekly kneeling at Thy Feet, I cast before Thy Throne
> The idols that I treasure most, and hail Thee God alone. (my emphasis)

Owning and verbally recognising God (through naming him, hailing him, and writing this verse) help fundamentally construct a privileged relationship. Prior to owning God through the taking of communion, Granger's speaker comes only 'obedient'; she's "trembling" and "conscience-stricken," complaining she's not worthy. But after partaking she finds peace and pardon

"Accept me Lord, for Thee I own" 169

and refreshment: "There's wine to drink, and bread to eat, and Christ to enter in." The suggestive phrase "there's . . . Christ to enter in" opens up two possibilities: the one, that Christ presents himself available to her (through the Host) for her to enter, like a room or a house, or a body; the other, that Christ stands ready to enter *her*. The poet makes the most of the ambiguities suggested by these metaphors of consumption and mutual penetration as she revels in the pleasures of "this sweet hour of fellowship with Thee."

Owning, then, links ideas of praising and possessing. Given Victorian women poets' frequent adoption of the paradigm of being a simple container or conduit for God's message, the assertion that God 'owns' a poet's words may be read uncomplicatedly as a statement that these words truly belong to God, are possessed by him, and are 'his words,' a statement that Havergal made explicitly. Chapter 2 has discussed women poets' preoccupation with charting the relationship of their words to the Word of God. However, devotional poetry of relationship expands its examination of what it means for a woman poet to 'own God in her words,' suggesting readings in which the woman simultaneously praises and possesses God, asserting ownership over God by writing about him, by *making him the subject of her verse*. The Christian's recognition or owning of God in effect *makes* him God.[27] In this way, this body of verse's exploration of 'owning' inches closer to the idea of comprehension, hinting that a Christian writer may be able actually to comprehend—or contain—her God.

Bennett's poem "A High Priest," which diagrams possession and knowing between Christian and God, argues that owning goes both ways.

> Lord and Master we will own Him,
>   Swift to recognise His claim:
> King of kings our hearts enthrone Him,
>   Blessed be His Holy Name!
> Yet new gladness finds expression,
>   And the rapture is increased,
> As we humbly take possession,
>   "We have such a Great High Priest!"
>
> "Blessing?" yearning heart that criest;
>   Stay, the Blesser comes to you!
> "Higher truth?" But this is highest,
>   We are in Himself—The TRUE.
> Not attainment, not acquirement,
>   But His fullness fully known;
> Guarantee for all requirement,
>   Jesus is upon the Throne.
>
> By a Priesthood all unchanging
>   Jesus meets our changing need:

170   *Christian and Lyric Tradition in Victorian Women's Poetry*

Naught from us His love estranging,
    Truly we are blessed indeed.
Lo, a covenant unbroken
    Spans the distance, "Till He come"—
Of the things which we have spoken,
    This, for aye, remains the sum.

In the first stanza the Christian speaker explicitly engages both meanings of owning: owning God or praising him as Lord; and taking possession of him, *having* him as High Priest. These dual meanings play alongside the twin operations of God himself claiming the Christian as *his* own, and the Christian recognising his claim. The poem's second stanza furthers the seeming paradoxes of the first by collapsing separate identities into each other, the speaker explaining, "We are *in* Himself" (my emphasis) and positing that the fullness of God is not a supplementary thing to be attained or acquired by the Christian, but rather something that may be completely internalised, as the Christian is internalised by God. The third stanza continues to evoke this intertwined existence, where naught 'estranges' and where covenants are ever unbroken. No longer separate entities, these mutually owning partners make one 'sum.'

As Bennett's poem demonstrates, women poets regularly explore the mirror operations of the owning relation, asserting that the God they own also owns them. They also often assert that God specifically owns their poetic works, as in Eva Travers Evered Poole's Preface to *Left Alone With Jesus* (1890). Poole notes the public's enthusiasm for her first volume (entitled *Lonely? No! Not Lonely,* and published in 1880) and rejoices in "the knowledge that God has already owned and blessed many of these embodied in this new volume, when sent forth in simple leaflet form" (v). Poole's preface argues that the successful publication and reception of a poet's works demonstrates God's *owning* them. God's recognition, in this formula, precedes (and possibly promotes) public recognition, and public success for the poet proves that God "owns and blesses" 'her' words— which are also 'His' words.

"So Earth Shall Know At Last . . . That I Am Thine"

As the previous discussion shows, owning is intimately bound to acts of recognition. Additionally, to own a woman has an undeniable sexual subtext, one which is played upon in devotional verse to suggest an expanded range of meanings for the relationship between woman and Lord (Bennett's "Though He Slay Me" is a gaspingly passionate case in point). For God to own a woman, then, conveys vouching for her, speaking for her, testifying to her acceptability and relationship with him; in Bennett's phrase, being her "Guarantee for all requirement." For God to own a woman's *verse*, as described in Poole's preface, implies acceptance and approval. What

"Accept me Lord, for Thee I own" 171

earthly approval is then necessary? As Margaretta Ayres Karr's preface to *The Heavenly Voice* illustrates, women poets often described publication as a secondary consideration, given that God has approved and purposed the work: "What was so divinely given and sanctioned for the uplifting of a soul to God, I offer without apology to [the] public . . . " (vi). Of course, making this kind of statement in her verse, or in a preface to her verse, serves to highlight rather than diminish the significance of a woman writer publishing her work for a wider audience. The discussion to this point has concentrated primarily on women's constructions in their devotional poetry of their standing before God. Clearly, however, these constructions undertake in significant ways the simultaneous construction of the Christian's standing before the world: specifically, the poem's production of an *I* speaking to God also produces a particular relationship with that speaker's human readers. Devotionality and didacticism, the aims of which seem at first glance almost antithetical, may in fact be seen to intersect in this body of verse in provocative ways. Devotional poetry's enjoining of 'speaking for oneself' also authorises and enables 'speaking for others,' as briefly suggested in the earlier discussion of the religious lyric. The authority of this speaking *I* demands consideration in the context of the broader question of how Victorian women poets figure their reward (spiritual, temporal, and specifically literary) in their negotiations with Christian discourse.

Surrendering one's will, or as Browne phrases it in "Submission," 'forgetting oneself,' has significant repercussions for the entwined romantic/erotic and literary ambitions articulated by the poem's speaker. Abject humility, and the expressed desire for nullification, complicate and are complicated by their voicing. This is particularly so when this voicing, directed to an omnipresent and omniscient God, is technically unnecessary: God already knows the desires of the poet's heart. Therefore these assertions seem to disprove that which they claim, for if the desire for total self-abnegation was true, it would contravene any assertion or indeed utterance. And yet Victorian women devotional poets continuously, repeatedly 'speak up.' These poets' expressions of abject humility are further complicated by their *public* voicing, their publication to a broader reading audience, and by their composition in a specifically regulated form, that of a lyric poem. Such a form is ineluctably attended by particular generic and formal expectations and, by meeting those expectations, the poem cannot avoid evincing conscious literary ambition. As Helen Gardner describes the key conflict within the religious lyric, "In all poetry which attempts to represent the intercourse between an individual soul and its Maker, there is a conflict between the ostensible emotion . . . and the artist's actual absorption in the creation of his poem and his satisfaction in achieving perfect expression" (*John Donne* xv–xvi). The androcentrism of Gardner's statement derives from her focus on seventeenth-century male lyric poets, but her critique is still suggestive for the case of nineteenth-century women poets. They, too, must negotiate the problematic intersection between sincere emotion

172 *Christian and Lyric Tradition in Victorian Women's Poetry*

and the act of creation, and their "satisfaction in achieving ... expression" indicates a persistent preoccupation with reception and recognition. Julia Walker has argued that the religious lyric's awareness of audience expectations effectively rang the death knell of the genre in the seventeenth century, but I contend that the devotional lyric as practised by nineteenth-century women can only be fully comprehended when its understanding of and particular ambitions for acting upon the reader are incorporated into its spiritual ambitions.

Melnyk argues that when Victorian hymns employ the first-person singular pronoun, "the congregational context change[s] the vision of subjectivity expressed ... replacing the individual conceived as autonomous and prior to community with an individual rooted in and defined in part by his/her communal attachments" ("Victorian Religious Women" 81). As the first part of this chapter argues, the individual speaking *I* of devotional verse stands distinct from the broader Christian body, but women poets also deploy that speaking *I* as a particular kind of teaching/testifying example before a broader community, turning private devotionality into a matter for (subtly self-aggrandising) display. Rossetti is a master at assuming a pose of submission which is also essentially self-display. A short, untitled lyric from *Verses* (1893) shows ownership going both ways in the speaker-Christ relation, but it also reveals the importance of audience to the construction of that relation.

> Lord Jesus, who would think that I am Thine?
>   Ah, who would think
> Who sees me ready to turn back or sink,
>   That Thou art mine?
>
> I cannot hold Thee fast tho' Thou art mine:
>   Hold Thou me fast,
> So earth shall know at last and heaven at last
>   That I am Thine.

There are unmistakably three parties in this poem: the speaking *I*, the directly addressed Lord Jesus ("Thou"), and the audience. Rossetti refers to the audience indirectly as those who bear witness to the relation between speaker and Jesus, whose recognition of that relation is passionately important to that speaker, revealed in her repeated references to those "who would think," he or she "who sees me," and the earthly and heavenly witnesses who "shall know at last." The speaker reveals herself as working to build multiple relationships. On the one hand, she appeals to Christ to save her, to cling to her despite her weakness, to make true the belief which she can only voice in the first stanza in interrogative uncertainty ("that I am Thine?"; "that Thou art mine?"). But on the other hand, she also indirectly appeals to that audience, at the outset so unpersuaded of her relation with

"Accept me Lord, for Thee I own" 173

Christ, for it ultimately to recognise that relation, and to grant her the ability to stake a certain claim, marked by her move from the interrogative to the assertive: "I am Thine."

Walker suggests that at the early stages of the religious lyric's development, with Donne's "La Corona," "the audience does not exist within the poem . . . there is only the implied possibility" (41). In the nineteenth-century devotional lyric, as Rossetti's verse demonstrates, the human audience is an inescapable presence within the poem, and in certain ways it rivals God himself as a significant interlocutor. A significant biblical text for many women poets is one that Adeline Braithwaite used as an epigraph for her volume of devotional verse, *Scripture Spoil in Sacred Song* (1886): "Speaking to yourselves in psalms and hymns and spiritual songs, singing and making melody in your heart to the Lord" (Ephesians 5:19). Another important intertext is Colossians 3:16: "Let the word of Christ dwell in you richly in all wisdom; teaching and admonishing one another in psalms and hymns and spiritual songs, singing with grace in your hearts to the Lord." These Pauline exhortations help devotional poetry's sincerity poetics expand its arena: as well as addressing her Lord, the devout speaker, seeking self-edification, addresses herself, 'singing and making melody in her heart.' Further, if the Christians addressed by Paul communally 'speak to yourselves,' and teach and admonish one another, the result is mutual witness and mutual edification; the Lord is far from the only audience. Victorian women literally *speak to themselves* in their psalms, hymns, and spiritual songs of devotion, taking on, by means of poetry that centres on an intimately speaking *I*, roles as spiritual speakers, exemplars, and advisers to each other. Isa Gillon Fergusson's "The Communion of Saints" (in *Parables in Song*, 1889) illustrates this idea earnestly and appositely:

> We are God's prophets, whether false or true,
> Writing our scrolls upon each other's hearts,
> Transcribing characters we call our own,
> Each on his neighbour's hidden register.
> These copies of our lives are handed down
> In ever widening circles. Pause and think
> How full of import is each passing thought
> That doth ennoble or degrade thy heart;
> It stamps its record on the page of life,
> And leaves it fouler, fairer than before...

For Fergusson, the soul is a page. The act of physically writing characters on paper correlates to the inculcation of moral character in others' souls, "in ever widening circles." Melnyk has specifically suggested as part of the definition of Victorian "religious writers," those who "saw themselves as writing for an imagined congregation of readers who shared their religious concerns" ("Victorian Religious Women" 73). For the sincerely speaking *I*

174   *Christian and Lyric Tradition in Victorian Women's Poetry*

of devotional poetry, the sense of congregation and responsibility to that congregation, while implicit, remains powerful.

Christina Rossetti took her role as spiritual advisor extremely seriously, as her brother recognised: William Michael Rossetti wrote, "she certainly felt that to write anything for publication [was] to incur a great spiritual responsibility" (*Memoir* lxvii). Rossetti's devotional volume *Letter and Spirit* shows her own sharp awareness that the writer's every word carries great weight:

> Our Lord hath said: 'That every idle word that men shall speak, they shall give account thereof in the day of judgment. For by thy words thou shalt be justified, and by thy words thou shalt be condemned'. (St. Matt. xii. 36, 37) This by itself suffices for our warning and/ guidance. (136–7)

Westerholm, D'Amico (*Christina Rossetti*), and Arseneau and Marsh have analysed Rossetti's very deliberate production of an authoritative voice in her devotional prose and verse,[28] and many other women poets felt a similarly heightened consciousness of their influence or speaking responsibility. They strove to follow that biblical blandishment to "teach and admonish one another," which in turn enforced extreme consciousness of the presence and pressing needs of the reader.[29] This sense of responsibility to the reader resulted in much devotional verse that, while not outwardly didactic (given its regular focus on the private and personal *I*), nonetheless insists upon being read as testimony, or the bearing of witness, characteristic of sincerity poetics. As such, this body of verse implicitly asserts its ability to guide other Christians. In this context, poems that relate great suffering and that expostulate about reliance on God take on new significance as audience-directed testaments, producing authority out of the unassailable proof, "I have felt." Caroline Noel's *The Name of Jesus, and Other Poems, For the Sick and Lonely* (1878) provides a pertinent example of such a devotional testament. The volume employs the characteristic strategy of negotiating an intimate relationship with God through the poetic vehicle of personal physical pain. However, Noel's volume, the preface of which solemnly records that twenty years of suffering were endured by the author, simultaneously builds relationship between the poet-speaker (this elision is directly invited by the preface) and the reader, who bears witness to the relationship the poet-speaker builds with God. Most of Noel's poems are uttered in the first person, and all are intimately phrased, as, for example, "He Laid His Hand Upon Me"; almost all focus on suffering and approaching death, with titles such as "The Yoke," "Chastisement," "In Pain," and "The Redemption of the Body." Noel predominantly uses a model of the soul complaining to God about the suffering He inflicts, only to reach a new understanding of what that suffering is intended to achieve.

"Accept me Lord, for Thee I own"   175

Noel points significant lessons in first-person poems that do not explicitly address the reader, but that implicitly and explicitly invite the audience to *look* and to *hear*. Readers bear witness to, and take lesson from, the speaker's testimony of her own looking and hearing. Her own struggles and desire to see clearly and to hear clearly, as, for example, in "Indwelling," cause her to plead with God to "Reveal Thyself," to "show Thy goodness and Thy power divine" and "show me the glorious beauty that is Thine," for she longs to "see Thine image glow." The speaker bemoans the fact that she can only hear his reassuring voice at a remove:

> Thou speakest in Thy works;
>   But, wondrous though they be,
> They have no voice . . .
>   . . . they cannot tell me Thou art mine.

And while she finds it "pleasant" "to hear Thy Ministers proclaim," the speaker is conscious of the communicative limitations of "Anthem, Litany, and Prayer . . . the melodies that float through choir and aisle." The speaker petitions God that she may see directly, and be directly told, and, like Rossetti's speaker in "Cried Out with Tears," "commune with Jehovah face to face." Noel displays the same concentration on visual and aural images in the poem "In Pain," in which the speaker petitions, "Heavenly whispers let me hear," for "To behold Thee will be Heaven." Veils and various forms of blindness and deafness recur throughout the volume as blocks to full comprehension of God; in "The Yoke," written as a dialogue between God and the speaker, God rebukes her as "thou short-sighted child."

For Noel, the devotional project is to look successfully, that is, to see; and to listen effectively, that is, to hear. By modelling this search in her poetry, she makes this devotional project her reader's, as she offers her own verse as something to be seen and heard, in itself an approach to Christ. Right seeing and right hearing may thus be understood as right *reading*. The poem "Day-Break" retells Peter's story in the first person, Noel making it her own testimony but simultaneously making it every reader's. The poem provides "St. John, xxi" as an epigraph: the final chapter of John's gospel, this passage tells of the risen Christ's appearance to his disciples, who have followed Peter's example and returned to their fishing boats. Impetuous Peter, who cannot at first distinguish the figure on shore, hears his Lord's voice and immediately jumps overboard in his haste to reach him. The first three stanzas of Noel's poem stress the misery and solitude of the speaking *I*, who initially is literally as well as metaphorically at sea, and benighted: "The night is dark . . . "; "my soul longs for light." In this state, all s/he can see is her/his own despicable nature: "my sins in all their shame appear." In the fourth stanza, a series of rhetorical questions draw in an implicitly addressed audience and universalise the plight of the speaker.

176 *Christian and Lyric Tradition in Victorian Women's Poetry*

Shall I be always thus, and fall,
    When highest good I seek,
With love so passionately strong,
    Yet treacherously weak?

By the sixth stanza, the singular pronoun has become the plural, inclusive "we," as the speaker wistfully locates assurance in hearing the sound of Christ's (now seemingly lost) voice: "It seems a dream . . . That we have heard Him breathing Peace,/ In that familiar tone." When the speaking *I* returns in the eighth stanza, this singular voice now reads as multiplied and generalised. The speaker longs to really see Christ, if he really is risen, and like Thomas wants to see "those pierced Hands." Speaker and devout reader join in the challenges facing them, which are difficulties of vision ("these baffling mists and blinding spray") that seem to encompass the modern condition as well as a Galilean lake.

And dimly on the distant strand,
    Just touched with morning light,
I see a Form—now half revealed,
    Now shrouded from the sight.

Peter's plight, which is the speaker's plight, has become the reader's plight—and a biblical intertext suggests this plight is in truth that of every Christian: I Corinthians 13:12 reads, "For now we see through a glass, darkly; but then face to face." When Christ's voice is finally heard in the poem, it is an invitation to "come and dine," an invitation that encompasses every Christian hearer and reader. The appeal of Noel's poem is to see, to hear, to read or follow this verse, and to come to Christ, in the words of the last line, "To be made one with Thee." The penultimate verse of Noel's source chapter (that is, verse 24 of John 21), is deeply suggestive for this poem, for it claims complete authenticity for the report borne by the book: "This is the disciple which testifieth of these things, and wrote these things: and we know that his testimony is true." In devotional verse that bears witness to the personal travails of the speaking *I*, Caroline Noel the Victorian woman devotional poet assumes the same kind of authentic authority as the biblical disciple, and the reader who is invited to see what she has seen is assured that 'her testimony is true.'

Appeals to look and to hear, abundant in Victorian women's devotional poetry, may thus be read as signs of the speaker's self-positioning before a reader who is 'taking instruction.' Most of Charlotte Elliott's volume *Hours of Sorrow* (1836) is made up of first-person verses about suffering, but in the introductory poem she explicitly dictates her relationship with her reader, which is undertaken through the writing and reading of such verses:

"Accept me Lord, for Thee I own" 177

> . . . The many scarcely taste the cup of bliss,
> Ere some rude stroke, e'en while its sweets they sip,
> Dashes it (oft for ever) from their lip.
> For such, for such alone, I tune my lay;
> They feel life's path a rough and thorny way;
> And, looking sadly round, no longer find
> Those who shed gladness on the track behind,
> Strewed it with flowers, illumed it with their smile,
> And toil, and care, and sorrow could beguile.
> These, as they pass along, depressed, forlorn,
> Suffering from man's neglect, perchance his scorn,
> Feeling the world no balsam can bestow,
> To soothe the aching heart, or medicine woe,
> May, midst their sorrows, lend a listening ear
> To strains whose purpose is their grief to cheer;
> To tell them where another heart found rest,
> Once, like their own, disquieted, unblessed,
> And where, though sought in vain on earthly ground,
> A balm of sovereign virtue may be found.

Elliott takes up characteristic figures of sight and sound as she charts what her readers need and what her verse can supply: her readers can no longer see gladness or even light on their path, but the poet/speaker instructs her audience that reading her poems will help them spiritually see and hear what they need.

Jane Euphemia Browne's "Renew a Right Spirit Within Me" (from *The Dove on the Cross, and Other Thoughts in Verse*, 1859) uses a different, assertively humble strategy for speaker self-display and direction of the reader's vision. Similarly to Noel's "Daybreak," which retells Peter's story to help position the speaker authoritatively before her audience, Browne takes over a male biblical voice, this time David. In a rewriting of Psalm 52 (in insistently perfect common metre), the speaker laments her inability to see God, or even see what she has done wrong. She then departs into an ultra-principled cataloguing of possible sins, which, in the stringency of the listing and disavowing of wrongdoings, presents what almost amounts to a demonstration of her own holiness.

> My Father, Thou hast hid Thy face;
> Why art Thou wroth with me?
> Take not from me Thy love and grace,
> Though I have grievëd Thee.
>
> Lord, I have communed with my heart,
> And I have tried to pray,

178   *Christian and Lyric Tradition in Victorian Women's Poetry*

Kneeling in solitude apart,
    Yet found not what to say.

If I have sinned through heedlessness,
    And injured or offended
Some little one whom Thou dost bless,
    Whom angels have attended;

If I have cherished in my heart
    Thoughts which Thou dost condemn,
Causing Thy Spirit to depart,
    Till I repent of them;

Oh, shew me where my error lies . . .

[. . .]

And in this faith I come to Thee
    To seek forgiving grace:
From secret sin, oh cleanse Thou me,
    And let me see Thy face.

In the very primness of the speaking *I*'s self-examination, and the matching formal perfection with which she clothes it, the speaker makes herself a spectacle of spiritual and metrical stringency. She laments her imperfections, but her verse tells another, less humble story.

In a related way, the apologetic prefaces that abound in volumes of women's devotional verses reveal as they disavow the poets' ambitions to work upon their readers. Winifred Iverson's preface to *God's Touch, and Other Poems* (1890) brims with third-person statements in which humility and assertion battle:

> . . . it only remains for the Author to say that, in publishing these few poems, her one desire has been, if possible, to help and stimulate the followers of our Lord Jesus Christ in the Divine life.
> Several of the poems have been printed separately, and have met with considerable acceptance, and thus it is hoped that their collection in one volume may be found helpful to some who may, perchance, find "heavenly treasure" in the earthly vessel.
> With no pretensions to literary excellence, but with the earnest prayer that our Lord and Master may accept and use them for His glory, they are sent forth in His service. (n.p.)

The preface claims the volume's sole aim to be "to help and stimulate" Christians in their walk—"helpful" is a word that comes up repeatedly in

"*Accept me Lord, for Thee I own*" 179

women's writing about their own devotional writing. Then Iverson ingenuously mentions the success of previous poems, only to again disclaim literary pretensions or ambitions, describing her art as an "earthly vessel" that may contain "heavenly treasure" which is emphatically not her own. She hopes for God's acceptance of her art—that he will *own* her.

The poem "Yea! Let Him take all" exemplifies Iverson's modest yet far-reaching aims. Exploring the entwined relationship of Christ and his redeemed beloved, each stanza meditates on a different word of the titular scriptural phrase, and each produces a self-addressed lesson: "Know I not . . . "; "Hush, my soul!" The first-person *I* becomes a teaching illustration, with the speaker's internal meditations deployed for the good of the reader, so that the self-address is simultaneously a testimony addressed to a listening audience:

> Yea! *let* Him take all,
> Know I not that He most surely
> Claims me His possession purely?
> Yet He waits for mine assenting,
> Waits my heart's entire relenting;
> Ay! but 'tis in glad surrender,
> Everything to Him I tender. (second stanza; emphasis in original)

As the poem ends in an apparent extremity of self-abandonment, it becomes clear from the mingling of first-person reflection and outwardly directed instruction and rhetorical questions that the speaker retains a very firm sense of her self and her mission:

> Yea! let Him take *all*!
> All—with nought of reservation;
> All—in perfect concentration:
> All! but what "the all" I proffer?
> What of worth can I e'er offer?
> Hush, my soul! shall aught restrain thee?
> Jesus gave His all to gain thee;
> So "let Him take all,"
> Who "all" desires,
> And with His own great love my poor heart fires. (emphasis in original)

Iverson's standing before her fellow "followers of our Lord Jesus Christ" is intimately related to—in fact constituted by—her self-described standing before the Jesus to whom she kneels and simultaneously compares herself. He gave all, so she offers all, presenting her poem as textual evidence of her self-tendering and the Lord's concomitant possession of her. Humble and proud, she states, "my poor heart fires" with Christ's own love; the "considerable acceptance" of her verse, noted in her preface, is thus simultaneously secured by and sign of her divine inspiration.

180 *Christian and Lyric Tradition in Victorian Women's Poetry*

Devotional poetry was one of the most popularly read and widely produced genres in the Victorian era, and this chapter has redefined that poetry and argued the particular significance of its deployment in the hands of its female authors. The defining element of Victorian women's devotional poetry is its creation and maintenance of a personal relationship between Christ and the poet-speaker. A redefinition focusing on relationality rather than on specific acts of worship or denominational emphases is important because the intimacy paradigm adopted by this verse (which reflects and contributes to the century's gradual move to a more loving and emotive Christianity) shows marked uniformity across the sectarian differences of the writers. Devotional poetry therefore demands re-evaluation as a distinct body of verse with its own distinct characteristics and ambitions.

I have suggested ways of engaging with this poetry that explore what it may offer to its women writers, without ignoring its problematic aspects. At an initial reading devotional verse does appear politically retrograde: a poetry of relationship, relentlessly focused on a woman's individual and personal bond with her God. In its assertion of emotive and specifically romantic attachment as the characteristic of faith-encounter between Christian and Lord, it also seems to eschew intellectual engagement. And further, devotional poetry's dominant paradigm of submission and suffering as characterising the relation between woman and Lord poses hurdles for feminist scholars trained to decry such oppressive models.

Yet this chapter has argued that devotional poetry does offer liberating possibilities for its female writers. The poets surveyed here react variously to the conundrum of creating relationship, through poetry that recognises the woman as an individual, desiring subject, but that also negotiates the potential rewards of submission to a dominating master. Far from apolitical, women's devotional verse is intimately concerned with power, status, and recognition. The Bride/Bridegroom paradigm from the Song of Solomon provides a particularly potent model for women poets looking for ways to privilege femininity and to re-imagine a romantic model that grants to the female partner status and agency. The development of the romantic pairing by a number of poets into an unsettling, occasionally violently imagined relationship of domination and suffering submission may fruitfully be read through frameworks that reveal the 'payback' of recognition for a voluntarily submissive partner. In the hands of poets like Christina Rossetti, Jean Ingelow, and Lucy Ann Bennett, the dynamics of a dominant/submissive relationship are interrogated with an emotional and psychological complexity that permits envisioning of a new, mutually fulfilling relationship with God. Across the spectrum of Victorian women's devotional poetry, depictions of striving submission reveal the stirrings of desire to reconstitute the relation between woman and Lord, and to create for women Christians recognition, status, and a degree of power.

Finally, spiritual ambition is ineluctably tied, in this body of work, to literary ambition. A particular characteristic of devotional verse is the deployment of 'sincerity poetics,' the elision between the dramatised speaker and the woman poet herself. Whether through expressions of groveling self-abandonment, through appeals to see, hear, and take example, and/or through displays of poetic and moral virtuosity which offer themselves as both record of and instruction in sanctity, women's devotional poetry reveals a powerful orientation towards a human audience as well as towards the partner-Christ. Devotional poetry helped create a community of Victorian women serving as mutual advisers and sages, enabling them to debate and to assert the standards for what it meant to be a Christian. At a fundamental level, devotional verse interrogates the terms of value in the construction of Christian identity, and valorises the feminine, childlike, and emotive. Enabling women poets to extend their claims as to what is 'mine' and as to their rights to enter and reshape religious discourse, devotional poetry ultimately enables women to expand the characteristics of a Christian. Victorian women produce out of devotional poetry liberatory models grounded on the primacy of the individual relationship with Christ. These models situate the (female) poet as Christian authority and sage, and allow her to participate in the construction of a communal, inclusive, expanded Body of Christ.

5 Virtue and Virtuosity
Style in the Victorian Woman's Religious Lyric

> And she could hear the deep-toned harmonies
> For ever chanted in creation's bounds,
> Unheard by duller ears:–for her whole soul
> Was as an echo, giving back the sounds
> With holy truth.
>
> —Jane Euphemia Browne, from "Light in Darkness"

Chapter 4 has discussed how devotionality in Victorian women's poetry, with its close links to cultural categories of sentimentality and femininity, has particular repercussions for the lyric genre in the period. The devotional mode, centred about expressions of intimacy and submissive humility, allows play with the dialectic of privacy and publicity, and permits the re-construction of the devout poet's standing before her earthly and heavenly audiences. Closer examination of the particular formal and linguistic choices in Victorian women's religious poetry will direct attention to how poets performed humility (spiritual and literary) through *style*, further complicating the relationship between the humble Christian and her public audience. Examining this body of work's characteristic aesthetics will also help assess the repercussions of a woman adopting the role of religious and poetic virtuoso. To this point, this book has analysed *what* Victorian women were saying in their religious poetry, examining their deployment of biblical source material and models, and has argued *why* they were writing religious verse, suggesting the benefits women sought from their choices of theme, genre, and mode. This final chapter considers the significance of *how* Victorian women were writing their religious verse, and examines what the stylistic and aesthetic features of this verse may reveal about women poets' aspirations in their negotiations with Christian and lyric traditions.

The Victorians themselves were deeply vexed by the question of how religious verse should be written. They struggled with how a religious or devotional poem should *seem* to its reader, and what ambitions could or should be communicated through its technical construction. Keble developed the concept of poetic Reserve to describe the way in which God works to veil His messages with seemly indirection; the poet, Keble suggests, should convey modesty of intent similarly veiled in Reserve. "It is required," Keble writes, " . . . in all poets, but particularly in sacred poets,

Virtue and Virtuosity 183

that they should seem to write with a view of unburthening their minds, and not for the sake of writing; for love of the subject, not of the employment" (*Occasional Papers* 88). For Keble, the poet should seem almost to speak involuntarily—and certainly should not draw attention to his own role through immodest or self-seeking literary flourish. He (Keble's poet is male) employs a veil of Reserve to ensure that no mindfulness of a public audience is displayed, and writes solely to 'unburthen' himself. In counterpoint to this view, the Reverend Horatius Bonar, himself a prolific and popular hymn-writer, saw the purpose of religious poetry as extending well beyond simply the (reserved) unburdening of a poet's heart. For Bonar, the intent to publish (literally, to make public) is indispensable to the moral purpose of a poet. Bonar's poet may be a man *or* a woman, and the poetic vocation means both to "sing her own song, in her own way, upon her own harp" *and also* to sing "for others." For Bonar, the working of a devotional lyric upon its reader is of central importance. In his introduction to Eliza Ann Walker's volume, *Hymns and Thoughts in Verse*, Bonar writes thus:

> The poet does not sing for himself, but for others; it may be for his fellow men at large, or for the Church of God; it may be for his own age, or for ages to come. Yet he does not the less on that account enjoy his song or reap its benefits. . . . Each hymn that has gone out from the most obscure minstrel has done its work, if it has taken possession of the Church, and helped to mould, or strengthen, or comfort, or build up a saint. It might not contain "thoughts that breathe and words that burn"; it might be plain and unpoetic—the merest utterance of intense spiritual feeling—but it took hold of men's ears and hearts. . . . Let the reader accept this little volume as that of one who has spoken from her heart; who has sung her own song, in her own way, upon her own harp . . . Again and again she has soothed herself and gladdened others with Christian song. (vii–ix)

For Keble, 'good' and religious poetry has a primarily inward, personal benefit, and how it should "seem" to external readers must be carefully regulated. For Bonar, 'good' and religious poetry is essentially outward-directed; while it does offer the poet himself or herself the benefits of 'soothing' and refining of the faculties, its greater significance lies in its work on others: it must aim for particular rhetorical effect. Bonar thus builds on but also departs from Keble's construction of poetry's nature as a safety-valve for the individual's overpowering emotions. Yes, Bonar writes, the poet should by all means soothe herself: utter intense spiritual feeling, speak from her heart, sing her own song—but she must also aim to gladden others with her Christian melody.

Beneath the surfaces of their differing messages about poetic purpose, both Keble and Bonar betray anxiety about the display of poetic virtuosity, the question of how pious verse should appear or *seem*. Keble warns against

184 *Christian and Lyric Tradition in Victorian Women's Poetry*

writing verse "for the love of the employment"; Bonar suggests, approvingly, that the most effective poetry may in fact be "plain and unpoetic," containing neither original thought nor vibrant phrasing nor stylistic flourish. Victorian women's religious poetry, in its negotiations between Keble's sincerity poetics of Reserve and Bonar's prescription of effective didacticism, both illustrates and seeks to respond to the anxieties engendered by the intersection of religious theme and display of poetic skill. Women poets took pains to demonstrate that they spoke from the heart, singing their own song in their own way, but the stylistic 'dress' of their work also suggests a love not just for the subject of their poems, but also for "the employment." Style becomes for Victorian women poets not just a means to an end, but also an end in itself.

Style's vexing relationship to artistic motivation has posed a central challenge for generations of religious poets and critics. In his introduction to *The New Oxford Book of Religious Verse* Donald Davie writes:

> For when a poet chooses a style, or chooses between styles, he is making a choice in which his whole self is involved—including, if he is a Christian poet, that part of himself which is most earnestly and devoutly Christian. The question is, for him: what sort of language is most appropriate when I would speak of, or to, my God? (xxviii–xxix)

Almost 150 years previously, in 1844, Elizabeth Barrett asked a very similar question to the one posed by Davie's ventriloquised, essentially male religious poet. Barrett explicitly engages with the problematic issue of who was entitled to treat sacred subjects and to speak of God, and *how* that person could do so. In her assertion that faith is essentially linked to lived experience, and that therefore it is not the exclusive territory of holders of church office—that is, men—but of all humans who live and experience faith, Barrett states firmly that as all are capable of experiencing devotion, all are equally entitled to utter that devotion. She also suggests that the form of utterance of that devotion should be divorced from the idea of 'fit' words and dictated forms; quotidian language, as long as it is devoutly uttered, is also acceptable language to clothe and praise God. Carefully, but nonetheless passionately, Barrett decries the generally held opinion,

> nearer to superstition than to religion, that there should be no touching of holy vessels except by consecrated fingers, nor any naming of holy names except in consecrated places. As if life were not a continual sacrament to man, since Christ brake the daily bread of it in His hands! As if the name of God did not build a church, by the very naming of it! As if the word God were not, everywhere in His creation, and at every moment in His eternity, an appropriate word! As if it could be uttered unfitly, if devoutly! (Preface to 1844 *Poems*, 1897 ed., xii–xiii)

Virtue and Virtuosity   185

Barrett defends her refusal of silence, her own utterance on sacred topics, on the grounds of heart-felt reverence: "by the principle of adoration, I . . . have been hurried into speech" (xiii). She also directs attention to the nature of that speech, and suggests its potentially democratic, inclusive, quotidian forms. Barrett turns Davie's formulation on its head: The question is, *for her*: what sort of language is most appropriate when I—a *woman*—would speak of, or to, my God? This chapter takes up the Davie/Barrett question and applies it to Victorian women, examining the language they used in their religious poetry and using those linguistic and stylistic choices as a lens through which to examine the development of concepts of the lyric and of the Christian in the nineteenth century.

The attention Victorian women poets paid to the 'exterior' elements of their verse, revealed in a wealth of linguistic, metrical, and stylistic ornamentation, indicates that style represents for these women a highly significant element of their project of self-definition as Christians and as poets. Rather than being torn, as McGann has suggested (*Poetics of Sensibility* 52), between separate poles of virtue and virtuosity, I contend that Victorian women poets sought to establish their claim to the former by demonstrating their poetic facility with the latter.[1] Women's many modest prefaces disclaiming poetic skill, or virtuosity, work paradoxically to foreground the value that these poets clearly place upon execution, as does the abundance of richly embellished technique that tends to weary a modern reader. This body of work's very vulnerability to particular stylistic criticisms may help identify the features that deserve re-evaluation. Victorian women's religious poems regularly present themselves as unmediated, sincere, artless effusions born solely out of response to God's greatness—Havergal's "The Song Chalice" being a case in point—but they are at the same time highly wrought works of art, packed with ornamental elements such as archaic diction, syntactic and figurative ornamentation, expostulations, ellipses, rhetorical questions, repetition, and elaborate and metronomically regular prosody. Undeniably, much of this body of work is aesthetically poor—belaboured, over-long, overly conscious of 'sounding poetical.' However, because this chapter is founded on the contention that Victorian women very consciously undertook 'aesthetic work' in their religious verse, I suggest that critics should therefore read these poems *as* aesthetic works, not apologetically but critically, to better explicate the particular ambitions voiced therein. When the workings of Victorian women's religious poetry are so foregrounded by the poets themselves, thoughtful readers should respond by asking what these workings are *working to achieve*. What might those aesthetic characteristics *do*, for women writers, and for the development of the genre? How do form and style in Victorian religious poetry help embody and promote women's ambitions to spiritual and literary standing? And what contribution do women poets make, through this particularly crafted verse, to both Christian and lyric traditions?

186   *Christian and Lyric Tradition in Victorian Women's Poetry*

These questions have, however, not really been formulated in Victorianist scholarship to this point, largely because the characteristic poetic ornamentation common to women's religious verse appears to post-Victorians as excessive, politically incorrect, even embarrassing. The relatively little modern criticism that has focused on such works has been dismissive of its lack of aesthetic quality, and generally has implicitly linked ornamental flourish with (insincere) emotional gush. David Cecil labeled "the average hymn [. . .] a by-word for forced feeble sentiment" (quoted Gardner, *Religion and Literature* 126). Llewellyn Jones labels the "spontaneous effusion" standard of women's poetry "mutterings," and more pointedly, as "anarchism of language" (199). Hoxie Neale Fairchild is particularly curmudgeonly in his dismissal of Victorian women's technical skill: "women poets of the Victorian Period proper had been granted the license to write messily and usually availed themselves of the privilege" (vol. 5, 33, n.36). As Jane Tompkins has trenchantly observed in her work on the nineteenth-century sentimental novel, both the affective and the devotional fell sharply from favour in the twentieth century:

> The very grounds on which sentimental fiction has been dismissed by its detractors, grounds which have come to seem universal standards of aesthetic judgment, were established in a struggle to supplant the tradition of evangelical piety and moral commitment these novelists represent. In reaction against their world view, and perhaps even more against their success, twentieth-century critics have taught generations of students to equate popularity with debasement, emotionality with ineffectiveness, religiosity with fakery, domesticity with triviality, and all of these, implicitly, with womanly inferiority. (*Sensational Designs* 123)

Tompkins' work on sentimental literature has significantly influenced my readings of the affectionalisation and devotionalisation of the lyric genre in the Victorian period. Informed critical readings of this body of work must, as Tompkins and Bourdieu have suggested in different ways, be aware of the political and literary assumptions underpinning the twentieth- and twenty-first-century denigration and neglect of much nineteenth-century sentimental, moralistic, and domestic literature. Unfortunately, even the more insightful studies of sentiment have tended to fall into the trap of avoiding the particular (particularly distasteful) role of religious sentiment. McGann, for example, omits from *The Poetics of Sensibility* any full consideration of religious sentiment, the relation of sentiment to the practice and imagining of Christianity, and in particular the possible deployment of sentiment in poetry for religious purposes. Our own largely uninterrogated bias, I contend, renders it all the more urgent to thoughtfully reassess the aesthetic characteristics and standards operating in the Victorian literary and religious context.

A further challenge for a critic attempting to reevaluate the function of stylistic features in Victorian women's poetry is posed by the vulnerability of such evaluations to charges of trying to identify an 'essential' female style.[2] I want to make clear that my point of inquiry in this chapter does not have to do with identifying a female style of religious poetry (it is readily demonstrable that key 'feminised' characteristics of religious poetry are also practised by male poets of the period). My inquiry rather has to do with how and why a style that was gendered feminine by the Victorians themselves came to be the expected style for religious poetry, and how women made use of this style both to develop the idea of the nature and role of the religious lyric in the Victorian period and to develop an idea of their own role as religious and literary virtuosi. Assessing how women poets used aesthetic features to help answer the persistent, potentially crippling question that they faced—how could they, as women, speak of God?—will help the modern reader better understand and better value the achievement of this body of verse. Both lyric and Christian traditions were influenced by Victorian women's verse, and the intersection of discourses of gender, poetry, and Christianity in the Victorian period reveals the suggestive inextricability of gender questions from aesthetic questions from questions of Christian faith, practice, and identity.

Fundamentally, the characteristic stylistic features of Victorian women's religious poetry are concerned with display. The conscious construction and display of decorativeness and obedience in this body of verse must be considered within a specifically Christian discourse. This highly stylised poetry works to demonstrate affective sincerity and to render the poet herself as well as her work an acceptable offering to the Lord, and may also be seen to be constructed like and operate like ritual: formal and formalised demonstrations of dedication and correctness that legislate divine response and acceptance. Stylistic practice further permits women Christian poets to foreground the importance of the immediate and personal into the impersonal and 'scientific' realm of theology, thereby incorporating a range of voices into monolithic Christian discourse. While the aesthetic features I identify and analyse in the course of this chapter's argument are not unique to religious poetry by women, these features are significantly wielded by female artists to help them challenge gendered constraints on the religious privilege and status available to women Christians in the Victorian period.

"Fripperies and Seductive Indulgences"

When Davie, Fairchild, and others decry the distinctive stylistic characteristics of Victorian women's religious poetry, to what features specifically are they referring? How can the particular aesthetic features of Victorian women's religious poetry be first described and then appropriately evaluated? A representative verse might help begin to anatomise the genre. The

188 *Christian and Lyric Tradition in Victorian Women's Poetry*

first three stanzas of "Jesus Saith . . . Follow Me," an anonymous poem printed in *The Christian Lady's Magazine* (vol. 1, 378), read:

> The sound hath fallen on mine ear,
>   I struggle to be free;
> And why should guilt, and doubt, and fear
>   Detain my soul from thee?
>
> On thee, O Christ! my guilt I cast,
>   A suppliant at thy throne;
> Thy blood can cancel all the past,
>   And thou my prayer wilt own.
>
> Lead, lead me on, my God, my King!
>   Yet, oh! the cup to drink,
> To tread the path of suffering,
>   My trembling soul doth shrink.

Into the third stanza alone are crammed two pairs of rhymes, two biblical allusions, rhetorical repetition, suffering ejaculation, sentence inversion, and archaic diction. The effort of fitting all of these poetic devices and words into a carefully conventional common metre stanza exhausts the energies of this slight verse; most modern readers would judge it unsatisfactory poetry, for the conveying of meaning has clearly been subordinated to embodying 'poeticalness.' (No straw man, this verse is entirely typical of the many hundreds of poems *The Christian Lady's Magazine* printed in its fifteen year run. A similar example of overwhelming poeticalness can be found in the next volume: "Lamentation of David Over Saul and Jonathan" [vol. 2, 25–27] so self-consciously fulfils the demands of the lyric that in eight double-quatrain stanzas it undertakes four separate apostrophes and emotes to the order of ten different metaphors for "dead.")

"Jesus Saith . . . Follow Me" exemplifies many of the features of Victorian women's religious poetry pilloried by twentieth-century criticism: primary charges include execution over substance, mawkishness, slight vocabulary and cliché phrasing, repetitiveness, metrical monotony, and ornamental excess. It embodies what might be labeled hyper-poeticisation, in which such elements as archaic diction, ornamental flourish, and metrical regularity are emphasised to the point of over-determination. Each of these elements deserves brief illustration.

To begin at a syntactic level: Victorian women religious poets make frequent and self-conscious use of archaic diction. Sometimes these word choices clearly echo the Elizabethan English of the Authorised Version of the Bible, particularly in the use of *thee*, *thou*, and '-eth' verb endings. Other poets draw both language and figuration from the ballad tradition; many others take their quaint language to the verge of baby-talk. Jane

Crewdson's delving into historical language, for example, aims to strike notes both of beauty and emotional appeal, but often tips the balance into excessively saccharine cuteness, as when she describes Christ as the "spotless lambkin" of God. Marianne Farningham is another enthusiastic proponent of the "t'wills" and "ne'ers" of decorative archaism; such archaic contractions often serve the dual purpose of 'beautifying' the verse and also, by eliminating syllables, preserving metrical correctness. Women persisted in using antiquated and consciously 'poetical' language throughout the period, as demonstrated in "A Question," which appeared in the *Women's Penny Paper* on February 1, 1890. It opens

> Ah, which methinks is best?
> The olden, deep unrest,
> Tumultuous yearnings of the impassioned soul, -
> The joy of the ideal . . . [3]

Often operating hand in hand with archaism in Victorian women's religious poetry is wordiness, or syntactic excess. Elizabeth Gifford's "Lilies" takes seriously the injunction of the biblical intertext, "consider the lilies of the field" (Matthew 6:28), and does so at considerable length, and with plenty of decorative archaisms:

> To such fair flowers He pointed, He who spake
> As spake none other; He interpreted
> For us their precious import, bade them bear
> Eloquent witness to a Father's love,
> Teach profound lessons of the mind of God,
> And speak of life and growth beyond their own,
> And promise food and raiment, and proclaim
> Vast stores of wealth for our incessant need,
> And set our anxious questionings at rest . . . (in *Poems*, 1897)[4]

Punctuating this characteristic voluminousness is a whole series of expostulatory effects, including such features as exclamations, ejaculations, invocations, sighs, Os, and ellipses. The already quoted *Christian Lady's Magazine* poem, "Jesus Saith . . . Follow Me," provides a rich illustration of this wealth of expostulation. In another example, Jean Sophia Pigott's "Not My Own" (in *A Royal Service, and Other Poems*, 1877) uses frequent italics as well as dashes and exclamation marks to convey emotional fervency, as demonstrated in the stanzas excerpted here:

> But this I have, and marveling at Thy grace,
>   I hesitate no more,—Thou lovest me!
> I *recognise* Thy right to this poor heart,
>   Thy right supreme, and yield it unto Thee.

190 *Christian and Lyric Tradition in Victorian Women's Poetry*

Oh! *reign* therein, and *keep* it wholly Thine;
    Make every pulse unto Thy blessed will
To beat so full, so true, that evermore
    My spirit Thou may'st sanctify and fill.
My Saviour and my Lord, to Thee I give
    My life, myself! . . . (emphasis in original)

Such poetic expostulations, which often read to a modern audience as emotional excess or even fakery, were in fact deployed by women poets to communicate just the opposite, emotional sincerity. 'More' was perceived by women poets, in this context, as distinctly 'better.'

A further decorative emotive feature, clearly linked to didacticism but also often detaching from any didactic aim, is that of the rhetorical question. Very frequently deployed in women's religious verse, the question mark occasionally loses connection to any discernable 'lesson,' becoming quite literally an ornamental extra. Eliza Hamilton was a prolific early Victorian poet, born in Dublin and raised Moravian; much of her work shows a strong Calvinist emphasis and at the same time a strong decorative urge. "Psalm LXXIII. 25" (in *Poems*, 1838) provides not the biblical paraphrase that might be expected from its title, but rather a meditation that ranges into the New Testament to supply a personal application of the message. The whole is studded with rhetorical questions that in their extended series seem utterly independent of any expectation of readerly response.

Here, in this wounding world,
    Whom, whom have we but Thee?
Is much of sweetness the reward
    Of all our blind idolatry?
We drink at love's bright fount;
    We drink, but do we thirst no more?
We bear a cross—but not the one
    Thou—Ever-blessed bore!
And do we easier find the yoke—
    And is the burthen light?
Lighter than thine? that thus we cast
    Thy pitying tears from sight!
Dost never weariness of heart
    Come over us like death?
Need we no rest unto our souls,
    No anchorage of faith? . . .

One of the most striking features of Victorian women's religious verse, and a particularly significant aspect of its aesthetic project, is its characteristic prosody. Extreme metrical regularity and *sameness* defines the overwhelming majority of this body of work. Certainly, variation does occur, and a number of female poets demonstrate highly conscious metrical manipulation in sonnets or other even more elaborate forms. However, the most frequently used stanzaic form throughout the broad corpus of women's religious verse is the regular quatrain, and the most frequent metrical scheme, common metre.[5] Mrs. Alexander's immensely popular *Songs for Little Children* (which contains "All Things Bright and Beautiful") offers perhaps the best known examples of hyper-orthodox metre and rhyme, but her regimented regularity is far from atypical. Lydia Denning, for example, in "The Redeemed shall return to Zion with Songs" (in *Songs of the Better Land*, 1868), demonstrates insistently regular rhyme and metre (in this case long metre), as well as many other characteristic features, including the devotional speaking *I*, cliché and repetitive phrases, and a wealth of 'sincere' expostulatory markers. The first four stanzas read as follows:

> O dear, delightful, happy day,
> When Jesus washed my sins away,
> When with His blood He made me white,
> And pure in His all-glorious sight!
>
> On this delightful day of days,
> To Thee I'll sing a hymn of praise,
> And tell this wondrous work of Thine,
> Thy loving-kindness how divine!
>
> This is the day when first Thy light
> Dawned on my soul so long in night,
> When first Thy praise employed my tongue,
> When first heaven's joyous songs I sung.
>
> O glorious day! O joyful hour!
> When my glad heart first felt Thy power,
> When first Thy saving grace I knew,
> Thy loving-kindness, Oh! how true …

Nor are such determinedly, jinglingly regular metres confined to the work of minor religious poets; they also appear in the verse of highly accomplished poets, including Elizabeth Barrett. Amongst Barrett's early, explicitly religious poetry may be found "Hymn," (in *An Essay on Mind and Other Poems*, 1826), which counsels readers to call on God, in almost unexceptionably regular common metre:

> Since without Thee we do no good,
>   And with Thee do no ill,
> Abide with us in weal and woe,—
>   In action and in will.

192   *Christian and Lyric Tradition in Victorian Women's Poetry*

In weal,—that while our lips confess
  The Lord who 'gives,' we may
Remember, with an humble thought,
  The Lord who 'takes away . . . ' (first two of seven stanzas)

Repetition underpins all these characteristic decorative formal features of Victorian women's religious verse, whether that repetition is of word or phrase, exclamation, rhyme, regular stress, or trope. For example, Eliza Hamilton's "Nothing Between" (in *Hymns for the Weary*, 1878) repeats the titular phrase three times in each of eight matching stanzas, as exemplified here:

Nothing between, Lord, nothing between,
Let me Thy glory see,
Draw my soul close to Thee,
Then speak in love to me,
Nothing between.

Jane Besemeres takes another frequently used approach, beginning each stanza (here the first three of six) with the identical phrase:

One is my Master, even Christ;
  No other do I see
Worthy of all my heart's deep love,
  And Christ says—'Follow me.'

One is my Master, even Christ;
  All other voices seem,
Save only as they echo His,
  Like voices in a dream.

One is my Master, even Christ;
  If He but guide my way,
Appointing all my daily work,
  How can I go astray? (in *Vanished Faces, and Other Poems*, 1884)

Marianne Farmingham's poem "Alone" (in *Lays and Lyrics of the Blessed Life*, 1860) begins every quatrain with a line that twice repeats that single word: "Alone, alone." Emma Muir's *God's Octave, and Other Poems* (1896) makes much use of reiterated phrases and incremental repetition: in "Trials not Troubles," for example, every alternate line of a two-page-long poem is "Nearer to Him," and in "Unselfishness," each triplet stanza ends with the one word, deeply indented: "Unselfishness." These repetitive effects, perhaps more than any other feature, tend to lend women's religious poetry of the period an appearance of uniformity which can, in the mass, seem numbing to a modern reader.

In the nineteenth century, however, decorative religious verse was a hot commodity. The tremendous popularity of the decorative religious poetry described here may be seen in its mass production and mass consumption in the period. Nonetheless, Victorian attitudes to the ornamented style also display ambiguity and unease. Poetic ornamentation was often denigrated in literary criticism, with critics' complicated attitude to decoration and flourish further troubled by correlations between style and gender. Nineteenth-century critics frequently identify decorativeness as profoundly feminine as well as essentially untrustworthy (or arguably, profoundly feminine *and thus* essentially untrustworthy). In an 1864 essay in the *National Review*, Walter Bagehot attempted to define and evaluate three styles of poetry, which he dubbed pure, ornate, and grotesque. "The definition of *pure* literature is that it describes the type in its simplicity," he writes, using Wordsworth as an example of that praised pure style. "The whole which is to be seen appears at once and through the detail, but the detail itself is not seen" (38). Ornate style, on the other hand, which "works not by choice and selection, but by accumulation and aggregation" (45), presents plenty of detail and description. This quantity of detail is visible in (and for) itself, not just acting as a conveyance to the 'true message' of the poem, and thereby producing "the conviction that [this verse] is not the highest art, that it is somehow excessive and overrich" (47). While Bagehot uses overblown passages of Tennyson's *Enoch Arden* to illustrate his criticisms of ornate art, his various descriptions of the ornate style clearly feminise it, as when he contrasts "a mist of beauty, an excess of fascination, a complication of charm" with the "simple, defined, measured" pure style, and compares the former to "moonlight" and the latter to "sunlight." In one heavily loaded phrase, Bagehot indicates that ornate art is not only feminine, but potentially morally questionable: "though the *rouge* of ornate literature excites our eye, it also impairs our confidence" (48; emphasis in the original). He does not wholly damn the ornate style, pointing out that it can describe "inferior" scenes that the pure style cannot, and that it aims to idealise. But in describing the style by analogy as a landscape "too soft, too delicate, too vegetable" (48), Bagehot clearly draws an implicitly gendered value judgment, and as clearly communicates his belief that the unreliable, feminine ornate style needs some (manly) stiffening up.

In an 1876 discussion of poetic construction and decoration that considers both men and women writers, the Victorian critic Edmund Clarence Stedman writes:

> The rule of architecture may safely be applied to poetry,—that construction must be decorated, not decoration constructed. The reverse of this is practiced by many of those writers, who are abundantly supplied with poetical material, with images, quaint words, conceits, and dainty rhymes and alliteration, and who laboriously seek for themes to constitute the groundwork over which these allurements can be displayed.

194   *Christian and Lyric Tradition in Victorian Women's Poetry*

> Having not even a definite purpose, to say nothing of real inspiration, their work, however curious in technique, fails to permanently impress even the refined reader, and never reaches the heart of the people,—to which all emotional art is in the end addressed. Far more genuine, as poetry, is the rude spontaneous lyric of a natural bard, expressing the love, or patriotism, or ardor, to which the common pulse of man beats time. The latter outlasts the former; the former, however acceptable for a time, inevitably passes out of fashion,—being but a fashion,—and is sure to repel the taste of those who, in another age, may admire some equally false production that has come into vogue. (289)

Emotional art is equated here with "curious technique," and denigrated as both evanescent and 'lacking'; execution over substance is roundly criticised. Stedman separates out having something to say, which is something *truly* felt, from mere technique and quirks of fashion, praising "simplicity and freshness" above all else. He deprecates "in the first place obscurity and hardness" (xv) and in the second, "that excess of elaborate ornament, which places decoration above construction, until the sense of originality is lost—if, indeed, it ever has existed" (xvi). Stedman uses a specifically and profoundly negative gendered term in relation to an overly decorated literary structure, describing himself as manfully and "steadfastly opposing *meretricious* efforts to attract notice by grotesque, fantastic, and other artificial means" (xvi, my emphasis). Like Bagehot, Stedman elides ornamentation with femininity, and with (specifically female) untrustworthiness.[6]

Interestingly, one of the few highly regarded female Victorian literary critics voiced a similar position in regard to decorative style. Alice Meynell, whose literary criticism was unique amongst women writers in its range, popularity, and influence, often used her critical introductions to poetic collections to communicate her views on poetic style and her personal preference for perfection of aesthetic achievement over epic range or grandiose ambition.[7] Of Elizabeth Barrett Browning, Meynell wrote, "her poetry has genius. It is abundant and exuberant, precipitate and immoderate; but these are faults of style and not deficiencies of faculties. When she is gentle she is classic and all but perfect" (quoted Evans 184). In her famous essay "Rejection," first published in the *National Observer*, October 24, 1891, Meynell offers a defense of her preferred refined, "gentle" literary style. She praises simplicity and discrimination (the word "rejection" serves Meynell as a close synonym for discrimination), noting both the sacrifices and rewards of exercising aesthetic editorialism. Herself a poet of extreme, almost oracular spareness, Meynell refuses what she terms "the joys of decorators," and asks, "when we write, what hinders that we should refrain from Style past reckoning?"—deliberately setting herself apart from the unwieldy past female "tradition" (*Rhythm of Life* 81). In many ways a more generous and a more judicious critic than her male counterparts, Meynell draws no implicit link between decorative and ornate writing and the writing of women. However, like her male counterparts, she denigrates decoration as facile and weak.

Alfred Miles, in contrast to Meynell, is both resolute and sweeping in his gendered evaluations of poets in *The Poets and the Poetry of the Nineteenth Century*. Miles draws a distinction between style displaying polish and style displaying enthusiasm, assigning both substantive thought and aesthetic polish to the domain of male poets, and enthusiastic feeling and the moral viewpoint to female poets. In assessing the work of Sarah Flower Adams, Miles counterposes "lyrical enthusiasm" to "the constructive faculty," judging that "the moral charm . . . takes precedence of the artistic, as is to be expected in the work of a true woman" (218). Echoes of this statement, "the work of a true woman," were frequently heard in the period. Less fine artists, women were held to always reveal themselves as women through their writing style.

Thus a 'feminised style' was problematically conceptualised and articulated by the Victorians. LaPorte has written thoughtfully of the nineteenth-century conflation of gender difference and literary difference, noting that "no tradition of writing in the nineteenth century is more self-consciously feminine than the poetess tradition" (160). The linking of gender and genre distinction was broadly assumed by the Victorians, who associated 'feminine writing' with subtlety of perception, tenderness of emotion, and sweetness of diction, as well as 'prettiness' of ornament. As LaPorte trenchantly notes, "Victorian models for women's and men's verse thus conditioned the production and reception of poetry" (161), even when practical instances of gendered generic difference evaded capture.[8] A 'feminine' style, after all, was definitely not restricted to female practitioners; Keble provided a significant exemplar of emotive and tender lyric verse, as well as extremely regular metricality,[9] and other male religious poets including Henry Francis Lyte, James Montgomery, and James Edmeston made frequent use of such staple elements of women's poetry as the devotional speaking *I*, expressions of expostulatory emotion, and various kinds of ornamental repetition. An example may be found in Edmeston's "Meditation Upon Christ" (in *Closet Hymns and Poems*, 1846).

> What wondrous words are those!
>   Yes—"Jesus wept!"
> How much do they disclose
>   Of all that slept
> Unspoken in the kind Redeemer's breast—
> Love, pity, sorrow, felt, though unexpress'd,
>   Yes, in those falling tears,
>   I volumes read,
>   Fill'd with what most endears
>   To me who need
> A Saviour, who I feel can always be

196 *Christian and Lyric Tradition in Victorian Women's Poetry*

Touch'd with affection, kindness, sympathy.

> I too am called to weep,
> And what relief!
> Christ hath an interest deep
> In all my grief:
> Yes, "Jesus wept!" sorrow he felt and knows,
> And feels and sympathises in my woes.

Additionally, overtly feminised evaluations were also frequently applied to male poets, particularly in the genre of religious poetry. The *Edinburgh Review*, for example, assessed the minor poet Bernard Barton in clearly domesticated, sentimentalised, and feminised terms:

> The staple of the whole poems is description and meditation—description of quiet home scenery, sweetly and feelingly wrought out; and meditation, overshadowed with tenderness, and exalted by devotion—but all terminating in soothing and even cheerful views of the conditions and prospects of mortality. (quoted in Miles *The Poets and the Poetry*, vol. 11, 71)

Stedman, in discussing Victorian hymnology, encompasses the work of male poets Keble, Lyte, Montgomery, Edmeston, Bowring, Milman, and Moir, as well as Sarah Flower Adams and Charlotte Elliott, with this group of attributes: "tender beauty of sentiment and expression . . . elaborate sweetness, refinement, emotional repose" (277). Such feminised markers attached to piety and to devotional poetry in the abstract, without necessarily indicating the author of that devotional poetry. Clearly, most of these attributes convey an overtly positive judgment, but it is also clear that when femininity is associated with specific issues of aesthetics, a semi-articulated anxiety hovers close to the surface.

On the one hand praising lyrical elaborateness and beauty as markers of piety and sincerity, and on the other decrying those same elements as 'artificial' and 'meretricious,' Victorian critics have particular difficulty with decorative lyricism in the specific context of religious poetry. In religious writing, rhetorical display unavoidably suggests self-seeking. Isaac Watts, the great eighteenth-century hymn-writer, stated he felt duty-bound to refuse aesthetic and stylistic temptations in composing his religious lyrics, writing of his own *Hymns and Spiritual Songs*, "some of the Beauties of Poesy are neglected, and some willfully defac'd."[10] Critics in the Victorian period echo Watts and other earlier writers, particularly Samuel Johnson, in decrying decorative aesthetic effects in poetry that seeks to treat God. Johnson's famous preface to the *Life of Waller* set up certain standards that have flavoured many subsequent commentaries on religious verse. "Of sentiments purely religious, it will be found that the most simple expression is the most sublime," Johnson wrote. "The ideas of Christian Theology are too simple for eloquence, too sacred for fiction, and too majestick for ornament; to recommend them by tropes and figures is to magnify by a concave mirror the sidereal hemisphere" (vol. 1, 292–3). As David Norton has shown, nineteenth-century commentators expressed their reverence for the language of the King James Bible in similar terms to those Johnson used, opining that the best possible language to speak of God is unimpeachably pure and simple. Thus an unsigned nineteenth-century appreciation of the Authorised Version describes its language as "distinguished by a general simplicity of expression, which the most uncultivated mind may comprehend, and the most cultivated admire,"[11] and an alternate translation of the Bible was criticised by the *Quarterly Review* in 1819 on the grounds that the translator had "no relish or perception of the exquisite simplicity of the original."[12] In the twentieth century, Donald Davie reveals his critical inheritance when he claims (rather controversially) that Christian poets throughout the ages have adhered to a poetics that exalts the plain style as the appropriate method of discussing divinity and a human's relation to the divine, eschewing elaborateness and decoration: "the only language proper for such exalted purposes is a language stripped of fripperies and seductive indulgences, the most direct and unswerving English" (xxix). Davie sees, it can be imagined, very little value in the characteristic Victorian woman's religious verse. Twentieth- and twenty-first-century reception of this body of work has been deeply influenced by dicta elevating simplicity as characteristic of the 'best' religious expression, and denigrating all "fripperies and seductive indulgences."

Popular but critically denigrated; practised by both men and women religious poets but gendered female in the most pointed criticism; Victorian poetic ornamentation deserves a closer, disinterested examination. Investigation of how the decorativeness of Victorian women's religious poetry functions must take into account its self-consciousness. Decorativeness in this body of work is *displayed*; it is a strategy. To better assess it, we should evaluate this poetry on its own terms, analysing its frequently self-reflexive nature in discussing itself as a work of art. In these poems, I contend, execution *is* substance, as stylistic features are used as a way of transforming the poem (and its producer) into decorative, feminised, acceptable offerings to the Lord. While the surface message of a woman's devotional poem may be self-effacing, the stylistic elements of that poem invite attention and, as tangible demonstrations of correctness, they assert their value as essential functions of the poem. Floweriness of phrase, versification, and trope may embody for modern readers Victorian decorative excess, but for Victorian women poets, these elements of form take on sacramental significance, as they postulate that form may communicate Truth. Just as individual poets' overt self-depreciation often conceals keen audience awareness and canny self-marketing, adherence to a decorative and consciously feminised stylistic model produces a means of expanding the woman's poetic role and spiritual status.

198   *Christian and Lyric Tradition in Victorian Women's Poetry*

Religious poems that comment upon themselves as artworks offer re-evaluations of the significance of decoration and the decorative artist in a Christian economy. Adelaide Procter's "One by One" provides an example of how a woman's verse may manoeuvre by means of style with a highly conventional theme, to produce provocative ambiguities and questionings of that theme, and ultimately to offer a reevaluation of both poem and poet. Formal elements in "One by One" repeatedly question and complicate the surface message, which is the popular theme of *vanitas mundi*: repetition, the primary aesthetic feature of the poem, communicates a message supplemental to – in fact, contradictory to – the surface message of disengagement from earth. Eight quatrains repeat seven times the formula "one by one," or a variation thereof. The poem begins:

> One by one the sands are flowing,
>   One by one the moments fall;
> Some are coming, some are going;
>   Do not strive to grasp them all.

The progression of stanzas, and their neatly identical forms (*abab* rhymes, trochaic tetrameter kept flawless with a deliberation visible in the accent mark in the word "armèd") serve to illustrate the theme of ever-fleeting, and thus endlessly repeatable, barely distinguishable moments. But the poem also complicates the theme by equating this message—enshrined in artfully arranged words—with a lasting artwork, thereby offering in the poem a reformulation of the biblical intertext, "Lay up for yourselves treasures in heaven." The poem both posits that intangible heavenly reward in the world to come and presents *in itself* an achieved treasure. The double themes of the poem are expressed most neatly in the sixth stanza:

> Every hour that fleets so slowly
>   Has its task to do or bear;
> Luminous the crown, and holy,
>   When each gem is set with care.

In a poem that advises the reader to be mindful of how fleeting moments are, and to live wisely by fulfilling "one by one thy duties," this poem stands as an act of both filling and retaining those slowly fleeting hours, by meeting its own advice of undertaking a needful task. The poem stands as a task completed and, in its paradoxical nature as on the one hand the spontaneous work of a minute and on the other an enduring work of art—a lasting ink imprint on white paper—it evades evanescence. The work of creating the poem is implicitly equated with the action recommended *in* the poem: forming a heavenly crown for oneself through right attitudes and duties fulfilled. Thus the excessive structuredness of this poem, its almost overdetermined formalism, illustrates the commended action of carefully setting a crown with gems, duly arranged; the poem describes and enacts a rite which grants its creator distinction as a privileged and potent spiritual minister.

Procter regularly deployed the trope of creating a crown or chaplet as a metaphor for composing poetry; she takes up this figure in many individual poems and it also lends the title for her 1861 volume, *A Chaplet of Verses* (as noted in Chapter 3, this was a devotionally themed collection produced to benefit a Roman Catholic refuge for destitute women). Comparisons between their own poetic work and other decorative arts appear regularly in women's religious verse, enabling women to comment more or less obliquely about the role and significance of their poetry. The arts used as metaphors vary widely, though certainly the most popular comparison is that drawn between poetry and song, often harp-accompanied. Other women sought out more unusual parallels: for example, both Procter in "The Carver's Lesson" and Bessie Rayner Belloc in "The Cathedral" take up the trope of stone-carving to meditate on the import of a possibly little-regarded but suggestively durable art form. Distinctions between ephemerality and lasting value underpin many more women's poems about art, and, in many of these, the implicit gendering of particular kinds of artistic creation becomes part of the critique. An anonymous contributor to the *Victoria Magazine*, in "Thoughts Suggested by a Line of Mrs. Barrett Browning's," uses the metaphor of spinning to critique the productions of a woman's life, all too often as devoid of substance as a "spider's web" instead of a spiritual, heaven-focussed "blest spinning well begun" (vol.6 454–5). Isa Gillon Fergusson's "Alpha and Omega" (in *Parables in Song*, 1889) deploys the similarly feminised figure of weaving to instruct the (female) reader to faithfully complete the task that God has assigned her: dedicatedly weaving fabric is the feminised equivalent of Paul's injunction to the Christian to "run the race."[13]

Such figures show Victorian women to be deeply conscious of the 'working' of their verse, and of how those workings relate to gender roles and to lasting renown. While these workings are often characterised by a degree of excess, a more illuminating lens through which to assess them is that of *deliberateness*. Although Fairchild's statement that Victorian women poets usually wrote "messily" suggests that technical and metrical precision was a rarity in this body of verse, in fact women religious poets frequently turned their extreme formal consciousness to the production of very finely wrought poetic forms. Such poems insist that their nature as aesthetic objects be read as part of their thematic message. Havergal, who uses a very specific metaphor for the production of art in "Life Mosaic," presents an apposite example of how the deliberately wrought form of a poem may interact with the content in such a way as to produce a message provocatively different from the explicitly stated theme.

> Master, to do great work for Thee, my hand
> Is far too weak! Thou givest what may suit—

> Some little chips to cut with care minute,
> Or tint, or grave, or polish. Others stand
> Before their quarried marble fair and grand,
>   And make a life work of the great design
>   Which Thou hast traced; or, many-skilled, combine
> To build vast temples, gloriously planned.
> Yet take the tiny stones which I have wrought,
>   Just one by one, as they were given by Thee,
> Not knowing what came next in Thy wise thought.
> Set each stone by Thy master-hand of grace,
>   Form the mosaic as Thou wilt for me,
> And in Thy temple-pavement give it place.

The sonnet's speaker indicates a feminine gender from the first line, as she humbly disclaims any ability to undertake "great work," for which, as for heavy labour, "my hand is far too weak!" The materials her master gives her are suitably diminutive, "little chips," and her tasks are feminised (tint, engrave, polish), as is her approach to the tasks, "with care minute." Havergal employs the rest of the octet to contrast her little work, described predominantly in monosyllables, with that of those masculinised, "many-skilled" and polysyllabic figures who sculpt marble and can "build vast temples, gloriously planned."

Yet Havergal uses form to complicate the surface theme of humility, most obviously in her choice of a highly wrought Petrarchan sonnet both to illustrate and defend her own art/lifework. She begins her defense at the turn of the sonnet, with the word "Yet," and implores God to accept her work, which she deprecates ("tiny," "just one by one,") even as she presents it as an acceptable offering. Again using a motif that frequently appears in her work, the speaker-poet suggests that God not only gives her the materials but also forms the design for what she produces, setting those finely wrought stones (or poetic lines) "by Thy master-hand of grace" into a mosaic destined to be given place "in Thy temple-pavement." In such a consciously designed poetic form as the sonnet, these mentions of "great design" have an unignorable self-referential element, underscored by the "care minute" the poet-speaker displays in the perfect rhyme scheme and the metrical deliberation (for example, in the trochaic substitutions of "Set each stone" and "Form the mosaic," which foreground God's activity within the poet's own). By troping on ornamentation, and also by using formal elements to complicate the sonnet's message, Havergal's poem demonstrates a complex combination of humility, self-deprecation, faith and obedience in action, a commitment to one's own art work, and an eye to eternal significance.

Repetition arguably functions as the single most significant stylistic feature of Victorian women's verse. The charge of repetitiveness, often (and absolutely fairly) leveled at nineteenth-century devotional poetry, deserves more scrupulous interrogation, as repetition is used by women poets to explore the particular outcomes of creating decorative artworks in a Christian economy. Particularly in the context of its linking of verse to prayer, and of its complex relationship to ritual, repetitive technique takes on added layers of significance because prayer and ritual, which may be beautifully crafted in and of themselves, are also directed towards achieving additional, specific desired ends. Decorative repetition takes many forms in these poems. Individual words, particular phrases, or certain tropes are repeated; grammatical and syntactic parallels drawn; and forms of incremental repetition constructed in which repeated structures are continually added to and continually re-evaluated. These many variants of repetition operate in multiple ways: as a way of structuring relationship with God, as a sign of conscious artistic production, and also, as they elevate the role of formal elements in relation to the poem's integral message, as an act of self-honouring assertion on the part of the artist. Poetic repetition in religious verse provides the poet with textual means of asserting spiritual control.

Drawing a suggestive parallel, the Victorian Stedman highlights repetition as he compares the poetry of Procter specifically and of women devotional poets more generally to the particular act of telling the rosary:

> . . . it is like telling one's beads, or reading a prayer-book, to turn over [Procter's] pages, so beautiful,–so pure and unselfish a spirit of faith, hope, and charity pervades and hallows them. These women, with their melodious voices, spotless hearts, and holy aspirations, are priestesses of the oracle. Their ministry is sacred. . . . (280)

The link between poem and prayer that Stedman makes here, a link made across the Victorian period, drew in part from the Tractarian-influenced expressive poetics that viewed the lyric poem as the emotional, unmediated outburst of a soul. The persistence of the paradigm is remarkable. At the start of the Victorian period the piously evangelical *Christian Lady's Magazine* printed numerous poems entitled "A Prayer," an entirely conventional choice—but at the end of the century the far less pious, far more radical *Women's Penny Paper* was still continuing the same practice. Popular poets from Lucy Bennett to Charlotte Elliott published poems with titles like "My Prayer" or "Prayer to the Saviour," and many other women entitled their poems with phrases from other, famous prayers, as, for example, Eliza Cook does in "Hallowed Be Thy Name" and "Thy Will Be Done." This seemingly unproblematised self-identification of lyric output as sincere, soulful, prayerful expression begins, however, to appear more complicated when the outcomes of the incantatory repetition employed by these poems are examined. Unexpected layers of meaning and assertiveness may be found when a poet constructs a devotional lyric in such a formally patterned and consciously repetitive fashion that it resembles, in Stedman's phrase, "telling one's beads."

202   *Christian and Lyric Tradition in Victorian Women's Poetry*

Many of these prayer-poems, which communicate an extreme consciousness of form and of the particular relationship of form and content, help poets seek to regulate the "interchange 'twixt earth and heaven."[14] In Emma Muir's volume *God's Octave, and Other Poems* (1896), the first-person singular pronoun predominates, as is typical of devotional verse, and similarly typically many poems are addressed directly by a speaker to her God, as prayers. The representative "Just as Thou Wilt" uses phrasal repetition as a means of regulating and thus controlling not only the poet-speaker's own expression but also the expressive answering capabilities of God himself.

> Just as Thou wilt, Lord,
>   Sickness or health;
> Just as Thou wilt, Lord,
>   Poverty, wealth;
> Just as Thou wilt, Lord,
>   If I'm only Thine,
> To serve Thee on earth,
>   Then in glory to shine.
>
> Just as Thou wilt, Lord,
>   Teach me the way
> Daily to seek Thee,
>   To serve and obey.
> Just as Thou wilt, Lord,
>   Shall all be the rest,
> For well do I know
>   That Thy way is the best.
>
> Just as Thou wilt, Lord,
>   Live Thou in me;
> Happy my life, Lord,
>   Joyous and free,
> To one so unworthy,
>   If grace be but given
> To tread the bright pathway
>   From earth up to heaven . . . (first three of five stanzas)

The dactylic dimeter wraps from line to line with a relentless forward movement; this metrical inexorability matches the repeated "Just as Thou wilt, Lord," which may be read as assurances directed to the Lord or equally to the self. Formally, the poem admits of no diversion from the "bright pathway" it traces: continually rearticulating the words that bind her and God in equal measure, the speaker will follow God's direction, and she assures herself (and reminds her Lord) of her inevitable reward. In this way, Muir's

Virtue and Virtuosity 203

prayer-poem demonstrates the contractual operation that Hannah More describes in *Bible Rhymes*:

> Mark, how the author's hallow'd lays
> Begin with prayer, and end with praise!
> Commerce, how sure! which, while it gives
> Due payment, rich returns receives . . .

"Commerce, how sure!" rejoices More, her poem (like Muir's) formalising the rules that structure the relationship between author and God in twin ways. These poets 'formalise' relations into law; at the same time, they enshrine those rules in regulated, poetic *form*, thereby granting themselves, as poets, legislative authority.

In this fashion, repetition of biblical words and specifically biblical promises may also serve to create affirmations of contract between the prayerful poet and the God who must respond.[15] Charlotte Elliott's "Hebrews XIII.5" begins:

> Promise of truth immutable,
> Whose preciousness no tongue can tell,
> Let me repeat and weigh thee well—
>   "Never will I forsake thee."

The poem progresses to nine further highly repetitive four-line stanzas, the first three lines of which rhyme uniformly in regular iambic tetrameter, and the fourth line of which takes the form of either "'Never will I forsake Thee'," quoted, to represent the words of God, or "Never wilt Thou forsake me," a line printed without quotation marks, representing the supposedly unmediated words of the speaker. The speaker's words in the first stanza, "let me repeat and weigh thee well," provide a key to the poem's ambitions. Although the poet-speaker uses the word "thee," she makes it clear she's repeating and weighing *the words of the biblical promise*, not God himself (she capitalises all pronouns relative to God); her focus in this poem is on words and their constructive power. The incantatory power that inheres in the words appears to be suggestively mobile, as the supplicant speaker both cajoles God to repeat these words to her: "Say to me, Saviour, from above . . . ", and comes close to commanding God: "Still wilt Thou, Lord, thus speak to me." Elliott's alternating use and omission of quotes around the key, repeated phrase show the words—and the instructional power—going from mouth to mouth. The final two stanzas illustrate:

> Never, though I may turn from Thee,
> Vile, profitless, ungrateful be,
> Still wilt Thou, Lord, thus speak to me—
>   "Never will I forsake thee."

204   *Christian and Lyric Tradition in Victorian Women's Poetry*

Lord, it is like Thee thus to speak—
No more I ask, no more I seek—
Thy covenant sure Thou wilt not break—
    Never wilt Thou forsake me.

God's words conclude seven of the ten stanzas; the speaker's, three; but the poem as a whole closes with the speaker's own voice. In the last stanza she reaffirms the promise to herself, and defines God as the one who says what it is that she wants and expects said: "Lord, it is like Thee thus to speak." Through controlling articulation, by means of formal repetitive effects, the speaker affirms her power over a discourse of redemption, commitment, and empowerment.

While repetition is an integral feature of the way these prayer-poems structure a seemingly humble address to an all-powerful God, repetitive textual effects are simultaneously inescapably self-referential. Poetic repetition may be seen to take on a circular function which, in addition to directing the mind outward to the God addressed, also continually draws attention to itself in a self-affirming round of not-the-same yet-the-same. Anthropologist Mircea Eliade, in *The Sacred and the Profane*, notes the circularity of the temporal space opened up by repetitive ritual: "Religious man lives in . . . sacred time, [which] appears under the paradoxical aspect of a circular time, reversible and recoverable, a sort of eternal mythical present that is periodically reintegrated by means of rites" (70). Procter creates this kind of "eternal mythical present" in her poetry's repeated invocations and appeals to God and to the Madonna; in a controlled, poetic stasis she can constantly reiterate and recreate relationship between her Lord and her speaker.[16] "The Peace of God," for example, directs a series of appeals to God the Father, presenting repeated petitions for peace amidst the world's clamour: "We ask for Peace, O Lord!" While the request formula adopts a position of humility, the repeated reformulation of the request foregrounds the central role of the Christian issuing it, granting her an undeniable degree of visibility and power. The knowledgeable speaker insists on defining the kind of peace that God should give, closing the fourth and final stanza:

Give us that Peace, O Lord,
Divine and blest,
Thou keepest for those hearts who love Thee best.

In poems like Procter's, circling about acts of petition that ultimately emphasise the petitioner's knowledge and degree of *self*-assurance, the poet does not direct the reader's thoughts to a future state; rather, she centres consideration on her present work, the poem, in which she herself dictates action, response, and relation.

Another way of examining the circular, self-sustaining function of decorative repetition within Victorian women's religious verse is to analyse how repeated acclamation and punctuation effects focus attention on the poem's construction. Elizabeth Gifford's "Another Comforter" (in *Poems*, 1897) meditates on the Holy Spirit, the "Comforter" to whom Christ referred in John xiv. 16–26 (the scriptural reference is presented as an epigraph). The poem's primary purpose, however, is serial and referential, rather than exploratory or analytical; exclamation marks punctuate the end of almost every line, resulting in a growing but particularly static pile of exclamatory accretions.[17] The real topic of Gifford's poem becomes not the object of recognition but rather the accumulating words of recognition and decoration, and their arrangement. The poem presents a litany of apostrophes, a rhyming series of acts of recognition that, ultimately, direct attention to the utterer of acclamation as well as to the deity acclaimed. The first stanza reads:

> Oh God, the Holy Spirit!
>   Oh Legacy of Christ!
> Oh Gift of God the Father!
>   Oh Blessedness unpriced!
> Oh Spring of life eternal!
>   Oh living, loving, Dower!
> Oh heavenly Inspiration!
>   Show forth in us Thy power.

This quoted stanza illustrates the general pattern, as a series of reverential ejaculations is occasionally and briefly punctuated with supplicatory invocations. The first four stanzas alone contain twenty-four exclamation marks; the total at the end of the poem's seven stanzas has reached thirty-two. These repeated acclamations continually conjure the Holy Spirit in an ongoing act of textual heraldry. Through repetition Gifford's poem undertakes decoration in two senses: in the sense of 'to do grace and honour,' and at the same time in the sense of 'to ornament and embellish'; the first process is undertaken by means of the second. The intensely heightened degree of repetitive embellishment in this poem suggests the ultimate subordination of the appeals for the Holy Spirit to act, to the repeated verbal acts of recognition undertaken by the poem's devout speaker. The circular self-regard of this poem elevates the role of decoration and that of the decorator.

Decorative repetition of all kinds may thus be read as a tool for formalising the relationship of God and speaker-poet-Christian-woman. In their conscious deployment of decorative or ornamental language, structures, and tropes, women's religious poems transform themselves *into ornaments*, and present themselves as a means of honouring and connecting with God. By examining poems' self-presentation as ornaments, decorative formal effects may be seen not as excrescences but as instruments fundamental to the 'work' of the poem. One of the two poems published in the initial issue of the *Christian Lady's Magazine*, the self-consciously entitled "Stanzas" (vol.1, 62–3), provides a particularly suggestive demonstration of the operation and particular ambition of poetic decoration, explored through theme and trope. A close reading reveals the intertwining of the ideas of presenting God with adornments or treasures, and being oneself an adornment or treasure for God.

"Stanzas"

Daughters of Zion! hither bring
    The best and dearest of your store;
A willing tribute to the King
    Your lips confess, your hearts adore;
His just demands with gladness meet,
And pour your treasures at his feet.

Ye that can frame a lasting wreath,
    With which to crown Immanuel's brow,
Search ye the gardens of the Lord,
    To grace and do him honour now;
I bring in aid a simple flower,
Trained in my lone and lowly bower.

No brilliant hue, no spicy scent,
    My humble home-born gift can boast;
Yet since I raised it for the Lord,
    The offering shall not all be lost;
If man the feeble weed disown,
He'll keep it for himself alone.

Names justly dear adorn your page;
    Mine may not claim a place with these;
A novice in the work of God,
    Unapt to teach, unskill'd to please;
My tribute is but meant to shew
Remembrance of the debt I owe.

A debt to heav'n of all I have,
    Of all I am, or hope to be;
A bond that binds me to the Lord,
    And to his church eternally!
Therefore I bring my little all,
Where'er I hear my Master's call.

Servants of Christ! I bid ye speed;
    God prosper ye, as ye shall try
To set forth truth, to cherish love,

Virtue and Virtuosity   207

To labour in simplicity:
Still echoing the angelic strain,
"Glory to God! good will to men."
                    H.

In these tidy six-line stanzas, the speaker appeals to the "Daughters of Zion" to bring "a willing tribute" to God.[18] The second stanza elides daughters of Zion with daughters of the nineteenth century, introducing a trope of peculiar importance to Victorian women's conception of their spiritual life:

Ye that can frame a lasting wreath,
    With which to crown Immanuel's brow,
Search ye the gardens of the Lord,
[. . .]
I bring in aid a simple flower.

The flower trope here works on two levels. That the "wreath" the speaker mentions refers to acts of poetic devotion is clear; not only is the context that of lasting tributes, but the fourth stanza specifically addresses the forum for publication in another statement of overt self-depreciation: "Names justly dear adorn your page;/ Mine may not claim a place with these." But the flowers in question also serve as figures for the author(s) of this/these poems. "I bring my little all," says the speaker self-abasingly, indicating her own identification with the simple flower "trained in my lone and lonely bower." In her address to the daughters of Zion, then, the speaker is telling these women authors to search for themselves in the gardens of the Lord; they *themselves* are God's treasures.

That these treasures are explicitly feminine, according to the normative contemporary standards of femininity, is made clear in a stanza which paradoxically transcends precisely those standards. The poet-speaker (who is a woman, who is a flower) describes herself as personally unadorned with worldly decorations of female graces, bright colors and sensually alluring odours: "No brilliant hue, no spicy scent,/ My humble home-born gift can boast." She notes that while man may "the feeble weed disown," hers is an acceptable offering to God, claimed as His own. The paradox of exaltation in humility plays out on several levels in this poem. We hear the poet depreciating her own work against the lasting wreath of other poets' work, and stating she is "unapt to teach"; yet she has the authority to rally them with a clarion call of encouragement. Her form does not please according to men's standards, but will be kept by God "for himself alone." By radically expanding the standard of humble femininity, the speaker arguably transcends that standard.

In the final stanza the speaker counsels the daughters of Zion to "labour in simplicity." Labour denotes working at, crafting, possibly

208 *Christian and Lyric Tradition in Victorian Women's Poetry*

producing an artifact. Yet the crafted object, like this poem, must appear unlaboured, artless, essentially poetic, natural. The sense of this line then reads equally well as "labour *at* simplicity"; the phrase describes both the spiritual goal for a Victorian woman, permitted to engage only in reflection, with no exegetical, critical engagement with complexities, and the model of the social role of the feminine woman, working hard to appear as natural (and naturally decorative) as possible. The artlessness here is truly studied. The word "trained" in the second stanza raises the question of the discipline necessary to produce a work of art that seems as naturally sprung as a flower, and thence provokes consideration of the formal, prosodic analogue to the poem's vaunted naturalness. Each six-line stanza rhymes meticulously *ababcc*. Each is carefully metrically ordered into iambic tetrameter with trochaic substitutions in the first foot of the apostrophising lines (which begin the first, second, and final stanzas), to appropriately interruptive effect. A trochee also conveys a declarative emphasis to begin the final line: "'Glory to God! good will to men.'" Quoting this angelic pronouncement at Jesus' birth, the poem arguably reapplies that declaration to itself; the poem hails itself as a glorious and finely wrought treasure, a glory to God.

This poem stands as representative of numerous other women's religious poems in which female spirituality is aestheticised through formal decorative effects and also through the trope of floral decoration. Presenting flowers to the king involves the presenter in a dialectic that grants considerable power, for the operation of presenting an offering implies a receiving as well as a giving, thereby enacting an essentially mutually participatory act. The first *Christian Lady's Magazine* volume's preface explicitly labels the attributes of the Christian lady's mind "flowers in a fair garden, to the praise of the hand which created and adorned them" (4). Precisely the same image is again discussed in one of the final volumes, eleven years later, which describes "The Garden of the Lord" and warns readers not to rejoice blindly in their "leaves and luxuriance," or "blossoms, however fair and beautiful"; they have a higher purpose (vol. 23, 451–54). Christ rejoices in the blossoms of the productive Christian, and in the fruit of righteousness that the blooms will eventually yield. Woman has been adorned – made beautiful, decorative—by God himself. She in turn may offer her moral and intellectual beauties back to Him.

What is more, in so far as flower arranging and presenting take the form of a kind of physicalised ritual, the woman poet ritualises herself, in that the act of offering becomes in itself the offering; the flowers do not merely metonymically represent the fruit of righteousness and acceptability, they are themselves the fruit, or the culmination of the process. The act of writing devotional verse, whether or not explicitly equated with raising or presenting flowers, is implicitly equated thus. This is no passive involvement in ritual but a writing oneself into ritual in a self-scripted form, in a direct appeal to the One to whom one offers poem, or flower, or self. While the female decorative role adheres completely to the conventions of Victorian religious discourse, examination of the trope and function of decoration in these poems reveals a broad landscape of possibilities for women. Within the prescribed role, women poets can seize relationship with the decorated One, a relationship that may move as far as identification with the God-worthy gift, or even acts of mutual recognition.

Through foregrounding the ornamental character of their highly crafted poetic texts, Victorian women work to recreate themselves as virtuosic Christians *and* virtuosic artists. Each of the consciously ornamental poems reviewed in this chapter demonstrates dedication and artistry through ornamental flourish but also, and in related ways, through extravagant metrical regularity. In their construction and maintenance of (literally) 'correct' measures, women deploy syntactic, prosodic, and stanzaic elements as means not just of displaying poetic skill but also as means of displaying moral virtue; in fact, the two kinds of display are inextricably linked. Elaborate versification should be read in these poems not just as performance of decoration, but also as performance of obedience.

The elaborateness of these performances in Victorian women's religious poetry has, unfortunately, occasionally obscured the seriousness of the poets' aims, but as I have argued, it indicates a particular strategy. For example, Elizabeth Gifford's striking poem "Thy God hath commanded" (in *Poems*, 1897) displays the speaker-poet's adherence to the commands of the title both formally and visually. The poem's full title is as follows (with the capitalisation and punctuation in the original): "THY GOD HATH COMMANDED THY STRENGTH." "HE ... GIVETH STRENGTH." The appended epigraph reference reads "Psalm lxviii. 28–35." As frequently occurs in Victorian women's religious verse, the poem's eagerness to indicate its biblical origins has given rise to an unwieldy, 'unpoetic' title, but particularly interesting in the case of Gifford's poem is the relation of the particular *body* of the poem to that title and to the expectations it raises. The stanzas that follow demonstrate through their exceptionally highly wrought form both their unassailably 'poetic' nature (that is, they present a defense of the poet's skill) and also, by means of that formal appearance, their fulfillment of God's commands (that is, they present a defense of the poet's obedience and dedication). Stanzas one to three read:

> Be strong! Be strong!
>   Thy God commandeth thee.
>   He wills thy blessedness
>   Through gladness or distress,
>   No wavering heart be thine,
>   Despair not, nor repine,
>   But ever fearless be,
> Be strong! Be strong!

210 *Christian and Lyric Tradition in Victorian Women's Poetry*

Be strong! Be strong!
　　Alas! How can it be?
　　　　So bowed are we with sin,
　　　　So clogged, without, within,
　　　　So faint are we, so frail,
　　　　Heart, nerve, endeavour fail,
　　Ah, then! Howe'er can we
Be strong, yea strong!

Be strong! Be strong!
　　Still the word comes to thee.
　　　　True all thy sad lament,
　　　　True thou art impotent,
　　　　And thy Lord knows it well,
　　　　Knows more than thou can'st tell;
　　Yet still He saith to thee,
Be strong! Be strong!

Immediately noticeable is the deliberate and evocative shape of each stanza on the page, reminiscent of pattern poetry. Gifford uses stanzaic form as a means of visually embodying and enacting the exhorted action: to be strong. Through systematic indentation and regulated line lengths, the eight stanzas are made to resemble a fence, or a row of shields; they stand as a stout bulwark demonstrating both how the reader *should be* strong, and how the poet-speaker *is* strong. Each stanza offers a (very slight) development of the theme, as Gifford presents a stanza's exposition of the command, then a stanza of self-analysis, then contemplations of God's knowledge, God's grace, and so on. However, development of a theme takes a secondary role in this poem to demonstration of the theme. To this end, Gifford uses syntactic repetition and rhyme scheme as well as stanzaic structure to formally as well as visually demonstrate 'being strong.' Each stanza is braced at either end with a pair of commands, "Be strong! Be strong!"; the rhyme scheme of *abccddeeba*, in which every stanza echoes the same *a* and *b* rhymes, connects each stanza to itself and to those preceding and following, like links in a chain; each stanza enacts a return to the beginning, in formal self-reinforcement. The rhetorical questions of stanza two are the only questions to appear in the whole poem; otherwise, every statement expresses firm belief, a firmness matched by the poem's construction and uniformity. While the poem's series of commands conveys an ineluctable didacticism, the eighth and final stanza, in its rather complicated depiction of the ultimate end of being strong, brings attention back to the poem's speaker/constructor herself. This final stanza foregrounds the point of the speaker-poet's construction of her poem and construction of herself as a Christian, which are revealed to be interrelated undertakings.

Be strong! Be strong!
   Stronger and stronger be!
      With cleansèd hands and heart
      Acting a witness' part;
      Using the Master's strength,
      Until thou come at length
   All perfectly to be
Made strong; yea, strong!

Gifford's message here at the close seems to be: be obedient, be strong, act the part, in order eventually to be made *perfectly* strong. Thus her poem demonstrates, through a display of textual, formal strength, her determination to act (write) the part, and her own self-assurance of her inevitable victory and heavenly translation.

In examining the performance of obedience through form in Victorian women's verse, prosody plays a hugely significant but generally misunderstood role. W. H. Auden, in his rather negative introduction to an anthology of minor nineteenth-century poets, views 'messy' Victorian poetry differently from Fairchild, writing, "I am continually struck by the contrast between the extraordinarily high standard of their prosodic skill and the frequent clumsiness and inadequacy of their diction" (22). Auden doesn't consider that the creation of meaning within many nineteenth-century poems is not undertaken solely through the verbal message. In the particular case of Victorian women's religious poetry, readers should be alert to the translation of message *into* form—in important ways, the prosody conveys the meaning. Nineteenth-century poetry's mismatch between words and their arrangement disappoints Auden; I suggest that re-viewing women poets' emphasis on formal arrangement (which sometimes, to be sure, works to the detriment of content), will reveal for interrogation the importance that women religious artists placed on demonstrating prosodic faultlessness, or metrical righteousness. As already mentioned in this chapter, scholarly readings of the nineteenth-century poetess tradition continue to be contentious, but the role of metricality in the performance of both gender and faith poses particularly interesting and suggestive questions. In *The Contours of Masculine Desire*, Marlon Ross traces in the verse of pre-Victorians Hannah Barbauld and Mary Tighe a link between prosodic regularity and the demonstration of feminine grace and virtue. He argues that the underlying assumption of these women writers is that, "if feminine temper must be even, steady, easy, correct, and fair, so must feminine poeticizing" (217). Ross explicitly links the regular line, which the nineteenth century came to particularly associate with femininity, to moral correctness.

Lydia Denning's poem "The Redeemed" (in *Songs of the Better Land*, 1868) vividly demonstrates this association of correct line and correct will, demonstrating obedience and righteousness through form. In six long metre stanzas of ladylike neatness and regularity of rhyme, she discusses how her

212   *Christian and Lyric Tradition in Victorian Women's Poetry*

'hymn of praise' demonstrates textually the same bending of her 'wayward will' as has been undertaken morally. The trammelling of the line reflects the ordering of the soul. Here are the first, second, and fifth stanzas:

> O dear, delightful, happy day,
> When Jesus washed my sins away,
> When with His blood He made me white,
> And pure in His all-glorious sight!
>
> On this delightful day of days,
> To Thee I'll sing a hymn of praise,
> And tell this wondrous work of Thine,
> Thy loving-kindness how divine!
>
> [...]
>
> When first Thou claim'st this heart of mine,
> *And bent my wayward will to Thine*;
> When, childlike, at Thy feet I bowed,
> And ever to adore Thee vowed. (my emphasis)

If salvation means a bending of the wayward will to the paths of Christian righteousness, then the formal corollary of salvation is the bending of the irregular line to the constraints of numbers and rhyme. Thus metrical hyper-regularity may be reevaluated not as poverty of invention or execution, but as a commitment to continue in the paths of righteousness.

Arnold Eisen has written from a twentieth-century, Jewish perspective on the relation of ritual to art, and the particular significance of ritual correctness for the religious practitioner.

> Ritual, we might say, touches life but is not life; it marks out bounds within which life can be lived well. It is a sort of art. We need that art because, no matter how complicated its details, it has one supreme advantage over life: *we can get it right*. I know that I will never live up to ethical ideals, even my own. . . . But I can get the Bach invention right, if I practice it long enough. I can leave Yom Kippur *Ne'ilah* service, after twenty-five hours of following the prescribed ritual, with the precious sense of having at least done that much right. The ritual gives us a sense of rightness that is meant to inspire us to try to attain it outside the bounds of art as well. (74; emphasis in the original)

Eisen suggests ritual, operating like art, may bring kinds of perfection within reach. In the light of this insight, Victorian women religious poets' deployment of prosody may be seen as an undertaking, within the bounds

Virtue and Virtuosity   213

of art, that communicates an aspiration to a practice and way of life outside art that is similarly faultlessly 'right.' Intense and elaborate prosodic regulation stands as an aspirational marker: it represents the poet's vision of a perfect obedience to the will of God that transcends representation, even as it draws attention to its own representation of perfectly observed boundaries. Metrical faultlessness presents the devout Christian with another way of communicating commitment and certainty, and thus the prosodic characteristics of Victorian women's religious verse—so often rigidly regular, so often almost distractingly elaborate—help both communicate and constitute the devout belief that characterises the content. Victorian women's religious poetry, within its many provocative negotiations, centres about a devout faith in God, and unwavering metre helps transmit that commitment to perfection and perfectability.

Almost all of Anna Letitia Waring's poems in *Hymns and Meditations* (1863) embody hyper-composition and hyper-obedience. The volume centers thematically and formally about obedience, submission, the perfection of God's intentions and the complete willingness of the speaker to rely utterly and solely on him. Many of Waring's verses read like patterned series or lists of assurances: I will do this, I will do that, I will never do this, and so on. This opening poem is perfectly representative of the whole volume, and illustrative of a textually expressed and evidenced obedience; its self-stated aim is "to please Thee perfectly."

> "My times are in Thy hand."—Psalm xxxi.15.
> Father, I know that all my life
>   Is portioned out for me,
> And the changes that are sure to come,
>   I do not fear to see;
> But I ask Thee for a present mind
>   Intent on pleasing Thee.
>
> I ask Thee for a thoughtful love,
>   Through constant watching wise,
> To meet the glad with joyful smiles,
>   And to wipe the weeping eyes;
> And *a heart at leisure from itself,*
>   To soothe and sympathise.
>
> *I would not have the restless will*
>   *That hurries to and fro,*
> *Seeking for some great thing to do,*
>   *Or secret thing to know;*
> *I would be treated as a child,*
>   *And guided where I go.*

214   *Christian and Lyric Tradition in Victorian Women's Poetry*

Wherever in the world I am,
　　In whatsoe'er estate,
I have a fellowship with hearts
　　To keep and cultivate;
And a work of lowly love to do
　　For the Lord on whom I wait.

So I ask Thee for the daily strength,
　　To none that ask denied,
And a mind to blend with outward life
　　While keeping at Thy side;
Content to fill a little space,
　　If Thou be glorified.

And if some things I do not ask,
　　In my cup of blessing be,
I would have my spirit filled the more
　　With grateful love to Thee—
More careful—not to serve Thee much,
　　But to please Thee perfectly.

There are briars besetting every path,
　　That call for patient care;
There is a cross in every lot,
　　And an earnest need for prayer;
But a lowly heart that leans on Thee
　　Is happy anywhere.

In a service which Thy will appoints,
　　There are no bonds for me;
For my inmost heart is taught "the truth"
　　That makes Thy children "free;" [sic]
And *a life of self-renouncing love,*
　　Is a life of liberty. (my emphasis)

Retaining the instantly recognisable structure of the common metre stanza, but increasing it by fifty percent and incorporating into its iambic regularity the occasional anapestic substitution (which communicates a rushing eagerness), the speaker illustrates the 'portioning out' of her life through the careful formal portioning of these stanzas. Her themes are constancy, seeking and following guidance, and disavowing grandiose ambition. She states she is "content to fill a little space" in the spiritual as well as literary arena; the poet's heart is "at leisure from itself" as it humbly follows the dictates of her great Original. Her formal choices illustrate the obedience, modesty, and containment of her theme, as she carefully and faithfully constructs the expected rhymes and rhythms of a poem that, with every word, dutifully acknowledges and follows the inherited laws of lyricism and hymnody. Each stanza demonstrates the speaker-poet's willing adoption of a spiritual and literary "service" which foregrounds its own "bonds" even as it announces "there are no bonds for me." For Waring, being obedient, through renouncing freedom (thematically and formally), allows her to claim "a life of liberty." Chapter 4 discussed the ways in which Victorian women demonstrated submission to the will of God through their poems, and explored the various forms of payback for that submission. As Waring's poem demonstrates, submission also has a formal corollary, in which liberty is paradoxically found through renouncing promiscuous prosody.

A 'Particular' Poetry

Victorian women's poetry may be described as *particular*, in two senses. It is 'particular' in that its characteristically ornamental nature renders every poem a highly individual artifact that invites appreciation of its own specialness. It is also particular in that it consistently focuses on individual and subjective experience. Aesthetic elements play an essential role in constructing both kinds of particularity. As argued in the preceding section, the typical Victorian woman's religious poem works in twin ways: it offers an aid to worship, a prayerful devotion directing the thoughts outward to God, and simultaneously it presents itself as a tangible, physical object directing attention inward to its own craftedness. On the one hand, formal verbal arrangement provides poets with a traditional way by which they may approach, describe, and make emotional contact with God. In this sense, poetic language is a means to an end; decorative language may be deployed in verbal acts of honour and adoration that glorify God. Annie Matheson's "Ecce Homo," for example, (in *Love Triumphant, and Other New Poems*, 1898), uses ringing anapests, lists of attributes, and regular exclamations to proclaim the beauty and power of a manly Christ.

> How little they know of His ardour and beauty,
>> His sternness of purpose and chivalrous might,
> His bitter rebuke for betrayers of duty,
>> His passionate purity, radiant of light!
>
> Redeemer and Poet, the Image and Splendour
>> Of God uncreated, by man unbeheld,
> The Potter whose touches are potent and tender;
>> The Worker in metal He only can weld!

The fact that Matheson hails Christ in her poem as "Poet" and praises his artistry communicates the poet's reverence for the artistic vocation. This self-reflexive reverence leads to the second, connected function of decorative

216 *Christian and Lyric Tradition in Victorian Women's Poetry*

poetic language: aesthetic effects can, at the same time as expressing worshipfulness, serve to emphasise the poem's own iconicity. Patternedness becomes self-sufficient; the artwork of the verse is its own apology; the performance of the ritual of recognition or adoration becomes not solely the means to an end but also an arguably rival end of that ritual.

The hyper-poeticisation of Victorian women's religious verse demands that even while the poems take as their explicit subject the dedication of the self to God, they should also be read as poems *about being poems*, insisting upon their own particularity and their own intrinsic literary value. In this way, women religious poets' expressions of self-consciousness, as, for example, in their highly wrought apologies for lack of poetic skill, must be re-evaluated. An example of such self-consciousness may be found in Charlotte Elliott's "Sonnet to the Harp" (in *Hours of Sorrow,* 1869).

> Poor tuneless harp! I take thee to my Lord;
> Though all unmeet to offer at his shrine,
> If he endue my hand with skill divine,
> Sweet melody shall breathe from every chord;
> And thou to that high use shall be restored,
> Which erst in sinless paradise was thine:
> I lay thee at his feet, no longer mine;
> The strings all mute till wakened at his word.
> Oh! thou wert formed in those unsullied days,
>   When joy, love, innocence, attuned each lyre,
>   To blend thy music with celestial lays;
>   And e'en my notes shall mingle with that choir,
>   If He, th' eternal soul of harmony,
>   Now, by his Spirit, deign to breathe on me.

Every element of this poem draws attention to its own craftedness. Adopting a highly constructed sonnet form (to which the title itself draws attention), the poem demonstrates that it belongs to a virtuosic literary and prophetic tradition, sounding echoes of Milton in its invocation to the Holy Spirit, and of the biblical prophet Jeremiah in its disavowals of skill to speak.[19] While the harp itself is the subject of the apostrophe, and the putative subject of the meditation as a whole is the Lord for whom this instrument seems "unmeet," the poem's centre of attention never really moves beyond itself. Carefully regular in rhyme and metrical scheme, full of decorative expostulations and archaic words and contractions, all the poem's stylistic elements undercut the conditional humility of the poem: "*If* he endue my hand with skill divine,/ Sweet melody shall breathe from every chord," suggests sweet melody is already, presently breathing forth within this poem. Highly wrought, the sonnet demonstrates even as it belittles its own fitness for "that high use"; the conventional expression of humility becomes reformulated through the particular form of its expression. Despite the speaker's claims that her artistry is "no longer mine," her art-work remains very insistently her own, directing attention to its own particularity and to her consummate craftsmanship. Ultimately, Victorian women's religious poetry, in its insistent, even over-determined stylistic and linguistic ornamentation, works to reevaluate the particular texture of the individual's experience and expression in relation to the intellectualised, 'universal' truth that may be represented therein.

Stylistic ornamentation clearly contributes to the intensely particular *subjective* nature of most Victorian women's religious poetry. As Scheinberg argues in her examination of the nineteenth-century 'poetry as theology' paradigm (which was developed most fully by Keble), the personalisation and lyricisation of Christian belief in the period helped re-imagine and democratise faith: "theology itself [was] also transformed from a high intellectual 'science' into something quite personal and local—and thus feminized" (*Women's Poetry and Religion* 48). The dangerous possibilities opened up by this intensely personal and local focus help explain the anxiety underlying contemporaneous denigrations of Victorian women's poetry, the subjective focus of which leads often to accusations of the verse 'missing' the heights of universal reach and applicability. Note that it is specifically the lyric, with its focus on the personally speaking *I*, that is particularly troublesome to this nineteenth-century critic.

> The poetry of women (unlike the novels written by women) has, from Sappho downwards, been almost entirely subjective and personal ... We presume women, in writing poetry, draw their style from other women, and thus miss that largeness and universality which alone compels attention, and preserves a work through all changes of sentiment and opinion. ("Poetesses," in *Saturday Review* 25: 679)[20]

The anonymous critic suggests here that all women poets write *like* women and *for* women; their verse is inescapably gendered and therefore partial, particular, the opposite of universal. I argue, however, that by means of the characteristic subjectivity and style here decried women poets are deliberately pursuing aims other than universality. This study has already suggested that Victorian women religious poets do quite knowingly "draw their style from other women," and they deliberately situate their verse in the self-referential and self-affirming body of religious work undertaken by other female poets, following the biblical injunction to "sing to one another in spiritual songs." This body of verse emphasises the significance of the individual contribution within a female spiritual community, as each self-consciously produces itself as 'poetical,' emotive, and feminine, and highlights its own intensely personal particularity. A vivid example of such a highly subjective, highly self-conscious poem may be found in L. H. S.'s "Alice" in *The Christian Lady's Magazine* (vol. 4, 431–33), which in a sea of emotional and stylistic froth recounts the dying words of a pious young lady:

218 *Christian and Lyric Tradition in Victorian Women's Poetry*

Sisters! there's music here,
  From countless harps it flows,
Throughout this bright celestial sphere
  Nor pause, nor discord knows;

The seal is melted from mine ear
  By love divine,
And what through life I pin'd to hear,
  Is mine! Is mine!

The warbling of an ever-tuneful choir,
And the full deep response of David's sacred lyre
  Did kind earth hide from me
  Her broken harmony,
That thus the melodies of Heaven might roll,
And whelm in deeper tides of bliss, my rapt, my
  Wondering soul?

This poem consciously draws on a particular figurative, linguistic, and sty-listic lexicon, and its scope (while it might seem narrow and mawkish to outsiders) and its terms of value would be instantly recognised and appre-ciated by its readership. "Largeness and universality," then, which in the *Review* critic's account seems to equate to the eschewing of contextualisa-tion, represents the opposite of these women's poetic aims: their poetry insists upon the recognition of its own contingency and consistently fore-grounds its own situatedness as an historical and cultural artifact.

As already quoted, Hemans herself explicitly defends the poetic associa-tion of religion, affection, and subjective experience in the Preface to her own *Scenes and Hymns of Life* (1834):

I trust I shall not be accused of presumption for the endeavour which I have here made to enlarge, in some degree, the sphere of Religious Poetry, by associating with its themes more of the emotions, the af-fections, and even the purer imaginative enjoyments of daily life, than may have been hitherto admitted within the hallowed circle. (vii)

Hemans sees her self-appointed task as the extension of religious poetry through the incorporation of the emotive, affective, and quotidian, expand-ing the "hallowed circle" of themes and treatments away from its mas-culine and intellectual exclusivity. Dame Helen Gardner has pointed out the universalising ambition characteristic of religious poetry (*Religion and Literature* 135), describing how it has traditionally sought to articulate an essential and unchangeable God-nature in essentially unchangeable lan-guage. However, Victorian women poets, following Hemans' lead, work

Virtue and Virtuosity 219

to extend that tradition, incorporating the expression of quotidian subjects and individual embellishments into a monolithic discourse. The subjective and personal, then, is deliberately deployed in Victorian women's poetry, at a thematic *and* a formal level, for purposes of which the *Saturday Review* critic seems quite unaware.

While the particularising project may be seen to be implicitly undertaken across the broad body of Victorian women's religious poetry, a number of women poets make their focus on particular, subjective, and quotidian experience entirely explicit, in both their subject and style choices. Some, certainly, seem to have internalised the view, articulated by the anonymous critic, that this subjectivity renders their work somehow secondary and less important. Marjory Kinloch's *A Song-Book of the Soul* (1892) includes a brief prefatory comment asking forgiveness

> for having placed, side by side, subjects so sacred and so common-place. If fault be found with the arrangement of the verses, the writer ventures to refer to the teaching of two poets now at their rest. The one says, "yet set not in thy thoughts too far our heaven and earth apart," and the other assures us that "our common air is balm."[21]

Elizabeth Barrett, more daring, refuses to utter apologies for bringing sacred and common-place together and asserts the value of that 'everyday' expression within religious experience:

> As if life were not a continual sacrament to man, since Christ brake the daily bread of it in His hands! As if the name of God did not build a church, by the very naming of it! As if the word God were not, everywhere in His creation, and at every moment in His eternity, an appropriate word! As if it could be uttered unfitly, if devoutly! (*Poetical Works* xii–xiii)

Barrett suggests that the quotidian in sacred expression, which she staunchly defends, may encompass the choice of both subjects and words, and that all of these choices are fitting, no matter how 'minor.' Barrett's passionate defense finds many poetic echoes, some modest, some less so. Many women poets, for example, follow the model of Havergal's already quoted "By Thy Cross and Passion," which rewrites the universal phrasing of Isaiah 53 into a purely individual meditation: "Wounded for *my* transgression, stricken sore,/ That *I* might 'sin no more'." Many more make implicit or explicit use of the intertext that Taylor's "God's Chosen Things" takes as an epigraph, a biblical text of tremendous significance for Victorian women poets: "God hath chosen the foolish things of the world... and the weak things . . . and base things . . . and things which are despised, hath God chosen". (I Cor. i. 27–28)

But all around despise,
     And scorn a word from me;
They know I am not wise,
     My nothingness they see.
"My child, wilt thou not learn that I must use
Such things as are 'despised': thus thee I choose."

Teach me this lesson, Lord,
     Teach me again, again!
Till on my heart Thy word,
     Graven with iron pen,
Remain; and thus contented, I may choose
To be weak, foolish, base, despised, that Thou may'st use. (stanzas 4–5)

Taylor here laments others' contempt for her "despised" words, but she assures herself that the Lord will respond by engraving in her his own word. She reminds herself that the words and the character she bears are chosen/ written by God himself, and therefore are intended for his special use. Countless other Victorian women construct similar defenses of their works and their words: they equate their own poetic works with insignificant daily tasks and simultaneously apologise for and elevate these quotidian, personal, and particular undertakings. Anna Letitia Waring's poem "My times are in Thy hand," for example (quoted in full earlier), petitions for help with or acceptance of the most mundane and repetitive service: "So I ask Thee for the daily strength. . . . " So does Procter's "One by One," also discussed previously, which links regular mundane tasks to the work of creating poetry: "Every hour that fleets so slowly,/ Has its task to do and bear." In the hands of Victorian women poets, every such equation of daily pious tasks and 'daily' poetic words works to foreground and valorise the particular and quotidian nature of the female Christian's experience of faith, suggesting that the concomitant quotidian expression is itself, in Barrett's phrase, "a continual sacrament."

Through this consistent poetic focus on the daily, the small, the personal, and the particular, explored both through subject and style, women religious poets consistently train attention on the present and the immediate, and thereby on their own presence and immediacy. By emphasising the particularity of the expression, the *whatness* of what is said, these poems focus on the here and now, and on the actions and capacities of this individual poet-speaker. Havergal's "Life Mosaic" focuses, through decorative versification and trope, on the works of art she humbly/proudly creates; Procter's "The Peace of God" emphasises through repeated requests what the speaker herself knows and is certain of. Such poems centre consideration on the speaker's ability to decide action, response, and relation, exchanging a rarefied, heavenly focus for an entirely present, practical focus on immediate, individual acts of engagement with God.

Fundamentally, then, the ornamental features of Victorian women's religious poetry may be seen as formal and stylistic corollaries of the incorporation of the personal into Christian texts. As they enlarge Christian discourse to include the personal and particular, these aesthetic elements, like the transformation of biblical sources reviewed in Chapters 2 and 3, contribute to a larger, polysemic, democratising project. Victorian women's verse challenges the nature of Christian discourse as an intellectualised monolith, as multiple individualised voices assert their own, particular, constructive contribution to the discourse, and their right to make that contribution. Northrop Frye's codification of the kinds of language and rhetoric employed in the Bible, in *The Great Code*, offers a model that suggests a way of re-conceptualising and re-evaluating Victorian women's contribution to the democratisation of Christian religious language. Frye describes the much-vaunted (by the Victorians) 'simplicity' of the Authorised Version of the Bible as essentially expressive of authority: he links 'simple' biblical language to the unqualified "rhetoric of command" (211). Frye points out that traditional, biblically based Christian discourse is depersonalised: "The voice of authority, when transmitted by a human being, is impersonal: another reason that individuality is of so little importance in the Bible" (212). Frye contrasts this traditional biblical language of authority, which he describes as "a discontinuous prose of aphorisms or oracles," with "continuous or descriptive prose [which] has a democratic authority" (212). In providing examples of such continuous or descriptive writing, Frye suggests that the New Testament epistles reveal more "running continuity" and therefore incorporate more individuality of expression. The voice of God, conveyed in the Bible through oracular, discontinuous rhetoric, is contrasted to "the voice of man" [sic], conveyed through more immediate and familiar language (214–5). As this chapter has demonstrated in some detail, immediate and familiar language, emphasis on the particular and the personal, and the foregrounding of emotive and descriptive immediacy, are all prominent characteristics of 'the voice of woman,' as it is represented in Victorian women's religious verse. The continuous, individual, immediate, and democratic mode of expression deployed by Victorian women poets disrupts and displaces the discontinuous authoritative structure identified by Frye as characteristic of traditional, biblically based religious discourse. Through transformations of biblical source material, the adoption of the devotional mode, and the practice of a highly ornamented decorative style, women's poetry of the period transfigures hieratic Christian discourse. Impersonal, aphoristic language is transformed in this voluminous, highly wrought body of work into the continuous style of personal relationship, a style which valorises the individual experience and the particular expression, and which allows the Victorian woman to write herself back into the Christian tradition.

Conclusion

Harriet Tilley's volume *Blossoms of Thought* (1850) displays particular consciousness of the role and privilege of poetry in Christian faith, and thoughtfully considers the importance of language in practising that faith. In particular, "Poesy" utters a defense of poetry that exemplifies and justifies a decorative Victorian religious verse.

> Sweet Poesy, the brightest, loveliest, best
> Of all the pow'rs which emanate from Him
> With whom all good and perfect gifts do rest.

> O 'tis a heav'n-sprung Science! earth could ne'er
> Produce a talent so transcending fair.
> 'Tis angels' language in the empyreal clime;
> And only God can teach this art sublime.

Tilley takes here a particularly religious approach to the traditional defense of poetry's Truth, claiming poetry has a "sacred mission" to smooth the difficulties of earthly life "and wing the soul for its ascending flight." For this author, poetry is literally unearthly, and a marker of its transcendence, or its heavenly provenance, is its *language*: "angels' language in the empyreal clime." As Tilley's own poem demonstrates, "angels' language" is characterised by familiar elements: archaic diction, syntactic and figurative gush, and expostulatory flourish. This poesy is a "fair" Science, sweet and lovely, inescapably feminine, an "art sublime" which transcends any earthly education. Tilley stands as a representative for a vast multitude of Victorian women poets who construct hyper-poetical, highly wrought lyric verse both to sanctify femininity and to feminise sanctity.

In analysing how and why Victorian women made the religious lyric peculiarly their own, this chapter has argued that this poetry allows women poets both to pose and to attempt to answer the question of how a woman writer can treat God. The challenging stylistic excess of so much nineteenth-century religious poetry, if read as a way of answering this question, may be seen as a legitimate form of expression, molded by cultural exigencies, and vividly eloquent about the conditions influencing its own formation. What modern readers tend to see as this body of work's greatest failing—what weighs it down into mundanity—paradoxically provides the means by which women could claim a kind of transcendence. The archaisms and voluminousness, the cliché prosody, the decorative accretions, and the relentlessly subjective focus so evident in this verse are, rightly read, means to an end. I have argued that ornamentation is a strategy in this body of verse, a strategy that makes use of available models of gender and affectivity. By translating Victorian literalisation of women's expressive lyrics into a religious context, women constructed and participated in a new kind of aestheticism, harnessing lyrical elements as personal ornamental offerings, and creating a new venue for encounters with God. This is a privileged venue: as performed decorative 'correctness' elides with performed obedience, women poets align their works with ritual observances and demonstrate their own 'rightness' before God.

I have also suggested that in the creation of an intimate, elaborately ornamented religious poetry, Victorian women offer a subtly differentiated version of biblical style, moving away from the authoritative, discontinuous, and oracular mode toward a personal, mediated, and continuous style. Women's poetry in the century develops into a distinctive devotional verse of relationship, emotive, non-intellectual, and immediate. Both endlessly self-replicating and also insisting upon the value of multiple individual viewpoints, women's decorative verse inserts a profoundly democratic polysemy into Victorian Christian discourse. The stylistic features catalogued and analysed in this chapter are not unique to women's poetry of the period (although they are certainly highly characteristic), but as deployed by women writers these features help challenge and expand gendered constraints on Christian experience and privilege.

In considering the contribution of lyric poetry to the feminisation of Victorian Christianity, and the contribution of Victorian Christianity to the feminisation of the lyric itself, this chapter has argued that the operation of poetic style is central to these intertwined cultural developments. The universalising impulse of critical approaches that have sought to dictate a 'proper' style for treating elevated religious topics have tended to de-historicise and decontextualise the unique religious experiences of individuals. I have aimed instead to describe and re-valorise the multiple operations of Victorian women poets' religious expression, through examining the context and the consequences of the stylistic choices these women made at a syntactic, formal, and figurative level. This body of verse, as it contributed to the development of the lyric, also had broad significance for the religious position and self-identification of women in the nineteenth century. The relationship of style to subject matter in women's religious verse is complex, contingent, and mutually constitutive: Victorian women's religious faith was crafted in part by the ways they wrote about it. Women's ideas about Christian belief, duty, and character, about the nature of God himself, and about their own nature as Christians and as writers, were all significantly shaped by their stylistic choices.

Conclusion

As long as inborn sin is felt,
Or penitence in tears shall melt;
As long as Satan shall molest,
Or anguish rend the human breast;
As long as prayer its voice shall raise,
Or gratitude ascend in praise;
So long God's poet shall impart
A balm to every broken heart;
So long the fainting spirit cheer,
And save the contrite from despair.

— Hannah More, *Bible Rhymes*

Thine is a lofty mission. Nothing less
Than God to glorify, and man to bless;
To raise poor grovelling Nature from the mire,
To give her wings, and teach her to aspire;
To nurse heroic moods; meek worth to cheer;
To dry on Sorrow's cheek the trembling tear;
And still be ready, let who will deride,
To take the lists on injured Virtue's side.
This is thy calling. Tasks like these
Claim and repay the soul's best energies.
Nor need'st thou fear, while thus employed,
That life should seem a burthen or a void.
Joys shall be thine man makes not nor unmakes;
Cheer, which the fickle world nor gives nor takes;
Unhoped-for streams that in the desert rise,
And sunshine bursting through the cloudiest skies!
From light to light thy steps shall tend,
Thy prospects ever brightening to the end;
Thy soul acquiring as it goes
The tone and feelings that befit the close.
Such path, O gifted one, be thine to tread!

— H. F. Lyte, "The Poet's Plea"

In *Godiva's Ride*, Dorothy Mermin wrote, "The center of Victorian discourse, in which all questions were implicated and to which all roads led, was religion" (107). This study has sought to explore the still under-examined importance of that religious centre to women's poetic work and to their own constructions of identity and mission. While it has long fallen

Conclusion   225

away from critical regard and notice, Victorian women's religious poetry was profoundly engaged in posing and suggesting answers to fundamental questions concerning faith, originality, authority, gender, and aesthetics. As the epigraphs from More and Lyte suggest, Victorian women could find in the role of God's poets much work, much honour, and much satisfaction, in an earthly as well as heavenly arena.

In this book I have called for and offered examples of multi-dimensional readings of women's religious verse that take into account the complex and productive interweaving of poetic, religious, and gendered discourses in the Victorian period. Over the past decades, feminist critical models have produced analyses that have illuminated women's historical struggles with androcentric textual and authoritative paradigms, but that haven't always been sensitive to the wide range of creative approaches taken by women working *within* traditional discourses such as that of Christian faith. I have sought to demonstrate that Christianity did not function solely as an oppressive force for Victorian women, but that it could also provide liberating avenues for expression and self-definition. Responses to Christian discourse other than protest and rejection were possible, and were in fact formulated by Victorian women poets, and this rich array of responses demands thorough and disinterested analysis.

This body of work has proved 'invisible' to us for decades due to our own critical preconceptions, not just concerning the constraints of traditional religion but also concerning the limitations of particular literary approaches. Convention and conventionality is broadly mistrusted in post-Romantic poetry and fiction, but in nineteenth-century women's poetry, convention is embraced, formalised, and ritualised; 'convention' becomes a strategy. It requires an entirely different hermeneutic, which this book has worked to outline. I have suggested that terms like *derivative* and *didactic* need to be re-interrogated in the context of a body of work that consciously and creatively negotiates with questions of authority and originality and conceptions of heavenly and earthly audiences. While Victorian women poets' use of biblical language and characters has proved little to modern critical tastes, these poets' inventive redeployments of traditional figures enabled them to reposition themselves within Christian texts that had historically rendered women silent and invisible. Further, Victorian women's search for expanded spiritual expression and recognition was intimately connected to the construction of new kinds of literary status, and both quests contribute to a re-imagining of gender roles within a Christian hierarchy. Victorian women poets, I have suggested, manoeuvre within Christian discourse in creative, unexpected, even radical ways, often within the most conservative seeming texts.

Throughout this study I have sought to explicate the importance of *poetry* to the Christian 'work' that women did in the Victorian period. Arguably the foremost genre for Victorian women negotiating with Christian discourse, lyric poetry offered women writers a uniquely enabling

226   *Christian and Lyric Tradition in Victorian Women's Poetry*

means of entry into an exclusive realm. In the Victorian period, women became poetical beings like never before, as cultural expectations of feminine domesticity, sentimentality, and piety could be directly manipulated into a construction of privileged, 'poetical' expression. In fact, these terms (feminine, domestic, sentimental, pious, poetical) approached interchangeability in the period; nineteenth-century literary commentaries reveal that 'being poetical' came to mean something very close to 'being a Christian woman.' The creative work of Victorian women poets fundamentally reshaped the categories of *poet* and *Christian*, their work also demanding that both categories be reconsidered through the lens of gender. Women's deployment of the religious lyric also influenced the development of that genre in the nineteenth century, contributing both to the feminisation of Christian experience and to the feminisation of poetry, refracting Victorian poetics in provocative ways.

I have also argued the importance in Victorian women's religious poetry of a devotional mode of expression, which played a significant role in Victorian women's negotiations with lyric tradition. Devotionality grew out of the increasingly relationship-focussed Christianity of the nineteenth century, with its many iterations of a companionable rather than juridical Jesus. These iterations did not merely provide models for a relational theme, but also contributed to the spread in lyric poetry of a mode that emphasised the loving, the sympathetic, and the empathetic; that sought to foreground its own (personal and textual) obedience and submission; that was expressive of humility; that simultaneously recognised the vastness of the divide between human and divine and longed for union. The devotional mode, intimate rather than public, emphasising the personal, immediate, and quotidian, was ineluctably linked to femininity as well as sentimentality. As such, it provided a uniquely enabling mode for Victorian women to promote themselves as natural, and naturally spiritual, poets.

And finally, this study has investigated the formal and stylistic corollaries of women's incorporation of the personal into Christian discourse. Deploying biblical phrases, epigraphs, or intertexts; incorporating instantly recognisable romantic models; composing batteries of repetitions and exclamations: the style of Victorian women's religious verse, often seeming so tedious to a twenty-first-century reader, reveals the sometimes surprising extent of women's creative and spiritual ambitions.

Voluminous and various as the body of Victorian women's religious verse undoubtedly is, it should nonetheless be considered as a distinct body of work, united about common concerns and particular common characteristics. Rightly viewed, the homogeneity of this poetry functions in several ways. The uniformity of topic, trope, and style that characterises women's religious verse has often been dismissed as unoriginality, but it should instead be examined for how it points both to itself and beyond itself. Women's poems consciously situate themselves within a vast, self-referential, and self-affirming body of work. Repetition and hyper-poeticisation helps this body of work create its own sacred authority, which reaffirms every contributor to the corpus as a Christian authority in herself.

One of the tasks of a conclusion is to summarise, briefly and with a hint of relief, the key contentions of the work; subsequent tasks include suggesting future directions for study and urging the reader to look further. However, the phantom undergraduate imagined in my introduction has lingered to the close of this study, and persists in asking, *why* should we look further? Fundamentally, I believe that the critical analysis of Victorian women's poetry needs to broadened and refocused, in a context that relocates the discourses of Christian religion from the margins to a central position in women's creative work. The tremendously important recuperative project begun in the eighties by Armstrong, Leighton, Reynolds, Mermin, and others has helped bring back into consideration the verse of many forgotten nineteenth-century women writers, and has reshaped both the Victorian canon and our understanding of the operation of canonisation. Certain Victorian writers, including Rossetti, Michael Field, and to a lesser extent Adelaide Procter, Alice Meynell, and Dora Greenwell, have attracted insightful studies from a growing number of literary critics. However, the full scope of these poets' oeuvres has sometimes remained inadequately examined. Feminist analysis has generally proved underequipped to assess the (in many cases substantial) Christian content of these poets' works, seeming to assume that Christian devotion is antithetical to political assertion, creative originality, and also aesthetic value. I hope that this book demonstrates the insupportability of this supposed antithesis, and I call for a broadened consideration of all the Victorian women poets we read and study. The faith and the faith-inheritance of poets like Barrett Browning, Rossetti, Hickey, Procter, Meynell, and others profoundly influenced every aspect of their work, their literary aspirations, and their conception of themselves as Christians, as artists, and as women. It must, therefore, be reincorporated into our scholarly inquiries. Further, I contend that we can only properly evaluate the achievement of leading Victorian figures if we have a fuller understanding of the work of the lesser known women amongst whom and for whom they wrote. Some decades ago Marion Shaw demonstrated that the language and structure of *In Memoriam* were deeply embedded in popular religious poetry of the period, and Patrick Scott suggested that Tennyson should be re-read through Keble to "gain new perspectives on the instabilities and continuities of early Victorian religion" ("Rewriting the Book of Nature" 141). We must now, I contend, apply this same kind of informed critical consideration to the works of Barrett Browning, Rossetti, and others, re-examining them as writers within a very particular creative and spiritual community. The literary context of women's religious verse in the Victorian period influenced everything these poets wrote, and it must inform our readings of them.

Well then, if we must look further, *where* should we look? At the outset of this work, I indicated the necessary, pragmatic limitations I had to place

228 *Christian and Lyric Tradition in Victorian Women's Poetry*

on the project's scope. The corpus of Victorian women's religious verse remains so vast, rich, and suggestive that it offers compelling material for many future studies. One possible future direction may lie in closer investigations into the distinctive approaches taken by women poets of the many different Victorian Christianities. Because a primary goal of this project was to suggest ways of analysing common concerns and features of this body of verse, examining denominational variations took a secondary role to investigating and theorising those overarching operations. However, scholars of theological history interested in elucidating the production and dissemination of particular doctrinal and sectarian positions will find a wealth of resources in the lyric contributions of Victorian women across the range of denominations. Study of the verse of women of divergent communities of faith, including Roman Catholics, Unitarians, or Arminian Methodists, may reveal how and why these women made use of particular liturgies or texts beyond the Bible, and how they may have constructed images of community peculiar to their own congregations. These findings may in turn shed new light on the contributions of these women to the construction and development of their communities of belief.

A second fruitful area for continuing investigation lies in the wealth of publishing outlets that existed in the Victorian period. The impact of those outlets on the creative and spiritual self-conceptions of their female contributors deserves a much closer examination than was possible in this book. How the periodical press shaped the development of women's religious poetry deserves a study of its own, a study that would explore a whole series of provocative questions about how the intersection of Christian discourse and periodical culture shaped the period's ideas of anonymity, sincerity, and professionalism.

Third, while the lyric genre stands as the pre-eminent form adopted in the body of Victorian women's religious verse, inquiry into how women poets deployed other poetic forms would give rise to a range of fascinating new investigations. For example, Victorian women's epic retellings of scriptural originals deserve close and serious analysis, as many make astonishingly inventive and bold manoeuvres with their sources. Elizabeth Barrett's *Drama of Exile* is one of few such biblical epics to have received any critical attention; Jean Ingelow's "Story of Doom," Barbara MacAndrew's "Ezekiel," George Eliot's "Legend of Jubal" and "The Death of Moses," and Sarah Greenough's "Magdalene," among many other examples, present fascinating creative reworkings of source material that may open new vistas upon the range of Victorian women's literary ambitions.

And fourth, the broader social implications of Victorian women's religious lyric verse demand further examination. In this study, I have concentrated primarily on women's constructions of a 'personal' Christian poetry, which, while it permitted significant re-imaginings of divine and earthly audiences, was generally deployed in the cause of *individual* spiritual and literary growth. Future studies may and should seek to relate the private and personal benefits of women's devotional poetry to the 'public face' and public ambitions of this body of verse, examining the processes by which religious poetry became a significant vehicle for Victorian women to express a voice in important social questions. As Melnyk, Flammang, Adams, and others have argued elsewhere, religion was not merely a private pastime for nineteenth-century women, but was also used to form, shape, and expand public personae and public action. The particular social uses to which religious *poetry* was put have, however, yet to be fully examined. Christian-themed verse was certainly deployed with both force and volume, for example, by temperance activists, anti-vivisectionists, and later in the century by suffragists. I have argued that women could, through authoring religious poetry, enter, extend, and redeploy Christian discourse, "authorising" themselves as privileged Christians. Answers to the question of how these gains, made through poetic negotiations, might enable the articulation of a specifically female voice of social protest and social influence, must belong to a future study.

I have been able to articulate in this conclusion only a few of the many possible future directions for studies into Victorian women's religious poetry. This book as a whole serves as a brief introduction to the creativity and complexity of Victorian women poets' transfigurations of their lyric and Christian inheritances. That creativity and complexity will, I hope, be explored in greater depth in future works.

Appendix

Victorian periodicals reviewed for religious verse, and library holdings consulted.

The Animal's Guardian.
      London. 1890–1897.
      British Library holds volumes 1 through 8, no. 3.

The British Mothers' Magazine.
      London, Edinburgh. 1845–1855.
      British Library holds volumes 1 through 11.

The British Women's Temperance Journal.
      London. Jan. 1886–Sept. 1892.
      British Library holds volumes 4, no.1 through 10, no. 117.

The Christian Lady's Magazine.
      London: R. B. Seeley and W. Burnside, 1834–1849.
      University of Virginia Library holds volumes 1 through 31 on microfilm.

The Christian Mother's Magazine.
      London. 1844–1845.
      British Library holds volumes 1 and 2.
Subsequently published as *The Englishwoman's Magazine.*
      London, Kendal, Bath. 1846–1855.
      British Library holds volumes 1 through 9.

The Victoria Magazine.
      London: Emily Faithfull, 1863–1880.
      University of Virginia Library holds volumes 1 through 36 on microfilm.

The Women's Penny Paper.
      London. 1888–1892.
Subsequently published as *The Woman's Herald.*
      London: 1892–1893.
      University of Virginia Library holds volumes 1 through 8 of the entire run, on microfilm.

Bibliography

Adams, James Eli. *Dandies and Desert Saints*. Ithaca and London: Cornell University Press, 1995.

Adams, Kimberly VanEsveld. *Our Lady of Victorian Feminism: The Madonna in the Work of Anna Jameson, Margaret Fuller, and George Eliot*. Athens, OH: Ohio University Press, 2001.

Adams, Sarah Flower. *Nearer, My God, To Thee*. Boston: Lee & Shepard, 1876.

Adams, William Henry Davenport. *Celebrated Englishwomen of the Victorian Era*. 2 vols. London: F. V. White & Co., 1884.

Alexander, Cecil Frances. *Hymns For Little Children*. London: J. Masters & Co., 1884.

——. *Poems*. Ed. W. Alexander. London: Macmillan & Co., 1896.

Altick, Richard. *The English Common Reader: A Social History of the Mass Reading Public, 1800–1900*. Chicago: University of Chicago Press, 1957.

Anderson, John M. "In the Churchyard, Outside the Church: Personal Mysticism and Ecclesiastical Politics in Two Poems by Charlotte Smith." *Seeing Into the Life of Things: Essays on Literature and Religious Experience*. Ed. John L. Mahoney. New York: Fordham University Press, 1998. 195–209.

Armstrong, Isobel. "The Gush of the Feminine: How Can We Read Women's Poetry of the Romantic Period?" *Romantic Women Writers: Voices and Countervoices*. Eds. Paula R. Feldman and Theresa M. Kelley. Hanover, NH: University Press of New England, 1995. 13–32.

——. "Msrepresentation: Codes of Affect and Politics in Nineteenth-Century Women's Poetry." *Women's Poetry, Late Romantic to Late Victorian: Gender and Genre, 1830–1900*. Eds. Isobel Armstrong and Virginia Blain. Basingstoke, Hampshire: Macmillan, 1999. 3–32.

——. *Victorian Poetry: Poetry, Poetics and Politics*. London and New York: Routledge, 1993.

Armstrong, Isobel, and Virginia Blain, eds. *Women's Poetry, Late Romantic to Late Victorian: Gender and Genre, 1830–1900*. Basingstoke, Hampshire: Macmillan, 1999.

Armstrong, Isobel, Joseph Bristow, and Cath Sharrock, eds. *Nineteenth-Century Women Poets: An Oxford Anthology*. Oxford: Clarendon Press, 1996.

Arseneau, Mary, and Jan Marsh. "Intertextuality and Intratextuality: The Full Text of Christina Rossetti's 'Harmony on First Corinthians XIII' Rediscovered." *Victorian Newsletter* 88 (1995): 17–26.

Auden, W. H., ed. *Nineteenth-Century Minor Poets*. London: Faber, 1967.

Auerbach, Nina. *Woman and the Demon: The Life of a Victorian Myth*. Cambridge, MA: Harvard University Press, 1982.

B., M. E. *The Young Child's Gospel; or, The Life of Our Lord in Easy Verse. Also Children's Morning and Evening Prayers and Hymns for a Week*. London: Jarrold & Sons, 1880.

234 Bibliography

Bagehot, Walter. "Wordsworth, Tennyson, and Browning; Or, Pure, Ornate, and Grotesque Art in English Poetry." *National Review*, 1 (1864): 27–66.

Bal, Mieke. *Death and Dissymmetry: The Politics of Coherence in the Book of Judges*. Chicago and London: University of Chicago Press, 1988.

———. *Lethal Love: Feminist Literary Readings of Biblical Love Stories*. Bloomington: Indiana University Press, 1987.

———. *Murder and Difference: Gender, Genre, and Scholarship on Sisera's Death*. Bloomington: Indiana University Press, 1988.

Balfour, Clara Lucas. *The Bible Pattern of a Good Woman*. London: S. W. Partridge, 1867.

———. *The Women of Scripture*. London: Houlston & Stoneman, 1847.

Barrett Browning, Elizabeth. *The Poetical Works of Elizabeth Barrett Browning*. London: Smith, Elder & Co., 1897.

———. *The Poetical Works of Elizabeth Barrett Browning*. Oxford: Oxford University Press, 1913.

Barrett Browning, Elizabeth, and Robert Browning. *The Brownings' Correspondence*. Vols. 1–8, ed. Philip Kelley and Ronald Hudson; vols. 9–14 ed. Philip Kelley and Scott Lewis. Winfield, KS: Wedgestone Press, 1984–1998.

Bateman, Josiah. *The Life of the Rev. Henry Venn Elliott*. London: Macmillan & Co., 1868.

Battiscombe, Georgina. *Christina Rossetti: A Divided Life*. London: Constable, 1981.

Beck, Mary E. *Bible Readings on Bible Women. Illustrated by Incidents in Daily Life*. London: S. W. Partridge, 1892.

Belloc, Bessie Rayner. *In Fifty Years (Poems)*. London: Sands & Co., 1904.

Bemis, Virginia. "Reverent and Reserved: The Sacramental Theology of Charlotte M. Yonge." *Women's Theology in Nineteenth-Century Britain: Transfiguring the Faith of Their Fathers*. Ed. Julie Melnyk. New York and London: Garland, 1998. 123–32.

Bennett, Lucy Ann. *Poetical Works of Lucy A. Bennett*. Ed. Mary Eley. London: Marshall, Morgan & Scott Ltd., 1930.

Bennett, Mary Anne. *Poems*. London: Griffith Farran & Co., 1894.

Besemeres, Jane. *Vanished Faces, and Other Poems*. London: James Nisbet & Co., 1884.

Bevan, Emma Frances. *Service of Song in the House of the Lord*. London: Hatchards, 1884.

Bevington, Louisa Sarah. *Key-Notes (Poems)*. London: Kegan Paul & Co., 1879.

Blain, Virginia. "Period Pains: The Changing Body of Victorian Poetry." *Victorian Poetry* 42:1 (2004): 71–79.

———. ed. *Victorian Women Poets: A New Annotated Anthology*. Harlow, England: Longman, 2000.

Blair, Kirstie, ed. *John Keble in Context*. London: Anthem Press, 2004.

Bloom, Abigail Burnham, ed. *Nineteenth-Century British Women Writers: A Bio-Bibliographical Critical Sourcebook*. Westport, CT: Greenwood Press, 2000.

Bonar, Horatius. *Hymns of Faith and Hope. First Series*. London: James Nisbet & Co., 1871.

The Book of Private Devotion, A Series of Prayers and Meditations; With an Introductory Essay on Prayer, Chiefly from the Writings of Hannah More. New York: William Robinson, 1845.

Booth, Catherine. *Female Ministry: Or, Woman's Right to Preach the Gospel*. London: Morgan & Chase, 1870.

Boothby, Cecilia Elizabeth. *Voices of Joy and Thanksgiving: A Collection of Sacred Poems for the Principal Festivals of the Christian Year*. London: Day & Son, 1866.

Bibliography 235

Bowra, C. M. "Christina Rossetti." *The Romantic Imagination*. London: Oxford University Press, 1950. 245–70.

Boyd, Nancy. *Josephine Butler, Octavia Hill, Florence Nightingale: Three Victorian Women Who Changed Their World*. London and Basingstoke: Macmillan, 1982.

Bradley, Ian. *Abide With Me: The World of Victorian Hymns*. London: SCM, 1997.

———. *The Call to Seriousness: The Evangelical Impact on the Victorians*. London: Jonathan Cape, 1976.

Bradstock, Andrew, Sean Gill, Anne Hogan, and Sue Morgan, eds. *Masculinity and Spirituality in Victorian Culture*. New York: St. Martin's Press, 2000.

Bradstock, Andrew, and Anne Hogan, eds. *Women of Faith in Victorian Culture: Reassessing The Angel in the House*. New York: St. Martin's Press, 1998.

Braithwaite, Adeline. *Scripture Spoil in Sacred Song (Poems)*. London: J. Nisbet & Co., 1886.

Breen, Jennifer, ed. *Victorian Women Poets 1830–1901: An Anthology*. London: Everyman, 1994.

Brewster, Emily. *Collect, Epistle and Gospel Teachings, for the Sundays of the Christian Year*. London: Skeffington, 1890.

Bristow, Joseph. "Coventry Patmore and the Womanly Mission of the Mid-Victorian Poet." *Sexualities in Victorian Britain*. Eds. Andrew H. Miller and James Eli Adams. Bloomington: Indiana University Press, 1996. 118–39.

———. ed. *Victorian Women Poets: Emily Brontë, Elizabeth Barrett Browning, Christina Rossetti*. Basingstoke, Hampshire: Macmillan, 1995.

Brontë, Anne. *The Poems of Anne Brontë: A New Text and Commentary*. Ed. Edward Chitham. London and Basingstoke: The Macmillan Press, 1979.

Brown, Annie Johnson. *Rejected of Men, and Other Poems*. London: Sampson Low & Co., 1890.

Brown, James Baldwin. *The Home: In Its Relation to Man and to Society*. 2nd ed. London: James Clarke & Co., 1883.

Browne, Jane Euphemia. *The Dove on the Cross, And Other Thoughts in Verse*. London: James Nisbet & Co., 1849.

Bruce, Charles, ed. *The Book of Noble Englishwomen; Lives Made Illustrious By Heroism, Goodness, and Great Attainments*. London: W. P. Nimmo, 1875.

Butler, Ann. *Fragments In Verse; Chiefly On Religious Subjects*. Oxford: Bartlett & Hinton, 1826.

Caine, Barbara. *English Feminism 1780–1980*. Oxford: Oxford University Press, 1997.

Campbell, Duncan. *Hymns and Hymnmakers*. London: A. & C. Black, 1898.

Carpenter, Mary Wilson. *Imperial Bibles, Domestic Bodies: Women, Sexuality and Religion in the Victorian Market*. Athens, OH: Ohio University Press, 2003.

Chadwick, Owen. *The Victorian Church*. 3rd ed. 2 vols. London: Adam & Charles Black, 1970.

Chapman, Raymond. *Faith and Revolt: Studies in the Literary Influence of the Oxford Movement*. London: Weidenfeld & Nicolson, 1970.

Charles, Elizabeth Rundle. *Sketches of the Women of Christendom*. London: Society for Promoting Christian Knowledge, 1889.

———. *The Women of the Gospels, The Three Wakings, and Other Verses*. London: T. Nelson & Sons, 1868.

Chesterton, G. K. "Alice Meynell." *Dublin Review* 172.1 (1923): 1–12.

Cheyne, Elizabeth. *A Little Book of Saints*. London: A. C. Fifield, 1906.

Choi, Sara. "Christina Rossetti's Dialogical Devotion." *Christianity and Literature* 53:4 (2004): 481–94.

236   Bibliography

Christ, Carol. "The New Feminist Theology: A Review of the Literature." *Religious Studies Review* 3 (1977): 203–12.

Clark, George Kitson. *The Making of Victorian England*. London: Methuen & Co., 1962.

Clark, Suzanne. *Sentimental Modernism: Women Writers and the Revolution of the Word*. Bloomington: Indiana University Press, 1991.

Cleaveland, Elizabeth H. J. *No Sect in Heaven*. London: A. W. Bennett, 1860.

Cobbe, Frances Power. *Rest in The Lord; And Other Small Pieces*. London: Pewtress & Co., 1887.

Collins, Thomas, and Vivienne Rundle. The *Broadview Anthology of Victorian Poetry and Poetic Theory*. Peterborough, Canada: Broadview, 1999.

A Commentary Upon the Holy Bible, from Henry and Scott. With Numerous Observations and Notes from Other Writers; Also Maps of the Countries Mentioned in Scripture, and Various Useful Tables. 6 vols. London: Religious Tract Society, 1835.

Cook, Eliza. *Poetical Works*. London: Warne, 1886.

Cooke, Elizabeth Harriet. *The Widow's Mite (Verses)*. London: R. J. Mitchell & Sons, 1874.

Cousin, Annie Ross. *Immanuel's Land, and Other Pieces (Poems)*. London: James Nisbet & Co., 1876.

Cozens, Emily. *A Collection of Original Poems on Various Subjects*. Wallingford: William Payne, 1875.

Craik, Dinah Mulock. *Poems. By the author of "John Halifax, Gentleman,"* etc. Boston: Ticknor & Fields, 1866.

Crewdson, Jane. *Lays of the Reformation and Other Lyrics, Scriptural and Miscellaneous*. London: Hatchard & Co., 1860.

Cunneen, Sally. *In Search of Mary: The Woman and the Symbol*. New York: Ballantine Books, 1996.

Cunningham, Valentine. *Everywhere Spoken Against: Dissent in the Victorian Novel*. Oxford: Clarendon Press, 1975.

———. *The Victorians: An Anthology of Poetry & Poetics*. Oxford: Blackwell, 2000.

D'Amico, Diane. *Christina Rossetti: Faith, Gender and Time*. Baton Rouge, LA: Louisiana State University Press, 1999.

———. "Eve, Mary, and Mary Magdalene: Christina Rossetti's Feminine Triptych." *The Achievement of Christina Rossetti*. Ed. David A. Kent. Ithaca and London: Cornell University Press, 1987. 175–91.

———. "Fair Margaret of 'Maiden Song': Rossetti's Response to the Romantic Nightingale." *Victorian Newsletter* 80 (1991): 8–13.

Daly, Mary. *Beyond God the Father: Toward a Philosophy of Women's Liberation*. Boston: Beacon Press, 1973.

Darton, Margaret E. *Words in Season for the Weary (in verse)*. London: Charles Gilpin, 1850.

Davie, Donald, ed. *The New Oxford Book of Christian Verse*. Oxford: Oxford University Press, 1981.

Davis, Natalie Zemon. *Women on the Margins: Three Seventeenth-Century Lives*. Cambridge, MA: Harvard University Press, 1995.

De Jong, Mary. "'With My Burden I Begin': The (Im)Personal 'I' of Nineteenth-Century Hymnody." *Puritanism in America: The Seventeenth Through the Nineteenth Centuries*. New York: Edwin Mellen Press, 1994. 185–223.

Denning, Lydia Louisa. *Songs of the Better Land: A Testimony to the Truth of the Gospel of Christ*. Bristol: C. T. Jefferies & Sons, 1868.

Dering, Robert, Mrs. *Gatherings from the Scripture. An Offering to Boys and Girls*. London: B. Wertheim, 1848.

Bibliography 237

Dieleman, Karen. "Elizabeth Barrett Browning's Religious Poetics: Congregationalist Models of Hymnist and Preacher." *Victorian Poetry* 45:2 (2007): 135–57.

Dix, Morgan. *The Calling of a Christian Woman and Her Training to Fulfil It.* New ed. London: Richard D. Dickinson, 1884.

Donaldson, Mrs. *Home Duties for Wives and Mothers, Illustrated by Women of Scripture.* London: William Hunt & Co., 1882.

Drane, Augusta Theodosia. *Songs in The Night and Other Poems.* London: Burns & Oates, 1876.

Drinkwater, John. *Victorian Poetry.* London: Hodder & Stoughton, 1923.

Edmeston, James. *Closet Hymns and Poems.* London: The Religious Tract Society, 1846.

Eisen, Arnold. *Taking Hold of Torah.* Bloomington: Indiana University Press, 1997.

Eliade, Mircea. *The Sacred and the Profane: The Nature of Religion.* Trans. Willard R. Trask. New York: Harcourt, Brace & Co., 1959.

Elliott, Charlotte. *Hours of Sorrow Cheered and Comforted.* London: J. Booth, 1869.

———. *Hours of Sorrow: Or Thoughts in Verse, Chiefly Adapted to Seasons of Sickness, Depression and Bereavement.* N.p., Nisbet, 1836.

———. *Selections From the Poems of Charlotte Elliott, With a Memoir by her Sister, E.B.* London: The Religious Tract Society, 1873.

———. *Thoughts in Verse on Sacred Subjects.* London: William Macintosh, 1869.

Elliott, Emily Elizabeth Steele. *Wayside Pillars. Religious Meditations in Prose and Verse.* London: Seeley & Co., 1866.

Ellis, Rowland. *Some Women of Scripture. Five Lenten Addresses.* London; Brighton: SPCK, 1881.

Engelhardt, Carol Marie. "The Paradigmatic Angel in the House: The Virgin Mary and Victorian Anglicans." *Women of Faith in Victorian Culture: Reassessing the Angel in the House.* Eds. Anne Hogan and Andrew Bradstock. New York: St. Martin's Press, 1998. 159–71.

Evans, Ifor. *English Poetry in the Later Nineteenth Century.* 2nd ed. London: Methuen & Co., 1966.

Everard, George. *Safe and Happy: Words of Help and Encouragement to Young Women.* London: William Hunt and Company, 1871.

Faber, Frederick William. *The Rosary and Other Poems.* London: James Toovey, 1845.

Fairchild, Hoxie Neale. *Religious Trends in English Poetry.* 6 vols. New York: Columbia University Press, 1939–1968.

Farningham, Marianne. *Lays and Lyrics of the Blessed Life, Consisting of Light from the Cross and Other Poems.* London: Benjamin Low, 1860.

Fearnley, Rachel Jane, and Harriet Ann. *Crumbs From the Master's Table.* N.p., Bradford, 1899.

Fergusson, Isa Gillon. *Parables in Song, and Other Pieces.* London: James Nisbet & Co., 1889.

Feuerbach, Ludwig. *The Essence of Christianity.* Eds. E. Graham Waring and F. W. Strothman. New York: Continuum, 1957, 1985.

Field, Michael. *Mystic Trees (Poems).* London: Eveleigh Nash, 1913.

———. *Poems of Adoration.* London: Sands & Co., 1912.

Fiorenza, Elisabeth Schüssler. *Bread Not Stone: The Challenge of Feminist Biblical Interpretation.* New ed. Boston: Beacon Press, 1985.

———. *In Memory of Her: A Feminist Theological Reconstruction of Christian Origins.* London: SCM Press Ltd., 1983.

238   Bibliography

Flammang, Lucretia A. "'And Your Sons and Daughters Will Prophesy': The Voice and Vision of Josephine Butler." *Women's Theology in Nineteenth-Century Britain: Transfiguring the Faith of Their Fathers.* Ed. Julie Melnyk. New York and London: Garland, 1998. 151–64.

Flowers, Betty S. "The Kingly Self: Rossetti as Woman Artist." *The Achievement of Christina Rossetti.* Ed. David A. Kent. Ithaca and London: Cornell University Press, 1987. 159–74.

Fontana, Ernest. "Mary Magdalene and the Pre-Raphaelites." *The Journal of Pre-Raphaelite Studies* 9 (2000): 89–100.

Francis, Emma. "'Healing relief . . . Without detriment to modest reserve . . . ': Keble, Women's Poetry and Victorian Cultural Theory." *John Keble in Context.* Ed. Kirstie Blair. London: Anthem Press, 2004. 115–24.

Fraser, Hilary. *Beauty and Belief: Aesthetics and Religion in Victorian Literature.* New York: Cambridge University Press, 1986.

Frye, Northrop. *Anatomy of Criticism.* Princeton: Princeton University Press, 1957.

———. *The Great Code: The Bible and Literature.* London: Routledge & Kegan Paul, 1982.

Gardner, Helen, ed. *John Donne: The Divine Poems.* Oxford: Clarendon Press, 1969.

———. *Religion and Literature.* London: Faber & Faber, 1971.

Gifford, Elizabeth. *Poems.* London: Eden Fisher & Co., 1897.

Gilbert, Sandra, and Susan Gubar. *The Madwoman in the Attic: The Woman Writer and the Nineteenth-Century Literary Imagination.* New Haven: Yale University Press, 1979.

Godwin, Elizabeth Ayton. *Songs Amidst Daily Life.* London: n.p., 1878.

———. *Songs For the Weary: The School of Sorrow and Other Poems.* London: n.p., 1873.

Granger, Mary Ethel. *Peace: A Thanksgiving After Holy Communion (in verse).* London: Swan Sonnenschein & Co., 1886.

Grant, Cecilia Havergal. *The Master's Smile, and Other Poems.* London: James Nisbet & Co., 1889.

Gray, Douglas. *Themes and Images in the Medieval English Religious Lyric.* London and Boston: Routledge & Kegan Paul, 1972.

Gray, F. Elizabeth. "Beatification Through Beautification: Poetry in *The Christian Lady's Magazine*, 1834–1849." *Victorian Poetry* 42.4 (2004): 261–82.

———. "'Syren Strains': Victorian Women's Devotional Poetry and John Keble's *The Christian Year.*" *Victorian Poetry* 44.1 (2006): 61–76.

Greenough, Sarah Dana. *Mary Magdalene, and Other Poems.* London: Chapman & Hall, 1887.

Greenwell, Dora. *Camera Obscura (Poems).* London: Daldy, Isbister, & Co., 1876.

———. *Carmina Crucis (Poems).* London: Bell & Daldy, 1869.

Gregory, John. *A Father's Legacy to His Daughters.* 1774. New York; London: Garland Publishing Inc., 1974.

Hamilton, Eliza H. *Hymns for the Weary.* 6th ed. Edinburgh: J. Taylor, 1878.

———. *Poems.* Dublin: Hodges and Smith, 1838.

Hamilton, Susan, ed. *Criminals, Idiots, Women and Minors: Victorian Writing by Women on Women.* Peterborough, Canada: Broadview Press, 1995.

Haskins, Susan. *Mary Magdalen: Myth and Metaphor.* Hammersmith, London: HarperCollins, 1993.

Havergal, Frances Ridley. *Kept for the Master's Use.* London: James Nisbet & Co., 1880.

Bibliography 239

———. *Letters by the Late Frances Ridley Havergal.* Ed. Maria Vernon Graham Havergal. London: James Nisbet & Co., 1885.

———. *The Poetical Works of Frances Ridley Havergal.* London: James Nisbet & Co., 1884.

Haycraft, Margaret. *Songs of Peace.* London: James Nisbet & Co., 1883.

Headley, Phineas C. *Historical and Descriptive Sketches of the Women of the Bible, Chronologically Arranged, From Eve of the Old to the Marys of the New Testament.* London: Partridge, Oakey, & Co., 1855.

Heimann, Mary. *Catholic Devotion in Victorian England.* Oxford: Clarendon Press, 1995.

Helsinger, Elizabeth K., Robin Lauterbach Sheets, and William Veeder, eds. *The Woman Question: Society and Literature in Britain and America, 1837–1883.* 3 vols. New York and London: Garland Publishing, 1983.

Hemans, Felicia. *Moral and Religious Poems.* Edinburgh and London: William Blackwood, 1850.

———. *The Poetical Works of Mrs. Felicia Hemans. Edited, with a Critical Memoir, by William Michael Rossetti.* London: E. Moxon, Son, & Co., 1873.

———. *Scenes and Hymns of Life, with Other Religious Poems.* Edinburgh: William Blackwood; London: T. Cadell, 1834.

Hickey, Emily. *Ancilla Domini.* London: n.p., 1898.

———. *Our Lady of May, and Other Poems.* London: Catholic Truth Society, 1902.

———. *Poems.* London: E. Mathews, 1896.

Hickok, Kathleen. *Representations of Women: Nineteenth-Century British Women's Poetry.* Westport, CT: Greenwood Press, 1984.

Higonnet, Margaret Randolph, ed. *British Women Poets of the Nineteenth Century.* New York: Penguin, 1996.

Hilliard, David. "Unenglish and Unmanly: Anglo-Catholicism and Homosexuality." *Victorian Studies* 25 (1982): 181–210.

Hobbs, June Haddon. "His Religion and Hers in Nineteenth-Century Hymnody." *Nineteenth-Century Women Learn to Write.* Ed. Catherine Hobbs. Charlottesville, VA: University of Virginia Press, 1995. 120–44.

Hogan, Anne, and Andrew Bradstock, eds. *Women of Faith in Victorian Culture: Reassessing the Angel in the House.* New York: St. Martin's Press, 1998.

Holy Bible, with copious marginal readings. And an abridged commentary by the Rev. T. Scott. Pocket edition. London: George Virtue, 1842.

Hope, Mildred Beresford. *Eucharistic Hymns for the Church's Seasons.* London: Novello and Ewer, 1892.

Howell, Agnes R. *Through the Woods: A Volume of Original Poems.* London: Hamilton, Adams and Co., 1875.

Howitt, Mary. *Ballads and Other Poems.* London: Longman, Brown, Green, and Longmans, 1847.

Hughes, Sheila Hassell. "'Eye to Eye': Using Women's Literature as Lenses for Feminist Theology." *Literature and Theology* 16.1 (2002): 1–26.

Hull, Amelia Matilda. *Royal Musings Concerning the King and His Work.* London: James E. Hawkins, 1884.

Ingelow, Jean. *One Hundred Holy Songs, Carols, and Sacred Ballads. Original, and Suitable for Music.* London: Longmans, Green, and Co., 1878.

Iverson, Winifred A. *God's Touch, and Other Poems.* London: Marshall Brothers, 1890.

Jameson, Anna. *Legends of the Madonna as Represented in the Fine Arts.* London: Longman, Brown, Green, and Longmans, 1852.

———. *Sacred and Legendary Art.* 2 vols. London: Longmans, Green, and Co., 1883.

240 *Bibliography*

Jay, Elisabeth. "Doubt and the Victorian Woman." *The Critical Spirit and the Will to Believe: Essays in Nineteenth-Century Literature and Religion.* Eds. David Jasper and T. R. Wright. New York: St. Martin's Press, 1989. 88–103.

———. *The Religion of the Heart: Anglican Evangelicalism and the Nineteenth-Century Novel.* Oxford: Clarendon Press, 1979.

———. "Women Writers and Religion." *Women and Literature in Britain 1800–1900.* Ed. Joanne Shattock. Cambridge: Cambridge University Press, 2001. 251–74.

Jenkins, Ruth Y. *Reclaiming Myths of Power: Women Writers and the Victorian Spiritual Crisis.* Lewisburg, PA: Bucknell University Press, 1995.

Johnson, Samuel. *Lives of the English Poets.* 3 vols. Ed. George Birkbeck Hill. New York: Octagon Books, 1967.

Jones, Llewellyn. *First Impressions: Essays on Poetry, Criticism and Prosody.* New York: A. A. Knopf, 1925.

Kachur, Robert M. "Envisioning Equality, Asserting Authority: Women's Devotional Writings on the Apocalypse, 1845–1900." *Women's Theology in Nineteenth-Century Britain: Transfiguring the Faith of Their Fathers.* Ed. Julie Melnyk. New York and London: Garland, 1998. 3–36.

———. "Repositioning the Female Christian Reader: Christina Rossetti as Tractarian Hermeneut in *The Face of the Deep.*" *Victorian Poetry* 35 (1997): 193–214.

Karr, Margaretta Ayres. *The Heavenly Voice: A Life of Christ in Blank Verse: His Work and Word in Sonnets.* New York: Eaton & Mains, 1905.

Keble, John. *Lectures on Poetry 1832–1841.* Trans. E. K. Francis. 2 vols. Oxford: Clarendon Press, 1912.

———. *Occasional Papers and Reviews of John Keble.* London and Oxford: James Parker, 1877.

———. *The Christian Year.* London: Ward, Lock & Tyler, n.d.

Kelly, John, and Eric Domville, eds. *The Collected Letters of W. B. Yeats.* 3 vols. Oxford: Clarendon Press, 1986–97.

Kendrew, Mary E. *Lyra Sacra.* London: Elliot Stock, 1894.

King, Harriet Eleanor Hamilton. *The Hours of the Passion and Other Poems.* London: Grant Richards, 1902.

King, Harriet Rebecca. *Thoughts In Verse Upon Scripture Texts, To Which are Added Miscellaneous Poems and Nursery Hymns etc.* 2 vols. London: W. J. Cleaver, 1842; James Nisbet & Co., 1846.

Kinloch, Marjory G. J. *A Song-book of the Soul.* London: Kegan Paul & Co., 1892.

Knox, Isa Craig. *Songs of Consolation.* London: Macmillan & Co., 1874.

Krueger, Christine L. *The Reader's Repentance: Women Preachers, Women Writers, and Nineteenth-Century Social Discourse.* Chicago: University of Chicago Press, 1992.

Kruppa, Patricia S. "'More Sweet and Liquid Than Any Other': Victorian Images of Mary Magdalene." *Religion and Irreligion in Victorian Society.* Eds. R. W. Davis and R. J. Helmstadter. London: Routledge, 1992. 117–32.

Landels, William. *Lessons for Maidens, Wives, and Mothers, From Some of the Representative Women of Scripture.* London: John F. Shaw and Co., 1865.

Landon, Letitia E. *The Easter Gift, A Religious Offering; By L. E. L.* London: Fisher, Son & Co., 1832.

Landow, George. *Victorian Types, Victorian Shadows: Biblical Typology in Victorian Literature, Art and Thought.* Boston and London: Routledge & Kegan Paul, 1980.

Lanser, Susan Sniader. *Fictions of Authority: Women Writers and Narrative Voice.* Ithaca and London: Cornell University Press, 1992.

Bibliography 241

LaPorte, Charles. "George Eliot, The Poetess as Prophet." *Victorian Literature and Culture* 31.1 (2003): 159–79.

Larson, Janet L. "Lady-Wrestling for Victorian Soul: Discourse, Gender, and Spirituality in Women's Texts." *Religion and Literature* 23 (1991): 43–64.

Lawrence, Mary Emma. *Hymns and Poems for Very Little Children.* London: Religious Tract Society, 1871.

Leighton, Angela. *Victorian Women Poets: Writing Against the Heart.* Charlottesville, VA: University of Virginia Press, 1992.

Leighton, Angela, and Margaret Reynolds, eds. *Victorian Women Poets: An Anthology.* Oxford and Cambridge: Blackwell, 1995.

Levi, Peter. *The Penguin Book of English Christian Verse.* Harmondsworth, England: Penguin, 1984.

Lewalski, Barbara Kiefer. *Protestant Poetics and the Seventeenth-Century Religious Lyric.* Princeton: Princeton University Press, 1979.

Lewis, Linda M. *Elizabeth Barrett Browning's Spiritual Progress: Face to Face with God.* Columbia, MO: University of Missouri Press, 1998.

Lyte, Henry Francis. *The Poetical Works of the Rev. H. F. Lyte. Ed., with a Biographical Sketch, by the Rev. John Appleyard.* London: Elliot Stock, 1907.

MacAndrew, Barbara. *Ezekiel and Other Poems.* London: T. Nelson & Sons, 1871.

Maison, Margaret. "Queen Victoria's Favourite Poet." *Listener* 73 (Apr. 29, 1965): 636–37.

Martz, Louis. *The Poetry of Meditation: A Study in English Religious Literature of the Seventeenth Century.* New Haven: Yale University Press, 1954.

Maskell, Eliza. *Gospel Themes: A Series of Sacred Poems.* London: Wertheim, Macintosh, and Hunt, 1860.

Mason, Emma. "'Her Silence Speaks': Keble's Female Heirs." *John Keble in Context.* Ed. Kirstie Blair. London: Anthem Press, 2004. 125–41.

Mathers, Helen. "Evangelicalism and Feminism. Josephine Butler, 1828–1906." *Women, Religion and Feminism in Britain, 1750–1900.* Ed. Sue Morgan. Basingstoke, Hampshire: Palgrave Macmillan, 2002. 123–37.

Matheson, Annie. *Love Triumphant, and Other New Poems.* London: A. D. Innes & Co., 1898.

McGann, Jerome. "Christina Rossetti's Poems: A New Edition and a Revaluation." *Victorian Studies* 23 (1980): 237–54.

———. *The Poetics of Sensibility: A Revolution in Literary Style.* Oxford: Clarendon Press, 1996.

———. "The Religious Poetry of Christina Rossetti." *Critical Inquiry* 10 (1983): 127–44.

Mellor, Anne K., ed. *Romanticism and Feminism.* Bloomington: Indiana University Press, 1988.

Melnyk, Julie. "'Mighty Victims': Women Writers and the Feminization of Christ." *Victorian Literature and Culture* 31.1 (2003): 131–57.

———. "Victorian Religious Women Writers and Communal Identities." *Australasian Victorian Studies Journal* 10 (2004): 70–90.

———. ed. *Women's Theology in Nineteenth-Century Britain: Transfiguring the Faith of Their Fathers.* New York and London: Garland, 1998.

Menteath, A. Stuart, Mrs. *Lays of the Kirk and Covenant.* Edinburgh: Johnstone & Hunter, 1850.

Meredith, Susanna. *Wanted: Deaconesses for the Service of the Church.* London: John F. Shaw and Co., 1872.

Mermin, Dorothy. *Godiva's Ride: Women of Letters in England, 1830–1880.* Bloomington: Indiana University Press, 1993.

242 *Bibliography*

Meynell, Alice. *The Rhythm of Life and Other Essays*. London: John Lane; Boston: Copeland and Day, 1896.

Miles, Alfred H. *The Poets and the Poetry of the Century*. 10 vols. London: Hutchinson & Co., 1891–1897.

Miles, Margaret R. *Image and Insight: Visual Understanding in Western Christianity and Secular Culture*. Boston: Beacon Press, 1985.

———. *The Image and Practice of Holiness: A Critique of the Classic Manuals of Devotion*. London: SCM Press Ltd., 1988.

Miller, Andrew H., and James Eli Adams, eds. *Sexualities in Victorian Britain*. Bloomington: Indiana University Press, 1996.

Milman, Henry Hart. *Milman's Poetical Works*. 3 vols. London: John Murray, 1840.

Montgomery, James. *Poetical Works of James Montgomery. With Life*. London: T. Nelson & Sons, 1863.

Moore, Virginia. *Distinguished Women Writers*. New York: E. P. Dutton and Co., 1934.

More, Hannah. *Strictures on the Modern System of Female Education: With a View of the Principles and Conduct Prevalent Among Women of Rank and Fortune*. Boston: James Loring, 1838.

———. *The Works of Hannah More, Including Several Pieces Never Before Published*. New ed. 11 vols. London: n.p., 1830.

Morgan, Sue, ed. *Women, Religion, and Feminism in Britain, 1750–1900*. Basingstoke, Hampshire: Palgrave Macmillan, 2002.

Morison, John. *Morning Meditations for Every Day in the Year: Or, the Christian Communing With His Own Heart*. London: Religious Tract Society, 1835.

Muir, Emma. *God's Octave and Other Poems*. Edinburgh: 'Printed for private circulation,' 1896.

Murray, Charlotte, Cecilia Havergal, and others. *Abiding In Thee: A Selection of Poems*. London: James E. Hawkins, 1888.

Murray, Charlotte. *More 'Messages' (Poems)*. Stirling: Drummond's Tract Depot, 1886.

Needham, Elizabeth Annabel. *Poetic Paraphrases*. London: James E. Hawkins, 1890.

Nesbit, Edith. *Ballads and Verses of the Spiritual Life*. London: Elkin Mathews, 1911.

Nixon, Jude V. *Victorian Religious Discourse: New Directions in Criticism*. Basingstoke, Hampshire: Palgrave Macmillan, 2004.

Noel, Caroline Maria. *The Name of Jesus, and Other Poems, for the Sick and Lonely*. New ed. London: Hatchards, 1878.

Norman, Edward R. *Anti-Catholicism in Victorian England*. New York: Barnes & Noble, 1968.

———. *The English Catholic Church in the Nineteenth Century*. Oxford: Clarendon Press, 1984.

O'Gorman, Francis. *Victorian Poetry: An Annotated Anthology*. Oxford: Blackwell, 2004.

Orr, Emily. *The Golden Year: Thoughts for Every Month*. London: SPCK, 1887.

Ostriker, Alicia Suskin. *Feminist Revision and the Bible*. Cambridge, MA: Blackwell, 1993.

Oulton, Carolyn W. de la L. *Literature and Religion in Mid-Victorian England: From Dickens to Eliot*. Basingstoke, Hampshire: Palgrave Macmillan, 2003.

Palazzo, Lynda. *Christina Rossetti's Feminist Theology*. Basingstoke, Hampshire: Palgrave Macmillan, 2003.

Palgrave, Francis Turner. *The Treasury of Sacred Song, Selected from the English Lyrical Poetry of Four Centuries*. Oxford: Clarendon Press, 1890.

Bibliography 243

Parkinson, William. *Poems*. London: Bell and Daldy, 1856.

Patmore, Coventry. "*Legends and Lyrics* and *The Wanderer*." *North British Review* 30 (1859): 221–27.

Paz, D. G. *Popular Anti-Catholicism in Mid-Victorian England*. Stanford, CA: Stanford University Press, 1992.

Peterson, Linda H. "Anthologizing Women: Women Poets in Early Victorian Collections of Lyric." *Victorian Poetry* 37:2 (1999): 193–209.

Petre, Catherine, Lady. *Sacred Verses*. London: n.p., 1864.

Pigott, Jean Sophia. *A Royal Service, and Other Poems*. London: S. W. Partridge & Co., 1877.

Pitman, Mrs. E. R. *Lady Hymn Writers*. London: T. Nelson & Sons, 1892.

Poole, Eva Travers Evered. *Left Alone With Jesus, and Other Poems*. London: James Nisbet & Co., 1890.

Pratt, Annis. *Archetypal Patterns in Women's Fiction*. With Barbara White, Andrea Loewenstein, Mary Wyer. Bloomington: Indiana University Press, 1981.

Prickett, Stephen. *Romanticism and Religion: The Tradition of Coleridge and Wordsworth in the Victorian Church*. Cambridge: Cambridge University Press, 1976.

————. *Words and The Word: Language, Poetics and Biblical Interpretation*. Cambridge: Cambridge University Press, 1986.

Prins, Yopie. *Victorian Sappho*. Princeton: Princeton University Press, 1999.

Probyn, May. *Pansies. A Book of Poems*. London: E. Matthews, 1895.

Prochaska, F. K. *Women and Philanthropy in Nineteenth-Century England*. Oxford: University of Oxford Press, 1980.

Procter, Adelaide Anne. *A Chaplet of Verses*. 2nd ed. London: n.p., 1862.

————. *The Poems of Adelaide Anne Procter, with an Introduction by Charles Dickens*. New York: Thomas Y. Crowell & Co., n.d.

Prothero, Stephen. *American Jesus: How the Son of God Became a National Icon*. New York: Farrar, Straus, and Giroux, 2003.

Purvis, June, ed. *Women's History: Britain 1850–1945, an Introduction*. London: University College London Press, 1995.

Raine, Rosa. *Verses for Church Schools*. London: Joseph Masters & Co., 1861.

Reardon, Bernard M. G. *Religious Thought in the Victorian Age: A Survey from Coleridge to Gore*. London: Longman, 1980.

Reed, John Shelton. "'A Female Movement': The Feminization of Nineteenth-Century Anglo-Catholicism." *Anglican and Episcopal History* 57 (1988): 199–238.

————. *Glorious Battle: The Cultural Politics of Victorian Anglo-Catholicism*. Nashville: Vanderbilt University Press, 1996.

Ricks, Christopher. *The New Oxford Book of Victorian Verse*. Oxford: Oxford University Press, 2008.

Roberts, Ellen. *Heathen Fables in Christian Verse*. London: James Nisbet & Co., 1860.

Robertson, Eric S. *English Poetesses: A Series of Critical Biographies With Illustrative Extracts*. London: Cassell & Company, 1883.

Robinson, A. Mary. F. *The Collected Poems Lyrical and Narrative of Mary Robinson. With a Preface and Portrait*. London: T. Fisher Unwin, 1902.

Roden, Frederick S. "Gender and Religion in Recent Victorian Studies Publications." *Victorian Literature and Culture* 31.1 (2003): 393–403.

————. "The Kiss of the Soul: The Mystical Theology of Christina Rossetti's Devotional Prose." *Women's Theology in Nineteenth-Century Britain: Transfiguring the Faith of Their Fathers*. Ed. Julie Melnyk. New York and London: Garland, 1998. 37–57.

244   Bibliography

———. *Same Sex Desire in Victorian Religious Culture*. Basingstoke, Hampshire: Palgrave Macmillan, 2002.

Rogal, Samuel. *Sisters of Sacred Song: A Selected Listing of Women Hymnodists in Great Britain and America*. New York and London: Garland Publishing, 1981.

Rosenblum, Dolores. "Christina Rossetti's Religious Poetry: Watching, Looking, Keeping Vigil." *Victorian Poetry* 20 (1982): 33–49.

Ross, Marlon. *The Contours of Masculine Desire: Romanticism and the Rise of Women's Poetry*. Oxford: Oxford University Press, 1989.

Rossetti, Christina. *The Complete Poems of Christina Rossetti. A Variorum Edition*. Ed. Rebecca W Crump. 3 vols. Baton Rouge, LA: Louisiana State University Press, 1979–90.

———. *Letter and Spirit. Notes on the Commandments*. London: Christian Knowledge Society, 1883.

———. *The Poems of Christina Rossetti. Chosen and Edited by William M. Rossetti*. London: Macmillan, 1904.

———. *Time Flies: A Reading Diary*. London: SPCK, 1885.

Rossetti, William Michael, ed. *Rossetti Papers 1862 to 1870*. New York: C. Scribner's Sons, 1903.

———. "Memoir." *The Poetical Works of Christina Georgina Rossetti*. By Christina Rossetti. London: Macmillan, 1904. xlv–lxxi.

Rouch, Martha Pearce. *Cathedral Rhymes, Suggested by Passages in the Liturgy and Lessons, By the Author of 'Recollections of Childhood' etc.* London: E. Churton, 1847.

Ruether, Rosemary Radford. "Feminist Interpretation: A Method of Correlation." *Feminist Interpretation of the Bible*. Ed. Letty M. Russell. Oxford: Basil Blackwell Ltd., 1985. 111–24.

Ruskin, John. *The Works of John Ruskin*. Eds. E. T. Cook and A. Wedderburn. 39 vols. London: George Allen, 1900–12.

Saffery, Maria Grace. *Poems on Sacred Subjects*. London: Hamilton, Adams, and Co., 1834.

Saunders, Emily Susan G. *The New Christian Year; Or, Thoughts on the Present Lectionary*. London: George Stoneman, 1891.

Scheinberg, Cynthia. "'Measure to Yourself a Prophet's Place': Biblical Heroines, Jewish Difference and Women's Poetry." *Women's Poetry, Late Romantic to Late Victorian: Gender and Genre, 1830–1900*. Eds. Isobel Armstrong and Virginia Blain. Basingstoke, Hampshire: Macmillan, 1999. 263–91.

———. *Women's Poetry and Religion in Victorian England: Jewish Identity and Christian Culture*. Cambridge: Cambridge University Press, 2002.

Schumacher, Michele M., ed. *Women in Christ: Toward a New Feminism*. Grand Rapids, MI: Eerdmans, 2004.

Scott, Patrick. "The Business of Belief: The Emergence of 'Religious' Publishing." *Studies in Church History* 10 (1973): 213–24.

———. "Rewriting the Book of Nature: Tennyson, Keble, and *The Christian Year*." *Victorians Institute Journal* 17 (1989): 141–55.

Sewell, Mary. *Church Ballads. (Second Series. On the Festivals)*. London: J. T. Hayes, 1868.

———. *Stories in Verse for the Street and the Lane, Being the Second Series of "Homely Ballads for the Working Man's Fireside."* London: n.p., 1861.

Shalkhauser, Marian. "The Feminine Christ." *Victorian Newsletter* 10 (1956): 19–20.

Shapcote, Emily Mary. *Mary: The Perfect Woman, One Hundred and Fifty Rhythms in Honour of the Mystical Life of Our Lady*. London: Manresa Press, 1903.

Bibliography   245

Sharp, Elizabeth Amelia. *Women Poets of the Victorian Era*. London: Walter Scott, 1890.

Shaw, Marion. "*In Memoriam* and Popular Religious Poetry." *Victorian Poetry* 15 (1977): 1–8.

Sigerson, Dora. *Verses*. London: Elliott Stock, 1893.

Skelton, Edith. *All Good Things Come to Those Who Wait*. London: Griffith, Farran, & Co., 1884.

Smulders, Sharon. "Feminism, Pacifism and the Ethics of War: The Politics and Poetics of Alice Meynell's War Verse." *English Literature in Transition 36.2* (1993): 159–77.

———. "Woman's Enfranchisement in Christina Rossetti's Poetry." *Texas Studies in Literature and Language* 34.4 (1992): 568–88.

Southey, Robert. *Sir Thomas More: Or, Colloquies on the Progress and Prospects of Society*. 2 vols. London: John Murray, 1829.

Spender, Dale. *Man Made Language*. London and Boston: Routledge & Kegan Paul, 1980.

Spurgeon, Charles Haddon. *Spurgeon's Sermons*. Retrieved from <http://www.spurgeon.org/sprmns.htm> on July 16, 2007.

Stedman, Edmund Clarence. *Victorian Poets*. Boston: James R. Osgood and Company, 1876.

Stevenson, Lionel. *The Pre-Raphaelite Poets*. Chapel Hill, NC: University of North Carolina Press, 1973.

Stewart, Susan. "Lyric Possession." *Critical Inquiry* 22 (1995): 34–63.

Stock, Sarah Geraldina. *Joy in Sorrow (Poems)*. London: John F. Shaw and Co., 1884.

———. *Life Abundant and Other Poems*. London: John F. Shaw and Co., 1892.

Streatfield, Sophia Charlotte. *A Little Garland of the Saints, and Other Verses*. London: A. R. Mowbray & Co., 1877.

Tamke, Susan S. *Make a Joyful Noise Unto the Lord: Hymns as a Reflection of Victorian Social Attitudes*. Athens, OH: Ohio University Press, 1978.

Taves, Ann. *The Household of Faith: Roman Catholic Devotions in Mid-Nineteenth-Century America*. Notre Dame, IN: University of Notre Dame Press, 1990.

Taylor, Barbara. *Eve and the New Jerusalem: Socialism and Feminism in the Nineteenth Century*. New York: Pantheon Books, 1983.

Taylor, Dennis. "The Need for a Religious Literary Criticism." *Seeing Into the Life of Things: Essays on Literature and Religious Experience*. Ed. John L. Mahoney. New York: Fordham University Press, 1998. 3–30.

Taylor, Georgiana M. *Lays of Lowly Service, and Other Verses*. London: Morgan and Scott, 1881.

Tennyson, George B. *Victorian Devotional Poetry: The Tractarian Mode*. Cambridge, MA: Harvard University Press, 1981.

Thompson, Rachel. *In Honour of a Triune God. Original Hymns and Poems*. Malmesbury: N. Riddick, 1890.

Threlfall, Jennette. *Sunshine and Shadow: Poems*. London: William Hunt and Co., 1873.

Tilley, Harriett Meston. *Blossoms of Thought, Poems*. London: Houlston & Stoneman, 1850.

Todd, Janet, ed. *British Women Writers: A Critical Reference Guide*. New York: Continuum, 1989.

Tompkins, Jane. *Sensational Designs: The Cultural Work of American Fiction, 1790–1860*. New York: Oxford University Press, 1985.

Townshend, Gladys Ethel. *In the King's Garden, and Other Poems*. London: John Long, 1906.

246 *Bibliography*

Trudgill, Eric. *Madonnas and Magdalens: The Origins and Development of Victorian Sexual Attitudes.* London: Heinemann, 1976.

Tucker, Herbert F. "House Arrest: The Domestication of English Poetry in the 1820s." *New Literary History* 25.3 (1994): 521–48.

Tuell, Anne Kimball. *Mrs. Meynell and her Literary Generation.* New York: E. P. Dutton & Co., 1925.

Turnock, Sarah Elizabeth. *Women of the Bible.* London: Geo. Burroughs, 1899.

Tynan, Katharine. *Ballads and Lyrics.* London: Kegan Paul & Co., 1891.

Upton, Bridget Gilfillan. "Feminist Theology as Biblical Hermeneutics." *The Cambridge Companion to Feminist Theology.* Ed. Susan Frank Parsons. Cambridge: Cambridge University Press, 2002. 97–113.

V., K. E. *The Circle of Saints: Hymns and Verses for the Holy Days of the English Calendar by K.E.V.* London: Swan Sonnenschein, & Co., 1886.

Valenze, Deborah M. *Prophetic Sons and Daughters: Female Preaching and Popular Religion in Industrial England.* Princeton: Princeton University Press, 1985.

W., M. O. *Rhymes from the Book and from Life. By M.O.W.* London: Simpkin, Marshall, Hamilton, Kent & Co., 1900.

W., S. E. *A Christian Woman: A Tract (in Verse) by S.E.W.* London: Henry James Tresidder, 1861.

Walker, Cheryl. *The Nightingale's Burden: Women Poets and American Culture Before 1900.* Bloomington: Indiana University Press, 1982.

Walker, Eliza Ann. *Hymns and Thoughts in Verse, by E.A.W.* London: William Hunt and Company, 1864, 1887.

Walker, Julia. "The Religious Lyric as a Genre." *English Language Notes* 25 (1987): 39–45.

Waring, Anna Letitia. *Hymns and Meditations, by A. L. W.* 10th ed. London: Alfred William Bennett, 1863.

Warner, Marina. *Alone of All Her Sex: The Myth and the Cult of the Virgin Mary.* London: Pan Books, 1985.

Watson, J. R. *The English Hymn: A Critical and Historical Study.* Oxford: Oxford University Press, 1997.

Westerholm, Joel. "'I Magnify Mine Office': Christina Rossetti's Authoritative Voice in Her Devotional Prose." *Victorian Newsletter* 84 (1993): 11–17.

Wilberforce, William. *A Practical View of the Prevailing Religious System of Professed Christians, in the Higher and Middle Classes in the Country, Contrasted with Real Christianity.* Philadelphia: Key and Biddle, 1835.

Williams, Jane. *The Literary Women of England.* London: Saunders, Otley, and Co., 1861.

Woosnam, Etty. *The Women of the Bible: New Testament.* London: S. W. Partridge, 1884.

Worton, Michael, and Judith Still. *Intertextuality: Theories and Practices.* Manchester: Manchester University Press, 1990.

Wright, Fanny. *The Books of the Bible in Verse.* London: n.p., 1908.

Wright, Marian Saunders. *Paraphrases on Sermons Preached by Professor Elmslie (In Verse).* London: Elliot Stock, 1891.

Zemka, Sue. *Victorian Testaments: The Bible, Christology, and Literary Authority in Early-Nineteenth-Century British Culture.* Stanford: Stanford University Press, 1997.

Notes

NOTES TO THE INTRODUCTION

1. Dame Helen Gardner's definition of religious poetry demands that poems so categorised display "that sense of commitment and obligation which is the essence of religion" (*Religion and Literature* 134).
2. Patrick Scott has demonstrated the considerable growth in religious publication in the nineteenth century: between 1801 and 1835, religious books made up 22.2% of books published, and between 1836 and 1863 this increased to 33.5% (224). Given that between these years legislative changes meant publishing in England increased exponentially, the overall numbers of volumes of religious content clearly skyrocketed.
3. There is much further critical work to be done on the interpenetration of discourses of religion and gender in the Victorian period, following on from the important work undertaken in edited collections by Bradstock and Hogan and by Bradstock, Gill, Hogan, and Morgan, as well as in monographs by James Eli Adams, Fred Roden, and others.

NOTES TO CHAPTER 1

1. For a fuller discussion of attendance figures at Church of England and Nonconformist services, see Reed "A Female Movement" 204–5, particularly n.14. See also Richard Mudie-Smith, *The Religious Life of London* (London: Hodder and Stoughton, 1904), for returns reporting church attendance.
2. From "In What Way Can Wives and Mothers Best Promote the Revival of Piety in the Church?" *The British Mothers' Magazine* IV (Dec 1848): 265–68.
3. For other treatments of Victorian women's religious prose, see Valentine Cunningham, *Everywhere Spoken Against: Dissent in the Victorian Novel* (Oxford: Oxford University Press, 1975), and Sue Zemka, *Victorian Testaments: The Bible, Christology, and Literary Authority in Early-Nineteenth-Century British Culture* (Palo Alto, CA: Stanford University Press, 1997).
4. For a classic discussion of the importance of *The Christian Year* in the Victorian period, see Appendix C to G. B. Tennyson's *Victorian Devotional Poetry*, 226–32.
5. Duncan Campbell reports of Charlotte Elliott that "more than a thousand letters . . . were found in her repositories after her death, giving thanks for light and blessing received from 'Just as I am'" (71).

248 *Notes*

6. See, for example, Charles LaPorte's "Atheist Prophecy: Mathilde Blinde, Constance Naden, and the Victorian Poetess," *Victorian Literature and Culture* 34:2 (2006): 427–41; and Marion Thain's "'Scientific Wooing': Constance Naden's Marriage of Science and Poetry," *Victorian Poetry* 41.1 (2003): 151–69.
7. See "Period Pains," 72.
8. Davie's statement is simply inaccurate, and his unselfconscious use of this standard goes some way toward explaining why of the 103 poets in his anthology, only eleven are women. Clearly Davie's selection would have included more women, particularly, one suspects, from the nineteenth century that saw such an outpouring of women's devotional verse, if it were not for his exclusionary stylistic standard of non-sentimental "artistry." To give Davie his due, despite the egregious use of the universal masculine pronoun whenever referring to "the poet," his inclusion of thirty-five poems by eleven women is certainly more representative than Peter Levi's 1984 edition of *The Penguin Book of English Christian Verse*, which includes, in its sweep from Old English to twentieth-century lyrics, an astounding total of just six poems by a mere four women; unbelievably, he excludes Christina Rossetti, arguably the greatest Christian devotional poet of the nineteenth century, saying that while she is a "lovely poet," not a single one of her poems is without "serious faults" (25).
9. See Matthew 17:2; Mark 9:2–3; Luke 9:29.
10. Williams' *The Literary Women of England* describes the Hymns for Children thus:
"These 'Hymns,' which connect the gratification of the eye with life's destinies and with just sentiments, have no peculiar adaptation to childhood, but are equally suitable for adolescence, or manhood, and still more so for womanhood. Mrs. Hemans's mental and moral perceptions were so uniformly clear and bright, that few intellects at any age could find difficulty in following their lucid track; nevertheless, she had not that particular faculty for instruction which consists in assuming the point of view of other and differently constituted minds in various stages of development. Her art consisted rather in wafting people gently away in her own stream, than in floating as a pilot on their rafts". (440)

NOTES TO CHAPTER 2

1. William Michael Rossetti may have had in mind a review in the Sydney *Bulletin* which praised Christina Rossetti's work but decried "all her useless baggage of religious verbiage" (quoted in *Poems of Christina Rossetti* xix).
2. For accessible reviews of the primary goals and methods of 'first-wave' feminist hermeneutics, see Christ, "The New Feminist Theology"; Fiorenza's afterword to the 1995 edition of *In Memory of Her*; Schumacher 170–73.
3. The first five cantos of Lucy Hutchinson's *Order and Disorder* were published in 1679; the rest remained in MS until Norbrook's edition in 2001. Rowe's *The History of Joseph* was published in eight books in 1736 and in ten books in 1737. I am indebted to Dr. Sarah Ross for these references.
4. This extract is taken from Part the Second: The Prophets. More's asterisked footnote reads: "See Pope's exquisite poem of 'The Messiah'."
5. James C. Livingston's *Religious Thought in the Victorian Age: Challenges and Reconceptions* (London: Continuum, 2007) offers a stimulating account of the variety of Victorian attempts to incorporate Christianity into a scientific worldview.

Notes 249

6. For a fuller discussion of the operation of religious poetry in *The Christian Lady's Magazine*, see Gray, "Beatification through Beautification," *Victorian Poetry* 42:3 (2004): 261–82.
7. See Mary Wilson Carpenter for a provocative discussion of the proliferation (and bastardisation) of biblical commentaries in the nineteenth century.
8. While I have not been able to locate the original of this passage, E. R. Pitman quotes Havergal as writing thus: "Writing is praying with me; for I never seem to write even a verse by myself, and I feel like a little child writing. You know a child would look up at every sentence and say, 'And what shall I say next?' This is just what I do. I ask that at every line He would give me, not merely thoughts and power, but also every word, even the very rhymes. Very often I have a most distinct and happy consciousness of direct answers" (74).
9. Jeremiah chapter 1, verses 6 to 9 reads: "Then said I, Ah, Lord GOD! behold, I cannot speak: for I am a child. But the LORD said unto me, Say not, I am a child: for thou shalt go to all that I shall send thee, and whatsoever I command thee thou shalt speak. Be not afraid of their faces: for I am with thee to deliver thee, saith the LORD. Then the LORD put forth his hand, and touched my mouth. And the LORD said unto me, Behold, I have put my words in thy mouth."
10. Many other women besides Mrs. Wright practised and signalled the transformation of male-derived instruction into feminine verse. Ann Butler (*Fragments in Verse, Chiefly on Religious Subjects*, 1826), like Wright, indicates that several of her poems drew inspiration from particular sermons, as for example "The Grand Inquiry," which is noted, "Composed after having heard the Rev. W. Marsh preach from 1 John iv.8." Somewhat similarly, Butler's "Difficulties Removed" presents an epigraph from Mark's gospel, and the epigraph bears a footnote: "Composed after hearing a sermon from the above text by the Rev. J. N. Goulty." Thus Butler's poems are appropriately bookended by anointed authority: the beginning and the end of her art is Christ—or, more specifically, Christ in man's voice.
11. For comparable complaints, see Psalms 6, 39, and 42.

NOTES TO CHAPTER 3

1. "England has many learned women, not merely readers but writers of the learned languages, in Elizabeth's time and afterwards—women of deeper acquirement than are common now in the greater diffusion of letters; and yet where were the poetesses? The divine breath ... why did it never pass, even in the lyrical form, over the lips of a woman? How strange! And can we deny that it was so? I look everywhere for grandmothers and see none." *The Letters of Elizabeth Barrett Browning*, ed. Frederic G. Kenyon (New York: Macmillan, 1897), vol. 1, 231–32.
2. Of course, innumerable sermons on the role of women in society were preached that drew on female biblical characters to endorse the traditional roles of women: "keepers at home," dedicated mothers like Hannah, good housekeepers like the woman of Proverbs, and so on. See Prochaska ns. 53, 54.
3. See Cobbe's "Madonna Immacolata," chapter 14 of *Italics* (London, 1864).
4. The figure of Eve, for example, received poetic treatments from Elizabeth Barrett Browning (most extensively and sympathetically in *A Drama of Exile*), Christina Rossetti, May Probyn, and Emily Shapcote, among others. In their various depictions, poets had to negotiate with Eve's cataclysmic contribution to the Fall, as well as her extraordinary status of Mother of Humankind.

250   *Notes*

5. Also, I would contend, this poetic body of work stands as a forerunner of the mammoth undertaking (in the United States) of Elizabeth Cady Stanton's *The Woman's Bible*, in the last years of the nineteenth century.

6. A number of feminist historians in the latter twentieth century have written disparagingly about the kinds of women's histories that began to be produced in the mid-nineteenth century, dubbing them the "women worthies" model and pointing to the ease with which the model could be made to serve conservative forces. More recently, however, historians Natalie Zemon Davis and June Purvis have sought to emphasise the polemical possibilities inherent in the "women worthies" model's production of exemplars for women, suggesting they worked to "reveal the range of women's capacity" (Purvis 2), and to argue that all could do what some had done, if given similar opportunities and means.

7. See Margaret Maison, "Queen Victoria's Favourite Poet."

8. William Michael Rossetti wrote that although his sister was not "hostile" to Catholicism, she was "firmly opposed to anything savouring of Mariolatry" (introduction to *Poetical Works*, lii). See D'Amico, "Eve, Mary, and Mary Magdalene" for a fuller discussion of Rossetti's treatments of these three figures, and particularly her heralding of Mary's humility.

9. Best-known for the multiply reprinted and translated *The Chronicles of the Schönberg-Cotta Family*, an historical novel about Martin Luther, Mrs. Charles also published numerous religious prose works for the Society for Promoting Christian Knowledge, and works of poetry.

10. Clara Balfour relates the wedding at Cana story in her volume *The Women of Scripture*, and she too emphasises the power of Mary's speaking. "A woman also was undoubtedly his first disciple, for when the Virgin mother ministered to him in infancy, and kept all his sayings in her heart, she was fulfilling the office of a disciple: and now we find her the first to proclaim his divine mission by counseling obedience to him. *Many volumes of sermons could not exhaust the richness of the sentence Mary uttered on this memorable occasion*". (259; my emphasis)

11. Haskins notes that in 1856 there were sixty such Magdalen homes, and fifty years later there were 308 (333).

12. Dante Gabriel Rossetti, John Keble, and Charles Kingsley, among others, wrote of the Magdalene's suffering tears. R. W. Dixon writes a more complex poem in his "Mary Magdalene" but this too ends with a portrayal of the Magdalene stunned, exhausted, and alone. For a more detailed discussion of nineteenth-century representations of the Magdalene, particularly in the visual arts, see Kruppa, "'More sweet and liquid than any other': Victorian Images of Mary Magdalene."

13. Haskins points out another identification, that of Mary Magdalene—Mariham in the *Pistis Sophia*—with the Old Testament figure of Miriam.

14. The (problematic) tradition identifying the Magdalene as the woman who anoints and dries Jesus' feet may also be reclaimed to propose the Magdalene as the only other woman beside the Madonna with an explicitly physical relationship with Jesus.

15. Dan Brown's *The Da Vinci Code*, an international smash hit, reinterprets the Holy Grail legend in the light of this alternate history.

16. Kruppa quotes an interesting extract from one of Spurgeon's 1855 sermons that suggests that the Magdalene's voice was indeed a source of some cultural fascination:

> When the grand orchestra shall send out its music, when the organs of the skies shall peal forth their deep-toned sounds, we shall ask, "what was that sweet note heard there, mingling with the rest?" . . .

Ah! Mary Magdalene's voice in heaven, I imagine, sounds more sweet and liquid than any other. (quoted 121)

17. Late in the period, the woman poet Vernon Lee rewrites the Magdalene as one of the three Magii. See Fontana 96–97.
18. Versions of this story may be found in three of the gospels: Matthew 9: 20-22, Mark 5: 25-34, and Luke 8: 43-48.
19. Rev.iii.14-22 (author's own footnote).
20. Col.iii.17 (author's own footnote).
21. For an in-depth study of Victorian women novelists' use of the Corinne figure, see Linda M. Lewis' *Germaine de Staël, George Sand, and the Victorian Woman Artist* (Columbia: University of Missouri Press, 2003).
22. The previous section of this chapter comments more fully on this misidentification. For the view of a contemporary biblical commentator, see Thomas Scott's comments on the identification of Mary Magdalene as the sinful woman, quoted above.
23. Charles develops this idea further in the prose work *Sketches of the Women of Christendom*, in which she keeps the two women of the two versions of the story distinct, closing with the words, "these two women . . . stand before us, shielded and crowned with His gracious praise." (73)

NOTES TO CHAPTER 4

1. For examples to illustrate this last point, see Barrett Browning's "Cowper's Grave" and "A Child's Thought of God," as well as Mary Kendrew's "As One Whom His Mother Comforteth."
2. See, for example, Melynyk's "Mighty Victims," which claims that "nineteenth-century women . . . coopt[ed] the central symbol of Christianity: they claimed as model and symbol a feminized version of Christ" (135). Sue Zemka, in *Victorian Testaments*, discusses what she calls the "feminine Christology" (102) popular in the second half of the nineteenth century, pointing to Sarah Stickney Ellis' comparison of women to Christ in the conclusion of *The Daughters of England* and writing in detail about Dickens' and Nightingale's linking of women and Christ figures. A classic study remains Marian Shalkhauser's "The Feminine Christ," *Victorian Newsletter* 10, (1957): 19–20. Jan Marsh, Georgina Battiscombe and many other Christina Rossetti commentators have drawn parallels between "Goblin Market"'s Lizzie and the salvific figure of Christ. Isobel Armstrong links *Aurora Leigh*'s Marion to Christ in *Victorian Poetry, Poetics, and Politics* (369). On the other side of the Atlantic, Stephen Prothero's *American Jesus* devotes an entire chapter to the nineteenth-century feminised Christ, showing how the figure grew out of Evangelicalism's focus on the humanity, gentleness, and emotionality of Jesus, and was perpetuated and developed by the iterations of the "Sweet Savior" of popular hymnody. Kathleen Margaret Lant looks at female Christs in the nineteenth-century American novel in "The Feminist Redeemer: Louisa Alcott's Creation of the Female Christ," *Christianity and Literature*, 40:3 (1991): 223–53.
3. Barbara Lewalski identifies the Psalms as "the compendium *par excellence* of lyric poetry" in the sixteenth and seventeenth centuries (39). For a full exploration of the use of the Psalms in early modern writing, see Rivkah Zim, *English Metrical Psalms: Poetry as Praise and Prayer, 1535–1601*, Cambridge University Press, 1987.

252 *Notes*

4. In "Victorian Religious Women," Melnyk argues that Victorian women's iterations of communal identity helped them construct an alternative literary subjectivity to that of the Romantic, individual, vatic poetic voice, and her analysis focuses particularly on the plural first-person pronoun, which she dubs the "homiletic we" in novels and the "congregational we" in poetry (which she sees as significantly shaped by the hymn tradition).

5. William Alexander, Bishop of Armagh, wrote an explicitly feminised definition of hymnody in a Preface to his wife Cecil Frances Alexander's *Poems*, writing that "a good hymn must be poetry: but poetry in essence and by suggestion, poetry with a timid air and tremulous voice, recognised by a look of bashful beauty, half hiding herself as if reverently afraid of distracting the gaze which should be turned upward, and robbing God of a portion of His tribute" (xxv–xxvi).

6. For Edmeston, the term 'closet' is clearly not solely a female domain. He sees the realm of the affections as privileged and more closely linked to metrical than prosaic expression; he also sees endurance as the lot of all Christians (not just women). Edmeston also has an interestingly conflicted attitude to privacy and publication that is not dissimilar to that voiced by some women poets: he gives voice to thoughts and feelings "which are not proper for singing in public" or even in front of family, so these poems are to be used for private devotion—and yet he publishes them unapologetically, indeed calmly confident in the approval of the wider reading public, the multiple "hearts of others" he imagines at the close of his preface.

7. Many so-entitled 'hymns' are quite literally unsingable and never did appear in congregational worship; for example, Jean Ingelow entitled a collection of verse *One Hundred Holy Songs, Carols, and Sacred Ballads. Original, and suitable for music* (1878). In this volume several poems are specifically labeled "Hymns," including "Hymns with a Burden" and "Double Hymns." Almost all display metrical and stanzaic complications that would render congregational singing a herculean task. I have only found one poem of Ingelow's that has been set to music and appears in several hymnals: the hymn "And didst Thou love the race that loved not Thee." Almost every Victorian woman poet penned a hymn at some point, though these may also have had additional titles. For example, Anne Brontë wrote "A Hymn" which was thus entitled in manuscript, though published in the sisters' 1846 joint volume as "A Doubter's Prayer." Many other poems with no aspirations to musical settings nonetheless gained such settings and, for good or ill, were lustily sung in congregation: the difficulties of singing "Lead, Kindly Light," for example, have been articulated a number of times. Further, as Edmeston's comments foreshadow, the texts of many hymns, published in hymnals and other collections, became the subject of personal reading, meditation, and thus devotional exercise for individuals in the privacy of their own home. Three leading studies of the hymn genre in the nineteenth century may be found in Susan Tamke's *Make a Joyful Noise Unto the Lord: Hymns as a Reflection of Victorian Social Attitudes,* Ian Bradley's *Abide With Me: The World of Victorian Hymns,* and most authoritatively, J. R. Watson's *The English Hymn: A Critical and Historical Study.*

8. John Spurr has written about the promotion of private devotion in the Restoration Church, and specifically notes the dangers inherent in private devotion's elevation of the individual view and belief, as "private prayer" could easily "play into the hands of the disaffected," becoming "the 'life and soul' of schism within the church" (*The Restoration Church of England, 1646–1689*, New Haven and London: Yale University Press, 1991: 340).

Notes 253

9. The gendering of devotionality has been a particular point of interest for scholars of the Early Modern Period and Renaissance. See for example Michael Schoenfeldt, "The Gender of Religious Devotion: Amelia Lanyer and John Donne," in *Religion and Culture in Renaissance England*, Claire McEachern and Debora Shuger (eds), Cambridge, England: Cambridge University Press, 1997, 209–33; Gary Ferguson, "The Feminisation of Devotion: Gabrielle de Coignard, Anne de Marquest, and François de Sales," in *Women's Writing in the French Renaissance*, Philip Ford and Gillian Jondorf (eds.), Cambridge, England: Cambridge French Colloquia, 1999, 187–206; and Susan Comilang, "Through the Closet: Private Devotion and the Shaping of Female Subjectivity in the Religious Recess," *Renaissance and Reformation/ Renaissance et Réforme*, 2003; 27 (3): 79–96.

10. More recently, Emma Mason and F. Elizabeth Gray ('Syren Strains') have analysed the ongoing influence on Victorian women writers of Keble's über-Tractarian *Christian Year*, arguing that this phenomenally popular text helped shape the devotional practices and productions of decades of faithful readers and writers.

11. For nineteenth-century Roman Catholics, Bishop Challoner's *The Garden of the Soul* (first published in 1755, but going into multiple editions), provided a kind of competitor to Keble's High Church *The Christian Year*. This vastly popular and revered book of prayers presented a traditional accompaniment to Roman Catholic services. It expanded throughout the nineteenth century, becoming more and more specifically Roman rather than universally Christian—a universality of appeal which the *Christian Year* continued to enjoy. *The Garden of the Soul* included two devotions, the Benediction of the Blessed Sacrament, and the rosary, which Heimann calls "this least intellectual of devotions" (62), pointing to its repetitiveness, simplicity, and accessibility to the unlearned and even illiterate.

12. In her valuable discussion "'A Music of Thine Own': Women's Poetry" in *Victorian Poetry, Poetics and Politics*, Isobel Armstrong carefully complicates the "often simple, often pious, often conventional" surface poem of Victorian woman's lyric, postulating a double poem beneath in which these conventions are problematised (324). However, Armstrong's treatment of the pious or specifically devotional lyric is fleeting at best.

13. Bradley in *The Call to Seriousness* sees the fundamental characteristic of Victorian Evangelicalism to be the fear of the wrath of God (22–23), but also argues that by the 1860s large numbers of Victorians were turning away from the more extreme manifestations of Evangelical doctrine.

14. See R. Gibson, *A Social History of French Catholicism 1789–1914* (London: Routledge, 1989), 144.

15. This 'gentling' was not isolated to British Evangelicalism; Richard Rabinowitz has shown in a study of nineteenth-century American Evangelicals that a broad shift in religious sensibilities took place in the period, as the emphasis within the Church moved from "doctrinalism" to "devotionalism," with an intimate relationship with Christ the "central fantasy" (*The Spiritual Self* 177; quoted Prothero 53–54).

16. Dorothy Mermin notes that "the main development of Victorian religious ideas [was] the replacement of dogmatic faith by a diffusive benevolence [that] affirmed feminine values" (125).

17. John Shelton Reed describes the sometimes negative Victorian views on the feminine "embroidering impulse" (206) and on women's enthusiasm for the particularly decorative observational emphasis of the Oxford Movement ("A Female Movement").

254   *Notes*

18. David Hilliard's article on Anglo-Catholicism and homosexuality examines the particular charges of effeminacy launched at the Tractarians and their followers, and the way in which the Victorians linked "masculine and feminine styles of religion" (191) to 'virile' Protestantism on the one hand and the flowery observances of Anglo-Catholicism on the other (see "UnEnglish and Unmanly").

19. See for example Revelation 19:7, 21:2 and 9; and the extended analogy of Ephesians 5:22–33.

20. For example, Charles Haddon Spurgeon preached many sermons on texts from the Song of Solomon, and consistently identifies the Bride with The Church or The Christian (and, when talking about that Christian in the individual, uses the masculine pronoun). See, for example, "The Incomparable Bridegroom and His Bride" (1886), and "A Song Among the Lilies" (1874).

21. It wasn't solely women who made use of the romantic partnership paradigm of the Song of Solomon, of course. One of Charles Wesley's most popular hymns was "Jesus, Lover of My Soul," which begins, "Jesus, lover of my soul, let me to Thy bosom fly," and in which the supplicating speaker later requests Christ to "Cover my defenseless head with the shadow of Thy wing."

22. Examples of poetic dialogues include Caroline Noel's "The Yoke," Karr's *Heavenly Voice* sonnet IX, Poole's "The Soul and the Saviour," and Rossetti's "O Lord when Thou didst call me."

23. Male writers also used variations on this theme: one of Charles Wesley's hymns petitions "Oh! Could I lose myself in Thee," and concludes "I loathe myself when God I see,/ And into nothing fall . . . "

24. Particularly difficult for a modern reader, though far from uncharacteristic of this particular strand of devotional poetry that sanctifies suffering, are the several poems in Darton's volume concerning the death of a child, in which Darton's speaker advises the mother to rejoice in this sign of God's love: "And who so favour'd or so bless'd as thou/ Thus for the Lord an offering to prepare?" (these lines appear in a poem entitled "In heaven their angels do always behold the face of my Father who is in heaven").

25. Frances Ridley Havergal wrote: "'O Master!' It is perhaps my favourite title, because it implies rule and submission; and this is what love craves. Men may feel differently, but a true woman's submission is inseparable from deep love." (*Memoirs of Frances Ridley Havergal,* by Maria Vernon Graham Havergal, London 1880, 343).

26. Her sister Mary Eley served as posthumous editor of Lucy's *Poetical Works* and attempted to clarify thematic groupings: most of the poems in the section Mary entitled "Consecration and Service," including "Separation Unto God" and "Friends of Jesus," meditate on being possessed or mastered by God.

27. Northrop Frye dubs this "the Feuerbach principle," meaning the process by which humans make God in their own image (*Great Code* 228).

28. D'Amico writes: "As Rossetti matured, she was attempting to change the poetic voice of her religious poems so that it might represent not just the personal expression of one soul but also that of her audience" (*Christina Rossetti* 160). I suggest that the personal/communal dialectic, while it may be a more pronounced characteristic of Rossetti's later verse, appears throughout her oeuvre.

29. Emma Jane Worboise, prolific Victorian novelist, wrote in the *Christian World Magazine*: "there is no profession more truly sacred than authorship; like the ministry, it ought to be a vocation rather than a profession [. . .] True and worthy authors [. . .] are dedicated to the noblest toil on earth! They rank with the ministers of God's Word, and in another way they do His work" ("'Inkshed' and 'Authorship': To Intending Contributors" vol.18,

Notes 255

1882: 34; quoted Melnyk "Victorian Religious Women" 73). The 'ministry' of another woman poet is illuminated by reports of Charlotte Elliott's influence, as noted in Chapter 1.

NOTES TO CHAPTER 5

1. McGann sets up a series of binaries that nineteenth-century women poets faced—between affect and affectation, between "the language of the heart" and "the tricks of art," and between virtue and virtuosity—but I argue that these terms were not necessarily mutually exclusive and that their intersection in these poets' work reveals suggestive ambition.
2. LaPorte rightly notes that the very concept of a poetess tradition has given rise to disagreement amongst modern critics, having been "warmly embraced by some, [while] the risk of facile categorization has been warmly repudiated by others" (160).
3. On occasion, women poets' use of archaic language is explicitly linked to aims of historical recuperation, as is seen in the religious verse of both the Irishwoman Dora Sigerson's *Verses* (1893) and Mrs. A Stuart Menteath's stoutly Scottish *Lays of the Kirk and Covenant* (1850). Both authors seek to recount and praise specific historical and cultural elements of their country's Christian faith.
4. Another wonderful example of combined archaism and voluminousness may be found in Rosa Raine's "Naomi and Ruth" (from *Verses for Church Schools*, 1861). Raine takes up Ruth's plangent, profound declaration to her mother-in-law, found in Ruth chapter 1, verses 16 and 17: "And Ruth said, Intreat me not to leave thee, or to return from following after thee: for whither thou goest, I will go; and where thou lodgest, I will lodge: thy people shall be my people, and thy God my God: Where thou diest, will I die, and there will I be buried: the LORD do so to me, and more also, if ought but death part thee and me." Raine proceeds to add semantic and stylistic ornaments of an order that transfigures those plain words:

> Entreat me no more, my loved mother, to leave thee,
> Nor follow thee hence to thy desolate home;
> Think not I can thus in affliction bereave thee,
> And suffer thee lonely and childless to roam;
> With sorrow and anguish thy sad heart is swelling,
> Amid all thy wand'rings with thee will I go;
> Thy lowly abode be the place of my dwelling,
> And mine the fond task to assuage thy deep woe.
>
> Forsaking the bonds of my kindred and nation,
> Thy people of Israel my people shall be;
> Thy GOD, Whom thou servest with deep adoration,
> In faith and obedience be worshipped by me.
> The links that unite us death only can sever,
> And then, may I calmly repose in thy tomb,
> The ties of affection unbroken for ever,
> In regions eternal again to resume.

5. The prevalence of common metre (quite closely followed in popularity by long metre) in the Victorian religious lyric provides another reason to reject

256 *Notes*

simplistic divisions between the poem and the hymn in the period, as discussed in Chapter 4.

6. In his study of the "feminising" influences of Tractarianism, John Shelton Reed quotes a number of Victorians who glibly (and generally negatively) elided femininity with the decorative impulse, as in the case of the Evangelical clergyman who wrote, "Is it not a well-known fact that any gorgeous show will attract people, especially the female portion of the community?" ("A Female Movement" 206–8).

7. Meynell wrote critical introductions to collections of verse by Christina Rossetti, Coventry Patmore, Wordsworth, Tennyson, Shelley, Cowper, Herrick, and Jean Ingelow, amongst many others.

8. LaPorte also notes that modern scholars have shown no agreement on the nature or even the nomenclature of the nineteenth-century poetess tradition, and points out the vulnerability of discussions of such a tradition to charges of gender essentialism. He also suggests, persuasively, that the ongoing debate about the poetess model amongst twentieth- and twenty-first-century critics "is built into nineteenth-century terminology" (176; n.2).

9. Georgina Battiscombe writes of Keble's poetry in *The Christian Year* that it "marches forward with a perfectly accurate but sickeningly regular beat" (*John Keble: A Study in Limitations* London: Constable, 1963, 107).

10. *Hymns and Spiritual Songs in Three Books*, 10th ed., 1728, ix. Quoted Victoria Burke and Elizabeth Clarke, *The 'Centuries' of Julia Palmer*, Nottingham: Trent Editions, 2001, xv.

11. Anon (Archbishop Richard Lawrence), *Remarks Upon the Critical Principles, and the Practical Application of those Principles, Adopted by Writers, who have at Various Periods Recommended a New Translation of the Bible as Expedient and Necessary* (Oxford, 1820), 161–62; quoted Norton 179.

12. As given in Henry John Todd, *A Vindication of our Authorised Translation* (London, 1819), 80; quoted Norton 178.

13. See I Corinthians 9: 24–27 for Paul's extended metaphor about the athletic Christian running the race of life.

14. This phrase appears in Hannah More's *Bible Rhymes*, ll.489–92.

> So praise, which we to God impart,
> Comes back in blessings to the heart.
> Gainful return, to man when given
> Such interchange 'twixt earth and heaven!

15. Armstrong, in *Victorian Poetry*, sees Rossetti's use of repetition as exertion of power but in a different way to that of creating contracts. Armstrong argues that Rossetti uses repetition as a strategy of restriction, as a way of engaging with and questioning expressive boundaries and conventions (see particularly 352).

16. Very often, the Roman Catholic Procter is concerned with her relationship to the Madonna. "The Names of Our Lady," for example, is constructed about a series of venerations: each stanza from three to seventeen begins with an italicised title for Mary: "Star of the Sea," "Help of the Christian," "Our Lady of the Rosary," and so on. Each verbal repetition or veneration of a title performs coronation; the titler (or crowner) is necessarily in this relationship granted a form of power.

17. Frye has linked "oratorical" religious verse to prayer specifically through its characteristic "rhetoric of parataxis, short phrases strung together" (*Anatomy of Criticism* 294).

18. Zechariah 9:9 instructs redeemed Christians to express joy at the coming of their Lord: "Rejoice greatly, O daughters of Zion; shout, O daughters of Jerusalem: behold, thy King cometh unto thee."

Notes 257

19. See Jeremiah 1:6, "Then said I, Ah, Lord GOD! behold, I cannot speak: for I am a child."
20. Quoted in Prins, *Victorian Sappho*, 174.
21. The former of these quoted passages, "Yet set not in thy thoughts too far our heaven and earth apart," is by F. W. Faber, from *The Styrian Lake and Other Poems*, 1842; the second, "Our common air is balm," is by Keble, in "First Sunday After Easter," in *The Christian Year.*

Index

A

Adams, Kimberly VanEsveld, 23, 89, 91, 115
Adams, Sarah Flower, 9, 139, 140, 196; "Nearer, my God, to Thee," 139, 140
Alexander, Cecil F., 64, 124, 191; *Hymns for Little Children*, 64
Altick, Richard, 13
Anderson, John M., 3, 38–39
Armstrong, Isobel, 20, 28, 35, 75, 253n12, 256n15
Armstrong, Bristow and Sharrock, 24
Arseneau and Marsh, 174
Auden, W. H., 211

B

B., M. E., 44, 64, 124, 129; "Mary Anointeth the Lord," 129
Bagehot, Walter, 193, 194
Bal, Mieke, 22, 32, 41
Balfour, Clara, 89, 90, 108, 135, 250n10
Barton, Bernard, 196
Belloc, Bessie Rayner, 199
Bemis, Virginia, 17
Bennett, Lucy Ann, 41, 127–128, 143, 159, 160, 167–168, 169–170, 180, 201, 254n26; "A High Priest," 169–170; "Let Her Alone," 127–128; "Subjection," 167–168; "Though He Slay Me, Yet Will I Trust in Him," 159, 160, 170
Besemeres, Jane, 192
Bevan, Emma Frances, 6
Bevington, Louisa, 24
Blain, Virginia, 11, 24, 25, 146–147
Blair, Kirstie, 20

Blind, Mathilde, 24
Bonar, Horatius, 13, 37, 141, 183–184
Book of Common Prayer, 13, 31, 55, 141
Book of Martyrs, The, 13
Booth, Catherine Mumford, 68; "Female Ministry; or, Women's Right to Preach the Gospel," 68
Bourdieu, Pierre, 29–31, 186
Bradley, Ian, 253n13
Braithwaite, Adeline, 44, 46, 69–70, 173; "Joseph," 69; "My Witnesses," 69–70
Breen, Jennifer, 24
Brewster, Emily, 124
British Mothers' Magazine, The, 14–15, 247n2
Brown, Annie Johnson, 119; "S. Mary Magdalene," 119
Brown, James Baldwin, 14
Browne, Jane Euphemia, 72–74, 145, 155, 177–178, 182; "Blessed are the Pure in Heart," 73–74, 145; "Renew a Right Spirit Within Me," 72–73, 177–178; "Submission," 155
Browning, Elizabeth Barrett, 5, 13, 17, 19, 36, 85, 96–97, 158, 184–185, 191–192, 194, 219, 220, 249n1; "Bereavement," 158; *Drama of Exile*, 228; "Grief," 75; "Hymn," 191–192; "The Virgin Mary to the Child Jesus," 96–97
Butler, Ann, 67, 249n10; "Difficulties Removed," 76–77
Butler, Josephine, 87
Bynum, Caroline, 162–163

C

Caine, Barbara, 88

260 Index

Campbell, Duncan, 139–140
Carpenter, Mary Wilson, 17–18, 22, 41
Cecil, David, 186
Chadwick, Owen, 3
Chapman, Raymond, 38–39
Charles, Elizabeth, 6, 81, 95–96, 97–98, 116–117, 123, 124, 128, 134, 250n9, 251n23; "The Crown," 95–96; "The Sisters of Bethany II," 128; *Sketches of the Women of Christendom*, 97–98; "The Unnamed Women," 134
Cheyne, Elizabeth, 67
Choi, Sara, 39
Christian Lady's Magazine, The, 6, 13–14, 45, 46, 48–49, 188, 201, 205–209, 249n6; "Alice," 217–218; "Do You Love Christ?", 49; "Jesus Saith . . . Follow Me," 188; "Stanzas," 205–209
Clark, Suzanne, 29
Cobbe, Frances Power, 17, 67, 88; *Rest in the Lord, and Other Small Pieces*, 67
Collins and Rundle, 25
Cook, Eliza, 201
Cousin, Annie Ross, 9, 41, 124, 143, 150–152; "Songs of the Beloved," 150–152
Cowper, William, 141
Craik, Dinah Mulock, 74–75; "David's Child," 74–75
Crewdson, Jane, 41, 189
Crosby, Sarah, 15
Cuneen, Sally, 91
Cunningham, Valentine, 26

D

Daly, Mary, 22
D'Amico, Diane, 174
Darton, Margaret E., 158, 254n24
Davie, Donald, 29, 184–185, 197, 248n8
De Jong, Mary, 139
Denning, Lydia, "The Redeemed shall return to Zion with Songs," 191, 211–212
Dering, Mrs. Robert, 44
De Staël, Madame, 131
Dieleman, Karen, 39
Dix, Reverend Morgan, 15–16, 104; *The Calling of a Christian Woman and Her Training to Fulfil It*, 15–16

Donaldson, Mrs., 87–88
Donne, John, 137, 166
Drane, Augusta Theodosia, 6, 92, 143, 149–150; "The Fairest Fair," 149

E

Edmeston, James, 140, 195–196, 252n6; "Meditation Upon Christ," 195–196
Eisen, Arnold, 212
Eliade, Mircea, 204
Eliot, George, 87, 228
Elliott, Charlotte, 21, 78–80, 158–159, 176–177, 196, 201, 203–204, 216–217, 247n5; "Go and Sin no More," 78–80; "Hebrews XIII.5," 203–204; "Just as I am, without one plea," 21; "Paternal Chastening," 158–159; "Sonnet to the Harp," 216–217
Elliott, Emily, 141
Elliott, Reverend Henry, 21
Englehardt, Carol Marie, 91
Epigraphy and footnoting, 46–50
Essays and Reviews, 44–45, 58

F

Fairchild, Hoxie Neale, 186, 199, 211
Farningham, Marianne, 189, 192
Fearnley, Rachel Jane, 67
Ferguson, Isa Gillon, 44, 173, 199; "The Communion of Saints," 173
Field, Michael, 81
Fiorenza, Elisabeth Schüssler, 22, 23, 40, 80, 88, 124–125; *Bread Not Stone*, 80; *In Memory of Her*, 124
Flammang, Lucretia, 87
Fletcher, Mary Bosanquet, 15
Flowers, Betty, 46
Francis, Emma, 20
Fraser, Hilary, *Beauty and Belief*, 19
Frye, Northrop, 138, 221, 254n27, 256n17

G

Garden of the Soul, The, 253n11
Gardner, Helen, 171, 218; *Religion and Literature*, 247n1
Gifford, Elizabeth, "Another Comforter," 205; "Lilies" 189; "Thy God hath commanded," 209–211

Index 261

Gilbert and Gubar, 27
Godwin, Elizabeth Ayton, 1
Gnosticism, 108
Granger, Mary Ethel, 133, 168–169; "Peace: A Thanksgiving After Holy Communion," 133, 168–169
Gray, Douglas, 139
Greenough, Sarah Dana, 109–111, 115, 131–132, 228; *Mary Magdalene and Other Poems*, 109–111, 131–132
Greenwell, Dora, 6, 17, 36, 120–123; "The Gang-children," 6; "Quid Dixit, Maria?", 120–123
Gregory, Dr. John, *A Legacy to His Daughters*, 16

H

Hamilton, Eliza, 190, 192; "Nothing Between," 192; "Psalm LXXIII.25," 190
Haskins, Susan, 107–108
Havergal, Frances Ridley, 6, 48, 51–58, 69, 136–137, 139, 140, 145–146, 154–155, 156, 157, 185, 199–200, 249n8, 254n25; "By Thy Cross and Passion," 145–146, 219; "Enough," 154–155; "An Interlude," 52; "Isaiah xxxiii.17," 69; *Kept for the Master's Use*, 136–137; "Life Mosaic," 199–200, 220; "Luke ix.13," 53–54; "The Song Chalice," 52–53, 157, 185; "Take My Life and Let it Be" (Consecration Hymn), 51, 136, 139, 140; "The Thoughts of God," 55–58; "Verses on Texts," 54–55
Heber, Bishop Reginald, 141
Heimann, Mary, 141, 143, 144
Helsinger, Sheets, and Veeder, 17, 18
Hemans, Felicia, 32–35, 85, 100–101, 113–114, 119–120, 129–131, 144–145, 218, 248n10; "Female Characters of Scripture," 85; "Mary Magdalene at the Sepulchre," 113–114; "Mary Magdalene Bearing Tidings of the Resurrection," 119–120; "The Memorial of Mary," 129–130; *Moral and Religious Poems*, 32; "Paraphrase of Psalm CXLVIII," 33–35, 45;

"The Penitent Anointing Christ's Feet," 129–131; "The Song of the Virgin," 100–101
Herbert, George, 137
Herbert, Mary Sidney, 137
Hickey, Emily, 9, 81, 92, 93–94, 98–100, 103, 133–134; "Any Child to the New-Found Mother," 93–94; "Her Assumption," 103; "An Offering," 133–134; "Our Lady's Crowns," 93; "She stands without, seeking to speak to Him," 98–100
Hickok, Kathleen, 27–28
Higgonet, Margaret Randolph, 24–25
Higher Criticism, 44–45, 57, 84
Hilliard, David, 254n18
Hope, Mildred Beresford, 103–104; "Festivals of the Blessed Virgin Mary," 103–104
Howitt, Mary, 9, 58–61; "Dives and Lazarus," 58–61
Hughes, Sheila Hassell, 23, 80
Hull, A. M., "The Bride," 149
Hutchinson, Lucy, 42
Hymn, 18, 33, 139–140, 172, 252n5, 252n7

I

Imitation of Christ, The, 141
Ingelow, Jean, 165–167, 180, 228, 252n7; "O Christ of God, in my good days," 165–167
Iverson, Winifred, 77, 178–179; "Yea! Let Him take all," 179

J

Jameson, Anna, 88, 106, 108; *Legends of the Madonna*, 88
Jay, Elisabeth, 3, 19, 26, 144
Jenkins, Ruth, 10, 19, 86
Johnson, Samuel, 42, 136, 196–197
Jones, Llewellyn, 186

K

Kachur, Robert, 17
Karr, Margaretta Ayres, 101–102, 171; *The Heavenly Voice, a Life of Christ in Blank Verse*, 101–102
Keble, John, 19, 182–184, 195, 196, 217, 227, 257n21; *The Christian Year*, 13, 20, 31, 247n4, 253n10, 256n9
Kendrew, Mary, 152–153; "Jesu, Thou art to me," 152–153

262 *Index*

King, Harriet E. H., 93, 160–161; "The Bride Reluctant," 160–161
King, Harriet R., 44, 65–67, 125–127; "2 Corinthians I. 3, 4," 65–66; "Mark XIV. 8, 9," 125–127
Kinloch, Marjory, 219
Krueger, Christine, 10, 18–19, 21, 86
Kruppa, Patricia, 107

L

Landon, Letitia, 117–118; "The Magdalen," 117–118
Landow, George, 46, 50
Lanser, Susan Sniader, 46
LaPorte, Charles, 86, 195, 255n2, 256n8
Larson, Janet, 21, 23–24
Lawrence, The Hon. Mary Emma, 64
Leighton, Angela, 27–28
Leighton and Reynolds, 24
Levi, Peter, 248n8
Lewalski, Barbara, 137, 138, 142, 251n3
Lewis, Linda, 21, 39
Lyte, Henry Francis, 112, 114, 136, 141, 149, 195, 196, 224; "The Complaint of Mary Magdalene," 112

M

Magnificat, The, 97, 100–106, 117
Mallett, Sarah, 15
Mary the Mother of God, 23, 52, 81, 86, 88, 89, 91–106, 110, 111–112, 115–116, 128
Mary Magdalene, 81, 86, 95, 106–123, 128, 131
Maskell, Eliza, 61–64; "The Foolish and the Wise Builders," 61–63; "The Unprofitable Servant," 63–64
Mason, Emma, 20
Mathers, Helen, 87
Matheson, Annie, "Ecce Homo," 215
McAndrew, Barbara, 228
McGann, Jerome, 185, 186, 255n1
Melnyk, Julie, 17, 18, 21, 86, 172, 173, 251n2, 252n4
Menteath, Mrs. Stuart, 6
Meredith, Susannah, 88
Mermin, Dorothy, 27–28, 224, 253n16
Methodism, 15
Meynell, Alice, 194–195, 256n7
Miles, Alfred, 195

Miles, Margaret, 16, 17, 90
Mill, Harriet Taylor, "Enfranchisement of Women," 20
Montgomery, James, 195, 196
More, Hannah, 15, 17, 42–44, 142, 203, 224; *Bible Rhymes*, 42–44, 203, 256n14; *Strictures on the Modern System of Female Education*, 15
Morgan, Sue, 142
Muir, Emma, 192, 202–203; "Just as Thou Wilt," 202–203

N

Naden, Constance, 24
"Nameless Woman, The," 123–134
Nesbit, Edith, 105-106; "Magnificat" 105–106
Nightingale, Florence, 85
Noel, Caroline, 118–119, 174–176, 177; "Day-Break," 175–176, 177; "Indwelling," 175; "Woman's Commission," 118–119
Nixon, Jude, 21, 39
Norman, Edward, 3, 143
Norton, David, 197

O

O'Gorman, Francis, 26
Orr, Emily, 141
Ostriker, Alicia Suskin, 22, 23, 31–32, 39, 80

P

Palazzo, Lynda, 21, 39
Paz, D. G., 3
Piggott, Jean Sophia, 66–67, 124, 189–190; "Divine Childhood," 66–67; "Not My Own," 189–190
Pilgrim's Progress, 13
Poole, Eva Travers Evered, 46–48, 170
Pratt, Annis, 27
Prickett, Stephen, *Romanticism and Religion*, 19
Probyn, May, 93
Prochaska, F. K., 87
Procter, Adelaide Anne, 24–26, 92–93, 198–199, 201, 204, 256n16; *A Chaplet of Verses*, 92, 199; "The Names of Our Lady," 92–93; "One by One," 198–199, 220; "The Peace of God," 204, 220

Index   263

Q
Quakers, 5, 15
Quarles, Francis, 42

R
Raine, Rosa, 64, 255n4
Reed, John Shelton, 3, 14; *Glorious Battle*, 3; "A Female Movement," 14, 247n1, 253n17, 256n6
Ricks, Christopher, 26
Robertson, Eric S., 28
Roden, Frederick, 21, 23, 148
Rosenblum, Dolores, 84, 164
Ross, Marlon, 211
Rossetti, Christina, 5, 8, 13, 16, 24–26, 38–39, 45–46, 81–84, 94, 111-112, 113, 115, 117, 143, 153–154, 159–160, 163–165, 166, 172–173, 174, 175, 180, 248n1, 250n8, 254n28, 256n15; "Cried out with Tears," 164–165, 175; "Feast of the Annunciation," 94; "I followed Thee," 81–84; *Letter and Spirit*, 16, 174; "Mary Magdalene and the Other Mary. A Song for All Maries," 111–112, 117; "Thou, God, seest me," 154; "What is that to me? follow thou me," 159–160; "Why?", 163–164
Rossetti, Dante Gabriel, 101
Rossetti, William Michael, 38, 174
Rowe, Elizabeth Singer, 42
Ruether, Rosemary Radford, 40
Ruskin, John, *Of Queens' Gardens*, 17

S
Salvation Army, 5, 15, 68
Saunders, Emily S. G., 6, 36–37, 95, 124; "The Accession," 6; "Annunciation of the Virgin Mary," 95; "Evening Hymn," 37
Scheinberg, Cynthia, 10, 20, 23, 39, 86-87, 89, 90, 96, 97, 100, 217; *Women's Poetry and Religion*, 23
Schumacher, Michele, 22, 155–156, 157, 160, 163
Scott, Patrick, 227, 247n2
Sewell, Mary, 65
Shapcote, Emily, 92, 93, 102–103; *Mary, the Perfect Woman* 93, 102–103
Shaw, Marion, 227

Sidney, Sir Philip, 137
Skelton, Edith, 6
Southey, Caroline Bowles, 13
Southey, Robert, 14
Spender, Dale, 27
Spurgeon, Charles, 15, 250n16, 254n20
Stedman, Edmund Clarence, 193-194, 196, 201
Stock, Sarah Geraldine, 48, 154, 157; "Whose I Am, and Whom I Serve," 154
Streatfield, Sophia, 67

T
Taves, Ann, 143
Taylor sisters (Ann and Jane), 33
Taylor, Barbara, 14
Taylor, Dennis, 4, 7
Taylor, Georgiana, 41, 80–81, 148–149, 156–157; "God's Chosen Things," 219-220; "Oh to be Nothing," 156–157; "The Path of Faith," 81; "Wilderness Rest," 148
Tennyson, Alfred, 227
Tennyson, G. B., 16, 137–138, 139, 143
Tilley, Harriet, "Poesy," 222
Tompkins, Jane, 29, 186
Tonna, Charlotte Elizabeth, 48
Transfiguration, 31
Trimmer, Mrs Sarah, 17
Trudgill, Eric, 106, 115
Tynan, Katharine, 93, 124, 144; "The Dream of Mary," 93

U
Upton, Bridget Gilfillan, 22, 40–41, 125, 128
Unnamed Woman, The *See* "Nameless Woman, The"

V
V., K. E., 94, 114–115, 117, 131; "The Conception," 94; "S. Mary Magdalene," 114–115, 131
Valenze, Deborah, 86
Victoria Magazine, 199

W
W., M. O., 78
Walker, Cheryl, 27
Walker, Eliza Ann, 132, 183; "The Penitent's Place," 132

264 Index

Walker, Julia, 172, 173
Waring, Anna Letitia, "My times are in
  Thy hand," 213–215, 220
Warner, Marina, 86, 88
Watts, Isaac, 42, 196
Wesley, Charles, 15, 41, 254n21,
  254n23
Westerholm, Joel, 174
Wilberforce, William, 14, 144
Women's Penny Paper, The (later *The
  Woman's Herald*), 6, 158, 189,
  201

Worton and Still, 50–51
Wright, Fanny J., 44
Wright, Marian Saunders, 70–72; "Elijah," 71–72; "Jesus Washing the
  Disciples' Feet," 72

Y

Yeats, William Butler, 144
Yonge, Charlotte, 17

Z

Zemka, Sue, 251n2